N. _____, _____

W9-BVQ-101

For Nora, for Gerald –

Recollecting so many

years of friendship

Peter

CAMBRIDGE STUDIES IN AMERICAN LITERATURE AND CULTURE

The divided mind

CAMBRIDGE STUDIES IN AMERICAN LITERATURE AND CULTURE
EDITOR: ALBERT GELPI, *Stanford University*

ADVISORY BOARD
NINA BAYM, *University of Illinois, Champaign–Urbana*
SACVAN BERCOVITCH, *Columbia University*
RICHARD BRIDGMAN, *University of California, Berkeley*
DAVID LEVIN, *University of Virginia*
KENNETH LYNN, *Johns Hopkins University*
JOEL PORTE, *Harvard University*
MIKE WEAVER, *Oxford University*

Other books in the series
ROBERT ZALLER: *The Cliffs of Solitude*
PATRICIA CALDWELL: *The Puritan Conversion Narrative*
STEPHEN FREDMAN: *Poet's Prose*

The divided mind
Ideology and imagination in America,
1898–1917

PETER CONN

CAMBRIDGE UNIVERSITY PRESS

Cambridge

London   New York   New Rochelle

Published by the Press Syndicate of the University of Cambridge
The Pitt Building, Trumpington Street, Cambridge CB2 1RP
32 East 57th Street, New York, NY 10022, USA
296 Beaconsfield Parade, Middle Park, Melbourne 3206, Australia

© Cambridge University Press 1983

First published 1983

Printed in the United States of America

Library of Congress Cataloging in Publication Data
Conn, Peter
The divided mind.
(Cambridge studies in American literature and culture)
Includes index.
1. American literature – 20th century – History and
criticism – Addresses, essays, lectures. 2. United States
– Civilization – 1865–1918 – Addresses, essays, lectures.
I. Title. II. Series.
PS223.C66   1983   810'.9'0052   82–23661
ISBN 0 521 25392 6

For Terry

"Lady, I take record of God, in thee I have had
my earthly joy."

Malory

Contents

Acknowledgments

I have been especially fortunate in the group of friends and colleagues who have read some version or other of this manuscript. They have responded to it and to its author with unvarying courtesy, shrewdness, and generosity. Joel Conarroe, Albert Gelpi, Daniel Hoffman, Randolph and Judy Ivy, Patricia Rose, Robert Storey, Gerald Weales, and Larzer Ziff have benevolently collaborated to make these pages better than they would have been.

I have been fortunate, too, in the students and other young persons who have assisted in different ways. My thanks to the members of English 305, who were subjected to some of my ideas and whose reactions improved them. Carol Kuniholm, whose own study of Henry James will soon be completed, deserves special mention. Robin Bender, Ellen Shevitz, and David and Steven Conn have labored cheerfully, and with professionalism beyond their years, at the business of preparing footnotes, indexing, and typing.

I am grateful to the staffs of several libraries, especially those of the University of Pennsylvania and of Bryn Mawr College; their efficiency was matched only by their unflagging good humor and patience. The skill, patience, and wisdom of the Cambridge University Press editorial staff have elicited my unvarying admiration. I am especially grateful for the sharp eyes and good advice of Andrew Brown, Liz Maguire, and Sandra Graham. I want to acknowledge as well the support of the University of Pennsylvania Research Foundation.

My reliance on previous scholars has been immense and is documented in the notes. In addition, I want to call attention to several books. Readers fortunate enough to be familiar with Samuel Hynes's *The Edwardian Turn of Mind,* Justin Kaplan's *Lincoln Steffens,* and Larzer Ziff's *The American 1890's* will recognize the influence of those books upon this one.

If the dedication to this book were not preempted by their mother, it would be offered to my four children: Steven, David, Alison, and Jennifer. During the years of our acquaintance, they have taught me much of what I know of communion and happiness and love.

My wife, Terry, neither typed nor proofread nor checked sources. She did take time from her busier schedule than mine to listen and suggest, to hearten and improve. For that, and for her other and far more important gifts, she knows my thanks.

Chapter 1

The temper of the times

The years from the turn of the century to the First World War were among the most eventful in American history. It is an era, therefore, whose essential definition has proven unsurprisingly but remarkably elusive. Commenting on the year 1901, in the chapter of his *Education* called "Teufelsdrockh," Henry Adams styled himself – with droll relish at the thought of the contradictions – a "Conservative Christian Anarchist."[1] Not all the members of this generation, nor even most of them, would have recognized their own likeness in Adams's particular paradox. But if we understand Adams's witty formulation properly and loosely, if we take it to summarize a profound internal dialectic, a conflict between tradition and innovation, between control and independence, between order and liberation, then we might accept Adams's phrase as an epigraph to the cultural history of this period.[2]

This is an era in whose literature, politics, painting, architecture, and educational styles we see our own preoccupations. And yet, despite Adams's testimony elsewhere in the *Education,* the year 1900 was not a moment when "history broke in halves" (p. 392), for we find backward-looking images and ideas contesting with the voices of prophecy, the reactionary coexisting with the subversive.

All ages are transitional; in all of them the past and the future restlessly inhabit the same cultural space. Yet because of the peculiar turbulence of the 1900s – because of its accelerating urbanization and industrialization; the genuinely revolutionary character of its technological enterprises; the struggle of its working class, its black people, and its women to achieve self-consciousness and autonomy; the decisive centralization being wrought in its economics and politics; the explosive growth of its mass media – for these reasons and more Adams's conception of this era as one of acutely divided allegiances and sensibilities will prove fruitful.

This is a period that historians, finding what they bring, have dis-

covered by turns to be "essentially" progressive, or conservative, or
radical, or nostalgic. A few preliminary examples will suffice. In "The
Origins of Progressivism," Stanley P. Caine writes with great confi-
dence that "Progressivism began with the breaking of chains of intellectual and religious thought that bound Americans in the late nineteenth
century to precepts and assumptions that militated against reform."[3]
But Lawrence Goodwyn, in his magisterial study of the Populists,
would precisely reverse Caine's judgment: The Progressive "moment"
occurred as the impulse toward truly radical democratic reform had
exhausted itself in the nineties.[4] Richard Hofstadter, still the best-
known if not the most reliable of the analysts of this period, conceives
of the years of the first Roosevelt's presidency as a time of genuine
reform stifled by the outbreak of World War I.[5] Resisting this view,
Gabriel Kolko finds the reforms delusory because they embodied a
successful conspiracy by plutocracy to protect its own interests.[6] And
Allen F. Davis corrects Hofstadter from a completely different angle,
by denying that the war killed progressivism and arguing that in fact it
revitalized the movement.[7]

And so on. The assured, individual judgments of the historians add
up, in a word, to collective confusion. These contentious, contradictory
assessments could be multiplied, and they will be, in the pages that
follow. Their preliminary purpose here is to attest, by virtue of their
sheer cacophony, to the mordant wisdom of Henry Adams. Like
Adams in the *Education,* this is a period pulled in several conflicting
directions and characterized by a variety of competing tones. In the
unsettled early years of this century, anxiety grappled with hope in an
equally matched struggle.

The conclusions offered us for these years by literary and cultural
historians are divided more symmetrically than those of economists or
political scientists into two conflicting stereotypes. The more familiar,
more durable view has perceived in these years a long afternoon calm,
finally and irrevocably shattered by the eruption of the Great War and
its aftermath. Russel Nye proposes a version of this opinion: "The
society of the twenties and thirties was no longer the orderly, self-
confident, secure society of the prewar years."[8] Donelson F. Hoopes, in
his authoritative history of *The American Impressionists,* announces that
"the First World War ended the dream of a rational world, and anarchy
lay waiting in the wings."[9] Orderly, self-confident, rational.

How absolutely inadequate this catalogue of adjectives is in summa-
tion of a period that opens with the assassination of a president; numbers among its most dramatic episodes the last of the Indian wars, the
sustained brutality of the Philippines repression, and the bloodiest labor
battles in United States history; records a thousand lynchings and a

score of serious race riots; enumerates thirty-five thousand industrial fatalities every year; and produces as one of its bestselling novels *The Jungle* (1906), with its scarifying scenes of American poverty.

To be sure, some of the men and women who lived through the prewar years found them to be secure and even rational. Those who did may have even been in a majority (the point is doubtful, unprovable, and irrelevant). But their existence obviously does not make the simplifications of Nye and Hoopes appropriate. In any case, the real source of this benevolent leveling of the early years of the twentieth century is the mythmaking talk of the years that followed. Nye's mistake is to take too seriously what people of the twenties said about themselves and their predecessors. The writers of the generation that luxuriated in being "lost" had short memories, made shorter by the temptation to prove their dark wisdom special, and not the legacy of those they followed.

Confronting the caricature of innocence drawn by writers such as Nye is its opposite. "It has been shown," says Loren Baritz, citing Henry May and Christopher Lasch, "that a significant part of the generation immediately before World War I was itself in rebellion against many of the same aspects of middle-class American life that the men of the Twenties were to find inhibiting, stultifying and suffocating."[10] This is closer to the facts of the case. We will certainly find evidence of rebellion across the prewar years. Yet, here again, how many men and women actually felt alienated from middle-class values is unknown and unknowable. Such behavior as the state and national voting habits of American men, to take just one example, suggests an abiding conservatism. And if *The Jungle* sold well, *When Knighthood Was in Flower* (1898) sold better. In any case, the more significant complexity that Baritz's estimate obscures is that the rebellion we will examine in the early twentieth century was far more often ephemeral than substantial, and was all of it inconclusive.

The truth about these years – if there is one – lies not with any of the particular political or cultural estimates itemized here, nor in between them. Yet all are rational deductions from the facts and artifacts of the time. All are the intelligent but partial conclusions resulting from rigorously selective transactions between historians and their evidence.

The chapters that follow are grounded in an effort to take quite seriously Lionel Trilling's admonition about the irreducible complexity of any cultural moment:

> The culture of a nation is not truly figured in the image of the current. [The specific target here is Parrington's *Main Currents*.] A culture is not a flow, nor even a confluence; the form of its exis-

tence is struggle, or at least debate—it is nothing if not a dialectic.[11]

The novelists and journalists, artists and philosophers, whose work is examined in the following chapters contain—sometimes in their encounters with each other, more often and more interestingly in themselves—large parts of the dialectic that defined early twentieth-century America.

The dialectic Trilling summarizes has presented itself, in a variety of particular forms, as the hallmark of American culture virtually from its beginnings. In an influential look back at the history of the American imagination, Richard Chase discerned what he called "a culture of contradictions." Chase's interest was in fictional form and genre, but he did his best to locate that question in the larger context of culture. If the American novel "tends to rest in contradictions and among extreme ranges of experience," that is because it expresses the unsettled, improvisatory, disorderly quality of American life itself.[12]

Chase's image of America's divisions was partly based in turn on the hypotheses of Marius Bewley. Chase cites Bewley's essay "Fenimore Cooper and the Economic Age," in which Bewley describes a characteristic tension in American literature that has followed from a split in American experience. "What was the nature of the division . . . ? It took on many forms concurrently; it was an opposition between tradition and progress or between the past and the future; between Europe and America, liberalism and reaction."[13]

What is true of the culture as a whole is true of its parts, and what has been true of the past continues true of the present. For instance, the dialectic explored in Chase's and Bewley's literary criticism defines the terms as well of Kai Erikson's sociology. *Everything in Its Path* is Erikson's piercing study of the devastating Buffalo Creek flood of 1972. In that book, Erikson describes his unsuccessful attempt to isolate the "core values" of the Appalachian mountain community wiped out by the flood. Instead of core values, Erikson discovered contrary tendencies, "lines of point and counterpoint," he calls them.[14] Self-assertion versus resignation; self-reliance versus dependence on the group; love of tradition versus a passion for individual liberty—these are among the contrary tendencies of the people of Appalachia. My interest here is in the pattern of contrariety and not in the enumerated details. Yet Erikson's litany is familiar and suggestive in its details as well: Appalachia recapitulates America, and Erikson's terms closely resemble those I used in the first paragraphs of this chapter.

The principal rationale of the essays that follow is to trace the particular contours of this conflict through the first two decades of this century. The essays neither insinuate nor depend on the claim that the terms of the early twentieth-century dialectic were unique.

And yet, I am frankly tempted toward the speculation that, while those years were not idiosyncratic in their leading themes, they did contain a cultural contrariety of unusual intensity. In the early years of this century, the forces of new and old, of experiment and resistance, collided with singular energy. To put it summarily, a revolution was occurring, but one that provoked and met a counterrevolutionary reply. Let me briefly sketch this proposition.

To begin with the first half of this hypothesis, a substantial case can be made for a cultural revolution in these years. A number of perceptive historians have discovered here what they regard as a profound and decisive shift. To pick a recent example, Marcus Klein declares that the America of the early twentieth century was an essentially new creation, though he hedges the assertion with qualifiers: "God does not work in decimals, and I would not wish to be insistent about dates, but it was some time approximately and conveniently at the turn of the twentieth century that an America which had had definitions in myth and idea – variable definitions but nevertheless antique and accepted ones – all but disappeared."[15] Henry May is even more emphatic: "Everybody knows that at some point in the twentieth century America went through a cultural revolution."[16] Klein and May have in mind a set of developments that had roots in the nineteenth century but that took climactic and undeniably "different" shapes after about 1900. These were not isolated episodes but large-scale movements and events, among which the most powerful were increases in the number and native countries of immigrants, advances in technology, the country's turn toward imperialism, and, perhaps least dramatic but most important, the success of organization and centralization.

Simply to rehearse these developments is to capture something of their revolutionary significance. We are interested, however, not merely in the facts themselves but also in the apprehensions of those facts by people who lived with them. No one witness is altogether typical, and I shall call on many in the next few pages, but the popular journalist Mark Sullivan is a reasonably good starting point. Sullivan lived the first half of his adult life in the opening decades of the twentieth century, and he later tried to re-create that period in his encyclopedically chatty history, *Our Times*. Through six volumes and several thousand pages, Sullivan lists and describes and summarizes everything he can think of – from presidential elections to bestselling books to fashions to the World Series. The thesis, for which all the items are evidence, is dizzying change: in the size and character of the population, in politics and political leadership, in the nation's international role, above all in the multiplied achievements of science and technology. Of course all such backward glances as Sullivan's will yield testaments of change. But, as the more detached and scholarly examples of Klein and May suggest, Sullivan's perspective has a good deal of merit.

America's population grew from about 75 million in 1898 to roughly 100 million in 1917. Dramatic as it is, this increase was less significant than two other phenomena that were contained within it. First, these years encompassed the highest levels of immigration into the United States, with 15 million aliens coming into the country. John Higham describes the escalating numbers of immigrants in the early twentieth century as "a fantastic . . . climb."[17] In 1907 alone, 1.25 million aliens arrived, the peak of the influx. By 1910, one-seventh of the U.S. population was foreign born; in several eastern cities the actual majority of the population consisted of first-generation immigrants and their children. Probably nothing like this more or less voluntary migration had occurred on such a scale, anywhere. Certainly nothing like it had been seen before in the United States.

Virtually all of the immigrants clustered in cities, and this identifies the second significance that stamped America's swiftly growing numbers. The cities received not only the bulk of the immigrants but also an immense flux of internal migrants, rural Americans of all sorts, including southern blacks, who abandoned their farms and villages and transformed the country in these years into a definitively urban society. The census of 1920 was the first to enumerate more people living in cities and towns than in the countryside. And concentrations within that concentration were becoming always denser. In 1890, there was just one city (New York) with a million inhabitants; by 1910, with the addition of Philadelphia and Chicago, there were three; and a fourth (Detroit) was approaching that figure in 1920. The twenty-five cities of 100,000 or more in 1890 had doubled by 1910 and nearly tripled by 1920. These population movements were as demographically decisive as they were unprecedented.

America's burgeoning multitudes found themselves by turns the beneficiaries and the victims of remarkable technological developments. These were the years in which Americans realized, whether with outrage or hope, that they were to live henceforth in an irretrievably man-made, machine-made world. Any number of illustrations suggest themselves, of which the once-glamorous story of the automobile is only the most familiar. In 1900, less than a decade after Charles Duryea and Henry Ford tested their first gasoline-powered vehicles, there were 8,000 automobiles in the United States, traveling on somewhat fewer than 150 miles of hard-surfaced roads. By 1915, two and a half million cars jostled each other on several thousand miles of good roads. What had been a novelty had become one of the principal technical and socio-logical phenomena of the twentieth century.

Though less significant for daily affairs, what Orville and Wilbur Wright achieved in December 1903 was unquestionably the most stun-ning act of applied science in this period. Flight was among the most venerable of human dreams, a symbol of the future and a resonant metaphor for liberation. In the unromantic, boxy clumsiness of dirty cloth, wooden struts, and noisy engine, the Wrights made the dream prosaically real.

Though much of modern science was being constructed in these years, most of the work was going on in Europe: Planck's quantum theory, Einstein's special and general theories of relativity, and Bohr's model of the atom are the most spectacular examples. Some Americans did see the new maps of modern thought, and a few even saw them being drawn firsthand (Freud delivered his epochal lectures on psycho-analysis at Clark University in 1909). What so profoundly altered the daily lives of Americans, however, was not the new formulations of science but the inventions of technicians and engineers.

Transportation, communications, health, recreation, the texture of public and particularly of private life, and the pace at which life was lived, were being altered. Advances in medicine, including especially improvements in neonatal care; drastic reductions in deaths from ty-phoid, influenza, and tuberculosis; and the indefatigable efforts of Harvey Wiley and others to secure healthier food and drugs added an astonishing five years to the American life-span in the first two decades of the century. In manufacturing, machines, not people, accounted for the one percent annual increase in productivity between 1889 and 1919.[18]

The wireless was perfected: In 1901, in Newfoundland, Marconi heard signals from Europe. Disk recordings, invented in this period, made the twentieth-century record industry possible. The number of telephones increased twentyfold in these years; transcontinental calls began in 1913, when New York and San Francisco were connected. Film, to give a final example, grew up in these years. The movies existed only on the margins of American life in 1898. The first com-mercially successful film, *The Great Train Robbery,* was produced in 1903. By 1915, D. W. Griffith and others had created both the tech-niques and the commerce of the modern movie industry.[19]

Mark Sullivan, trying to find a vocabulary equal to the march of technological progress, was driven to trite but instructively strenuous hyperbole: "It would be interesting to compare, item by item, man's earliest longings for those things he deemed impossible, the fancies with which his imagination played in the Arabian Nights Tales and other myths and fairy-stories, with the things that became actualities" in the years after 1900.[20] The more prosaic wonders included household appliances, which flatly redefined the terms of daily existence (at least for the middle class). In 1900, only lighting was a widely available application of electricity. In the next two decades, electric irons, vacuum cleaners, washing machines, toasters, refrigerators, and sewing machines were developed. Electricity was also applied, with far-reaching results, to underground, surface, and elevated railways.

The home, the workplace, and the movement between them changed fundamentally. So, too, did the country's international agenda. The years around the turn of the century were the "busiest and most seminal period in American foreign policy" since the 1840s.[21]

The opening event in this busyness was the Spanish–American War, and the principal result of the war was that, in the years 1898–1899, the United States "suddenly became a colonial power."[22] Within two years, the election of 1900 was contested in large measure as a plebiscite on imperialism, and McKinley's solid victory indicated that after a century and more of resisting foreign entanglements, many Americans were ready to endorse an expansionist diplomacy. In 1898, Judge H. H. Powers summarized what he took to be a remarkable about-face:

> A year ago we wanted no colonies, no alliances, no European neighbors, no army and not much navy . . . . Our rôle in the world was to be *nil,* and the rest of the new world that of the dog in the manger. The Monroe Doctrine was construed as requiring no constructive action on our part toward the civilized world. The Washington Doctrine was frankly interpreted to mean national isolation. Our position on these points might be questionable, but it was not equivocal. We at least know our own minds.
>   To-day every one of these principles is challenged, if not definitely rejected.[23]

The causes of this suddenly shifted attitude have been the subject of disagreement for many years. E. L. Godkin, also writing in 1898, suggested with an ironic sigh that Americans had simply discovered imperialism to be fun:

> The ease and celerity with which Dewey did his work, fairly turned people's heads, coming on us, as it did, at a time when the capture of even a tramp steamer filled some of us with frantic joy. It seemed so easy to destroy a fleet that we all rushed to the conclusion that it must be just as easy to rule a far-off province. So we fell to shouting and yelling for distant islands to govern.[24]

Manifest Destiny, Social Darwinism, capitalist expansionism, the influence of European pro-imperialist propaganda – these are among the explanations later historians have offered for America's changed understanding of its proper world role.

Theodore Roosevelt in particular was fond of "scientific" talk on the theme of Darwinist imperialism. Though he conceded that "there is no exact parallelism between the birth, growth, and death of species in the animal world, and the birth, growth, and death of societies in the world of man," he nonetheless insisted that "there is a certain parallelism. There are strange analogies; it may be that there are homologies."[25] The analogy that most interested Roosevelt likened a thriving species in the animal world, which flourishes through struggle and conquest, to the triumphant march of "the white race" across the face of the earth. To expand is to live; to stay at home is to demonstrate oneself unfit in the global contest. Echoing generations of British apologists for imperialism, Roosevelt declared that the United States was obliged to carry its higher civilization to those whom it would rule: "In the long run there can be no justification for one race managing or controlling another unless the management and control are exercised in the interest and for the benefit of that other race" (p. 104). This, Roosevelt actually believed, was the most precise way to describe the American occupation of the Philippines.

Senator Albert Beveridge, an even more tenacious proponent of expansion than Roosevelt, stripped off the veil of pious philanthropy when he made the case for imperialism. In a famous speech in the Senate in 1899, Beveridge announced that "God has not been preparing the English-speaking and Teutonic peoples for a thousand years for nothing but vain and idle self-contemplation and self-admiration. No! He has made us *the* master organizers of the world to establish system where chaos reigns . . . . He has made us adepts in government that we may administer government among savages and senile peoples." Like Roosevelt, Beveridge always included an appeal to vigor and virility: "We will renew our youth at the fountain of new and glorious deeds."[26]

We shall have several occasions to return to the racial and sexual implications of such talk in later chapters. For now, Beveridge's reference to Americans as "master organizers" and his emphasis on system and government provide a transition to the last of the major changes being wrought in early twentieth-century American culture. The pattern that impressed itself across the whole of that society consisted in what Samuel P. Hays, agreeing with many others, has called "the organizational revolution."[27]

Hays does not overstate the situation. Organization, as a model and as an idea, permeated both America's institutions and its imagination. Busi-

ness, in its structures and capitalization, led the way. The merger movement, begun in earnest in the 1890s, ended decades of search for economic order in the rewards of consolidation. By 1900, nearly 75 "trusts"
had a capitalization of $10 million or more; a thousand mergers had been
recorded in the previous year. The real and symbolic climax occurred in
1901, when J. P. Morgan organized U.S. Steel as the first billion-dollar
corporation. The constituent parts of this colossal industrial combination
included 200 factories and transportation companies, 1,000 miles of railroad, over 100 blast furnaces, and 75 ore boats. U.S. Steel employed
over 170,000 workers and soon controlled 60 percent of America's steel
capacity. Its significance, whether exemplary or sinister, depended upon
the observer's politics, but the sheer scale of the enterprise made it a
major national preoccupation. Since, as Everett Dirksen pointed out
some time ago, a single billion dollars no longer seems like so much
money, we need to put Morgan's coup in the proper frame to appreciate
its magnitude: U.S. Steel's initial capitalization of $1.4 billion was three
times the annual expenditure of the United States government.

Predictably, evangels of organization appealed to natural law in their
enthusiasm. "You might as well," announced Rockefeller's counsel,
Samuel C. T. Dodd, "endeavor to stay the formation of the clouds, the
falling of the rains, or the flowing of the streams, as to attempt by any
means or in any manner to prevent organization, association of persons,
and the aggregation of capital to any extent that the ever-growing trade
of the world may demand."[28] In Frank Norris's *The Octopus,* Dodd's
fictional contemporary, the railroad president Shelgrim, preaches much
the same gospel: "Try to believe this – to begin with – that railroads
build themselves. . . . The wheat grows itself. . . . The wheat will be
carried to feed the people as inevitably as it will grow."[29]

The fictional Shelgrim and the factual Dodd speak, of course, only
on behalf of the monopolists. However, with suitable adjustments,
their ideas and even their flamboyant rhetoric accurately capture one of
the commanding themes of the early twentieth century. Visions of
organization entranced practically all of the constituencies and interests
of American society. As capital consolidated itself, for example, labor
struggled to organize and meet it. The American Federation of Labor,
founded in 1886, had enrolled only 278,000 members by 1898. By 1904,
that figure had risen to over one and a half million, a sixfold increase.
That kind of success provoked energetic opposition – the National Association of Manufacturers financed a nationwide anti-union campaign,
predictably labeled "the American Plan," and predictably abetted by the
U.S. Supreme Court (cf. the Danbury Hatters Case, 1908) – and union
membership grew more fitfully in the years after 1905. But the Industrial Workers of the World's "one big union" summed up an ideal

cherished by much of American labor, including that gigantic majority of workers who feared or despised the IWW itself.

On the farms, the early years of the century saw the continued appeal and intermittent success of the cooperative movement. For obvious reasons, farmers had even more trouble than labor in organizing against organized capital. In many parts of the country, especially in the South, the extortionate crop-lien system created as much dependence and defeat as the factory system of the Northeast and the Midwest. Nevertheless, the vision of organization reached many farmers as well.

In city halls and statehouses, organized politics – aptly named "machines," with roots reaching back into the Gilded Age – fought to hold on to what they had against the more recently gathered forces of organized reform. The target of the reformers was the invisible and sinister alliance between government and business. Yet, in an irony we shall have several occasions to contemplate in the pages that follow, the reformers' own objective was to run government *as* a business. The Progressives in particular wanted to adopt the organizational model of the corporation and bring to politics the efficiencies of scale and good management that were enriching the country's bankers and industrialists.[30] "City business is like any other business and needs precisely the same kind of organization, management and control," according to Benjamin Parke DeWitt.[31]

On the national level, the years of Theodore Roosevelt's presidency encompassed the establishment of twentieth-century administrative government and of more methodical, if more rigorously selective, mechanisms of regulation. Roosevelt also did what he could to centralize authority in the executive.

Similar impulses toward organization motivated many other groups throughout the society. In 1909, for example, the National Association for the Advancement of Colored People was founded. Its general purpose was to enable blacks to accomplish collectively what they were failing to do as individuals: blunt the edge of a ruthless racism that was becoming more deeply embedded in law and custom all over the United States. By 1912, the General Federation of Women's Clubs, which had been founded in 1890, had attracted a million members. Organized into political- and social-action groups, and into labor unions, women began to deal more aggressively with the large assortment of issues that affected them.

The culmination of a half-century's development in the organization and specialization of knowledge also occurred in these years. America's "science and scholarship, once fostered and sustained by regionally isolated learned societies, became centered in an expanding network of national organizations for the advancement of specialized knowledge."[32]

A whole range of social questions, for instance the rehabilitation of young delinquents, was typically reconsidered in the light of the organizational paradigm.[33]

In some ways the climax of the organizational imperative – and in any case one of the most far-reaching developments of these years – consisted in the absorption of modern technology by corporate capitalism. As David F. Noble has elegantly and exhaustively demonstrated, industrialism was transformed in the years around the turn of the century by the rise of technology and the interrelated emergence of the modern corporate model. The former geometrically enhanced the ability of capitalism to produce, and the latter provided a solution to the dangers of unregulated markets.[34]

When Horatio Winslow took over as editor of *The Masses* for the magazine's fifth issue, his first editorial was entitled "Organization." Winslow elaborated a graceless but revealing mixture of metaphors to make his point, and he spoke not merely for the socialists and cooperators of his own persuasion when he did so:

> To realize how thoroughly organization has burrowed into and transformed today's society is hardly possible; to add up its influence and untangle its crossed strands would be as difficult and as bewildering as to trace in a mature plant the effects of certain grateful spring rains. It is enough to say that definitely and surely organization had touched every art, science and industry in the world.[35]

The awkwardness of Winslow's prose should not obscure the accuracy of his judgment. A more recent and scholarly observer reached more or less the same conclusion. George Woodcock's long and authoritative history of anarchism, after detailing for over 450 pages the careers and beliefs of the leading figures in that movement, concludes with what might be called the counterstatement: "The real social revolution of the modern age has in fact been the process of centralization, toward which every development of scientific and technological progress has contributed."[36]

Given developments like these, it is with some justice that historians and critics such as Marcus Klein or Henry May have found nothing less than a revolution in early twentieth-century America. The scale and scope and speed of change were unprecedented. And yet to see only change is at last to see too little. This was a revolution that provoked a counterrevolutionary cultural response – which is, after all, more predictable than paradoxical. One would expect that a time of genuinely traumatic change would surely be a time as well of heightened reaction.

The accelerating shocks of the future were met by the redoubled claims of the past. Documenting that simultaneity of future and past is the task of the rest of this book.

George Santayana declared at least part of the thesis when, writing in the midst of these years, he described America's two "mentalities": "one a survival of the beliefs and standards of the fathers, the other an expression of the instincts, practices and discoveries of the younger generation."[37] Santayana's implication – that the divisions of America's mind followed the cleavages of age – simplifies the matter, as we shall repeatedly see. But the contention he describes, between surviving beliefs and new discoveries, was pronounced.

Consider briefly, to anticipate the arguments of the following chapters, the encounter between just one of America's preeminent older values and the "new discoveries" we glanced at earlier. All of those revolutionary developments conspired with each other in opposition to the venerable mythology of individualism. The gigantism of American cities, the entry of machines into every corner of life, the pervasive spread of the organizational ideal – all these contributed to the actual and imaginative diminishment of the individual. Further, the landscape that had bred the American hero was disappearing. The frontier had closed, the last Indian war had been fought. By 1912, the last continental states would be organized out of what had been (more picturesquely) "territories."

Simultaneously, however, and surely as a direct reaction against these tendencies, the myth of individualism was never more tenaciously embraced than in these years. "Collective man" was not compatible with the requirements of the American imagination. The simultaneous decline and strength of the ideal of the individual can be illustrated in all sorts of ways, among them the dialectical meaning of "success." Taken impersonally and even abstractly, business and its industrial system – its masses of laborers, its increasingly complex technologies and structures – were figured in repugnant, subhuman symbols such as the octopus. On the other hand, the capitalists themselves were often taken as models of success, exemplary individuals descended from pioneers and frontiersman who spent the same quantities of courage and savvy on changed battlegrounds. What seemed, from one perspective, to suffocate individualism became, from a different vantage point, a cause to reaffirm the idea of the individual.[38]

Theodore Dreiser's writing over a brief period at the turn of the century exemplifies this divided response. In 1900, in *Sister Carrie,* Dreiser created an enduringly powerful image of the organized brutality of capitalism and its virtual abolition of the individual. The Brooklyn trolley strike, the pathetic shifts of the poor, the soup kitchens, the

decline of Hurstwood into shabby suicide add grim stroke to stroke in a
memorabale portrait of corporate capitalism from the harassed viewpoint of its victims. Yet Dreiser, just a year before *Sister Carrie* appeared, had been listed in the first edition of *Who's Who in America,*
where he is described as a journalist who has written, among other
things, "Studies of Contemporary Celebrities." The citation is accurate.
The reference is to Dreiser's interviews with a collection of the rich and
famous for the magazine *Success.* In those pieces, in tones ranging from
the admiring to the adulatory, Dreiser celebrates the economic and
social victories of such men as Philip D. Armour, Marshall Field, and
Andrew Carnegie.

To move from these sketches to Dreiser's first novel is to be
wrenched from the sunlight of Horatio Alger into the half-light of
Jacob Riis. The coexistence of both worlds in Dreiser's work is a tribute
of sorts to his imaginative spaciousness. But it also discloses something
of the complex ethical and political forces contending against each other
in these years. On the one hand, hero worship, infatuation with men of
action and results, a need to affirm individual will against the gathering
hegemony of impersonal force. On the other hand, the unshakable
conviction that the age of force and collectivity has arrived, and a
deepening fear that human will is inevitably reduced to gesture.

If Dreiser is one index to this tension, popular culture enacted the
conflict indirectly in the rise of the western novel. Significantly, the
western flourished in the same years as the frontier closed, and it
reached its classic formulation just after 1900, in Owen Wister's *The
Virginian* (1902). The western combined myth and exotic detail to dramatize a way of life that was already disappearing.[39] We have seen that
some of the imaginative space once occupied by the frontiersman was
taken over by buccaneering capitalists. However, the vanishing cowboy
endured, too, not in his own person, but in the evermore glamorized
and simplified fantasies of story and film.

The subjects we have touched on in these pages will take their place as
well among the principal concerns of the following chapters. The dia-
lectics into which these questions shape themselves will be our particular point of entry.

We shall be surveying a landscape of divided consciousness for which
Paul Laurence Dunbar, in 1901, created a strikingly appropriate image.
Dunbar set the action of his third novel, *The Fanatics,* in Dorbury,
Ohio, and Dorbury is methodically described as a "border town," a
place therefore representative of "the schizophrenia of a mind pulled in
two separate directions."[40] The word "schizophrenia" is a little strong,
though I shall use it myself once or twice in later chapters. Be that as it

may, Dunbar's symbolic geography has broad application. The whole
of America in the early 1900s was a border town, a region poised
between the contending facts and images of past and future.

The study of this border region offered in the following pages is
emphatically *not* intended as a survey, either historical or literary. Some
time ago, Daniel Boorstin made an observation about these years that is
relevant to my purposes. The years from the end of reconstruction to
the outbreak of World War I, wrote Boorstin, have

> too often been described as if individual human beings had gone
> underground and the nation had been taken over by vast eco-
> nomic movements. The lack of dramatic focus in this period has
> tempted historians to treat it abstractly, as if Americans did not
> resume their individual lives until another war aroused them.[41]

This is a bit categorical, but it was roughly correct at the time Boorstin
wrote it, and it still is. My own interest is precisely in the human beings
who lived through these years. Generalizations about the forces – economic and other – that acted on these women and men are altogether
necessary to my arguments. The generalizations must emerge, however, between and from specific analytic engagements with a series of
individual figures and documents.

Most of the materials studied here are artistic: literature especially,
along with painting, music, and architecture. I share with Clifford
Geertz the point of view that art should be addressed as "a cultural
system." Art is deeply expressive of ideological transactions within a
society and may offer insights otherwise less accessible. Works of art
"materialize a way of experiencing."[42] At the same time, art is not
merely a "reflection" or a superstructural phenomenon, in a reductively
Marxian or in any other materialist sense. In Geertz's terms, the relationship between works of art and the society in which they are produced is neither mechanical nor instrumental but "ideational."[43]

These assumptions account for the fairly wide scope of the essays that
follow. They move between works of art in different forms, and between art and other sorts of information afforded by the events of the
period. My objective in approaching these years from a set of different
vantage points is to determine what can be affirmed about the culture as
a whole.

If the focus is broad, however, the method is confined most of the
time to the reading of texts. This is not merely to say that most of the
chapters are devoted to writers of one kind or another, though that is
the case. Nor is it only to recognize that what are often too casually
called "contexts" are themselves nothing more than reconstructed texts,
though that too is the case. It is also to acknowledge that even those

pages devoted to nonliterary subjects, to politics and music and the
visual arts, are based in texts. I more often present acounts of what the
several artists said about their work than appraisals of the buildings and
music and paintings themselves. This is, I realize, a controversial way
of proceeding, and in part it confesses my methodological limits. More
important, however, I agree with the architectural historian Robert
Macleod, who believes that "a consideration of the ideals and intentions
of the designers is more illuminative of their architecture than is conventional stylistic" analysis.[44]

I take it that what is true of architecture is also true of the other arts.
While the makers of art may not be able to tell us everything we need
to know about the art they make, they can tell us a very great deal.
Futhermore, since my interest is precisely in the interactions between
ideas and cultural performance, such testimony is indispensable.

In tracing some of the imaginative patterns that recur in the early
years of the century I have tried diligently not to slide into the sort of
easy "historicism" that Karl Popper derisively defined. "Historicism,"
wrote Popper, "is out to find The Path on which mankind is destined
to walk; it is out to discover The Clue to History."[45] I am not interested
in finding either the Clue or the Path. Rather, I am absorbed in trying
to reproduce the experience of these years and to ascertain the meaning
they had for those who lived through them.

To that end, I have set out a cluster of different but I trust finally
complementary objectives. In the essays that follow, I undertake to
reread some familiar texts, to recover some forgotten texts, to illuminate disparate people and forms by studying them in proximity to each
other, to examine a small number of examples that I claim to be representative, to assess each example in some detail, to locate the imaginative work of this period in some of its economic and political contexts,
to suggest a few connections between the early 1900s and earlier and
later American periods. The particular figures and texts are those that
have interested me. My job is to demonstrate the reasons for my interest and the larger significance of my choices.

The several chapters are tied together primarily through my engagement with the dialectical thesis I have been outlining in these opening
pages. That is to say, though the emphases and strategies of my exposition vary considerably from chapter to chapter, all of them undertake to
explore not the main currents but the crosscurrents of American political and imaginative life. However, I have tried in two other ways as
well to conform the parts of the discussion to the whole. First, many of
the particular topics discussed in one or another chapter – socialism, for
instance, or the position of women, or architecture, or painting – are
also introduced in other chapters, in connection with other topics. Sec-

ond, still another set of subjects – among them the legacies of Puritanism; medievalism and the Gothic revival; the implications of science and
technology; the significance of immigration; the genre and meaning of
romance; the geographies of pastoral – punctuate the essays. These latter
subjects form, as it were, an alternative table of contents.

A final word, about the matter of dates and "periods." Perhaps most
obviously, the two dates in my title identify two wars and the years
between them. It is true that those wars, and their consequences both
for politics and the imagination, are introduced periodically in the following pages. The wars of 1898 and 1917 were events of the most
widely recognized importance at the beginning and end of the period I
am interested in. However, the significance of these dates does not
reach beyond such small distinctions. In a study of this sort, any such
dates, whatever their elementary necessity, can quickly become decep-
tively precise. They are in fact little more than frank conveniences,
intended to locate more or less accurately the roughly two decades of
my interest.

Chapter 2

The triumph of reaction:
Henry James

The aging Henry James speaks, in these year, most clearly in the accents of conservatism, in a voice that modulates easily and often into unnuanced reaction. James was seventy when the First World War broke out, and he met it with apocalyptic anguish. Less than a week after the shells began exploding, on August 5, 1914, James summarized what he took to be the ethical and psychological meaning of the war in a letter to Howard Sturgis. The letter includes this widely quoted passage:

> The plunge of civilization into this abyss of blood and darkness by the wanton feat of those two infamous autocrats is a thing that so gives away the whole age during which we have supposed the world to be, with whatever abatement, gradually bettering, that to have to take it all now for what the treacherous years were all the while really making for and meaning is too tragic for any words.[1]

But the sound of shocked surprise here is misleading. Long before the war reduced the Europe of James's old age to a charnel house, he had declared himself against all the forces and instruments of "the whole age," of modernity itself. For him, the war was rather a climactic symbol than a revelatory disruption, the violence – writ almost incalculably large, to be sure – that seemed increasingly the hallmark of modern culture.

Graham Greene, one of James's finest critics, and one of the most attentive to James's imagination of evil, suggested decades ago (in an essay of 1937, "Henry James: The Private Universe") the social sources of the particular corruption James traces through the late stories and novels. In those fictions, Greene writes, James's egotists are figures rooted in widespread cultural derangement: "These later Jamesian characters . . . form the immoral background to that extraordinary period

18

of haphasard violence which anticipated the First World War."[2] In other words, the war did not reverse but actually ratified James's own prewar vision of disaster.

THE LATE FICTION

Near the end of *The Wings of the Dove,* as if to mark sympathetically the crimes committed against Milly Theale, Venice is transformed: "It was a Venice all of evil . . . ; a Venice of cold, lashing rain from a low black sky, of wicked wind raging through narrow passes, of general arrest and interruption."[3] In keeping with the mythic design of the whole novel, the storm punishing Venice is heightened: Not just Milly but civilization itself is engulfed by the forces set in motion by the quintessentially modern lovers, Kate Croy and Merton Densher. The ocean threatens to submerge the historic piazza of Saint Mark's: "There were stretches of the gallery paved with squares of red marble, greasy now with the salt spray; and the whole place, in its huge elegance, the grace of its conception and the beauty of its detail, was more than ever like a great drawing-room, the drawing-room of Europe, profaned and bewildered by some reverse of fortune"(II:285).

In part, profaned and bewildered Venice is expressive of Merton Densher's sorrow as he looks at it: psychology as politics. Like fictional geographies from Poe's Germany to V. S. Naipaul's Asia, James's Venice is a region of the mind. But in equal part this is a Venice whose growing disorder is itself affecting Densher: politics as psychology. If the passage sounds prophetic, it intends the manner of significant prophecy, as a vision not of the contingent future but of the facts of the present. In those facts James discovered what seemed to him dislocations and deformities of which the threatened Venice of *The Wings of the Dove* is only the most memorable emblem.

James's first guide to Venice was Ruskin, and Ruskin's example offers an interesting gloss on the urgency of the scene we have been looking at, as well as an insight into James's developing temperament as he confronted the new century. James knew Ruskin's work well, and from early on. It is not surprising that the young James, a neophyte art critic in the sixties, should have been on familiar terms with the books of the most influential aesthetic theorist in English in the nineteenth century. In 1869, when James visited Venice for the first time and found himself utterly (and, it would prove, permanently) enchanted, Ruskin's prose had much to do with the spell James found himself under. "It was not Venice in its detail," writes Leon Edel, describing James's visit of discovery, "but Venice in its totality that fired his imagination. With Ruskin . . . in his pocket, he walked or floated through the city."[4]

In a long, impassioned letter to his brother William (September 25, 1869), Henry quotes from *Modern Painters* on the significance of the ducal palace and on the shrewdness of concentrating in Venice on the study of Veronese, Tintoretto, and Bellini. He writes of Tintoretto's supremacy and includes a specific act of homage to Ruskin's prose: "I'd give a great deal to be able to fling down a dozen of Tintoretto's pictures into prose of corresponding force and color. I strongly urge you to look up in vol. 3d of Ruskin's *Stones* (last appendix) a number of magnificent descriptive pages touching his principal pictures."[5]

James had met Ruskin for the first time just a few months before his pilgrimage to Venice, and the younger writer's responses to the older one ironically foreshadow James's own spiritual trajectory over the succeeding three decades. After James had been taken by the Nortons to dinner at Ruskin's, he wrote his mother: "This was extremely pleasant. Ruskin, himself, is a very simple matter. In face, in manner, in talk, in mind, he is weakness pure and simple. I use the word, not invidiously, but scientifically." In specifying Ruskin's "weakness," James proposes a hypothesis that has considerable value for explicating his own emotional situation after the turn of the century. "He has," writes James, "the beauties of his defects; but to see him only confirms the impression given by his writing, that he has been scared back by the grim face of reality."[6]

James goes on to say that what Ruskin had been scared *into* is a "world of unreason and illusion." Terms that strong have no applicability to the James of the last novels. But the "greasy" stones of Venice that Merton Densher crosses in *The Wings of the Dove* are an image of fear provoked by the grim face of reality, one among many such images in the prose of James's last years. Like Ruskin, James reacted with aesthetic and moral alarm to a landscape and a social order being recreated by the engineering of technology and democratic politics.

In the late novels, the massive intensity of James's concentration on the relationships among his central characters virtually seals them off from the world at large. Edith Wharton, a friendly if by no means uncritical reader of James's fiction, recalls in her memoirs the frustration she felt each time she found herself caught up in the densely centripetal worlds of the late novels. "What was your idea," she asked James, "in suspending the four principal characters in *The Golden Bowl* in the void? What sort of life did they lead when they were not watching each other, and fending with each other?" James responded to the question with a look of pained surprise and the disturbed denial

"My dear—I didn't know I had."[7] Nevertheless, Wharton is surely correct in her assessment. The society in which late Jamesian characters move is powerfully implied in their relationships, but it is only implied. Scenes of such direct general purport as the rendering of storm-menaced Saint Mark's are infrequent, and such statements as they afford are typically symbolic.

In a number of the short stories of the 1900s, James engages the state of contemporary civilization less obliquely. "The Papers," for example, a long, undervalued tale that was never serialized and was published for the first time in the collection *The Better Sort* in 1903, brings to a strident climax James's lifelong quarrel with Fleet Street.

Maud Blandy and Howard Bight are a pair of popular journalists; their job is to create publicity for citizens who might otherwise remain obscure. They epitomize one of James's preoccupying fears throughout his career, and one that emerges with special poignance in the late years: the making public of what ought to be private. Maud and Howard represent not merely Fleet Street but much of what James understands to be the frighteningly distinctive epistemology of the twentieth century: The newspapers "were all the furniture of their consciousness."[8] Such a mental life is the stark antithesis of James's chiefly treasured values. For James the richest life is lived most inwardly. The growing dominion of the newspapers, in whose columns life is stripped of its interiority altogether and presented in simplified outwardness, is thus not merely a symptom of cultural decay; it is decay's monument. In "The Papers," James anticipates the twentieth century's increasingly reductive transactions between the media and its celebrities. The most famous man in England, Sir A. B. C. Beadel-Muffett, K.C.B., M.P., had done absolutely nothing except to *be* the most famous man in England. He is, Howard and Maud agree, "Magnificent": "It is genius," declares Maud, "to get yourself so celebrated for nothing—to carry out your idea in the face of everything. I mean your idea of *being* celebrated. It isn't as if he had done even one little thing" (p.23). The emptiness of a "life" lived solely in the pages of the daily press, and the reduction of life thereby to nothing more than public entertainment, systematically reversed James's professed conceptions of humanity.

From one point of view, Beadel-Muffett is a comically rendered recapitulation of John Marcher. Marcher, as James himself described him in his notebook reflections on "The Beast in the Jungle," is the man whose distinction resides in having nothing whatever happen to him; his obscure life ebbs away in shadows. Beadel-Muffett, Marcher's farcical apotheosis, accomplishes as little but ascends into the brilliantly lit pantheon of British journalistic fame.

The comedy of "The Papers" is harsh. James's contempt for all his characters – and for the masses of the public who make such careers possible – is palpable throughout the tale. From time to time, indeed, the comedy lapses altogether, and James's revulsion from the culture of Fleet Street erupts nakedly. "The press," observes Howard Bight at one point, "is the watchdog of civilization and the watchdog happens to be – it can't be helped – in a chronic state of *rabies*. Muzzling is easy talk; one can but keep the animal on the run" (pp. 63–4). The papers are a diseased animal, and the new civilization they simultaneously protect and ravage is diseased as well.

In no other fiction does James quite so directly image his dissent from the consciousness of the new century. By the time the story ends, human lives have become "new meat flung to" the papers, which "roared and resounded" like carniverous animals (p. 103).

Journalism, and what it represents and forebodes for the threatened fate of private persons, embodies much of the loud, vulgar, undiscriminating new world that – to use his words about Ruskin – "scared back" Henry James. What he is scared back into is often an anxious but unspecified plea for the private, the personal, the cultivated. But in "The Great Good Place," appropriately published in *Scribner's* in January 1900, James details the particular locale of his retreat.

George Dane, unlike Sir A. B. C. Beadel-Muffett, has accomplished a good deal; he is a hugely productive and as hugely successful novelist. But the outcome for Dane is that he lives more and more of his life in the glare of publicity and under the multiplying burdens of celebrity. His personal existence seems to him to be slipping away; he stands on the edge of illness and breakdown. After a short sleep one morning, Dane awakens in an altogether unfamiliar place: a place of rural retirement, peopled by mysterious but benevolent figures, a place of obscurity, of silence, of privacy. The setting is a "cloister"; it reminds Dane of "old convents" seen in Italy, of "some great abode of an Order, some mild Monte Cassino, some Grande Chartreuse."[9] Dane's companions are the Brothers; the most intrusive sounds are those of "slow, sweet bells" (p. 21). R. W. B. Lewis has written of James's characteristic use of a displaced religious language in his fiction.[10] This is an example of that displacement, but it goes beyond James's characteristic practice. "The Great Good Place" is James's modest contribution to the factitious medievalism of his generation.[11] It recalls, three decades later and now with unintended pathos, James's earlier judgment on Ruskin's "world of . . . illusion."

Nothing of technology, of the urban, of the industrial – nothing even, impossibly, of bad weather – approached Dane and his few companions: "They sat in silence a little, seeming pleasantly to follow, in the view of the green garden, the vague movements of the monster – madness, surrender, collapse – they had escaped" (p. 24). In this "good place," as in much of sentimental pastoral, the natural scene is "methodized," James's predictable version of which is to image the setting by means of an analogy of art. The countryside surrounding Dane's cloister resembles "some old Italian Picture, some Carpaccio or some early Tuscan, the representation of a world without newspapers and letters, without telegrams and photographs, without the dreadful, fatal too much" (p. 33). In this gigantically mystified rural seat, the individual personality reemerges: "The inner life woke up again, and it was the inner life, for people of his generation, victims of the modern madness, mere maniacal extension and motion, that was returning health" (p. 32).

However, if "The Great Good Place" illustrates James's address to the new century opening around him, it discloses much more than James's disgust at what George Dane calls "the wild waters . . . of our horrible time" (p.24). For the perfection of the demi-paradise that James constructs resides above all in negation – a negation not just of the detested loud world outside the garden, but of self. Dane "couldn't . . . easily have phrased" the charm of the place: "It was such an abyss of negatives, such an absence of everything" (p. 19). A victory like this contains its own defeat, since, as James knew better than most American writers before and after him, the self detached from other selves ceases to exist. Thus, when Dane declares to himself that "the real exquisite was to be without the complication of an identity" (p. 32), he is in his own view only elaborating his polemic against the modern world. However, he is at the same time inevitably celebrating the chillingly nihilistic triumph of self-negation. "I am," says he, "nobody. That was the fun" (p. 29). This is the portrait of a man "scared back" out of life itself.

The drama of "The Great Good Place" never rises to the grandeur of the contemporaneous *Wings of the Dove*. Nevertheless, Milly Theale's encounter with the question of her own identity is significantly similar to George Dane's. In the famous scene in Book Five, when Milly stands before the Bronzino portrait, when she declares, "I shall never be better than this" (I:221), what Milly is emphasizing above all about her painted likeness is that "she was dead, dead, dead." Milly's apotheosis, as James calls it, grows out of the paradox that shapes her whole career. As she expresses it herself: "Since I've lived all these years as if I were dead, I shall die, no doubt, as if I were alive" (I:199). Milly's tone is blithe, but her aphorism sums up a bitter truth. Her existence reaches toward meaning only as life itself slips from her.

After her second visit to Sir Luke Strett, she offers a more discursive analysis. The great doctor, she muses, had found out "literally everything. . . . it was truly what she had come for, and . . . for the time at least it would give her something firm to stand on. She struck herself as aware, aware as she had never been, of really not having had from the beginning anything firm. It would be strange for the firmness to come, after all, from her learning in these agreeable conditions that she was in some way doomed; but above all it would prove how little she had hitherto had to hold her up. If she was now to be held up by the mere process – since that was perhaps on the cards – of being let down, this would only testify in turn to her queer little history" (I:236). Milly has simply existed, without definition or purpose, and she gains her identity only in the act of losing it.

This has the intensity of allegory: Through Milly's doom, James images the fatality of innocence, its necessary defeat by evil, by experience, indeed by life itself. But that last phrase is sinister, for it suggests that life is the enemy. Sinister as well, therefore, is Milly's almost jovial acceptance of her death sentence and her embrace of the Jamesian logic of ultimate renunciation. Milly's life resembles a self-inflicted wound, from which the negation that is death becomes a release. She is annihilated in the struggle between mutually exclusive alternatives. Paradox expands to encompass tragedy as not-being comes to seem the only supportable mode of being.

A day or so after this visit to Sir Luke, Milly watches the brilliant Kate Croy lead a lively conversation. Kate is at her best, and Milly says of herself that she "was never at her best – unless indeed it were exactly, as now, in listening, watching, admiring, collapsing" (I:276). The observation is offhand, but the last word accurately abbreviates Milly's entire history. She is at her best in more or less exact ratio as she ceases to be.

One final image to complete this account of Milly's poignant destiny. Sitting alone in Sir Luke's spacious consulting room, Milly notes in turn the furnishings and decorations. She predicts that she will become familiar with all the ornaments, the many items "presented in gratitude and long ago." Above all, she lingers over the many photographs of the doctor's grateful former patients: "She should be as one of the circle of eminent contemporaries, photographed, engraved, signatured, and in particular framed and glazed, who made up the rest of the decoration" (I:237). All unwitting, Milly has devised a glancing recapitulation of the scene before the Bronzino portrait, but with a thickened texture of fatality. Where at Matcham she had accepted the proposition of others that she resembled the framed and gilded lady – a lady who struck her principally as dead – here in Sir Luke's office it is she who turns herself into an art object. This paragraph follows directly upon Milly's decision that she is doomed, and it fittingly commemorates her commitment to the oneness of transcendence and dissolution.

Characters as different from one another as Milly Theale, George Dane, and Sir A. B. C. Beadel-Muffett document, in their radically diverse ways, Henry James's profound and deepening alienation from his own time and place. Other characters of his later fictions, whatever their particular concerns, further amplify James's quarrel with modernity.

In "The Birthplace," James's splendid comic anatomy of bardolatry, the main character, Morris Gedge, is found as the story opens peering bitterly around the cramped Midlands cottage in which he and his wife are living. He weeps at the sight of what he calls their "prison," "so grim with enlightenment, so ugly with industry, so turned away from any dream."[12] One hears in the first two phrases an abrupt, symmetrical condemnation of two hundred years of modern history: the enlightenment of the eighteenth century, the industry of the nineteenth.

The "dream" of the final clause is, of course, the older England, specifically the putatively "merrie" England of the Renaissance. It is an England still and only to be found in "the great green woodland" (p. 405) of Shakespeare. Shakespeare is conceived by his late-Victorian worshippers, including Morris Gedge, in essentially pastoral terms. The green world of the poet is the antithesis of the tasteless vulgarity that comprises for Gedge the substance of his own epoch.

The story's comic irony rests on Shakespeare's ultimate elusiveness. Because so little can be verified, the curators of his birthplace, along with the hordes of visitors – the latter at once credulous and grasping – are licensed to invent just about any "facts" that suit their hero-worshipping fancy:

> "Don't they want also to see where He had His dinner and where He had His tea?"
> "They want everything. . . . They want to see where He hung up His hat and where He kept His boots and where His mother boiled her pot." (P. 437)

Morris Gedge at first resists these pressures to revise, to embroider, to mystify the past. However, scholarly tentativeness doesn't suit the tourists. Word of their dissatisfaction reaches his employers and, under the threat of dismissal, he relents. The story's sadly comic conclusion shows him as he has become: the most grandiloquently hypocritical of all the lecturers, overtopping all his predecessors in the kind and number of ersatz Shakespearean details he invents. The results of his excesses, needless to say, are multiplied receipts for the birthplace and a raise in his own salary.

Along with its comedy, "The Birthplace" discloses James's considerable sympathy with Morris Gedge, with the revolt against "enlightenment and industry," with the retreat into the fictive "great green woodland." Above all, the peculiar angle of vision from which James explores the hagiographic mythology of "Shakespeare" makes of the story another document attesting to its author's preoccupation with the interplay between being and absence.

A visitor to the shrine, significantly an American, offers the beginnings of an alternative hypothesis to Shakespeare's absence from the place. Rather than forcing Shakespeare's presence through the invention of a fictional story to fill the house, the American draws a moral precisely from the poet's irreducible inaccessibility. He says to Gedge:

> "I'm interested . . . in what, I think, is *the* interesting thing – or at all events the eternally tormenting one. The fact of the abysmally little that, in proportion, we know."
>
> "In proportion to what?" his companion asked.
>
> "Well, to what there must have been – to what in fact there *is* – to wonder about. That's the interest: it's immense. He escapes us like a thief at night, carrying off – well, carrying off everything. And people pretend to catch Him like a flown canary, over whom you can close your hand and put Him back. He won't *go* back; He won't come back. He's not" – the young man laughed – "such a fool! It makes Him the happiest of all great men." (Pp. 435–6)

Once again James suggests a felicity measured in absence. Shakespeare's superlative happiness depends on his more or less complete escape from the crowds and confines of his own home. We shall look at a more complex Jamesian transaction between birthplace and betrayal when we take up *The American Scene*. For now, note that under the pressures of what we might call Henry James's imagination of escape, his preeminent interest in the artistic careers of both the historical Shakespeare and the fictional George Dane really has nothing to do with art at all. Rather, James is drawn to the personal question of the successful writer's ability to sustain a private existence. In both stories, the one comic, the other visionary, life consists in evasion and absence. And, in "The Birthplace" as in "The Great Good Place," evasion ultimately involves the denial of identity. Morris Gedge makes this clear when he takes his visitor's suggestions a step further:

> "There is no author; that is for us to deal with. There are the immortal people – *in* the work; but there's nobody else."
>
> "Yes," said the young man – "that's what it comes to. There should really, to clear the matter up, be no such Person."
>
> "As you say," Gedge returned, "it's what it comes to. There *is* no such Person." (P. 439)

He is the happiest of men: There *is* no such person.

Henry James's anguished argument with his times finally led him, in two of his last completed major works, into moral confusion and despair.

The "ambiguity" of *The Golden Bowl* is a commonplace. Though occasionally critics address other subjects – the novel's style, or its adumbration of the international theme, for example – the bulk of the enormous critical literature surrounding this enormous book is given over to moral assessments of its four main characters, with special attention to Adam Verver and above all, to Maggie. Terms like "saint" and "witch" recur in critical essays discussing Maggie Verver, and such language rather baldly identifies the dichotomous conclusions readers have been arriving at for decades. The fact that a whole generation of skilled and intelligent critics has worried so insistently about the novel's moral stance perhaps bears more pondering than the wildly various judgments they have announced. It suggests that James has cloaked the quite serious moral issues he has taken up in *The Golden Bowl* in an opaque, barely penetrable veil.

Consider briefly the fact and significance of James's moral elusiveness with respect to one character in the novel, Adam Verver. His very name bespeaks rather the simpler dimensions of fairy tale than any more substantial realities. "Adam Verver" is a miniature encyclopedia of several of America's most self-congratulatory myths: prelapsarian and youthful, unspotted and robust. And much we are told in the book is intended to amplify those insinuations.

Indeed, as both Yvor Winters and F. O. Matthiessen complained a good many years ago, there is a split between morals and manners in James's protrayal of Adam Verver. To put their quite different if complementary opinions summarily: Adam's alleged benevolence cannot plausibly be the outcome of his posited background and environment. He is presented to us as the most successful of all the plutocrats, as successful – by unspoken parallels that had to be in the minds of James and his readers – as Andrew Carnegie and J. P. Morgan. He has survived and triumphed in a struggle that every observer of American business, regardless of political preference, understood to be enacted in the Darwinian jungle of American capitalism. The qualities necessarily implicated in success on Adam Verver's literally fabulous scale, brutality and energy and tenacity, are precisely those that the novel labors to disguise, to transform, or flatly to deny. Instead of drawing Adam in the plausible lineaments of his history, James simply pronounces him to be a spirit ruled principally by sensitivity, domestic piety, and innocence itself.

Where, logically, Verver must resemble the Theodore Roosevelt of Henry Adams's imagining – "pure act . . . wielding unmeasured power with immeasurable energy"[13] – he is given to us as a figure mainly passive, worked on by others, more than a little vulnerable, a potential victim in need of protection. Of his three decades of titanic commercial battles we are told nothing, except through a clichéd metaphor to which James gives a religious twist: "He had come out . . . at the top of his hill of difficulty, the tall sharp spiral round which he had begun to wind his ascent at the age of twenty, and the apex of which was a platform looking down, if one would, on the kingdoms of the earth."[14]

James himself, perhaps in embarrassment, calls it "the greatest of wonders" that such a gentle soul should "ever have got, as the phrase was . . . to where he was" (I:127). But that objection is immediately dissolved in another religious image: "The spark of fire, the point of light, sat somewhere in his inward vagueness as a lamp before a shrine twinkles in the dark perspective of a church" (I:127). He tends toward the altruistic rather than the self-serving, recognizing his own claims only after those of others have been attended to: "This amiable man bethought himself of his personal advantage, in general, only when it might appear to him that other advantages, those of other persons, had succesfully put in their claim" (I:125–6). Incapable of malice himself, he cannot even discern it in others: "His eyes . . . saw Mrs. Rance approach with an instant failure to attach to the fact any grossness of avidity of Mrs. Rance's own" (I:131).[15]

My reference earlier to the fairy-tale aura bathing Adam Verver was deliberate. As readers of James know, it was regularly his practice, with whatever degree of awareness or irony, to adapt to his complex novelistic purposes the elements of fairy tale. Thus, to instance familiar examples, the orphaned girl, the fairy godmother, the miraculous fortune, and the exotic metamorphoses out of which both *The Portrait of a Lady* and *The Wings of the Dove* are constructed.

In the case of *The Golden Bowl,* however, James has in a sense reversed himself. The very facts of Adam Verver's entire adult life are suppressed in order that cause may be detached from effect and that Verver may retain the uncorrupted simplicity that precedes experience. Where, say, Isabel Archer's career moves away from the simplifications of her premises toward the complex grandeur of maturity, Adam Verver's supposable complexity is simply erased on behalf of an impermeable virtuousness. Or, to put the matter in different terms, James's novel indirectly documents Max Weber's critique of America's derivatively Puritan confusion between moral and material achievement. Adam Verver, serenely superior to all his antagonists in both money and integrity, has been rewarded in wealth for his ethical strength, and vice versa.

Surely it is prudent to resist taking such a gratuitously asserted benevolence as Adam Verver's very seriously. Yet a question far more fundamental than its mere probability vexes Adam's innocence. Stated simply, Adam Verver is a good man only intermittently and partially. It is an oblique tribute to James that the logic of his character at last escapes the sentimental simplifications impressed upon it initially; yet the effect is more perplexing than assured. As we watch Adam act upon others, the self-sacrificial, figuratively Christlike martyr to the sacredness of human relationships gives way to a different figure, a calculating connoisseur of people as objects, a complacently manipulative collector. If it were only the Prince who was to become (in Maggie's words) "a part of [Adam's] collection . . . a rarity, an object of beauty, an object of price . . . a *morceau de musée*" (I:12), then something like retribution might be involved. But it is not just the Prince. Everyone Adam comes in contact with is estimated, assayed. He selects a friend, a son-in-law, a wife under the same criteria as those he applies to Old Master paintings and rare furniture.

This is Adam Verver's grotesque error: He has translated the ethical grounds of action into aesthetic ones. As the narrator himself observes in an extraordinary passage of comment:

> Nothing perhaps might affect us as queerer, had we time to look into it, than this application of the same measure of value to such different pieces of property as old Persian carpets, say, and new human acquisitions. . . . As [this measure] had served him to satisfy himself . . . both about Amerigo and about the Bernardino Luini he had happened to come to knowledge of at the time he was consenting to the announcement of his daughter's betrothal, so it served him at present to satisfy himself about Charlotte Stant and an extraordinary set of oriental tiles of which he had lately got wind. (I:196–7)

A paragraph like this requires only a little gloss, and the narrator immediately supplies it himself: Adam's "was all, at bottom, in him, the aesthetic principle." The idea of beauty, followed by its appropriation, governs Adam's existence. In such an ethical world, reciprocity must yield to the demands of possessorship, generosity must give way to calculation, and love to taste. James does not flinch from demonstrating the inhumane consequences of Adam's aesthetic principle. What it leads to, along with much else, is this image of Charlotte, following Adam through the art galleries at Fawns:

> Charlotte hung behind, with emphasized attention: she stopped when her husband stopped, but at the distance of a case or two . . . ; the likeness of their connexion would not have been

wrongly figured if he had been thought of as holding in one of his pocketed hands the end of a long silken halter looped round her beautiful neck. (II:287)

Properly situated, Adam Verver proves to be the lineal descendant, not of Christopher Newman or Isabel Archer or the rest of James's American explorers in Europe, but of Rowland Mallett or the scheming antiquarian in "The Aspern Papers." Above all, Adam Verver descends from Gilbert Osmond, who "thought Miss Archer sometimes of too precipitate a readiness. It was a pity she had that fault, because if she had not had it she would really have had none; she would have been as smooth to his general need of her as handled ivory to the palm."[16] Osmond's metaphorical ivory unmistakably foreshadows Adam's silken halter.

To notice the similarity between Adam Verver and Gilbert Osmond, however, is only to underline the moral welter of *The Golden Bowl*. For while that novel concedes Adam's inhumanity, it continues to insist on his worthiness. Moreover, where *The Portrait of a Lady* is peopled with large numbers of characters who both exemplify and enunciate a standard of behavior better than Osmond's, no such comparative norms oppose Adam Verver. Whatever their defects, *The Golden Bowl* seems to suggest that Adam's principles are the best that can be hoped for. And this in turn suggests that, in the twenty years separating the two novels, the dimensions of moral possibility have shrunk. To phrase that statement more exactly, what have shrunk are the dimensions of Henry James's ability to imagine moral achievements more ennobling than those of Adam Verver.

Ruth B. Yeazell, in her uncommonly shrewd analysis of *The Golden Bowl*, offers a hypothesis concerning Maggie's role in the book that I think can be more generally applied. "Maggie Verver's victory preserves the civilized forms of her world and the closed shape of her novel, but beneath the surface of these lingering nineteenth-century fictions, imposed at such tremendous cost, we feel an almost unbearable strain."[17] The victory, the strain, and the cost are James's, too.

THE AMERICAN SCENE

In 1904, past sixty and after a twenty-year absence, Henry James returned to America for a few months. He landed at Hoboken on August 30, spent the fall mainly in New England, and then in the first half of 1905 traveled over a large portion of the United States, from New York City to as far south as Palm Beach and Saint Augustine, through

Indianapolis and Chicago to California, Oregon, and Washington. It was professedly a voyage of rediscovery, and James hoped it would prove a voyage of recovery as well. Out of his months of observations emerged *The American Scene,* a massive, brooding monument to James's despair over modernity, a memorial carved in the furthest final reach of James's immensely complex late style.

It was James's well-known habit, in his late manner, to submerge both description and analysis in image making. The "vast bright Babylon" that is Paris in *The Ambassadors,* hanging like "some huge iridescent object, a jewel brilliant and hard" in the air of Lambert Strether's discriminations, comes to mind,[18] as does the page-long evocation of the Prince as a fantastic pagoda in *The Golden Bowl.* This stylistic habit recurs in *The American Scene,* pushed in fact a step beyond the practice of the novels to create the book's most striking and curious feature: In *The American Scene* only buildings speak. Page after page, and chapter upon chapter, James's recorded conversations are not with people but with buildings, buildings of all sorts, from homes to hotels, cafés to museums. The effect is odd, disconcerting. Human speech is eradicated from the book and replaced by the monologues of shop fronts and tenements.

A street of fine New England houses explains itself: "We are good, yes – we are excellent; though if we know it very well, we make no vulgar noise about it: we only just stand here, in our long double line, in the manner of mature and just slightly-reduced gentlewomen seated against the wall at an evening party."[19] Trinity Church, obscured by ever-larger and even more numerous skyscrapers, tearfully complains of its fate: "Yes, the wretched figure I am making is as little as you see my fault – it is the fault of the buildings whose first care is to deprive churches of their visibility" (p. 78; Plate 1). From across the dangerously busy Fifth Avenue, the Waldorf-Astoria beckons: "*Un bon mouvement,* therefore: you must make a dash for it, but you'll see I'm worth it" (p. 101). And so on, in scores of examples.

Several inferences may be drawn from this peculiar technique. It would, for instance, be relevant though at best partial to recall Edith Wharton's subversive question about the hermetic isolation of the few main characters in *The Golden Bowl.* In *The American Scene* isolation has become complete: Save for James's, the setting is otherwise empty of human voices.

More usefully, the technique of *The American Scene* conforms – albeit reductively – with James's lifelong commitment to reading the surfaces of his surroundings. The perceivable outsides of buildings and objects may be said to "speak" in all of James's fictions, though usually not between quotation marks. For James, the indefatigable analyst of tex-

National City Bank, 52 Wall Street, greatest financial institution of America, founded in 1812 on present site; purchased the Custom House for $3,000,000; will remodel the historic structure and occupy it when the Collector of Port moves to new building on Bowling Green. Since James Stillman became President of the bank in 1891 its business has grown enormously, revolutionizing banking conditions. Capital and surplus, $42,480,726; deposits, $255,468,356; assets, $317,436,471; cash in vaults May 29, 1905, $57,927,780. Known as the Rockefeller Bank.

PLATE 1. Trinity Church, as viewed between the commercial structures of Wall Street. (Reprinted from the 1905 edition of *King's Views of New York*.)

tures and surfaces, architecture documents better than any other evidence the core of a society. What it reveals about his natal country is the essential rootlessness and voracious pecuniary appetites of American life.

The urgency that drove James to make explicit the sermons in stone and clapboard he heard across the United States derived from his continued feeling of shocked betrayal at what American architecture revealed: the hastiness and shallowness and greed of American civilization. There is thus an obvious tactical function to the talking buildings of the book. James slyly enhances the authority of his angry pronouncements against American culture by dramatizing his opinions as the confessions of American artifacts themselves. In this way, it is not James who discerns the empty and unpromising quality of American society. It is the society itself that admits – sometimes gleefully, sometimes sorrowfully – to the charge. "Oh, yes," declare the overblown new "villas" on the Jersey shore, "we were awfully dear, for what we are and for what we do" (p. 8). The "detestable" tall new building looming over the Boston Athenaeum threatens its refined neighbor: " 'Exquisite' was what they called you, eh? We'll teach you, then, little sneak, to be exquisite! We allow none of that rot round here" (p. 233). The shop fronts of Boston grimly disavow any interest in excellence: "Oh come; don't look among us for what you won't, for what you shan't find, the best quality attainable; but only for that quite other matter, the best value we allow you" (p. 235).

Beyond their ostentation and vulgarity, beyond their lack of aesthetic distinction and their typical inappropriateness to their sites, what America's buildings confess to most insistently is their own transience. And in that they give voice to the major theme of *The American Scene:* James's collision with and revulsion from "the dreadful chill of change" (p. 232). The inescapable poverty of American culture is most vividly exposed by the impermanence of its creation, by the fact that permanence is never even considered. America is pastless and restless in equal measure. Its structures manifest a turbulent, frightening energy, improvising temporary solutions to practical problems, and to one problem above all, the acquisition of wealth.

At first glance, the indictment seems to resemble James's earlier, famous attack on American civilization in *Hawthorne* (1879). In that book's often-quoted catalogue of absences, James enumerates the "items of high civilization" missing from American life: "No sovereign, no court, no personal loyalty, no aristocracy, no church, no clergy, no army, no diplomatic service, no country gentlemen, no palaces, no castles, nor manors. . . ," and so on, for half a page.[20] *The American Scene* does echo that estimate of America's deficiencies, sometimes quite closely. Speaking of the American school, for example, James writes that the school has a colossal presence, "a presence which profits . . . by the failure of concurrent and competitive presences, the failure of any others looming at all on the same scale save that of Business, those in particular of a visible Church, a visible State, a visible Society, a visible Past" (pp. 134–5).

In fact, however, whatever premises James's later book shares with the one he wrote a quarter-century before, *The American Scene* is entirely different in its tone and consummated design, and the difference defines with precision the older James's enlarged despair. What James had felt was missing from America in 1879 was a past; what he finds missing in 1905 is the possibility of America *ever* constructing a past. The paradox here is only superficial. *The American Scene* pictures a society so devoted to getting and spending, so divorced from any consciousness of its own history, as to be trapped forever into the improvised experiments of the present. James passes his fears and suspicions most summarily in review when he transcribes his walk up Fifth Avenue and his conversations with "certain exorbitant structures" (p. 111), those bloated mansions scattered up and down the avenue by the dozen or so most emphatically "arrived" of New York's early twentieth-century *arrivistes* (Plate 2).

The ersatz châteaus and castles are emblems of New York's particular kind of "newness," the very sign of whose energy is that "it doesn't believe in itself." It is a self-propelling novelty whose mission is "to gild the temporary, with its gold, as many inches thick as may be, and then, with a fresh shrug . . . of its splendid cynicism for its freshly detected inability to convince, give up its actual work" (p. 110). Like demented Belascos, but working through their millions on the scale of cities rather than stages, America's rich blend the realities of history and society toward the requirements of their illusions. In James's eyes, they accomplish only the revelation of their money, their insecurity, their ignorance.

Typically, James reserves the decisive statement of his theme to be spoken by the scene itself – this time not by the buildings he is looking at but by the very "voice" of New York, speaking *to* the buildings. The lines are suffused with the passion of a jeremiad, and they bear quoting at length. James introduces the passage by describing the pity he felt, again and again on Fifth Avenue, when he learned that "such and such a house, or a row, is 'coming down' " (p. 112). The moral of the endless building and tearing down "rings out like the crack of that lash in the sky, the play of some mighty teamster's whip." At this point James falls silent, and the moral is explicated by the other voice:

PLATE 2. Fifth Avenue looking north from 65th Street, with the J. J. Astor house at the corner, 1898. (Reprinted by permission of the Byron Collection, Museum of the City of New York.)

"No" – this is the tune to which the whip seems flourished – "there's no step at which you shall rest. . . . I build you up but to tear you down, for if I were to let sentiment and sincerity once take root, were to let any tenderness of association once accumulate, or any 'love of the old' once pass unsnubbed, what would become of *us,* who have our hands on the whipstock, please? Fortunately, we've learned the secret for keeping association at bay. We've learned that the great thing is not to suffer it to so much as begin. Wherever it does begin we find we're lost; but as that takes some time we get in ahead."

Note that the dictatorial "I" has modulated into an oligarchic "we." The snarling collective voice goes on to reveal that the secret to defeating "association" is to build only on an inhuman scale, to build skyscrapers. The voice warns New York's buildings:

"You shall 'run,' all, without exception, to the fifty floors. We defy you even to aspire to venerate shapes so grossly constructed as the arrangement in fifty floors. You may have a feeling for keeping on with an old staircase, consecrated by the tread of generations . . . but how can you have a feeling for keeping on with an old elevator, how can you have it any more than for keeping on with an old omnibus?"

That the old elevators and old buses of Paris, of London, even of New York elicit today the same wistful nostalgia as old staircases at the turn of the century is a phenomenon outside our present concerns. What does concern us is the misanthropic, downright savage delight James invests in this prophetic voice of destruction:

"You'd be ashamed to venerate the arrangement in fifty floors . . . even if you could; whereby, saving you any moral trouble or struggle, they are conceived and constructed – and you must do us the justice of this care for your sensibility – in a manner to put the thing out of the question."

The malevolent oration winds up with a return from the matter of ugliness to the even more conclusive question of transience. The sky-scrapers will be constructed in such a manner

"that there shall be immeasurably more of them, in quantity, to tear down than of the actual past that we are now sweeping away. Wherefore we shall be kept in precious practice. The word will perhaps be then – who knows? – for building from the earth-surface downwards; in which case it will be a question of tearing, so to speak, 'up.' It little matters, so long as we blight the super-stition of rest." (Pp. 112–113)

Everything about this speech, even its moment or two of metallic, tight-lipped humor, is angry and embittered. Indeed, the prevailing tone arches beyond anger or fear and unmistakably toward the excess of paranoia. I use the word not in a clinical sense but in the analogic political sense once proposed by Richard Hofstadter.[21] And in that sense, James's terror is shaped into detailed paranoiac terms. He is not simply afraid. His nightmare is grounded in the scheming of intelligent, self-serving conspirators, the nameless "I" and "we" of the passage, uttering their commands in the scream of the whip, confidently allow-ing a glimpse into their secrets. The authors of the conspiracy are unnamed not merely because they are more than legion but because they are the very spirit of the place itself, of New York, of the United States as a whole.

Further, what is true for America in 1905 will soon be true for the rest of the world. What James calls "the force of the American example" (p. 160), "the fruit-bearing action" (p. 102) of the American precedent, ensures that the barbarism of modernity will swiftly accomplish its destructive march around the globe. The most acute suffering of the paranoid victim follows the discovery that "they" are not only in control, but in control everywhere. There can be no escape, anywhere. James has been betrayed by his natal home; he will inevitably be betrayed by his adopted home; he has in fact been betrayed by history itself.

The months of James's visit in 1904–1905 were among the most frenetic in the muckraking and reform movements. At an almost daily rate, books and articles exposed the political corruption and economic deformities of American society, and strategies for correction appeared almost as frequently – from the palliatives of federal regulatory legislation to more violent proposals. To list even a tiny handful of the exposés published between 1904 and 1906 is to recapture an echo of those clamorous years: Edward Bok's "The 'Patent-Medicine' Curse"; Lincoln Steffens's *The Shame of the Cities;* Thomas Lawson's *Frenzied Finance;* Ida M. Tarbell's *The History of the Standard Oil Company;* Charles Edward Russell's *The Greatest Trust in the World;* Robert Hunter's "The Children Who Toil"; David Graham Phillips's *The Treason of the Senate;* Eugene V. Debs's "Arouse, Ye Slaves!"; Upton Sinclair's *The Jungle.* E. W. Kemble's great cartoon, "Death's Laboratory," a gaping skull whose teeth are formed of patent-medicine bottles, appeared in *Collier's* on June 3, 1905. The Industrial Workers of the World met in convention for the first time in 1905, with Debs, Daniel De Leon, Lucy Parsons, Mother Jones, and others on the platform. The Niagara Movement was organized in 1905 by W. E. B. Du Bois, F. L. McGhee, W. M. Trotter, and others. Legislation creating the Food and Drug Administration was signed by President Roosevelt in 1906.

Almost nothing of this national ferment appears in *The American Scene.* To be sure, Philadelphia provokes a comment, a wryly apocalyptic image of "a society dancing, all consciously, on the thin crust of a volcano" (p. 285). But Philadelphia was perhaps the most systemically venal of all American municipalities, or so it seemed to contemporaries. (With bemused resignation, Steffens subtitled the Philadelphia chapter of *The Shame of the Cities,* "Corrupt and Contented.") However, James's occasional glimpse only underscores the more typical absence of politics – of current "topics" generally – from his book. (In June of 1905, while Big Bill Haywood was addressing the delegates gathered at that founding convention of the IWW in Chicago, James was delivering the commencement address at Bryn Mawr, speaking on "The Question of Our Speech.")

Part of the reason for James's indifference to political and economic issues we have already seen. He was frankly bewildered by the turmoil of American life. He had through his entire career disqualified himself as an analyst of "downtown," of the domains of finance and industry. His encounter with those worlds now more than ratified his disqualification; it left him numbed. At the same time, James would defend his omissions and emphases. He would appeal, for one thing, to the prerogative he had long insisted upon for all writers to choose their material. As he wrote in "The Art of Fiction" (1884): "We must grant the artist his subject, his idea, his *donnée*."[22]

More important, James would argue that his way into American society, through its sensitive indirections, would at last map out a surer guide to the substance of American politics than would a more direct reportage of current events. There is much to be said for James's view. Certainly, whatever the difficulties of its style, *The American Scene* remains today more readable, more provocative – and, on a whole range of items, more instructive – than contemporaneous and later surveys more clotted with fact. Further, without indulging in too precious a logic, if the key lesson taught by American civilization is its ultimate absence, if America is indeed "crowned not only with no history, but with no credible possibility of time for history" (p. 77), if all the events and items and objects that might be recorded would only repetitiously declare how "expensively provisional" they were (p. 77), then there is little reason to record them.

As we have seen, the political substance James felt so overwhelmingly was the willed impermanence that marched across the American landscape like a deranged giant, crushing the life out of history and sowing the seeds of "monstrous phenomena" (p. 83): of skyscrapers built on an inhuman scale; of trolleys, those "cars of Juggernaut in their power to squash"; of the darkened canyons of masonry, resembling "black rat-holes, holes of gigantic rats" (p. 109). The excess of these images, as some of the earlier citations have shown, is typical.

The calculated transcience of American culture expressed for James what he called "*the will to grow* . . . everywhere written large, and to grow at no matter what or whose expense" (p. 54; James's italics). Energy itself proves to be the agent of vile change. In another paranoid figure, the "thousand hits and misses" of the will to grow are rendered as "the very screeches of the pipe to which humanity is actually dancing" (p. 54).

James transforms America's faith in sheer energy into the chiefest charge in his indictment against the United States and against modernity. He sees energy, the will to grow, as insatiable appetite, grue-somely engorging itself on literally everything in its path, resistless power at its own service, leaving behind what James calls a "vision of eternal waste" (p. 113), a vision extending into whatever future he can see.

The will to grow inspired James with a fear of the boundless, of the gaping, of the void. His entire aesthetic commitment abjures the "sub-lime," the undifferentiated in any form, and rather rests in closure, in human scale, in limits and boundaries. Where Americans famously la-mented the passing of their western frontier, the "enclosing" of the country more or less commemorated by Frederick Jackson Turner in 1893, James – if he had addressed the matter at all – would have wel-comed that enclosure.

Fittingly, one of the few changes James discovered that he could greet with pleasure was the fence that had been built, since he was last there, around Harvard Yard. The fence confers the "especial decency of the definite, the palpable affirmation and belated delimitation of College Yard" (p. 62). Though high, the iron palings are "still insufficiently high"; but that makes a minor defect. What the fence blessedly repre-sents, the cherished idea it bravely stands for, is opposition to "the land of the 'open door.' " This familiar phrase is reconstructed by James's use of it. Its meanings are etched in a series of widening concentric circles that encompass respectively the aesthetic, the social, and the political testaments of *The American Scene*.

James provides the aesthetic significance of the open door when he complains that such a door "may make a magnificent place, but it makes poor places" (p. 62). The Harvard fence, on the other hand, this "drawing of the belt at Harvard," exemplifies a principle of exceptional importance for James: "the way in which the formal enclosure of ob-jects at all interesting immediately refines upon their interest, immedi-ately establishes values" (p. 62). Whether or not the enclosure is im-pressive from without, "from within it is sovereign" (p. 62). Limits define spaces, and the consequent values established are even more authoritative for the people within the spaces than for those excluded.

This aesthetic discussion is already beginning to impinge on the social meaning of the open door. A hundred pages later, describing his expe-rience of a New York club, James brings that social definition into more elaborated focus. A "splendid structure," a "palace for scale and decoration," the club shared the universal American affliction: It was a "house with almost no one of its indoor parts distinguishable from any other" (p. 166).

In almost all American buildings, from the public institution to the private home, James is struck by "the indefinite extension of all spaces and the definite merging of all functions"; he lurches between laughter and horror as he repeatedly encounters "the enlargement of every opening, the exaggeration of every passage, the substitution of gaping arches and far perspectives and resounding voids for enclosing walls, for practicable doors, for controllable windows" (p. 167). In short, what James calls the "essence of room-character" is systematically obliterated, and erased with it is any chance for concentration, for solitude, or for conversation, for "the play of the social relation at any other pitch than the pitch of a shriek or a shout" (p. 167).

James is vexed and saddened, but he is as well finally enlightened by "this diffused vagueness of separation between apartments, between hall and room, between one room and another, between the one you are in and the one you are not in, between place of passage and place of privacy" (p. 166). What these aimlessly open interiors illuminate for James is not merely the manners of the American people but their deepest "conception of life": The passion for democratic forms precludes any design of genuine interiors. The "instinct is throughout . . . that of minimizing, for any 'interior,' the guilt or odium or responsibility . . . of its *being* an interior. The custom rages like a conspiracy for nipping the interior in the bud" (pp. 166–7; James's italics).

Thus – and James is altogether in earnest here – the supremely representative American building is the hotel, "a synonym for civilization" (p. 102). James asks if the "hotel-spirit may not just *be* the American spirit most seeking and most finding itself." The hotel symbolized for James the very stuff of human restlessness, defying any margin of personal stability, sitting luridly at the very heart of metropolitan crowds and noise, decorated in imitation of something or other or of several things at once. The hotel stands as a parody of Jamesian conceptions of civilization at every point. One need only recall my earlier comments on "The Great Good Place" to comprehend just how brutally antithetical to his values James reckoned the New York hotel to be.

The political connotations James attaches to the open door are declaring themselves. The impulse toward gregariousness and the correspondent absence of discriminations in American interiors follow from the nation's allegiance to classless fellowship and its putative intolerance for inequality. The endless vistas inside American houses "correspond, within doors, to the as inveterate suppression of almost every outward exclusory arrangement" (p. 166).

James's argument, as he makes clear in several places, is with democracy itself. This is the power that levels the landscape of the American scene, confuses the interior spaces of its improvised structures, repudiates the idea of the past, and marches blindly ahead oblivious to what

James considered to be the vital truth of the "old discrimination in favour of the private life" (pp. 102–3). James had no sooner landed at Hoboken in 1904 than he found a "great presence" bristling on the dock, a presence "that shakes the planks . . . to an inordinate unprecedented rumble" (p. 54). It is "the monstrous form of Democracy," and James warns his readers at the outset that this monstrous form will "project its shifting angular shadow . . . across every inch of the field of his vision" (pp. 54–55). Then, in another of those images of paranoia in which *The American Scene* abounds, James conjures up the democratic spirit: "It is the huge democratic broom that has made the clearance and that one seems to see brandished in the empty sky" (p. 55). Destruction, emptiness, the void are for James the terminology at once of democracy and its artifacts.

So we return to the open door and the outermost of its circles of meaning. Almost as potently as its slipshod architecture, the immigrants express for James the perverse leveling, the failure of distinctions, the accelerating but pointless force of American democracy. The years of James's absence from the United States – he had sailed to Europe in 1883 – had seen upward of twelve million immigrants arrive on these shores; this in a population, by 1900, of just seventy-five million. Further, the annual rate of immigration was increasing and would reach a dizzying peak of 1.25 million in 1907, just two years after James's visit. In the early 1900s, Americans were startled by the realization that upwards of three-quarters of the population of New York, Chicago, Cleveland, and Boston consisted of immigrants or the children of immigrants.

As important as these remarkable numbers is the changing composition of those who came in the 1880s and later. These were the years of the so-called new immigration, when eastern and southern Europeans and Slavs, including large numbers of Jews, replaced the northern and western Europeans of the earlier (and much smaller) influx.

This is the open door James would close. Everywhere he looked, in New York, in Boston, in Philadelphia, he found looking back at him "the ubiquitous alien," the alien utterly in possession of James's country. "There was no escape from the ubiquitous alien into the future, or even into the present; there was an escape but into the past" (p. 87). A full trolley car is "a foreign carful; a row of faces, up and down, testifying without exception, to alienism unmistakable, alienism undisguised and unashamed" (p. 125). Comradeship with the immigrant is beyond contemplating: "There is no claim to brotherhood with aliens in the first grossness of their alienism" (p. 12). The country even tastes, metaphorically, of the alien. James detects everywhere a "sauce," of which he asks: "Is not the universal sauce essentially *his* sauce, and do we not feel ourselves feeding, half the time, from the ladle, as greasy as he chooses to leave it for us, that he holds out?" (pp. 117–118).

The vulgar stereotyping of "greasy" in this angry rhetorical question is unhappily typical of James's treatment of the immigrant throughout *The American Scene*. Searching for what he calls " 'my' small homogeneous Boston of the more interesting time," he finds only "gross little aliens . . . in serene and triumphant possession" (p. 231). Rutgers Street on the Lower East Side is the "swarming of Israel" (p. 131). Walking the streets of the Jewish ghetto is like finding oneself "at the bottom of some vast sallow aquarium in which innumerable fish, of over-developed proboscis, were to bump together, for ever, amid heaped spoils of the sea." The fire escapes of the tenements most resemble "the spacious organized cage for the nimbler class of animals in some great zoological garden. This general analogy is irresistible"; and James goes on to elaborate the analogy with distressing relish. The cage of the fire escapes

> seems to offer, in each district, a little world of bars and perches and swings for human squirrels and monkeys. The very name of architecture perishes, for the fire-escapes look like abashed afterthoughts, staircases and communications forgotten in the construction; but the inhabitants lead, like the squirrels and monkeys, all the merrier life. (P. 134)

Obviously, the failure of sympathy disclosed here is total. The amused complacency with which James denies the simple humanity of the people he inspects serves in a sense as his revenge against them for dispossessing him from his country.

James, who was received as something of a celebrity wherever he went, was personally escorted around Ellis Island by the commissioner of "this wonderful service" (p. 84; Plate 3). It was here, thrust into the midst of an army of "the inconceivable alien" (p. 85), that James had one of his greatest shocks. He recoiled from what he saw as if he had "seen a ghost in his supposedly safe old house" (p. 85). And it is under the impact of that shock that James advises America to close its open door:

> Is not our instinct in this matter, in general, essentially the safe one—that of keeping the idea of the country simple and strong and continuous, so that it shall be perfectly sound? To touch it overmuch, to pull it about, is to put it in peril of weakening; yet on this free assault upon it, this readjustment of it in *their* monstrous, presumptuous interest, the aliens, in New York, seemed perpetually to insist. (P. 86)

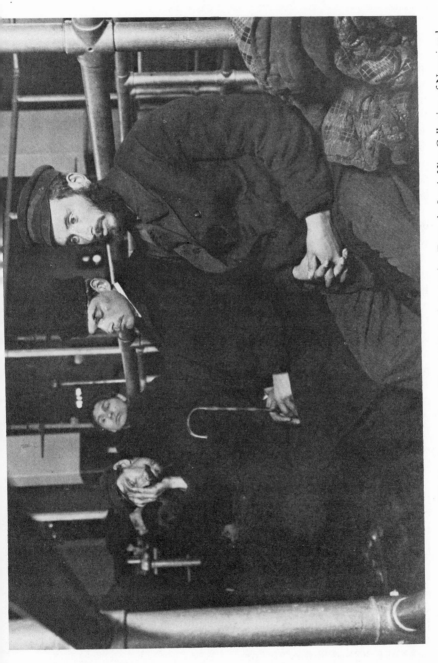

PLATE 3. Jewish immigrants at Ellis Island, 1905. One of Lewis Hine's photographs. (From the Lewis Hine Collection of Naomi and Walter Rosenblum.)

James's nativist hostility to the new immigrants can be counted as his contribution to the vehement debate that engrossed the nation in the early 1900s. Responses to immigration, and demands of all sorts to *do* something about it, remained one of the preoccupations of the entire period – understandably, perhaps, in view of the statistics cited earlier and the unprecedented human upheaval they imply.

I review this debate in the following chapter. What we shall attend to now is another, a more private and ironic, aspect of James's resistance to "the ubiquitous alien." The irony lies in the poignant fact that the most patently ubiquitous of the aliens in *The American Scene* is Henry James. Even more inescapably than the immigrants he despised, James's life shaped itself into a pattern of exile.

"My choice," he had written with ebullience in 1881, "is the old world – my choice, my need, my life. . . . My work lies there – and with this vast new world, *je n'ai que faire*."[23] That choice of the old world was of a piece with his multiple repudiation of the United States: as a subject, as a cultural resource, as a home. However passionate his European pilgrimage was, though, he would never find himself as one with any of the civilizations across the Atlantic. If, as he wrote to Morton Fullerton in 1900, the "port from which I set out was, I think, that of *the essential loneliness of my life*," it was a loneliness that followed him to his grave.[24] As he continued to Fullerton: "It seems to be the port also, in sooth, to which my course again finally directs itself."

In *The American Scene,* James's loneliness is brought to a climactic, excruciating pitch. Repelled and frightened by the inchoate present of America, fearfully convinced that there was to be no refuge in the future, James proposes that the only escape is into the past, the "pleasanter, easier, hazier past" of childhood memories and associations. But James discovers that the American conspiracy against him checkmates even his nostalgia. Some of the book's most moving passages record James's emotions when he confronts the remorseless erasure of the evidences of his own American life. A "high, square, impersonal structure," proclaiming its complete indifference, now stands on the expropriated site of James's house of birth on Washington Square. James confesses with mild self-mockery that he had imaginatively erected a commemorative mural tablet in his own honor during his years of absence. The smile dies on his lips when he finds that the wall itself that would have borne the inscription has been smashed. The effect on James, for whom settings and personal identities were always so intimately intertwined, was literally traumatic: He felt he had "been amputated of half [his] history" (p. 91).

The issues we have been reviewing are not merely speculative nor safely separate. Lying in the rubble left behind "the heavy footprints . . . of a great commercial democracy" (p. 92) is James's own exterminated past. The story of his betrayal by his home continues through the New York and New England sections of *The American Scene,* reaching an extraordinary finale in James's return to Ashburton Place, near the State House in Boston. He has come in search of a "pair of ancient houses" (p. 228), one of which had been his father's. Miraculously, though they are surrounded by the new tall buildings – "the horrific glazed perpendiculars of the future" – the old houses have survived, honest, sober, and respectable, "a conscious memento" (p. 229). James is instantly rapt into the past; he re-lives "on the spot" two years of far-away youth, a period toward the end of the Civil War, which included the beginnings of his literary career. It is precisely the kind of consolation and refreshment he has sought, until now, without success.

But the entire episode proves mere prologue to a monstrous practical joke. When James comes back to Ashburton Place just a month later, "to see if another whiff of the fragrance were not to be caught," the old houses are gone. He finds only "a gaping void, the brutal effacement, at a stroke, of every related object, of the whole precious past." The ancient home clung to its perilous existence for over forty years for no other purpose, it seems, than to multiply James's grief at its destruction. It was, he writes, "as if the bottom had fallen out of one's own biography, and one plunged backward into space without meeting anything."

The generalization James goes on to reach summarizes the whole text of his complaint against America with almost aphoristic concision: "If I had often seen how fast history could be made I had doubtless never so felt that it could be unmade still faster." In short, like the America he has renounced, he too has become pastless, and the security of his own existence seems threatened. Looking at the wreckage before him, James again blames the immigrant: "I had the vision, as filling the sky . . . of a huge applied sponge, a sponge saturated with the foreign mixture and passed over almost everything I remembered and might still have recovered" (p. 232). The logic of this charge seems at first elusive – the immigrants, after all, have little to do with the decision making of corporate America – but in fact James's charge follows rigorously. The aliens are not merely the omnipresent creatures, they are as well the symbols of democracy: of mobility and change, of crudely open doors leading out toward vertiginous vistas, of skyscrapers looming with sinister design over cowering private lives, of the trampled past.

With a mixture of relief and despair, James sailed back to England in July of 1905. He was not to return, though America and New York remained much on his mind in the decade of life that remained to him.

New York reverberated through the childhood reminiscences of the autobiographical volumes he began to write. The city also figures in several of his last tales and gives its name to the collected and revised "New York Edition" of his works.

Above all, the American tour evidently planted the seeds of the intense and suggestive late story "The Jolly Corner," a tale of radically literal dividedness that can serve as a suitable conclusion to our consideration.

The story's hero, Spencer Brydon, is a native New Yorker who returns to the city after a thirty-three-year absence in Europe. His purposes are initially commercial; he is to oversee the conversion of a building he owns into apartments. But he lingers, attracted more and more strongly to his other property, his own boyhood home – a large, anachronistically elegant townhouse, empty now of all furnishings and of the three generations of Brydons who lived and died there. He is drawn back to this ancestral home on its "jolly corner" and tries to catch the fading echoes of bygone years, tries to puzzle out what his life would have been if he had lived it in that house in that American city, if he had not made Europe his choice. Brydon becomes increasingly absorbed in the mystery of this "alternative destiny." He confesses to his friend, Alice Staverton, that he is at last

> wholly taken up with one subject of thought. It was mere vain egoism, and it was moreover, if she liked, a morbid obsession. He found all things come back to the question of what he personally might have been, how he might have led his life, and "turned out," if he had not so, at the outset, given it up.[25]

Brydon's preoccupation at last takes particular and concrete form: He decides that his alter ego, the ghost of his other life, is hiding somewhere on the premises of his old home. Thus Brydon's nocturnal visits, and his continuous wandering through the corridors and rooms. In a reversal that James seems to have enjoyed, the man haunts the ghost.

Recalling the imagery of *The American Scene,* the climax of "The Jolly Corner" is organized by means of the doors of Brydon's house. He becomes convinced of the ghost's presence when he returns to a door that he had left open and finds it closed. And he finally encounters the ghost standing in the shadow of a door that he had left closed and that now stands open. In the dimness of the pre-dawn hallway, Brydon takes in "his other self" (p. 225): a hard, acute figure, a grizzled head shielded by a wounded hand. The ghost, Brydon decides in recoil and disappointment, is "a stranger," not his own identity but an evil intruder, "odious, blatant, vulgar" (p. 226).

In this extraordinary meeting between Brydon and the other self he searches for and then rejects, James has sketched as vivid a portrait of the divided mind as we shall find in these chapters. The ghost can be taken as James's reaffirmation of his life's choices. Had Brydon remained in New York, he would have been a "success," a builder, a millionaire. He would have even anticipated "the inventor of the skyscraper" (p. 197). But he has chosen otherwise, and his repudiation of the ghost recapitulates and ratifies the lifelong decision he has made. Recall, however, that the ghost is in residence. And thus, in an irony that critics have not sufficiently apprehended, Brydon's old home becomes a trap and a trick. It is transformed from a refuge into the scene of his betrayal. The action is not unlike that of *The American Scene.*

In considering the transactions between James's aesthetic choices and his political commitments, a concluding hypothesis suggests itself. "Scared back," to quote for the last time young Henry James's assessment of aging John Ruskin, "scared back by the grim face of reality," fully at rest in no culture or country, convinced in any case of the bankruptcy of the future, James did have access to one "great good place," an enduring and unassailable place of retirement. James retreated into the remarkable late style, into a preoccupation with form, into a mountingly single-minded concern with technique. This is the outcome, in the three great final novels, in the two dozen stories written after 1900, in the volumes of autobiography, above all in *The American Scene,* of Henry James's anxious and finally desperate encounter with the modern world.

And yet, if James retreated from the modern world, the example of his life and his art was charged with significance for a younger generation that would in turn create the modern movement. Writers like Joseph Conrad, Ford Madox Ford, and T. S. Eliot revered what they understood to be the vast integrity of James's aesthetic dedication. Hugh Kenner gives over the opening paragraphs of *The Pound Era* to a jaunty reconstruction of a London afternoon through which young Ezra and old Mr. James walk together, in the general direction of the evening and modernism.[26] Kenner's implication is just: James belongs at the beginning of the story. Pound himself, we recall, evoked the Master in a section of Canto VII:

> And the great domed head, *con gli occhi oneste e tardi*
> Moves before me, phantom with weighted motion,
> *Grave incessu,* drinking the tone of things,
> And the old voice lifts itself
>   weaving an endless sentence.

I shall have more to say about the meaning of modernism in Chapter 8. For now, it will suffice to observe the irony of James's relation to his time. He had wanted to be America's Balzac. Driven from that ambition by his shock at what modern culture offered to his studious eye, he presided over the making of what would prove to be that culture's major aesthetic achievement. It is a pattern that we shall see confirmed again more than once in the pages that follow. James was an accomplice to the future, in spite of himself.

Chapter 3

Restoration as reform:
David Graham Phillips

An extraordinary group of investigative journalists, they had been relentlessly at work since the 1890s detailing in their newspapers and magazines the crimes of American business and politics, but they became "the
muckrakers" on the evening of March 17, 1906. President Roosevelt,
who had at first read their stories with interest and a measure of admiration, had decided that the whole group, and especially Thomas Lawson,
Upton Sinclair, and David Graham Phillips, had turned into extremists
and were on the way to becoming more disruptive of society's good
order than the evils they exposed. As was usually the case, Roosevelt
indulged his impatience more or less immediately. In a Gridiron Club
speech that he hoped to keep off the record, the president offered his
audience an extended comparison between the journalists and "The Man
with the Muckrake" in John Bunyan's *Pilgrim's Progress.*[1] Roosevelt
lashed the reporters with Bunyan's description of his muckraker: "the
man who could look no way but downward with the muckrake in his
hand, who was offered a celestial crown for his muckrake, but would
neither look up nor regard the crown he was offered, but continued to
rake to himself the filth of the floor." Rumors concerning the speech,
mostly accurate, began to circulate immediately; when Roosevelt repeated his attack, in public this time, on April 14, its central metaphor
instantly became headline news across the country. It was, in Louis
Filler's phrase, "what the reactionary journals had been looking for since
the exposures had first begun."[2] Roosevelt's victims at first met his
assault with outrage and alarm; soon, though, they adopted the term and
marched under its banner with mordant pride. They were by no means
the first investigative reporters America had produced. The Gilded Age
had numbered Mark Twain, Henry Adams, and Henry Demarest Lloyd
among its powerful critics. What did distinguish the muckrakers, apart
from their numbers and their access to a greatly enlarged audience, was
their intermittent alliance with organized political reform. Muckraking,

according to Justin Kaplan, "served as the leading edge of a political movement, progressivism."[3]

The man who especially provoked Roosevelt was David Graham Phillips. Phillips's articles (there would eventually be nine in all) under the collective title *The Treason of the Senate* had begun appearing in *Cosmopolitan* on February 15, just a few weeks before Roosevelt's outburst. Roosevelt told Lincoln Steffens that his principal target had been Phillips, not investigative reporting as such (though he named no one in any version of the speech). The president defended his overheated rhetoric by saying that he had spoken out to console "poor old Chauncey Depew," senator from New York, a useful ally of Roosevelt and a man whom Phillips had vilified in his first article as "an opportunist in politics and plunder." To Roosevelt, all this smacked of an excess of zeal or worse. To Phillips, more wounded than flattered by the singular presidential attention being paid him, the "muckraker" speech only proved Roosevelt's own opportunism. Phillips was as proud a man as Roosevelt would encounter: The reporter agreed to a subsequent meeting of conciliation only after the president had invited him three times.

The vigor of Roosevelt's hostility suggests that Phillips had achieved a certain preeminence. Louis Filler, the best-informed judge of these matters, tends to agree. Where other muckraking articles stopped with specific indictments, " 'The Treason of the Senate,' " writes Filler, "went the entire way" (p. 255), went beyond the enumeration of individual items of misfeasance to detect the decay of the entire system. Phillips's articles "represented the high point of muckraking in its exposure phase" (p. 257). Certainly one proof of Phillips's achievement comes immediately to mind. The single reform demanded throughout his series – the direct election of senators – was adopted within a few years. The Seventeenth Amendment, needless to say, had a host of sponsors and well-wishers, from the populists to the bosses of several city machines; but Phillips deserves his share of the credit.

Phillips initially undertook the series only grudgingly. His ambition had always been literary rather than journalistic. By 1905, he had already given up his career as a newsman and had published his first several novels. When Bailey Millard, Hearst's new editor at *Cosmopolitan*, came to Phillips with the proposal to muckrake the Senate, Phillips declined, suggesting William Allen White as better qualified. More than a little irony attaches to Phillips's reluctance, since whatever reputation remains to him three-quarters of a century later derives almost solely from his nine articles exposing the Senate rather than his twenty or so novels.

This series was announced in a breathless editorial: "A searching and unsparing spot-light . . . will be turned upon each of the iniquitous

PLATE 4. This photograph of David Graham Phillips appeared at the beginning of the first installment of *The Treason of the Senate* in the March 1906 issue of *Cosmopolitan*.

figures that walk the Senate stage."[4] Even by the more freewheeling editorial standards of its time, *The Treason of the Senate* is unquestionably an incendiary document. Ellery Sedgwick, the editor of *Leslie's*, who thought of himself as cautiously enlightened, damned Phillips as a socialist. That, as we shall have several occasions to observe in the pages that follow, is a ludicrous overstatement. Nonetheless, the dashing young man who stared reprovingly out at the public from the midst of his exposés accomplished a good deal in his series (Plate 4). Phillips invented the term "the Interests" to describe the massing of collusive political-economic powers; he discerned the essential identification between the two major parties (Democratic minority leader Arthur Gorman is simply "the left arm of the monster"); he detected the limits of even the few exceptional senators, such as Robert La Follette; he demanded that senatorial elections be transferred from state legislatures to the people.

As that last item illustrates, Phillips had in mind improving the system, not overturning it, and certainly not exchanging it for socialism. Indeed, as we shall see, aside from variants of received pieties, not much that might go by the name of ideology or theory contaminates Phillips's work.[5] His beliefs combine a sincere outrage against the manipulation of the "people" by the monied interests; a moist-eyed nostalgia for pre-urban simplicity and the superiority of Jeffersonian agrarian values; a strenuous moralism grounded on a quite specifically Christian fascination with bold distinctions between good and evil; an impatience with the details of political analysis, along with a concomitant failure of curiosity about institutions as such; and an irrepressible tendency to admire the "great man," the unconstrained and dominating individual who might simply set things right.

In all this, Phillips is typical of his muckraking and reforming generation. He was a representative figure; and this, even more than his distinctive achievement, identifies his importance for our purposes. To define David Graham Phillips aright is to understand much of the intellectual and political tenor of his era; and the best place to find Phillips is not in his reporting but in his novels. I want to read a few of those novels and suggest some of the ways in which they may illuminate the possibilities and the limits of the reform imagination. From time to time, I shall allude to Theodore Roosevelt, whose career and attitudes instructively complement Phillips's fiction.

In the opinion of *The Arena,* one of the leading radical magazines of the period, Phillips's *The Plum Tree* (1905) was "the most important novel of the year." Having begun with that estimate, the author of the eight-page, double-column review immediately exceeded it: *The Plum Tree* "is in our judgment far and away the most important novel of recent years, because it unmasks present political conditions in a manner so graphic, so convincing and so compelling that it cannot fail to arouse the thoughtful to the deadly peril which confronts our people" (June 1905, p. 663). Theodore Roosevelt read the first half of *The Plum Tree* and wrote to Owen Wister that the novel was "very widely read," "very popular," and not "healthy." Its original readers were titillated by *The Plum Tree* as a *roman à clef;* and as an antiquarian rogues' gallery, the book still repays interest. In retrospect, however, the novel seems less assured than it did to its contemporaries and is for our purposes more revealing in what it fails to say than in what it declares. To a greater extent than its author seems to have realized, *The Plum Tree* is a deeply disillusioned testament, the record of a corruption at last too profound for reform. Though intended as a prescription for progressive change, this novel finally suggests that the sources of America's political deformities lie beyond the remedy of procedural rearrangements – they lie in the province of the American character itself. According to *The Plum Tree,* the America of 1905 has experienced such a complete fall from its first grace that optimism is necessarily contrived, activity leads necessarily to corruption, and idealism resides only with the hypocrites and the feebleminded. In such circumstances, reform has become irrelevant; yet revolution remains unthinkable. Phillips occupies the untenable terrain bounded by this dilemma. Desperately in need of a resolution, Phillips appeals to a messianic figure. But that, as we shall see, reveals more of political and moral debility than of hope or of strength.

The novel's action is thus rich beyond its author's intentions. Indeed, *The Plum Tree* may be read as a transcript of the struggle between Phillips's residual, idealizing aspirations and his growing despair. The book represents the multiplying distance between what Phillips continues to long for and what he predicts – whether consciously or not – the outcome of America's history will be.

This debate can be said to capture something of the decisive failure of progressivism in the prewar decade, as that movement's commitment to elitism and order held in substantial check much of its innovative energy until the moment for conclusive change had passed. Phillips's moderation – and in this again he is representative – was impelled by the suspicion that 1905 would see revolution in America. As we shall see in the next chapter, that forecast, though disproven in the event, was perfectly sensible. To recall just one incident here, the murder of labor's notorious enemy, former governor Frank Steunenberg of Idaho, who was blown up by dynamite wired to the gate of his home on December 30, 1905, sent spasms through the commonwealth. When Bill Haywood and other officials of the Industrial Workers of the World went on trial for the murder in the spring of 1907, *The Outlook* magazine editorialized quite accurately that "the eyes of the entire country are centered on Idaho. It is no ordinary murder trial. Important issues, some of them without a parallel in the history of the country, are involved."[6]

This leads us back to Phillips's dilemma. *The Plum Tree* dramatizes a political establishment just about as corrupt as the system's more radical

critics claimed. Yet Phillips is committed above all to keeping the
peace. The characters in *The Plum Tree* are arrayed along a moral spectrum; but all of them, and especially the narrator-protagonist Harvey
Sayler, who stands ambiguously at the center of that spectrum, summarize a prediction about the ultimate limits of progressive ideology.

Let us concede at the outset that *The Plum Tree* is only partially
successful as an imaginative work. The storytelling is regularly defeated
by polemic, and the characters are just as regularly cut off from coherent patterns of motivation and judgment. Keeping the book off-balance
is Phillips himself, anxiously lurching about trying to find some outcome more satisfactory to his lingering idealism than the hard logic his
own insight demands.

Phillips has no trouble identifying the lesser complexity of simple
graft and deceit. The villains of this novel are drawn with the stark and
sentimental assurance of melodrama. Unsurprisingly, since for Phillips
American politics *was* melodrama, his accents in *The Plum Tree* are
indistinguishable from the rage of his muckraking journalism. Boss Bill
Dominick receives his supplicants while seated in state in his saloon, on
one side of him his bought judge, on the other side the owner of the
city streetcar franchise. Dominick is "a huge, tall man, enormously
muscular, with a high head like a block, straight in front, behind and
on either side; keen, shifty pig eyes, pompous cheeks, a raw, wide
mouth."[7] He offers a hand that is "fat and firm, not unlike the flabby
yet tenacious sucker of a moist sea-creature." (p. 19).

Phillips marches a whole brigade of larger and smaller rascals
through the pages of *The Plum Tree*. As the leading businessmen and
politicians of America, most of them recall, as Dominick does, the
broad-brushed exposés of muckraking journalism. Glancing at a dinner
table crowded with them, Harvey Sayler is wrought up to overstatement: "It was hard for me to keep my disgust beneath the surface.
Those 'gentlemen' assembled there were among the 'leading citizens' of
my state; and Roebuck [the foremost of the group in both dignity and
wickedness] was famous on both sides of the Atlantic as a king of
commerce and a philanthropist" (p. 346). "Liars, cheats, bribers; and
flaunting the fruits of infamy as honors, as titles to respect, as gifts
from Almighty God!" (p. 346).

It was, of course, the operating principle at the heart of progressive
reform that the alliance Phillips here pictures between politics and rapa-
cious commerce (as distinguished from benevolent commerce – that distinction meant much to reformers) was the chief evil of contemporary
American life. The political influence of bad businessmen was understood to be itself the source of the other evils that were destroying
public institutions, from the law to education to the church. If that

analysis of America's troubles were accurate, then solutions would not be far to seek. Corrupt business should be disentangled from politics, municipal and state machines should be vigilantly suppressed, public-spirited managers should replace self-serving bosses: the itemized agenda, in short, of progressive reform. If the ills devouring America's substance were matters of wicked men and wounded institutions, the men could be turned out and the institutions nursed back to health.

This is the point of view Phillips intends in *The Plum Tree*. It underlies the funny scene that directly follows Sayler's angry assessment of these "leading citizens." The dinner disintegrates into a brawl, with the youngest of the robber barons, knocked from his chair by a hurled teapot, crashing backward and taking the whole table with him: "Half the diners, including Dominick, were floored under it" (p. 356).

The scene is a combination of satire – "that repulsive mess of un-masked, half-drunken, wholly infuriated brutes" (p. 356) – and fantasy – would that the corruption of American society might be transformed into self-consuming grotesquerie and laughed away.

But the novel knows better. What troubles Phillips lies close to the bone of America's political life. The allegorical tableau in which the malefactors of both wealth and government are crushed under the table of justice is cathartic, but it stops far short of analysis. Among other things, it underestimates the complicity of the nation's citizens in the predations practiced upon them. "The misgovernment of the American people is misgovernment by the American people," Lincoln Steffens wrote in *The Shame of the Cities,* and Steffens had in mind not merely or even mainly the apathy of average citizens.[8] He meant to assail what he called the "conceit" that "deplores our politics and lauds our business" (p. 3). For Steffens, the big businessman was "the chief source of corruption." By far the most disruptive of Steffens's implications involves the irrelevance of nicely differentiated moral judgments of the behavior of individual businessmen. The commanding structure of capitalism is on the way to being revealed.

Thus we understand the sharply conflicted responses to business in this period. On the one hand, the businessman appears as the archetypal American, his values those most cherished by the culture: enterprise driven by efficiency, practicality enlivened by daring. "The successful businessman," reported Theodore Roosevelt, looking back at the turn of the century from the vantage point of 1913, "was regarded by everybody as preeminently *the* good citizen. The severe newspaper moralists who were never tired of denouncing politicians and political methods were wont to hold up 'business methods' as the ideal which we were to strive to introduce into political life."[9] Against this more or less traditional admiration stood by 1905 the fitfully emergent recognition, documented by one muckraking article or book after another, that "in all cities, the better classes – the business men – are the sources of corruption" (*Shame*, p. 40). The solution, in a word, has become the problem. More and more observers were compelled by Steffen's accuracy: Business was *not* the trustworthy adversary of politics; it was in fact the master, and politics the puppet.

The movement toward federal regulation is instructive. Despite the immense circulation during these years of loosely applied Darwinian metaphors to describe business competition, the largest of the corporations worked hard and generally with success to control competition, and thus to insulate American capital from the more rigorous possibilities of the marketplace. The plutocrats might announce – might even believe – that "the growth of a large business is merely survival of the fittest," as John D. Rockefeller put it in his legendary Sunday School address. But what Rockefeller professed to see as "merely a working out of a law of nature and a law of God" was what businessmen also labored energetically to ensure through the more pedestrian laws of cities, states, and nations.[10]

In the opinion of *The Plum Tree,* the supremacy of business had been established within less than a generation: "The dominion of the great business interests over politics was the rapid growth of about twenty years" (p. 184). An assortment of groups and people, to be sure, among them farmers, wage laborers, blacks, women, and immigrants, had understood these realities for a long time. But as the insight was more widely shared, it collided with the correlative realization that no other solution than the appeal to the techniques of business could elicit majority assent. Thus, the moral-political imagination of America was trapped between mutually unacceptable alternatives.

At its most fundamental, the struggle is not only over the means of production but over consciousness. The technology that has permitted the multiplication of wealth and its concentration also permits the increasingly efficient manipulation of minds. As Harvey Sayler explains, in the tone of someone sharing a discovery: "We hear much of many wonders of combinations and concentration of *industrial* power which railway and telegraph have wrought. But nothing is said about what seems to me the greatest wonder of them all – how these forces have resulted in the concentration of the *political* power of upwards of twelve million of our fifteen million voters; how the few can impose their ideas and their will upon widening circles, out and out, until all are included" (p. 209).

Phillips is talking about the scale and speed offered by technology to the few who would exercise both external and ideological control over the many. Here and elsewhere in *The Plum Tree* he approximates the insight into what the Italian Marxist Antonio Gramsci, would later call "ideological hegemony." By this, Gramsci referred to a system of control, both technological and otherwise, so complete that its victims consciously assent not only to their condition but to the values that inform it.[11] The mass of Americans, contends Harvey Sayler, find themselves "sunk in the most hopeless, if the most delightful, slavery – that in which the slave accepts his lowliness as a divine ordinance and looks up to his oppressors and plunderers as hero-leaders" (p. 337).

That measure of inertia, within the framework of the ideological impasse described previously, obviously makes the possibilities for reform slight. And indeed, whatever its intended design, Phillips's novel does not seriously entertain reform as an alternative. What emerge out of Phillips's analyses of American corruption are two quite different responses that together exemplify the trap into which the reform impulse would necessarily fall when disillusioned by the manifest inability of gradualism to produce substantial change. Lacking a coherent, much less a systematic, method of social and political evaluation, Phillips – and many of the reformers of his generation – declines by turns into wishful thinking and cynicism.

Senator Hampden Scarborough of Indiana, the political hero of several of Phillips's novels, represents Phillips's wishful response. Possessed of flawless political skill and relentlessly upright character, Scarborough brings into the novel a combination of virtue and talent uncomplicated by any defect whatever.[12]

Scarborough acts out of "a literal belief in democratic institutions and in the inspiring . . . principle of exact equality before the law" (p. 188). Phillips pays tribute to Scarborough's merits by electing him to the presidency at the end of the novel and insisting that Scarborough has not compromised himself to win.

But Scarborough has no program and he clearly has no chance against the kind of systemic corruption *The Plum Tree* has spent so many pages revealing. Whether Phillips understands it or not, Scarborough's election cannot resolve the American dilemma dramatized in the book. Rather, it is a ritual by means of which Phillips would console himself against what his own insight and logic have taught him. Phillips is making a gesture of a vaguely therapeutic sort, and it is even more vaguely but unmistakably antinomian. Scarborough, untainted by participation in the machinations of American political institutions, finds within himself the standards and the strength to take the measure of those same institutions. He will put America's house in order, prophesies Sayler, "Senate or no Senate" (p. 263).

He will not, needless to say. But the rhetoric of righteousness, unsupported by the baggage of any conceptual or programmatic details, has always titillated America's dissidents. Scarborough is peripheral; it is significant that the novel ends before his presidency begins. He is a figure of sentimental appeal, yet properly understood he is an image not of hope but of despair, since he is not an inhabitant of this world at all but of myth and romance.

Scarborough will prove epiphenomenal; he will not endure. What will endure are the hegemony of business over politics and the voluntary cooperation of the people in their subservience. Out of that reluctant and perhaps only half-conscious recognition Phillips fashions his most interesting character, the narrator, Harvey Sayler. As moral actor, Sayler occupies a ground midway between the simple virtue of Scarborough and the equally simple viciousness of Dominick and Roebuck and the rest. Sayler, that is to say, is the one character who rises to moral complexity in this novel and is the one who illustrates most interestingly the intractable problems facing Phillips and his contemporaries.

Sayler's beginnings are those of the conventional melodramatic hero. His earliest childhood memory is of his upright father, defeated by the nascent post–Civil War political machine, dying of a broken, virtuous heart, and lamenting, "Prosperity has ruined my country!" (p. 14). That vignette, complemented by Sayler's nostalgic, idealized recollections of his self-sacrificial mother and underscored by his honest childhood poverty, makes a familiar preparation for the portrayal of an unequivocating reformer: one whose integrity will be tempered by adversity and whose struggle against corruption will be energized by the need to revenge his parents for their suffering at the hands of conspiratorial politics.

In the book's most novel twist, however, it doesn't work that way. Sayler begins as a crusader against wickedness but goes on to sell himself, to assorted vested interests and at increasingly high prices, until he himself becomes the biggest of the bosses. Yet he never quite turns into what he and Phillips despise. For one thing, he never deceives himself about his moral choices, and he never fails to judge himself correctly. For another thing, he never altogether abandons his ambition to perform some general good. So, throughout the novel, Sayler appears as a divided figure: more and more securely tied to the organized plunder he had set out to combat, yet at the same time politically and morally superior to all the alternatives save Scarborough. And since, on the terms of the novel's own logic (if not its yearnings), Scarborough does not represent a plausible outcome, Sayler embodies the most realistic limits of political and social optimism. Sayler's depression is genuine, not feigned, when he discovers the necessity of "those compromises between theoretical and practical right which are part of the daily routine of active life, and without which active life is impossible" (p. 26).

Phillips does a bit more than dramatize through Sayler the familiar insight that standards of private morality are more or less axiomatically incompatible with effectiveness in the public arena. The details of Phillips's version of this conundrum are particularly relevant to his generation. Sayler's values are those of the progressive movement: reason, moderation, efficiency, above all system. Even at his least ambiguously corrupt, Sayler is efficient: "I reduced the payments for legislation to a system, instead of the shameless, scandal-creating and wasteful auctioneering that had been going on for years" (p. 133).

Despite Phillips's obvious irony here, Sayler's cynicism is instructive with respect to the ideological dilemma America faced at the turn of the century. Sayler accurately voices Phillips's contempt for the common people, his essentially aristocratic inclinations. Sayler locates himself midway between "our country's two opposing elements of disorder – the greedy plunderers and the rapidly infuriating plundered" (p. 186). If the common people cannot be trusted to play a role in their own liberation, if change must therefore be imposed from the top down, then the impulse toward reform must necessarily direct itself either into the celebration of messianic figures such as Scarborough or into debilitating alliances with entrenched forces.

From this follows the basically conservative, and even more basically aimless, nature of Phillips's address to reform. The exploited many are no more worthy of his allegiance than the exploiting few. If the plutocrats and bosses are revealed, in the dinner brawl we looked at earlier, as beasts, so also are "the masses . . . short-sighted, unreasoning and in nose-rings" (p. 185). Sayler's policy of "moderate and practical patriotism" (p. 187) consists at last in making the status quo more rational. Trapped in an ideology of submission, the oppressed majority can no more conceive of radical change than the reformers can: "The people . . . always reason that it is better to rot slowly by corruption than to be frightened to death by revolution" (pp. 174–175). The very premises of social analysis in Phillips's world, even as they fail to generate meaningful change, remain potent enough to exclude revolution.

Late in the novel, Sayler makes a glancing reference to the one form of revolution that would be admissible, and in doing so he makes what is in many ways the most revealing statement in the book. Testifying on behalf of a generation, Sayler declares that "legitimate" revolution would consist in reconstructing "what the republic used to be" (p. 232). In order to be allowed entry into this ideological world, Sayler implies, revolutionary energy has to be channeled impossibly (but safely) backward rather than forward. What Phillips expresses through his narrator is a deeply nostalgic yearning, part of the pastoral longing that simulta-

neously marks and inhibits the progressive imagination in its collision
with the complex problems of urban and industrial America.

One analysis of the failure of turn-of-the-century reform movements
attends particularly to the dissonance between the agrarian Populist and
the urban Progressive agendas. Undeniably, the thunder on America's
left in these years was as often as not the echoes of battle between farm
and city. To cite an example from the farthest-left reaches of the controversy, the stiffly dogmatic Marxist Daniel De Leon loudly opposed
any alliance between city workers and farmers. "The greatest misfortune," he wrote editorially in *The People* (June 7, 1891), "would be the
merging of the Eastern proletariat movement into that of the western
farmers."[13]

Among more centrist Progressive reformers, however, a measure of
emotional and spiritual continuity can be discerned beneath the surface
of the itemized political debates they engaged in with their agrarian
predecessors. This continuity is again demostrated in *The Plum Tree,* in
its middle-western hero Scarborough. The reform imagination, as revealed in this novel, lacked a native tradition of sustained and analytic
(as opposed to intermittent and emotive) dissent. It shared in the mythmaking veneration of the early republic that continued in 1900 to play
the role of the civil religion. It thus inevitably undermined its thrust
toward the future in ritual invocations of the past. The history Phillips
invokes—"what the republic used to be"—like history in all pastoral,
offers entry into simplified, reactionary landscapes: what Raymond
Williams calls "a mystified past."[14]

This is the web of unspoken assumptions that gives imaginative birth
to Scarborough. He is a reincarnation of those earliest leaders who
imposed vision and will and virtue on a less tumultuous society. Phillips's half-buried syllogism proposes that by re-creating such a leader he
will re-create such a society. Scarborough's unlikely election has less to
do with the logic of secular politics than with Phillips's quasi-theologi-
cal reading of history. Calling up that sanctified past is a gesture whose
irrelevance is no more striking than its sincerity.

The Plum Tree shows Phillips at once unwilling to talk himself into
reform, unable to accommodate himself to the idea of revolution, and
even unequipped—because of a failure of both ideological nerve and
analytic apparatus—to pursue his outrage coherently. Phillips's problems in that novel afford a paradigm of general significance for the
quality and texture of social debate in the American 1900s.

The pattern recurs in Phillips's novels. *The Great God Success* was his
first novel (and the only one he published pseudonymously—under the
name "John Graham"—to evade his contractual obligation to do all his

publishing in the New York *World*).[15] It isn't clear that Phillips intended to insult either Joseph Pulitzer or Charles A. Dana in his novel; it is clear that he was trying to set out what he took to be a tough-minded appraisal of American life. The novel's protagonist, an Alger-like editor named Howard, is as good a newspaperman as America is likely to produce. And, like Harvey Sayler, Howard is corrupted, and inevitably so.

Howard's spectacular rise as a newsman follows in part from his manipulation of the quintessential tabloid style, a simple, straightforward prose: "He began at the beginning. . . . Where others were hysterical, he calmly and accurately described, permitting the tragedy to reveal itself instead of burying it beneath high-heaped adjectives."[16] He writes like that not for detached aesthetic reasons but out of a sociopolitical commitment to reform on behalf of the "common man." As he explains to his paper's chief political reporter, a man named Jackman: "I am writing for the masses." Jackman responds: "You're right. We don't need literature on this paper – long words, high sounding phrases and all that sort of thing. What we want is just plain, simple English that goes straight to the point" (p. 29).[17]

What would Howard actually have the masses do? They should not organize themselves, or act out of any separate class consciousness. Rather, the lower class should join with the enlightened professionals in exclusively electoral action. After denouncing all of the genuinely radical reformers as either hypocrites or naïfs, Howard turns "his attention to the real problem, a respectable administration for the city – a practical end which could . . . be accomplished by practical action" (p. 176). Howard here illustrates his commitment, in other words, to the largely unprogrammatic solution represented by "decent men."

Jacob Riis elaborated the consummate version of this point of view in his worshipful volume, *Theodore Roosevelt the Citizen,* published in 1904, just three years after *The Great God Success.* Riis's account is unreservedly messianic. He writes that after Roosevelt has finished his work in Washington, he should return to New York City as mayor: "That year I would write the last chapter of my 'battle with the slums,' and in truth it would be over."[18] Riis nowhere descends to a technical discussion of what Roosevelt might *do* to overcome the slums (slums that probably contained, let us remind ourselves, even more of New York's population than the "other half" memorialized in the title of Riis's earlier book). No, Roosevelt's presence alone would simply cause the slums to evaporate like noisome dew under the sun of his personality. One recalls again Henry Adams's rather more fearful but congruent summary of Roosevelt as "pure act."

Phillips's hostility against Roosevelt is beside the point here. Whether Phillips actually had Beveridge in mind or even himself, it is Roosevelt who most completely embodies the values inscribed across the pages of this book. Thus, Howard is congratulated for remaining always cautiously conservative in his indictments, for attacking only plunder, while defending property (p. 183). His editorials are "not dangerous or demogogical because they were just and were combined with a careful avoidance of encouragement to the lazy, the envious, the incompetent and the ignorant" (p. 182). This is the very stuff of Rooseveltian reform: The greatest vehemence is reserved, in this catalogue of vices stereotypically associated with the poor, for the victims.

Roosevelt, mesmerized by his own furious activity, never understood how his contemptuous estimate of those he pitied (the pity was genuine enough, though sporadic) disabled his efforts to find institutional solutions to their problems. But the structure of *The Great God Success* itself reveals Phillips's disquiet with the widely shared Progressive electoral-managerial strategy. At the very moment Howard is moving New York in that direction, his own moral decline begins. It accelerates throughout the rest of the novel, growing in more or less direct proportion to this rise in wealth and influence.

Phillips addresses through Howard's career a turn-of-the-century version of a classic American dilemma. On the one hand, he remains loyal to the sort of ethical pattern discerned in American culture most famously by Max Weber.[19] Howard is a man of genuine talents, among them that preeminent progressive virtue, intelligence. (Intelligence is invoked repeatedly in *The Great God Success*, without a hint as to its particular application.) Howard is also possessed of real if modest literary skill, and he demonstrates above all a devotion to hard work: "work, incessant, self-improving, self-developing" (p. 93). Labor on Howard's scale – his productivity resembles Phillips's own – deserves its rewards. And in a world whose imagination, regardless of the details of ideological debate, is preoccupied with money, money can be the only meaningful reward. Yet on the other hand, Phillips distrusts wealth, believing in good moral fundamentalist fashion that money, even if it can be gained licitly, brings ethical self-destruction sooner or later. For Phillips, then, as for so many other Americans, and perhaps especially those of his generation, money is a powerful symbol, but simultaneously of good and evil, of virtue rewarded and vice triumphant.

By the novel's close, Howard has sold all the integrity he possessed and has appropriately left journalism altogether for a tour as American ambassador to England. Only then, at the very end of the book, does Phillips completely renounce Howard and subject him to the heavy-handed satire he reserves for irredeemably corrupt politicians. In the last scene of the novel, a splendid new portrait of Howard is hanging in the Spring Exhibition of the Royal Academy. An Englishman tells an

American friend what he deduces about the ambassador's character from the painting. "I see – a fallen man," says the Englishman. "He was evidently a real man once; but he sold himself." The Englishman adds, "Nothing could have kept him down. His face is almost as relentless as Kitchener's and fully as aggressive, except that it shows intellect, and Kitchener's doesn't" (p. 197).

The most striking thing about this scene is how much it manages to avoid confronting by translating political and social issues into a whole set of alternative vocabularies. The analogy of art, which gives a visual and "documentary" permanence to the revelation about Howard; the comparison with a British leader, which places Howard in an international setting and also insists on his commensurately large scale; the narrowly moralistic texture of the judgment expressed by the Englishman: All of these elements allow Phillips to discharge the burden of his spleen through emotionally satisfying but ultimately evasive figures and tactics.

Like Harvey Sayler in *The Plum Tree,* Howard is among the best of the probable products of American public life in the year 1900. Like Sayler, too, Howard provides Phillips with a reasonably interesting satiric target. Finally, like Sayler, Phillips's portrayal at last precludes the need or even the possibility of a consecutive analytic engagement with American problems.

Much of the same outcome can be observed in most of Phillips's other political novels. *The Second Generation* (1906), for example, was labeled "socialistic" upon its publication.[20] In fact, the novel is not merely *not* socialist; it is probably antisocialist. It offers an object lesson on the improbability of the socialist alternative for the progressive imagination. The moral hero of *The Second Generation* is Hiram Ranger, an aging but still powerful factory owner, simple in his habits despite his wealth, honest in his dealings despite his interests, a plain man whose hard work has brought him success – in a word, a good capitalist. Anti-intellectual in the familiar populist manner,[21] Ranger periodically denounces American colleges, and usually Harvard by name, for their absorption in book learning. Ranger's definition of a true university is the one he learns from his friend Mark Hargrave, president of the Tecumseh Agricultural and Technical University in Indiana: "A university in fact as well as in name, which would attract the ambitious children of rich and well-to-do and poor, which would teach them to live honestly and nobly, would give them not only useful knowledge to work with but also the light to work by."[22] Heir to an "iron Inheritance" (p. 69) from the Puritans, Hiram Ranger seeks to merge the theoretical and the applied. Therein would reside for Phillips, as it does for Henry Adams in the opening chapters of his *History of the United States* and for George Santayana in *Character and Opinion in the United States,* the peculiarly American character in triumph. The very name of Hargrave's university is intended as a compact polemical statement, and it succeeds with an excess that veers toward self-parody: not only the yoking of "technical" and "agricultural," but the doubled reference of "Tecumseh" to both the courageous leader of the Shawnee who had fought his great and losing battle in Indiana and the Civil War hero William Tecumseh Sherman. All of the arts of peace and war, speculative and practical, would be taught at Hargrave's school.[23]

Adams viewed the young President Roosevelt with nervously amused contempt; and Phillips regarded Roosevelt – or professed to – with unqualified contempt. But a good many of the citizens of that generation saw in Roosevelt the apotheosis of the active intellectual. The patently fearless hero of San Juan, Roosevelt was also the author of a dozen books (some of them, for instance his study of naval strategy in the War of 1812, considered authoritative). Chasing rustlers across the Dakota Badlands in winter, he used what leisure he could find to read Constance Garnett's translation of *Anna Karenina*. (He caught the rustlers. And, while his opinions of Tolstoy's novel were mixed – Tolstoy "is a great writer," but Anna's history is not "healthy" – he liked it well enough to read *War and Peace* later in the same year, during the round-up.[24]) America has had a few other presidents capable of tracking rustlers through a blizzard, and one or two who read Tolstoy. Roosevelt is the only one who did both, and more or less simultaneously. Like the American romance and its heroes, Roosevelt moved "among extreme ranges of experience." Chief Magistrate and Chief Gunslinger, he embodied at once the claims of state and individual. Roosevelt himself summarized his ideological dividedness when he said that he couldn't be sure whether he was a "conservative radical" or a "radical conservative."[25] If Roosevelt had been on speaking terms with Henry Adams, they might have discussed the president's enrollment in the "conservative Christian anarchist" party.

Roosevelt, in his youth and restlessness and daring, his personal incorruptibility (an integrity girded by modest wealth), his allegiance to what can be described only as a masculinized version of the intellectual life, made good for millions of his countrymen a cherished collective self-perception.[26] Above all, Roosevelt represents perseverance and work, and this preeminent commitment Phillips expresses in *The Second Generation* with near-Rooseveltian exuberance. "Work or rot – that's life" is Hiram Ranger's opinion (p. 47). This inelegant but widely accepted motto of rugged individualism lies near the heart of Phillips's ethics in this novel; eventually and typically, it overwhelms any other

competing motives. For Phillips, the moral question of personal idleness is more pressing than the moral and political questions raised by
Hiram Ranger's factories.

Like all of American industry, Ranger's factories are prodigally destructive of human life. In 1906, the same year *The Second Generation*
was published, the muckraker William Hard revealed in his article
"Making Steel and Killing Men" that in just one plant of the U.S. Steel
Company 46 men were killed and 598 wounded in a single year. During the two decades from 1888 to 1908, American railway workers died
at a rate of 328 every year. It was estimated that in all industries at the
turn of the century, upwards of 35,000 persons were killed every year
and over half a million injured. Hiram Ranger's factories – his flour mill
and cooperage – between them employ just under a thousand men, and
they contribute their share to the appalling total of American industrial
murder. An upright and plain-speaking physician, a Dr. Schulze,
whose practice consists largely of caring for injured laborers, summarizes the human destruction going on in Ranger's buildings: "Several
men are killed every year in those works – and not through their carelessness, either. . . . And forty or fifty are maimed . . . hands lost, legs
lost – accidents that make cripples for life. That means tragedy – not the
wolf at the door, but with his snout right in the platter" (p. 168).

Yet despite his periodic outbursts of sympathy for those anonymous
victims, Phillips's predominating admiration is finally for the masterly
Ranger, whose *personal* virtues he emphasizes and the impersonal consequences of whose actions he minimizes. Comment of Dr. Schulze's sort
is altogether rare in the novel; much more routine is Phillips's concentration on Ranger's character and intentions. As for Roosevelt, so for
Phillips and much of his generation: The most fundamental elements of
political reform lie in moral renovation. Thus, as we shall see in a
moment, Ranger's gallant qualities lead inevitably – at whatever cost in
plausibility – to benevolent social ends.

Phillips shows himself occasionally capable of economic and institutional analysis. He proposes, though glancingly, that all necessity is
material (p. 181), and he even offers an accurate paraphrase of Marx's
theory of surplus value. As if to prove that his sentimentality reaches
downward and not just upward, Phillips grants the theoretical statement to an idealized worker named Lorry Tague – "huge, deep-chested,
tawny, slow of body and swift of mind" (p. 226). Tague is a cooper
who was once, but only briefly, an assistant foreman: "I was no good
at it. I couldn't 'speed' the men. It seemed to me they got a small
enough part of what they earned, no matter how little they worked.
Did you ever think, it takes one of us only about a day to make enough
barrels to pay his week's wages, and that he has to donate the other five

days' work for the privilege of being allowed to live? If I rode I'd be living off those five days of stolen labor" (p. 230).

As Marx wrote in *Capital:* "The fact that [only] half a day's labour is necessary to keep the labourer alive does not in any way prevent him from working a whole day. Therefore the value of labour-power, and the value which that labour-power creates in the labour-process, are two entirely different magnitudes."[27] The difference, of course, represents exactly the capitalist's profit, what Lorry Tague calls the "stolen labor" that the worker pays for "the privilege of being allowed to live."

Phillips seems to have understood the conclusion if not the details of Marx's conception of surplus value. Interestingly, from time to time even Phillips's imagery resembles Marx's. In a well-known passage in the *Critique of Political Economy,* Marx wrote: "As values, all commodities are only definite masses of congealed labour-time."[28] One of Phillips's characters finds similar language for the same idea: "You see, money is coined sweat" (p. 286).

The main point to notice about *The Second Generation,* however, is that Phillips's working people, having ingested this much of Marx, do nothing whatever to *act* upon their insight. Lorry Tague, for example, sustains his personal integrity by remaining a common laborer. Having named the enemy, he resigns himself to stoical cooperation with it. It is enough for him to document his *moral* superiority to the system; it is not his responsibility to change it.

Phillips, like most of the dissenters of his generation, finally turns away from the implications of radical analysis and contents himself with the venerable American ceremony of the antinomian gesture. Out of the tension bounded by Phillips's sincere desire to make things new without overturning what is, emerge pastoral nostalgia and the unlikely but sublime creation of what amounts to enlightened capitalism. Arthur Ranger, at the novel's close, carries out the plan of his now-dead father Hiram by building a university next door to the barrel-works and linking the two. The "crowning vindication" of the scheme does not lie in the resultant cultivation of the workers, though this more or less instantly occurs. Rather, the Ranger idea proves its value in the factory's multiplied profits. Two generations of Rangers collaborate to demonstrate that "sane and shrewd utopianism would produce larger dividends" (p. 262). Only capitalist profit, in other words, can sanctify the liberation of the working class.

But that liberation is itself, of course, ephemeral. The assorted and conflicting ideological tendencies visible in this novel come together in a striking, altogether revealing image near the end. The Rangers' cooperative factory-university is described as having "gardens all round, big windows, high ceilings . . . no smoke or soot, a big swimming pool

for winter or summer" (p. 296). Here, at the climax of several generations of American outrage against the invasion of our gardens by machines, Phillips turns the whole theme on its head. As described in this
novel, the machines of Hiram and Arthur Ranger have simply become
the garden; the factory is absorbed hurtlessly into the green world of
pastoral.

In itself, the image is neither patently deceitful nor historically
groundless. The increasing use of electricity to power industrial plants
was permitting the construction of factories that were less noisome
environmental intruders than most. Some newly built turn-of-the-
century industrial buildings were sited in rural locations, and some
were enclosed within landscaped parks. An English visitor, Budgett
Meakin, toured one such plant and praised "the handsome buildings –
surrounded by well-kept lawns, overlooking on the one side the river,
and on the other a park-like village, inhabited by the employees. The
Natural Food Company's plant at Niagara Falls was lit to brightness by
30,000 panes of glass and was set in a ten-acre park overlooking the
falls."[29]

Phillips's countrified factory, then, is tied, though somewhat tenu-
ously, to a set of historical facts. However, the enthusiasm with which
Phillips embraces his image reveals the short reach of his industrial
critique. Glass and gardens were, and remained, the infinitesimal exception to the manufacturing rule; and they had in any case only a little to
do with the deeper dilemmas of America's economic life. The real
purpose of the Rangers' plant in *The Second Generation* is more therapeutic than political, justifying Phillips's sudden amnesia about the mul-
titude of issues he himself has raised. To dissolve all the turmoil and
blood of America's class struggle in the prettification of a single barrel-
works, to absolve American capitalism of its crimes solely through this
device, is, as Phillips himself declares, "utopianism" indeed. Whatever
its sentimental appeal, such an image in such a context – against the
background of Dr. Schulze's census of the industrial dead – bespeaks
intellectual fatigue. Recognizing with his contemporaries that the triumph of the machine over American life was no longer a disputable
matter, recognizing therefore the futility of the Luddite attack on the
machines of the modern world, Phillips seeks to evade their threat by
domesticating what he cannot defeat. "Gardens all round . . . no smoke
or soot": A resolution that is not and could not be earned is decreed.

This is perhaps the place to set Phillips's oxymoronic and self-defeating "urban pastoralism" in a corrective context. Though the Puritans
declared their purpose to found "a city upon a hill," though they took
much of their theology from Augustine's *City of God,* though their
great and influential English contemporary John Bunyan sent his hero

in search of the Celestial City, nevertheless the powerful, traditional Western current of feeling against the city flows unabated through American intellectual history from its beginnings. Phillips, in the subterfuge through which urban is magically metamorphosed into rural, encodes a history of back-looking prejudice, an entire system of mystified pastoral assumptions and values. Predictably, the tradition had grown even stronger in the face of America's accelerating urbanization through the nineteenth century. The American liberal Protestant leadership, for example, would harness New England religious energy in the service of the secular city, but it would guide the city according to agrarian, Jeffersonian principles. The disjunction is self-evident.

Certainly, antagonism toward the city was reinforced by the increasingly foreign-born character of America's city population. The interaction between culture and society is economically revealed in the exceptional American popularity of Ruskin in the latter half of the nineteenth century. The historian Albert Fine is accurate but actually understates the matter when he concludes that "part of the extraordinary receptivity of American audiences to the writings of . . . Ruskin can be attributed to his expressed hatred of commercialism and the cities that nurtured it. Urban life, Ruskin believed, was a violation of the laws of nature and incompatible with great civilizations."[30] In fact, the phenomenon of Ruskin's popularity had a double significance both as cause and effect, at once resulting from and impelling the nation's psychic retreat from its cities.

In these familiar ways, Phillips's anti-urbanism proceeds along a well-marked, well-worn path. The corrective context I spoke of earlier, on the other hand, was developing in the early years of the twentieth century a contrary response, an exuberantly pro-urban affirmation. Ruskin and his disciples notwithstanding, the new urban ideologists recognized the necessity of city and civilization to each other, indeed their congruence: They noted that the two words derived from the same Latin source, and they framed their optimism in allusions to the great city-states of history. They looked back, however, not in the manner of Phillips and other pastoralists for a literal but impossible place of preindustrial retirement. Rather, they sought in history models to adapt to the future; and the adaptations would be measured by the calipers of democracy.

Frederic C. Howe studied at Johns Hopkins in the 1890s and served as adviser in the early 1900s to Tom L. Johnson, the creative and indefatigable and radical mayor of Cleveland. Howe's book *The City: The Hope of Democracy,* published in 1905, is the ebullient testament of the pro-urban reformers. "To the city, we are to look for a rebirth of democracy. . . . The city is the hope of the future. Here life is full and eager."[31] Jane Addams, founder of Hull House, and one of the most gifted organizers in the cause of reform in this period, similarly conceived of the city in benevolent terms. Addams inserted the rise of the city into her loosely conventional evolutionary meliorism, regarded it therefore as providentially given, and set about defining it in consolatory ways.[32]

So, while Phillips's pastoralism continued to represent the more prevalent attitude toward the city among reformers – and, one speculates, among the populace at large – the contest over the definition of America's spirit was being more interestingly engaged.

Phillips was periodically and wrongly acclaimed or denounced as a radical, specifically a socialist. If any of his novels might in fact be called socialist, it would be the late work *The Conflict* (1911). What so distinguishes this book is not the presence in it of the affluent, half-hearted reformer David Hull, a self-conscious, self-appointed, upper-class custodian of "the masses." Hull is a fairly typical Phillips character. Against Hull is contrasted, however, what seems to be a genuine radical. Victor Dorn is not only for the working class but of it, and he brings to his commitments a revolutionary perspective. Thus, the progressive excoriation of corruption is allied in this novel with at least glimpses of a more fundamental critique.

The factories of this book's Remsen City, unlike those of *The Second Generation*, are not subjected to romantic transformation. They are limned in outrage, with a particular emphasis upon the divisions of class, upon the gulf both materially and in consciousness separating rich and poor:

> The old Galland homestead was at the western end of town – in a quarter that had become almost poor. But it was so dignified and its grounds were so extensive that it suggested a manor house with the humble homes of the lord's dependents clustering about it for shelter. To reach it Jane had to ride through two filthy streets lined with factories. As she rode she glanced at the windows, where could be seen in dusty air girls and boys busy at furiously driven machines – machines that compelled their human slaves to strain every nerve in the monotonous task.[33]

The worker as wage slave, bound to the mechanism of industry, is prominently part of the derivative Marxian rhetoric of the period. Admittedly, American observers would have drawn the analogy between chattel slaves and laborers even if Marx had never written. Nonetheless, the acknowledgment of Marx's insight in this connection goes back at least as far in American polemic as the work of George Fitzhugh, where it appears, ironically, as part of a defense of slavery. (Fitzhugh's *Cannibals All! or Slaves without Masters* first appeared in 1857.) Making children the victims of the factory system is historically apt if not statistically accurate, since the abuses associated with child labor wrote perhaps the bloodiest of all the dark pages of this era. In addition, the children lend melodramatic urgency to the scene Phillips sketches.

The most revealing moment in the passage, however, lies in its casual insinuation that the noisome factory, and the system it represents, are somehow un-American: To reach it we have passed by a manor house surrounded by the cottages of the lord's dependents. Phillips posits a substantial if specious likeness between industrialized Remsen City and a feudal landscape. Whatever it lacks in logic, the parallel discloses much of Phillips's ideology. He is playing off one pastoral myth against another. We had occasion to refer to Ruskin earlier. His is only the most elaborate example of the re-creation of feudalism as the positive term in anti-industrial manifestoes; the pattern is routine throughout English and Continental writing of the nineteenth century. In those European versions of pastoral, the politics of feudalism is welcomed as a part of the larger retreat from the modern world.

Phillips is combining his own pastoralism with his nationalism to deflect responsibility for the American scene away from American sources. In his supremely typical American revision of pastoral, the serfdom of twentieth-century American laborers fades into that of medieval peasants; what had seemed to be analogy is in fact working to mystify. And implicit in the careless but deliberated identification of worker and peasant, needless to say, is the alternative pastoral assertion of America's own agrarian mythology. Despite his overt hostility to Ruskinian typology, then, Phillips's resort to the past is no less escapist than that of his European predecessors and contemporaries. He is indulging again the fantasy of a return to "what the republic used to be," to cite once more that key phrase from *The Plum Tree*.

Phillips was by no means alone in his polemical redefinition of "feudalism." The architect Louis Sullivan, for example, construed the term in more or less the same way. To Sullivan, feudalism in his day meant "roughly, the men who had money and power."[34] And Phillips's friend and idol, Albert Beveridge, regarded his senatorial enemies as feudal lords. According to Claude Bowers, Beveridge believed that Nelson Aldrich was promoting an "idea of government . . . remote from the earlier American concept. It went back to feudalism, and [Aldrich] envisioned nothing less than a moneyed feudalism, with a few men at the top dictating the destiny of society and resting on the broad foundation of the masses confiding blindly in the superior wisdom of their master."[35]

Whatever the merits of the feudal analogy, note that the choice here, as it always is in Phillips, too, is not between past and future but between alternative pasts. Aldrich's alleged feudalism specifically betrays "the earlier American concept." A page out of Herbert Croly emphasizes the general applicability of this perspective to the meaning and fate of progressivism. A few years after the critical election of 1912, Croly tried to sort out the significance of Woodrow Wilson's victory in a book called *Progressive Democracy*. In a shrewd piece of close reading, he quotes and analyzes Wilson's own prophetic summoning of the future heralded by the New Freedom: "We are witnessing," Wilson proclaimed, "a renaissance of public spirit, a reawakening of sober public opinion, a revival of the power of the people, the beginning of an age of thoughtful reconstruction, that makes our thought hark back to the great age in which democracy was set up in America." Croly seizes immediately upon the paradox that turns Wilson's vision precisely on its head. "Remark," Croly observes caustically, "how every phrase of this version of a doctrine which is called progressive confronts the past and turns its back upon the future. Progressivism is not a new birth of public spirit; it is a rebirth. It is not an awakening of public opinion to something novel; it is a reawakening. It is not aimed at an unprecedented vitalizing of democracy, but at its revival along traditional lines. A 'thoughtful reconstruction' is promised; but the 'thought' which prompts the revision 'harks back to the great age' of primitive American democracy. The projected reconstruction is only a restoration."[36] As in Phillips's fiction, forward and backward become interchangeable.

This sort of intellectual muddle is rather typical, as we have seen, of Phillips. Nonetheless, with the character Victor Dorn, the spine of *The Conflict*'s dissent is stiffened, at least apparently. Dorn goes considerably further than Phillips's other dissidents in maintaining a systematic and radical critique of American conditions. He understands the fundamental insight of twentieth-century capitalism into the advantages of large-scale organization, and he understands the need therefore for any alternative economic and ideological system to devise comparable organizational strategies. He has written a broadside, "a plea to workingmen to awaken to the fact that their *strikes* were stupid and wasteful, that the way to get better pay and decent hours of labor was by uniting, taking possession of the power that was rightfully theirs and regulating their own affairs" (pp. 50–51).

Yet Dorn's attention is deflected at last from the task he proposes here by a series of evasions, tangential narrative paths his creator is led

into by his own lack of ideological or critical assurance. Pastoral, as we
have seen, is such a detour. So also is the elaborate but ultimately
pointless love story that actually engages most of Phillips's interest.
Though it is pointless, the love story is revealing, for its predominance
serves to emphasize the essentially romantic nature of Phillips's politics.
Revolution in Phillips's hands becomes an adventure. Victor Dorn is a
heroic man, but his heroism is circumscribed within his creator's limits.
The progressive will as revealed in this novel is poised in frustrated
suspension between the suspicion that the palliatives of reform are inadequate and the continuing fear of any violent rupture in the status
quo. Thus, whatever Dorn might have accomplished in some other
novelist's hands (if I may put the point that way), in Phillips's he
accomplishes nothing at all: He is permitted to behave in a ceremonially
heroic way. One escapade succeeds another; Dorn outfaces or out-
smarts bosses and plutocrats and their hired thugs as well, but he effects
no change whatever. Nor could he. Whether Phillips consciously understood the mechanism of displacement or not, his ultimately irrelevant political point is that Dorn's exaggeratedly splendid personal qualities ratify his verbal dissent; nothing more is needed. (The equations
might be written the other way around in a literature growing out of a
more robustly intellectual tradition.) We saw earlier how Phillips's
resolute anger at the sight of abusive American factories collapsed into
the misdirection of feudal references. That microcosmic failure predicted the more central evasion summed up in the character Victor
Dorn. Dorn's superb combination of radical eloquence and frontier
courage leads only to himself. The book's apparent interest in America's institutions wavers and fades, and we are left to admire the American romance hero, the familiar loner who stalks across our culture from
near its beginnings.

If Dorn is less radical than he is intended to be, the novel he appears
in is by a considerable measure less realistic. Costume melodramas of
one sort or another – pseudohistorical tales with interchangeable plots
set variously in the Middle Ages, the Italian Renaissance, and colonial
America – possessed a sizable share of the American reading market in
the early 1900s.[37] In the view of a number of commentators in this
period, the most significant development in literary fashion was the
increasingly ineluctable triumph of romance (with its "spirit of idealism") over the challenge of realism. Such an assessment may seem
ironic in retrospect, but it was not eccentric. Maurice Thompson, in an
essay in *The Independent* (1900), spoke of "a veering of popular interest
from the fiction of character analysis and social problems to the historical novel and the romance of heroic adventure. We have had a period of
intense, not to say morbid, introversion directed mainly upon diseases

of the social, domestic, political and religious life of the world. . . . it has run its course."[38]

David Graham Phillips professed contempt for romance. Predictably, he insists on several of the more familiar items on the realist agenda. We have already seen something of his view of literary style. He takes his subjects from the ranks of ordinary, contemporary citizens and through them examines an impressively long list of current political and social problems. He looks more or less unblinkingly at the corruption around him and eschews not only the gauzy apparatus but what might be called the gauzy tone of popular costume epics.

In short, Phillips's aesthetics have a fairly manifest political basis; his subjects and techniques follow directly from his commitments. Given such attitudes, the irony of his actual literary performance proves virtually complete, and it affords a commentary on the limits of political realism in this period. Victor Dorn, rather obviously, had leapt straight from the pages of a romance into the world of *The Conflict*. Swashbuckling, a virtuous picaro, Dorn is as appealing – and at bottom as politically irrelevant – as the thousands of knights, musketeers, condottieri, and minutemen who pursue each other across the pages and chapters of turn-of-the-century romance fiction. It can even be argued that such characters transcend irrelevance in their political implications: They, and the plots they inhabit, are conservative in the unexceptional manner of all formula fiction. Dorn thus embodies a paradox, and one that I am proposing is representative of the divided mind of American dissent in this period. Even in a novel that tries to maintain a serious inquiry into the structures of American corruption, the poverty of available intellectual and fictional materials subverts the novelist's conscious design; revolutionary impulses exhaust themselves not merely in compromise but in apolitical adventure.

Phillips's uncertainty is codified unintendedly in his language, which is sometimes blandly Rousseauean, at other times naïvely Marxist, in its accents. "Organize," demands Victor Dorn. "Think! Learn! Then you will rise out of the dirt where you wallow with your wives and children. Don't blame your masters; they don't enslave you. They don't keep you in slavery. Your chains are of your own forging and only you can strike them off!" (pp. 52–53). Kenneth Lynn, in his fine chapter on Phillips, comments that this speech is a "beautiful example of what could happen to the *Communist Manifesto* when it got into the mouth of an Alger hero."[39] Lynn is only half right. For in its American incarnations, the *Manifesto* almost always sounded as if it had gotten into the mouths of Alger heroes, even when the speakers were uncompromising socialists. Listen to Eugene V. Debs, speaking on behalf of the Industrial Workers of the World in 1905: "We Industrial Workers are doing what we can to increase your discontent. We would have you rise in revolt against wage slavery. The workingman who is contented today is truly a pitiable object. Victor Hugo once said: 'Think of a smile in chains,' – that is a workingman who . . . is satisfied with his lot; he is glad he has a master, some one to serve; for, in his ignorance, he imagines that he is dependent upon the master. The Industrial Workers is appealing to the working class to develop their . . . capacity for clear thinking. You are a workingman and you have a brain and if you do not use it in your own interests, you are guilty of treason to your manhood."[40] Compare that with Victor Dorn (whose name is surely derived from Eugene Victor Debs). The rhetorical resemblance cannot be denied even if, as I have been trying to show, Phillips's radicalism finally dissipates into versions of pastoral and romance.

Aside from its exuberance, Dorn's Debsian speech contains more than a hint of an insight into the trap of ideological hegemony. Later in *The Conflict*, that hint is developed when Dorn explicates the false consciousness of the working class: "Only a small part of the working class as yet is at the heart of the working class. Most of us secretly – almost openly – despise the life of work, and dream and hope a time of fortune that will put us up among the masters and idlers. . . . The false and shallow ideas that have been educated into us for ages can't be uprooted in a few brief years" (p. 140).

Given both the scale of the task and Phillips's own background, Dorn is inevitably a journalist. His crusading socialist weekly, *The New Day*, commemorates that whole galaxy of radical dailies, weeklies, and monthlies – *The Advocate, The American Non-Conformist, The Appeal to Reason, The Call*, the *Jewish Daily Forward*, and so many others – that sprang up around the country in the eighties and nineties and provided the best chance for the oppressed and discontented people of rural and urban America to organize and educate themselves.

The first task of those who rule, according to Lawrence Goodwyn, is "the creation of mass modes of thought that literally make the need for major additional social changes difficult for the mass of the population to imagine."[41] Goodwyn has the American turn of the century specifically in mind, and his book *The Populist Moment* pays tribute to the same struggle Victor Dorn describes: that of working people to transcend the ideas that have been inculcated into them. Significantly, the strategy Dorn pursues is exactly the one outlined by Goodwyn in his history of populism: the independent press, supported by the lecture system. The lecture system, through which citizen orators carried the gospel of dissent to thousands of communities, was "the essential democratic communications network within the movement."[42] Similarly, the Citizens League, led by Victor Dorn, relies chiefly upon "the influence of their twelve hundred men, their four or five thousand women and young men and girls, talking every day and evening, each man or woman or youth with those with whom he came into contact" (p. 268). Dorn calls this league "the army of education."

My point in underscoring these parallels is to propose that, in *The Conflict*, Phillips has rendered the techniques of dissent in historically reliable terms. And Phillips goes further than most populists or progressives in tracing the roots of his critique to the work of Marx. Victor Dorn identifies Marx as second only to Christ in the history of liberty: "It won't be long before there are monuments to Marx in clean and beautiful and free cities all over the earth" (p. 62). Most significantly, however, despite the occasional paraphrase of Marxian discourse, it is the *figure* of Marx, and not the revolutionary materialist doctrine, that actually holds Phillips's imagination. Like Dorn himself, Marx appears here more as a romantic hero than as an agent of fundamental and violent change. Marx hovers over the action of the novel as a benevolent, paternal personality, not as the prophet of apocalypse.

In a word, Marx is sentimentalized. Four pictures, we are told, hang on the wall of the offices of *The New Day*. In keeping with Dorn's ascetic temper, the pictures are appropriately "lithographs, cheap, not framed, held in place by a tack at each corner." The pictures include "Washington–then Lincoln–then a copy of Leonardo's Jesus in the Last Supper fresco–and a fourth face, bearded, powerful, imperious, yet wonderfully kind and good humored" (p. 59). Such is the Karl Marx of *The Conflict*. By an all-too-visible sleight of hand, similar to that by which Hampden Scarborough is awarded the presidency at the end of *The Plum Tree* and Hiram Ranger's factories are made part of the green world in *The Second Generation,* a new day is simply decreed. Despite its designed optimism, what is done to Marx in this novel, like the similarly gratuitous gestures of hope in Phillips's other books, is in fact best understood as an unintended confession of despair. Nostalgia, hero worship, a nearly self-effacing absorption in a benevolent personality: These are the marks of a politics that has failed.

In speaking of the conservatively circumscribed imaginations of many progressive reformers (he is specifically describing the doctrines of the Harvard economist Willard Fisher), Goodwyn concludes that their "sophisticated despair, grounded in the belief that hierarchical American society could, perhaps, be 'humanized' but could not be fundamentally democratized, became the operative premise of twentieth-century reformers."[43] This is a compelling generalization, and it applies with uncanny accuracy to David Graham Phillips's political novels.

If Phillips has retained any visibility at all in the decades since his death in 1911 (besides that connected with *The Treason of the Senate*), it is based on his interest in the "new woman" question. Phillips's novels are, at least by turns, indisputably alive to the systematic oppression of women in early twentieth-century American society. Phillips's theme is everywhere power, and his explorations were unblinking enough to permit him to see the powerlessness of women: in politics, in the marketplace, above all in the family. The leading female character in *The Conflict* evidently has her author's approval when she offers this estimate of marriage: "–to marry one of these men, with their coarse physical ideas of women, with their pitiful weakness. . . . These were the creatures who ruled the world and compelled women to be their playthings and mere appendages" (p. 6). Scattered across Phillips's writings, passages such as this indicate his at least occasional awareness of women's fate in the peculiar institution of marriage.

In the end, however, what is true of the politics in Phillips's novels is true as well of the sociology of sexual relations he portrays: Unsupported by an articulate or coherent ideological perspective, tempted indeed toward many of the oppressive idealizing clichés that dominated perceptions of women, Phillips's undeniably progressive sympathies propel him toward nothing more than intermittent glimpses of alternatives to the status quo. More than many of the writers of his time – certainly more than most of the male writers – Phillips understood the cruelties practiced upon women by traditional marital and domestic structures. Several of his novels dramatize the situation with uncommon insight. Yet without exception, Phillips's outrage ultimately evaporates, leaving the traditional structures intact. The gestures Phillips indulges in his political novels – in which, for instance, machines within gardens are arbitrarily denominated green – find analogies in those novels that have sexual relationships as their subject.

One novel and one play can stand here for all of Phillips's work on this theme. The novel, *The Price She Paid* (1912), documents Phillips's tough-minded understanding of the condition of women in America at the turn of the century. Told largely from the point of view of its heroine, Mildred Gower, the novel records her efforts, following her virtual impoverishment upon the death of her father, to build a life of financial and moral independence, to assert and maintain her equality, not in the abstract theater of abstract statement, but in the workaday arena of getting and spending. She would cultivate her talents, pursue her own career, and dispose of herself on her own terms.

The book is distinguished in several specific ways by a subversively radical analysis of the position of American women. To begin with (it is also the novel's major achievement dramatically), Phillips looks long and hard at the meaning of marriage for women. He offers a sustained exploration, from the woman's point of view, of the legalized slavery into which contemporary marriage can degenerate. In a society dominated by commercial values, in which access to commercial opportunities is denied to women except through subordinate alliances with men, and in which in the worst case women themselves become commodities, there is a powerful likeness between marriage and prostitution.[44] This grim assessment of sexual relations constitutes the main argument of *The Price She Paid*. The novel's considerable dramatic success lies in Phillips's ability – more in evidence here than in most of his novels – to invent a series of images and episodes through which to give life to his ideas.

Mildred's grasping mother and stepfather organize her marriage to the repulsive but rich General William Siddall, a figure whose literary genealogy encompasses the villains of sentimental melodrama, but a figure here of exceptional vivacity. Phillips actually uses Siddall to subvert the most important sexual premise of melodrama by embodying the evil male threat in the husband, not the rapist or seducer of tradition. With that corrosive piece of casting, Phillips uses convention against itself: The nightmare of safely familiar romance becomes the reality of sexual politics.

We first meet Siddall presiding over a stupefyingly excessive dinner in his grotesquely ornate New York mansion. He is "entertaining" Mildred and her parents, and he spends the evening evaluating Mildred for purchase. "He buys a woman," judges Mildred, "as he buys a dog or a horse."[45] Impressed by what he sees, Siddall announces himself willing to marry Mildred – "if the goods are up to the sample" (p. 61).

Mildred Gower is perfectly aware of her repugnance for the General and for the social system he represents. Yet she is also willing to marry him, and thus willing both to ratify his pretensions and to strengthen the system. Her willingness derives not merely from her material need but from the partialness of her rebellion. The system she loathes also defines her own ideology, thus dividing her against herself. Whatever stirrings of revolt she might feel are necessarily frustrated, at the beginning of the novel, by her inability to conceive of any alternative organization of sexual relations other than those that have imprisoned her. Under such circumstances, revolt would be pointless at best and ironically self-destructive at worst.

Mildred's freedom is constricted by the twinned realities of her economic powerlessness and her consciousness of herself as a commodity. Her life with Siddall is designed by Phillips as a supremely typical case, virtually an allegory of the limits of marriage for women. Siddall is incalculably rich, and he insists that Mildred have everything she desires – except a dollar of her own or an inch of autonomous space.

Mildred is, in other words, the ultimate kept woman, who lives in the greatest possible luxury in just the proportion in which she relinquishes all claims to independence.

After a few months of marriage to the General, Mildred walks out, risking both poverty and his particular revenge. It is a genuinely courageous and genuinely rebellious act; it overpowers the moral equilibrium that has held her disaffection captive to her material wants. If Mildred is spared the harsh consequences she foresees, that has to do – typically – with Phillips's failure of nerve, not Mildred's. For the rest of the novel, Phillips shields his heroine from the more plausible results of her choice. Here, as so often in his novels, he is caught between his premises and his wishfulness. Having used his main character to demonstrate both how deeply corrupt the American sexual domain is and how inescapably it holds captive the women in it, Phillips simply decrees a more or less happy ending: something to reward Mildred's intelligent energy and honest striving, one feels, rather than the fate that the novel's own logic would produce.

The novel's outcome – Mildred, contentedly alone, working diligently to establish herself in a successful singing career – is attractively forward-looking, even feminist, but not coherent. Put it this way: Phillips needs to manipulate both his heroine and his story to ensure the "emancipated" outcome he desires. But such manipulation amounts to another species of evasion, to the substitution of wish for logic. Further, whether he intended the result or not, the threat offered to convention by Phillips's heroine is rendered nonthreatening by the spheres to which her work is reserved. She does work hard, her incipient career is a real one, her chances for success are good (indeed, too good: The novel's last line tells us that "she laughed and rushed away to fresh triumphs" [p. 379]). But Mildred is a singer, demonstrably peripheral to the economic forces that shape American society, and her role remains essentially "feminine": ornamental, apolitical, a matter of leisure time and surplus cash. The clear implication is that Mildred embodies a dissent bounded rather strictly by the sexual presuppositions of her time.

Those boundaries are made even more visible in Phillips's handling of Mildred's marital career. After spending most of the novel worrying about General Siddall's return or retribution, Mildred learns – to her quite old-fashioned shock – that the General had married her bigamously. His first, undivorceable wife is languishing in a mental institution. The *deus ex machina* permits Phillips to titillate the reader, but it also permits him to end Mildred's union in exactly the most sentimentally satisfying way: Her bad marriage is not merely over, it never existed. As the marriage magically evaporates, much of its significance as social criticism evaporates as well. In a peculiar way, what had seemed subversive turns at the last minute into a reaffirmation of convention.

Phillips observes of one of his lesser characters, late in the novel, that she fails to understand Mildred's quest for independence because she "lived in the ordinary environment of flapdoodle and sweet hypocrisy and sentimentality; and none such can more than vaguely glimpse the realities" (p. 373). The comment is surely intended to apply to the whole novel: Phillips considers his portrait of a lady free of flapdoodle and hypocrisy. And, up to a point, it is. From contemporary sexual relations he draws inferences about the inherent oppressiveness of American domestic institutions that could make *The Price She Paid*, despite its nonpolitical subject matter, a political study of considerable general significance. In the event, however, Phillips's own glimpse of reality is veiled by disabling sentiment. What he intends as unreservedly progressive emerges as a dialectic in which the conventional and conservative eventually overtake the radical. As in the political novels themselves, the rhetoric of dissent leads finally to its own exhaustion.

It may be worth glancing here at the difference between David Graham Phillips and Theodore Dreiser. Phillips is overtly addressing social and political issues in all his novels, and from a designedly progressive point of view. Yet in *The Price She Paid* and in his other books, Phillips's radicalism is restrained and defeated by what prove to be his ideological presumptions. Dreiser, altogether apolitical and mawkishly sentimental, created in *Sister Carrie* a plot similar to that of Phillips – the sexual adventures of a young midwestern woman who makes a stage success in New York – but Dreiser's story turned out to be explosively threatening in its implications for the established order. Dreiser's novel actually asked the questions that Phillips circled around, about the definition of morals, about the relationship of literature to social problems, about the premises of a sexist society and politics. The formula through which Mildred Gower is rewarded is at last as traditional as those of *Pamela* and the Horatio Alger tales. (Mildred herself does bravely oppose the definition of "virtue" in its narrowest sexual-pecuniary sense, but it's that sense her novel affirms in the end.) There is, needless to say, nothing traditional about Carrie Meeber's reward.

Though the shape of its plot is altogether different, Phillips's play *The Worth of a Woman* reveals at its center the same thematic ambivalence as *The Price She Paid*. Diana Merivale, a young woman of uncommon energy and intellect, gives voice throughout the play to Phillips's conception of a more humane relation between men and women than convention allows, a relation of genuine equality. The focus here is specifically sexual: Resisting the urgent protestations of family and friends, Diana refuses to marry the amiable young lawyer, Julian Burroughs, with whom she has had an affair and by whom she finds herself pregnant. One after another, Diana enumerates and demolishes all the arguments traditionally associated with such moments. In doing so, she assails virtually every cliché and stereotype surrounding female sexuality: that women are necessarily "victimized" by freely chosen sexual love, that sexual desire is masculine and sex something "done to" women, that marriage is a suitable or sensible "reparation" for pregnancy.

Diana stands in the antinomian highway, insisting on the primacy of her independence, denying that her value as a human being is implicated in her virginity or in its loss, declaring that it is the prevailing commercial understanding of marriage, and not sexual love freely given and received, that corrupts the integrity of women. At one point Preacher Woodruff sanctimoniously tells Diana, "Women are led by their emotions. *You* were." To which Diana replies with the bitter question, "And what are men led by?"[46]

Sexual love, Diana argues, is neither a sin nor a crime. A loveless marriage would be. She demands for women what American culture has always conspired to deny them, by denouncing the split between sexual law and custom and real sexual ethics. Her polemic, generalized, not only opposes externally devised codes against internally derived perceptions of right, it strenuously indicts the former while exulting in the latter. From early in American thought, this juxtaposition has been the graph on which individual responsibility has been charted. What makes Diana Merivale's version of this proclamation novel, even modestly revolutionary, is her vigorous defense of her autonomy as a woman, as an actively, interestedly, exuberantly sexual woman. Her self-assertive vitality would give the lie to the entire array of formulas in which women are imprisoned by American culture.

The play's structure also deals rather inventively with the consequences of dramatizing dissent in a female figure. It is a critical commonplace to note the number of dissident heroes whose search for alternative sources of order leads them on either literal or symbolic quests for fathers. *The Worth of a Woman* reverses that commonplace. Diana Merivale has a father, whom she deeply reveres and who has in fact tutored her in independence. He has often quoted to her the familiar epigram of personal liberty: "Resist much, obey little" (p. 76). Once he learns of Diana's pregnancy, however, his rebellious spirit melts under the sun of convention, and his advice proves to have been somewhat theoretical. Diana justifies her refusal to marry by appealing to her father's own teaching: To marry, she declares, "would be false to all you taught me" (p. 91). To which Merivale responds – after a quite brief pause – in the accents of rigidly orthodox melodrama: "Either you marry him or he dies." Preacher Woodruff begins the marriage ceremony on that last word.

It is at this point that Phillips further alters the usual pattern of American romance. Instead of either yielding or fleeing – the typical responses of American male heroes – Diana stands her ground and argues her case. And, after a considerably protracted debate, she wins. Merivale concedes Diana's ethical superiority, embraces his daughter on her terms, and throws the almost-wed Julian Burroughs out of the house. In other words, the father in this tale has, all unwitting, been engaged in a moral journey and has discovered moral truth in the wisdom of the child. Pedagogical roles are exchanged, and thus even more emphatically the legitimacy and logic of Diana's revolt against convention are affirmed. Here the third act closes.

If *The Worth of a Woman* ended with this scene, with Merivale assenting to his daughter's definition of her sexual and human rights, its final tone would be univocal. There is, however, a short fourth act in which Phillips changes direction and squanders much of the purpose he has brought to the issues at stake in the play. Julian Burroughs, who had left the stage "slowly, as if dazed and blinded" at the end of Act III, and who has been relieved of the need to "do his duty" by Diana, returns. Educated by Diana's courage, Julian has now grown into a true love for her, accompanied by true respect. He proposes marriage on these mutual and uncoerced terms, and Diana accepts. The logic of Phillips's characters is not at risk here: Neither Diana nor certainly Julian is drawn with sufficient dimension to make the play's outcome implausible. What is at risk – what risks, in fact, being reduced to farce – is the integrity of Phillips's vision. Diana's rebellion has been real, and her bill of particulars against the sexual hypocrisy of her era has been a ringing declaration of female independence. At the last, however, Phillips denies her both the coherence of her point of view and the need to endure the harsher consequences of her position. By providing her with a husband, Phillips characteristically undertakes to have it both ways: to embrace both revolt and respectability.

Sacvan Bercovitch, in *The American Jeremiad,* brilliantly revises Perry Miller's version of early New England's attitude toward its mission. Bercovitch observes, to begin with, that the lament over the colonists' moral and spiritual decline commences immediately upon the first settlement and not, as Miller would have it, with the second and third generation. Bercovitch quotes Thomas Shepard, crying out, just six years after the *Arbella*'s landing, "We never looked for such days in *New-England. . . .* Are all God's kindnesses forgotten?" Further, the

American jeremiad has its readily discernible sources in the Protestant English preaching of the fifteenth and sixteenth centuries, and that in turn can be traced back to the traditions of the medieval pulpit.

Bercovitch's reconstruction of the jeremiad's tone is perhaps even more important than his reordering of its chronology. The Puritan preachers did not simply scourge their hearers: They continually reaffirmed the mission even as they excoriated backsliding from it. Their devotion to the errand grew, if anything, more intense rather than less as time went on. Thus, the New England jeremiad, though fervid indeed in its denunciation of colonial decline, is precisely distinguished by its equally zealous and optimistic countertheme, its "affirmation and exultation."[47]

This doubled structure of the jeremiad has persisted in American culture. Bercovitch tracks its presence in the work of several major nineteenth-century writers, and he glances at a number of twentieth-century authors as well. The pattern he describes fits David Graham Phillips and the ideology of progressive reform down to the ground. Mingling rebuke and affirmation, exposure and assent; mourning the lost and more perfect past yet loudly optimistic that the future will see a restoration; insisting on the sacred exclusivity of America's destiny and relying on the efficacious convergence of individual and communal election; ratifying in the end a conservative political and social agenda: As he endorses and presses these themes, Phillips makes a representative contribution to America's distinctive, jeremiad vision of reform.

Chapter 4

It couldn't happen here:
the failure of socialism in America

THE SCARLET EMPIRE

There is no crime. There are large numbers of people in prison, but they are political deviates, widely understood to be insane, and labeled "atavars." Periodically, at great festivals attended by the entire population of the country, and for which national holidays are decreed, the most notorious and intractable of the imprisoned malcontents are dragged from their cells and grotesquely executed.

The time is 1900; the place is the lost continent of Atlantis. Surviving in some unexplained fashion under the Atlantic for centuries since a cataclysmic earthquake buried it, Atlantis has developed into a full-fledged "Social Democracy." What that means, in David Parry's novel *The Scarlet Empire* (1906), is that Atlantis is a complete and perfect hell, a thoroughgoing dystopia: a place of relentless and ruthless leveling, of mediocrity canonized, of joyless, uniform gray.

All men being equal, in Atlantis they are forced to be equal in every microscopic detail. Money and private property have long since been abolished, as have any and all appurtenances of status based on skill or intelligence. Every citizen of Atlantis eats the same number of ounces of identically prepared fish gruel and seaweed each day. Everybody wears the same dully colored, crudely stitched clothing and lives in uniformly miserable hutches.

Recently, the Atlantean parliament has been legislating equality in whatever realms of individuality have managed to evade leveling. To mock the implications of equality, Parry nurtures to full, awful fruition every outrageous excess he can conceive; the recent history of Atlantis is made a ludicrously literal chronicle of egalitarianism. All the citizens wear verbometers around their necks. If anyone speaks more words each day than the national quota, punishment follows. "It is not just," pronounces a loyal member of this society, "for one individual to talk more than another – it is not in consonance with the fundamental idea of equality."[1]

All laws must forward this perverse vision of social democracy by enforcing greater and greater uniformity. A selection of Atlantean laws includes the following:

> A Bill to Regulate the Trimming of Finger Nails.
> A Bill Requiring the Use of the Left Arm as Much as the Right.
> A Bill Providing for the Equal Use of the Maxillary Muscles on Both Sides of the Mouth in the Act of Masticating Food.
> A Bill Requiring Every Individual to Laugh Aloud Once Every Hour, and Providing Inspectors for the Enforcement of the Act.

As these preposterous items suggest, Parry's satire against social democracy is not especially restrained.

David Parry's splenetic novel is an extreme but by no means unique document in the debate over socialism at the turn of the century. By casting his account in utopian terms, Parry hoped to take advantage of the extraordinary popularity of the utopian genre, which had been "perhaps the most widely read type of literature in America" in the 1890s, though that popularity was on the wane in the 1900s.[2]

The utopian apparatus permits Parry to indulge his antisocialistic anger uninhibitedly and to dramatize his terrors with unabashed apocalyptic urgency. Thus, early in the novel, the emasculating consequences of socialism are denounced in a relatively trite figure: "This damnable Democracy, which, like an octopus with a million tentacles, is throttling the manhood of our entire race" (p. 87). In the novel's sensational scenes of execution, however, this tired simile is transformed into bizarre fact. The condemned prisoners – convicted of the crime of individualism – are marched into a huge amphitheater, which is crowded with thousands of their bloodthirsty socialist fellow citizens. To the ear-splitting applause of that mob, the victims are pushed through an airlock in the base of a huge transparent sea wall. Waiting on the other side, ready to ingest them before they can even drown, lurks a nightmarish creature:

> I looked quickly and at that moment an incredible monster seemed to dash itself at the amphitheater. I saw two immense eyes, a cavernous mouth and a dozen great arms or tentacles all flattened against the transparent wall.. . . . its body was as large as a whale's and covered with scales that glistened in the light. Its arms reached apparently a hundred feet in length and seemed as large around as a man's body. But most terrifying were its eyes, which looked like concave lenses about five feet in diameter, and

the mouth, capacious as a hogshead, which contained teeth like those of a crocodile. (P. 258)

The octopus. David Parry's reactionary, utterly forgotten, near-hysterical response to Frank Norris's widely read novel of just three or four years earlier (Plate 5). Writing in 1927, Mark Sullivan offers this gloss on the origin of the octopus as a political figure: ". . . synonymous with *The System* – the first use of it may have been a visualization of the trusts thrusting tentacles out over the country from Wall Street. (Or was the word inspired by a map of the Standard Oil's pipe-lines criss-crossing the country? Or by a map of the railroads? Or did Frank Norris, the novelist, invent it, or appropriate it from general use?)"[3] The burden of Sullivan's comments is that, though the source of the most familiar of all the symbols of the American 1900s is ambiguous and probably pedestrian, the decisive reading of the symbol was that formulated by Norris. The octopus, for Norris and for most of his contemporaries, was an apposite emblem of the stranglehold in which corporate America had embraced its citizens. For Parry, driven in the opposite direction by a fear and loathing apparently even greater than Norris's, the octopus became not merely an emblem of the people's suffocation by the socialist state but an emblem he is compelled to translate into a phantasmagoric reality.

The absurd Atlantean parliament is called the Vorunk, and the barbaric festivals of execution are the feasts of Kuglum. The terms sound faintly and derisively Slavic, which is consistent with Parry's xenophobic reaction against what he understood to be the eastern European roots of American socialism, roots being watered at the turn of the century by the tidal wave of "new immigrants" arriving in the United States each year. *The Scarlet Empire* was published literally at the height of immigration into this country. Equally important, as we noted earlier, the places from which immigrants came had changed: Great Britain, Germany, the Scandinavian countries, which had provided the majority of immigrants through most of the nineteenth century, were replaced by Italy, Greece, Poland – by what a contemporary observer called the "Hebrew centres."[4] The typicality of Parry's fulminations are captured in John Thomas's generalization about American attitudes toward the new immigrants: "All the ethnic groups arriving in such great numbers after 1880 . . . were viewed at one time or another as dissidents and potential bomb throwers in need of the ministrations of cultural counter-revolutionaries teaching a kind of 'Americanism' indistinguishable from conformity."[5]

The mounting xenophobia of the early 1900s, of which *The Scarlet Empire* is only a small instance, was about to instigate the exhaustive

The attacks of the monster made the vast assemblage frantic with delight.

PLATE 5. This rendering of David Parry's octopus was one of ten illustrations provided by Herman C. Wall for the first edition.

Dillingham Commission inquiry, which would in turn form the allegedly factual basis for the restrictive immigration laws of the following
decades. Parry nicely illustrates the subordination of logic to bigotry so
characteristic of nativist hysteria in his interesting if rather odd view
that prerevolutionary Russia offered the closest contemporaneous approach to a government of social democracy. What Parry has in mind
with this hypothesis is surely not the rigidly stratified hierarchical structure of the czarist regime but the immobilized masses of poor peasantry
at the bottom of the system. Taken with any historical seriousness,
Parry is warning that socialism leads not forward but backward into
medieval feudalism. But there is no reason to search for a historically
serious significance here. Parry invokes czarist Russia, the most determinedly antisocialist government in the world, not because the connection makes any ideological sense but to fuel his polemic with the energy
of prejudice. It is only a further irony that Parry's attack on the conformity of socialism is ultimately at the service of a theology of American
conformism.

Thus, the savagery of Parry's ridicule – and in this he is representative – emerges out of the doubled sources of his anger: His quarrel is
not merely political or economic but ethnic and racist as well. (The
anti-Semitic overtones of *The Scarlet Empire*, though muted, are unmistakable.)

Parry is so confused by his own rage that his satire regularly threatens to defeat itself. Consider the caution against equality expressed in
such "socialist" Atlantean legislation as the "Short Step Bill." This is "a
measure to limit to ten inches the length of the step in walking or
running. . . . owing to the varying lengths of the legs of different
individuals, some would cover a much greater distance in one step than
others, and this certainly did not seem in accord with complete equality" (p. 318). Putting the case most generously, one might argue that
Parry is using slapstick comedy to laugh his readers out of any socialist
temptations they might be feeling. (Note that the New York *Times,* in
a brief review, spoke of the book's "amusing imaginative material."
The radical journal *Arena* took the novel's grotesqueries as a serious
affront and published a three-page, double-column rebuttal called
"Parry and His Book."[6])

Whatever their merits, Parry's excesses do underscore his anger. For
him, the image appropriate to the regimented equality of Atlantis is the
prison: "The whole race has been placed on the same dead level as that
which obtains in our penitentiaries" (p. 174); Atlantis is nothing more
than a "radium-lighted dungeon of the sea" (p. 79).

There is, by the way, a fragilely slender plot that surfaces from time
to time throughout Parry's four hundred pages of social commentary.

John Walker, an impoverished, good-hearted, but fatally naïve young socialist, in despair at the evils of capitalist America, attempts suicide by throwing himself off the Coney Island Pier into the midwinter Atlantic. He doesn't drown (even though his pocket is weighted down with a copy of *The Iniquities of the Capitalist Régime*). Much to his astonishment and initial delight, he is rescued by an inhabitant of the "socialist utopia" Atlantis. Using Walker as his point of view, Parry is able to manufacture a crude *Bildungsroman:* Walker learns, as it were, the true lesson of socialism and by the end of the novel has made his commitment to good, old-fashioned American capitalism. We learn that after his escape from the Atlantean dungeon, Walker will return to the United States, change his name, and devote his remaining years to the accumulation of a large industrial fortune.

More or less predictably, Walker's escape from Atlantis is apocalyptic. Accompanied by the inevitable and darkly beautiful atavar Astraea, Walker commandeers a derelict submarine from the Atlantean museum, hammers it into working order, slips through an airlock, and floats to the surface. In the manner of all adventure tales, the submarine is attacked by the monstrous octopus. Walker fires his torpedoes, intending to hit only the beast, but both the monster and the city it symbolizes are doomed. "There directly before my eyes was the brilliantly-lighted amphitheater with a torrent of water pouring into the arena and thousands of creatures like ants struggling with the flood!" (pp. 393–394). The mixture of catastrophism and utopianism is a relatively common one, of course: Since the book of Revelations, at least, the pattern recurs in millennial literature. It permits one to pause long enough to do stern justice to one's enemies before setting up the new paradise. In a sense, *The Scarlet Empire* interestingly reverses that traditional chronology: Walker's torpedo allows David Parry to blow up the future he fears in order to celebrate the status quo.

The enemy is socialism, and with a grand gesture David Parry has swept it away. Swept away as well is socialism's agent, the immigrant, the exotic foreigner, the Other. Swept away finally is the most fearsome nemesis of all, organized labor.

Throughout the novel, Parry insists on the particular responsibility of organized labor in creating the social-democratic system he portrays as so appalling. The million omnipresent inspectors who peer into every cranny of Atlantean life to enforce the laws of mediocrity are the administrative and ideological heirs of the union's walking delegates. The principles that inform the "damnable Democracy" all have their genesis in an Atlantean labor movement strikingly similar in its agenda to that of the United States at the turn of the century. A dissident doctor, Walker's confidant throughout the book, outlines the chronology:

But for the Federation of Labor the Social Democracy would never have been. It was the Federation that paved the way. It passed laws providing that the State should fix wages and hours of labor. It declared what should constitute a day's work in all industries, it limited the number of men who could be permitted to learn the various trades and occupations . . . (P. 209)

From the eight-hour day to the Short Step Bill. For David Parry, the dominoes would topple irresistibly and violently.

Parry, as it happens, was more of an archetypal than a typical enemy of socialism and organized labor. Aside from being a self-proclaimed millionaire capitalist who had lectured across the country against the eight-hour day, and aside from living in the deliciously named Golden Hill section of Indianapolis, Parry was serving at the time of his novel's publication as president of the National Association of Manufacturers. He was thus in some sense the ultimately authoritative spokesman for American big business, though his anger is a reliable index as well to the reactions of more ordinary Americans. Indeed, in the combined simplification and venom of *The Scarlet Empire* lies the first answer to the question of American socialism's failure. A nationwide, prepotent hostility met turn-of-the-century socialists, an opposition forged out of elements and creeds so heterogeneous that they agreed on nothing except their unified hatred for socialism.

To conservatives and capitalists, of course, socialism was immoral in its denial of the sacrosanct myth of individualism. Christians assumed the atheism of socialists, and moralists of all denominations condemned what they took for granted was socialism's espousal of free love. To nativists, socialism was a foreign creed and to anti-Semites, specifically Jewish. To the progressives, with their commitment to stability and gradualism, socialism was anarchic and mindless; to the reformers it was too radical and to the pragmatists too dogmatic. To much of organized labor, socialism threatened to ignore or even to exacerbate working conditions rather than improve them; and to the larger portion of labor outside the union movement altogether, socialism was irrelevant. In short, Americans of virtually every persuasion could agree on their common and apparently instinctive antipathy for socialism, and they did.

The routine virulence of American antisocialism and the perception of socialism as the evil toward which other evils tended suggest how representative a text *The Scarlet Empire* is, after all. We glanced earlier at Richard Hofstadter's analysis of "the paranoid style" in American politics and culture. Hofstadter takes his illustrations from moments in American history other than the one we are considering. But the reaction of the great majority of Americans to socialism, their fear of "a vast and sinister conspiracy" against their nation and its values, rather convincingly exemplifies Hofstadter's point.[7]

SECTS AND SECTARIANS

The United States has historically been, of course, a country given to chiliastic self-indulgence. We have produced ranters and apocalyptic prophets in every generation since the first Anglo-Saxon occupation. Michael Wigglesworth wrote the earliest American bestseller to welcome "the Day of Doom" nearly two and a half centuries before the escalating labor wars of the late nineteenth century provoked Senator John J. Ingalls to announce that "we are on the verge of revolution."[8] Nevertheless, and with all this proviso by way of preface, the prospect of a full-scale and decisive upheaval seemed especially conspicuous in the early years of the twentieth century. Selig Perlman has argued that the Pullman strike of 1894 brought the American labor movement, and American society, to a genuine turning point: "The Pullman strike marks an era in the American labor movement because it was the only attempt ever made in America of a revolutionary strike on the continental European model. The strikers tried to throw against the associated railways and indeed against the entire existing social order the full force of a revolutionary labor solidarity."[9]

Whatever the merits of Perlman's generalization, it is undeniable that the two decades from Pullman to the First World War were years of recurrent revolutionary alarms. And socialism was recurrently identified – hopefully or fearfully, according to the politics of the observer – as the most likely engine of revolt. Yet this prevalent consciousness was founded upon a complete misunderstanding of the political life of socialism in America in this period, and specifically upon an enormous overestimation not only of socialism's appeal but of its coherence as well. By means of a thoroughly American process of mystification, the socialist enemy was exalted and enlarged, it was made homogeneous, it was awarded a degree of single-minded purpose out of any proportion to reality. Indeed, the second answer to the question of American socialism's failure resides precisely in the utter disarray within "the movement" itself.

The zealotry of socialism, like the zeal that marches to any evangelical calling, proved itself by dividing into a new sect for each shade and nuance of opinion. With this, socialism participated in the genius for fragmentation universally at work among radicals. In his history of the Wobblies, *American Syndicalism* (1913), John Graham Brooks quotes a delegate to the founding Industrial Workers of the World convention of 1905. The delegate enumerates four kinds of "theorists" in attendance at that first meeting. There were parliamentary socialists, of two types: impossibilist and opportunist. There were anarchists, again of two types: Marxian and reformist. There were industrial unionists. And there were what Brooks's informant calls "labor union fakirs."[10] To suspicious or fearful outsiders, they were all radicals or anarchists or "reds." To themselves, on the contrary, they were distributed along a political scale calibrated with microscopic fineness.

The myriad ancestors of turn-of-the-century socialism virtually guaranteed the movement's internal divisiveness: Marx; Ferdinand Lasalle, the founder of German social democracy; the anarchist Mikhail Bakunin; the utopians Edward Bellamy and Laurence Gronlund; nineteenth-century American communitarians of several complexions.

Morris Hillquit, the philosophical voice of the Socialist Party of America, published in 1903 his *History of Socialism in the United States*. It is an important book, providing as it does an extended effort to define and defend the specific differences between the Socialist Party and all of its current and past rivals on the left. Part One of Hillquit's volume consists of an extraordinary catalogue of nineteenth-century radical movements and groups. For well over a hundred pages, the Shakers, the Harmony Society, the Zoar Community, Bethel and Aurora, the Oneida Community, the Owenites, the Fourierites, the Icarians, and many more are passed in review, a poignant roll-call of abandoned dreams and forgotten dreamers.[11]

Hillquit's intention is by no means, of course, disinterested or antiquarian. He is trying to detach his own party from the adhesive of these massed precedents; but he achieves much the reverse. Thus Hillquit's Part Two, "The Modern Movement," not only inadvertently documents much of the genetic linkage between the older and newer radicalism, but it also reveals within the new movements the same rage for orthodoxy and the same talent for schism that typified the earlier radical experiments. The conflicts between the original German and the later American adherents of the Communist International; between Daniel De Leon and a succession of opponents for control of the Socialist Labor Party; between De Leon and Eugene V. Debs for authority over the socialist agenda as a whole; between the socialist labor movement and the reformists, exemplified supremely by Samuel Gompers of the American Federation of Labor; between elements of the radical labor movement itself (e.g., the De Leon vs. Chicago factions of the IWW, or Debs vs. Bill Haywood on the utility of violence); between the Social Democracy of America and the Social Democratic Party; between socialists who would include and those who would exclude

blacks; between and among the factions within Hillquit's own Socialist
Party of America: These are just a few of the internal struggles that
contained the left within its own turmoil during these years.[12]

At a relatively obvious level of generalization, most of these conflicts
matched revolutionaries against reformers. But that dichotomy is far
too simple to account for the psychological welter on the left in this
period, because every sect saw itself as the truest of the believers and its
rivals as fanatics or opportunists. Thus, after the disappointing presidential election of 1908 (Debs received just over 420,000 votes, practically no increase from the Socialist tally in 1904), A. M. Simons, editor
of the Chicago Daily Socialist, wrote a letter to William English Walling
opening for discussion the possibility of replacing the Socialist Party
with a Labor Party on the English model. Attacking the Socialist left,
Simons wrote: "On the one side are a bunch of intellectuals like myself,
Spargo, Hunter and Hillquit; on the other side a bunch of never-works,
demagogues and would-be intellectuals, a veritable 'Lumpen-Proletar-
iat'."[13] Four years later, Walling himself, a leader of the Socialist
Party's left wing but by no means its most radical voice, devoted a long
section of his "explanation" of contemporary socialism to a denunciation of Victor Berger. Berger had been the cofounder with Debs of the
short-lived Social Democracy of America in 1897 but had spent the
1900s in acrimonious opposition to Debs, pursuing a "pragmatic Marxism." In 1910, Berger became the first Socialist elected to the United
States Congress. To Walling, Berger's successes are not socialist achievements at all but delusory compromise and a species of routine American
self-promotion. Walling's contempt for Berger's "Milwaukee socialism" is ratified in his view by the welcome Berger received in the
capitalist press.[14] So much for the myth of the "monolithic" left.

E. J. Hobsbawm, in his intelligent analysis of modern revolution,
discerns in the trajectory of events in France at the end of the eighteenth
century the shape of "all subsequent bourgeois-revolutionary politics . . . [a] dramatic dialectical dance [that] was to dominate the future." In Hobsbawm's summary, the moderate reformers mobilize the
masses against the forces of reaction. The masses then push beyond the
moderates toward a more radical agenda, and the moderates split into
two factions: conservatives, who join with counterrevolutionary elements, and a left wing, which attaches itself to the radical masses.[15]

This has a relevance to the political and intellectual developments we
are considering. The politics of the turn-of-the-century American left
was choreographed rather broadly as an episode in the "dialectical
dance" Hobsbawm speaks of. A crucial difference, though, and another
reason the incipient socialist revolution failed in America before rather

than after it occurred, lies in the relative detachment of the nation's masses. Instead of providing the single-minded vanguard of radical action, the working class and the poor enacted the dialectic over change within themselves. In the end, for such reasons as those we have been examining in this chapter, caution and gradualism took almost as firm charge of the bottom as of the upper ranges of America's social-economic pyramid.

THE ROMANCE OF SOCIALISM

We have been asking why socialism failed in America in the 1900s. Another of the answers lies in the transformations inflicted upon social-ist ideology by many of its most influential literary and intellectual proponents. I referred in Chapter 1 to Clifford Geertz's notion of the "ideational" relation between art and the culture from which it emerges. In fact, the case could be made that politics, no less than literature, may be addressed as an institutionalized and formal expres-sion of the imagination. Leaving that vexed issue moot for the mo-ment, and conceding that the failure of socialism as a political move-ment is not identical with the limits of literary socialism, I merely assume that they are intimately connected and that an analysis of social-ist fiction can illuminate political events.

To hazard an anticipatory generalization, socialism was typically re-defined and re-created even in the hands of sympathetic advocates. Its leading themes were simplified, subordinated, and often suppressed on behalf of a familiar American avoidance of ideology matched by an equally familiar embrace of adventure and romance. It was more often true than not that socialism became the verbal apparatus rather than the substance of the fictions produced by its own adherents. The pattern we have already traced in David Graham Phillips's "socialist" novel *The Conflict* proves typical and recurrent. What is putatively socialist turns out to be the blending of a very diffuse compassion for society's ex-ploited with unprogrammatic messianic hopes.

Written over twenty years after the event, *The Cage* is at once Charlotte Teller's reconstruction of the Haymarket riot and her reverential memorial to Haymarket's executed anarchists. The trial of those men, according to Teller's narrator, was a "conspiracy," and their conviction led to "the murder, by the State, of seven innocent men."[16] The date of Teller's witness is partial proof of the ineradicable impression Haymar-ket made on the American conscience. Memories of the bombing and

of the subsequent executions remained green for decades, a frightening
and yet exhilarating episode to socialists and others on the left, who
saw in the event, as Teller did, the murderous power of the state.

An earlier and more famous denunciation of the trial and its outcome, of course, was that of William Dean Howells. Writing immediately after the executions (in a letter, apparently never sent, to Whitelaw
Reid), and anticipating the charge of Teller and many others that the
conviction was a conspiracy, Howells declared, "We have committed
an atrocious and irreparable wrong. . . . Under the forms of law, their
trial has not been a trial by justice, but a trial by passion, by terror, by
prejudice, by hate, by newspaper."[17] And, anticipating Teller's charge
of state murder, Howells wrote in January 1888 to Hamlin Garland that
the anarchists had been "civically murdered . . . for their opinions."[18]
In the same letter, Howells confided that his "horizons have been in-
definitely widened" by the Haymarket episode. That widening encompassed above all Howells's adoption of a version of socialism. Under
the influence of Gronlund, Thomas Kirkup, and Tolstoy, Howells had
been moving toward a socialist perspective for some time before Haymarket. The bombing and execution did not initiate but undoubtedly
hastened that leftward movement, in part by demolishing Howells's
residual economic optimism.

The socialism that Howells espoused was more ethical than economic, more intuitive than ideological. In this, it was paradigmatically
predictive. Howells's utopian romances, nostalgic and vaguely human-
istic, are rural settings that provide the space and time for individual
fulfillment. Such a socialism amounts essentially to a "barn-raising,
housewarming kind of cooperation between rural neighbors."[19]

As we shall also see in the case of the writers who followed him, the
half-hearted nature of Howells's socialism had nothing to do with
timidity. He could act with brave decisiveness when he was sure of his
ground. His intervention in Haymarket itself, for example, stands out
as what one of his biographers calls a "lonely act of courage," since it
exposed him to a torrent of abuse.[20] After the turn of the century, when
he was in his sixties, Howells worked actively with William James and
Mark Twain in the anti-imperalist campaign that opposed American
aggression in the Philippines; he marched in support of women's rights;
he took part in the creation of the National Association for the Advancement of Colored People. Furthermore, if Howells appears at best
a tentative socialist, he himself spoke of the socialists as having "nothing definite or practical to take hold of."[21] The explosive fragmentation
of socialism, examined in the second section of this chapter, proves that
Howells was, in one sense, simply right.

In any case, the conflicting social and political attitudes Howells exhibited broadly foreshadow much of the socialist writing of the period we are concerned with. Kenneth Lynn offers a useful summary: "In his personal and artistic despair, Howells in the nineties had become more painfully aware than ever before of the reservations in his social radicalism, of the ambivalence in his democratic commitment."[22] Though the details would differ in each case, Howells's reserved radicalism and his ambivalent commitment foretell the intellectual and political style of the novelists who adopted the socialist cause in the early 1900s. Howells's back-looking utopias, for example, recur in the alternately radical and less-radical fictions of numbers of reformers and would-be revolutionaries. And Howells's outlook forecasts an even more significant symptom of the ideological ambivalence of romance in putatively socialist literature.

"The curious thing about these leading Socialist 'fictioneers' is that they were the most romantic novelists of their time."[23] Alfred Kazin did not have Charlotte Teller in mind when he wrote that generalization (neither she nor her novel is mentioned in his study). But *The Cage* illustrates as well as any novel from these years the characteristic tendency of American political fiction to dissolve into romance.

Teller's politics are resolutely democratic-socialist. Her novel's title, like that of Upton Sinclair's successful novel *The Jungle,* published a year earlier, is intended as a multilayered metaphor encompassing the fate of America's working class and its poor. Poverty, the mean streets of the Chicago slums, the wage slavery in which labor is bound, the laws that enshrine and ensure the domination of the many by the few: Each of these is a cage. The last and most literal of the book's cages is the huge and gloomy prison within whose walls, in the novel's final chapter, the Haymarket anarchists are executed.[24]

The story's political plot is woven around the efforts of an Austrian socialist, a man aptly named Eugene Harden, to organize Chicago's lumberyard workers into a militantly efficient union. From the moment Harden enters, however, that plot is absorbed into several versions of romance. To begin with Harden is physically and intellectually heroic, outscale, a near-superman. He has, we are told on first seeing him, the "head of an Atlas" (p. 22). Furthermore, Harden is an aristocratic and affluent man who has voluntarily chosen to take part in the workers' struggle but who cherishes his distance from them. Finally, his motive, he announces immediately, with only partial irony, is based on the "excitement" and the "romance" of the battle (p. 33).

Throughout the novel, we observe Harden primarily from the point of view of young Frederica Hartwell, whose response to the socialist is preponderantly emotional and only marginally ideological. Frederica is a woman who more or less automatically sentimentalizes everything

and everyone with whom she comes in contact. She lives in the slums
with her minister father, but only because of their altruistic desire to do
so. Reverend Doctor Hartwell represents Teller's conception of the
irrelevance of Christian consolation. He has given up a secure, middle-
class parish for a slum mission, but his congregation, which is made up
of the massively exploited men who work in Alexander Sloane's lumberyard, utterly ignores his services. Ironically, the millionare Sloane
provides the money to support Hartwell's ministry, a self-indicting
corruption that Teller repeatedly insists on.

Frederica is her father's daughter. The blighted tenement landscape in
which she lives, for example, becomes an incongruous pastoral:

> She found her hours of beauty every day in the city. At the close
> of a hot day, when the sun at the end of the street changed into
> golden mist the dust rising from the day's traffic and lit up the
> windows of the houses, she held her breath in enjoyment of it.
> Moonlight falling on the one tree before the house, or on the
> flower boxes on the back porch, was full of subtle promise to her;
> and on rainy days when the smoke from the factory chimneys
> swung low over house roofs, she thought she lived in the gods'
> twilight. (Pp. 43–4)

The genealogy of that moonlight can be traced, of course, directly back
through generations of romance writers. The squalid houses themselves, and the roseate lenses through which Frederica views them,
summarize between them the epistemologies that compete against each
other in *The Cage*. Charlotte Teller is certainly aware of the self-
hypnotic limits of Frederica's vision. But, as we have already begun to
see (e.g., in the initial portrait of Eugene Harden), whatever may have
been its conscious purposes, the novel relentlessly veers toward the
sentimental pole of its debate.

Early in Frederica's relationship with Harden, they attend a concert
of Wagner's music. Virtually intoxicated by what she hears, Frederica
creates a quintessentially romantic identity for herself, as a Valkyrie, a
war-woman clothed in silver armor and riding a white horse (pp. 95–
101). Harden has been lecturing her on socialism, and on the need for
men and women to take direct action against oppression. The image of
the mythic war-woman is a reductively antithetical response: theatrical
and evasive, superficially different from the Christianity of her father
but finally apolitical or even reactionary in a quite similar way.

To the extent she can see evil at all, Frederica is possessed of real
sympathy for the society's victims and of an equally real capacity for
outrage in the face of the excesses of capitalism. But those qualities are
routinely subordinated to her more fundamental, stereotypically ro-

mantic motives. Thus, though the novel reaches intermittently toward the form of an education, in which Frederica does indeed approach a somewhat more sophisticated and more militant commitment, that pattern collapses regularly into the adventure of matchmaking. A major example of the book's self-negating ambivalence occurs early in the novel, when Teller transcribes one of Harden's organizing speeches. It is a shrewd and even powerful piece of oratory, explicitly linking the insights of Marx to the circumstances of Chicago; the effect on the large audience of workingmen is deservedly successful. (Harden actually quotes the *Communist Manifesto* at least once, without identifying the source.) The point of view from which we watch and hear Harden in this scene, however, is that of Frederica, who is sitting in a distant gallery. Her thoroughly nonpolitical response to Harden's rhetoric serves rather completely to deflect the ideological energy of the moment. Frederica is deeply moved, but in an undisguisedly personal way; she succumbs not to Harden's socialism, but to his "magnetic vitality" (p. 119). She falls in love.

A different episode with a similar significance is contained in a brief chapter near the middle of the book called "The Day of Independence." At dawn of this day, Frederica slips out of her father's house, having pledged herself to find a job, earn her own living, and never again eat a "breakfast bought by Mr. Sloane's money" (p. 163). Frederica's troubles in finding work at all, the sordid propositions she receives in the course of her interviews, and the poorly paid drudgery she finally undertakes in a hat factory all contribute to Teller's impassioned attack on turn-of-the-century urban wage slavery. But the sentimental antidote quickly follows. Frederica returns home to find Harden, who now, instead of preaching socialism, proposes marriage. All of Frederica's devotion to independence evaporates in love: "The surrender was intoxication" (p. 173). Ironically, the preceding twelve hours have indeed comprised *the* day of Frederica's independence. She gives herself to Harden without a backward glance. The episode recapitulates the shape of her career throughout the novel.

As we have noted along the way, *The Cage* does incorporate a political plot of some consequence. In it, Eugene Harden successfully organizes a hundred thousand Chicago workingmen; demonstrations are followed by strikes; Alexander Sloane conspires to burn his own lumberyard as a means of discrediting the union; and, finally, police battle citizens in the Haymarket riot. Or, as a condescending reviewer wrote in *The Independent:* There is " 'the strike,' which is always the climax in socialistic fiction, and then comes the throwing of the inevitable bomb. After that we have the chaos out of which all socialists evolve their order."[25]

Actually, patronizing as it is, this résumé concedes too much. It is not a socialist order that evolves in this book. Rather, the novel's socialism is absorbed into a relatively conventional domestic resolution. This perspective eventually reduces the story's political conflicts to the margin, where strikes, riots, and trials serve as complications in the matchmaking tale.

Teller's shifting perspective is revealed in the book's final chapter. "The Day of the Law" is the day of the Haymarket executions. Teller's rendering of that event is oblique – we stand with the sympathetic thousands in a chill rain outside the prison – but undeniably moving. The silent crowd faces the same massed police whose clubs and guns had provoked the riot to begin with. The entire scene is a tableau of justice perverted.

However, to define the focus of Teller's outrage accurately is also to recognize its narrow reach. She insists on the specific innocence of all the Haymarket prisoners. Teller is almost surely right in this verdict, but what is historically right proves to be thematically and politically inept. For the ironic result of Teller's concentration on the guiltlessness of the anarchists is that the ideological commitment they embody is suppressed if not repudiated. Through hundreds of pages, the issue has been the evil of capitalism and all its institutions. Suddenly that issue is submerged in the moral tribute paid to the executed men. Thus, though it is humane, Teller's sympathy causes the field of her analysis to shrink, from the structural to the personal. To put it in terms of the geography of her last chapter: The prison no longer symbolizes an oppressive deformity in the class structure of American society. Rather, the prison becomes merely the setting for a tragic but particular mistake: the execution of seven wrongly convicted men. What is offered as radical commemoration is deflected into something more like another version of America's recurring and unprogrammatic antinomian protest.

Teller's unintended but decisive retreat from the political position she has endorsed throughout the novel is underscored in the book's final scene. The last chapter turns directly from the spectacle at the prison to linger over the romantic attachment between its two main characters. The effect of the execution on Frederica and Eugene Harden is politically imperceptible. Instead, Teller reports that their passion, which had for some months been cooled, is at this moment rekindled: "A flame had sprung from her to him" (p. 337). The novel ends with their embrace.

Arthur Bullard's *Comrade Yetta* (1913) also ends with the embrace of its married radicals, but the event has a far more complex significance than in Charlotte Teller's socialist romance.[26] *Comrade Yetta* is Bullard's testament to Jewish labor and Jewish socialism. It also bears witness to the irrepressible ambivalence that shaped the concrete responses of American socialists to the conflicting demands of theory and culture.

The novel tells Yetta Rayefsky's story. She is an immigrant who begins her American life in New York City, in her father's secondhand bookshop on East Broadway. Father and daughter have emigrated from central Europe after their home in the ghetto of Kovna was destroyed and Yetta's mother and brother killed in a pogrom. Within a few years, Yetta's father also dies (of tuberculosis), and she is reduced from shabby gentility to poverty. She finds herself living with distant and indifferent relatives, who take the few dollars she earns each week working in a sweatshop. Bullard documents Yetta's four years "on the rack" of overwork and despair with angry energy.[27] She labors ten to twelve hours each day, with a dozen other women, making vests. She is harassed by her pushing boss Jake Goldfogle, himself only a step ahead of bankruptcy. She barely escapes being kidnapped and installed in a whorehouse.

Yetta's suffering in these early chapters serves to dramatize New York's turn-of-the-century corruption. Bullard is especially outraged by the commonplace alliance of pimp and politician and police, and by the reality of life in New York for poor women. Throughout these opening chapters, Yetta's reactions are cast in understandably escapist and thoroughly romantic terms. Having no pleasures at all, she finds even modest pleasures immense. The window of the mean apartment she lives in, for example, faces a settlement house. Through its open front door she catches glimpses each Saturday night of the dance she is forbidden to attend. She sees a "fair garden, lit with the sunlight of laughter, a garden where blossomed the wondrous flowers of music, of joy – of Romance" (p. 21). Trapped within the mutually reinforcing ideological and sexual-economic restrictions of her society, Yetta can imagine only one way out: "She had sore need of a Prince in Silver Armor" (p. 22).

Bullard's use of these treacly clichés is an earnest of his intention to repudiate the values they imply. In the novel's next major episode, the attractive and still utterly naïve Yetta becomes the target of a pimp named Harry Klein. Klein works mightily, for several chapters, under the guise of a respectable courtship, to add Yetta to his string. After finally realizing what is happening and escaping entrapment by the slenderest hair's breadth of melodrama, Yetta recalls the event this way: "He had come to her singing the Song of Songs – like a Prince in Shining Armor riding forth to rescue her from the Giant Greed" (p. 128). In fact, Klein has proven a procurer and a thug, and in itemizing in scarifying detail his brutality to the women in his house, as well as his protection by the law, Bullard not only subverts the language of romance, he turns it into its opposite. In its first half, *Comrade Yetta* is a book in which romantic illusion collapses into the sordid reality it usually conceals.

And yet, taken as a whole, *Comrade Yetta's* exploration of the intertwined categories of politics and aesthetics is not so resolute or so straightforward as these early chapters would suggest. To begin with, the epistemology of romance has a tenacious hold on Yetta's mind, and her near-rape and captivity at first adapts itself readily to the contours of sentimental drama, to the tones of pathos and tragedy. It is only after a more or less accidental encounter with a group of reformers and socialists that Yetta begins to comprehend her own experiences at or near the bottom of American society in political terms.

Ideologically awakened, she first goes to work for the reformist Woman's Trade Union League (WTUL), becoming the protégée of its director, a woman named Mabel Train. Mabel is an aggressive and talented administrator, essentially middle-class in her values and very comfortable in her well-furnished private life. She represents what proves to be only a stopping place on Yetta's intellectual journey. Mabel's WTUL does sensible work, but it is institutionally conciliatory, and Bullard's impatient attitude toward such groups is indicated by his portrait of the league's advisory council, many of whose members are in the grip of an anticipatory radical chic: They "liked to be thought odd, and found in labor unions a piquant fad" (p. 125). Eventually, Yetta will leave behind the piecemeal and half-committed politics of the WTUL, and, in line with Bullard's relatively dogmatic conception of the irreconcilable difference between the classes, she will leave Mabel behind as well.

From early on, Yetta (probably loosely modeled on Clara Lemlich) shows large talents for oratory, organization, and journalism, and she develops all of them as the story progresses. She does a successful tour writing a labor page for the yellow New York *Sun* and resigns when her editor refuses to print her exposé of a department store that places major advertising in the paper. Realizing that she has moved further left, she joins the ailing socialist daily, the *Clarion* and, doubling as executive and reporter, manages to improve both its quality and its circulation. At the end of the novel, she has married the *Clarion's* editor, Isadore Braun, and borne two children. It is Isadore whom she is embracing in the book's final scene.

The marital passion of *Comrade Yetta*, unlike that of *The Cage*, is intended to complement rather than evade the book's socialist politics; the intention partially succeeds. Bullard's plot makes Yetta's choice of a husband an act of almost allegorically straightforward significance. For much of the novel, Yetta directs her unrequited passion toward a man named Walter Longman, older than she, rich, a handsome gentile, a thoroughly accomplished amateur philosopher and philologist. The language of romance, which had been discredited earlier, in Yetta's encounter with Harry Klein, is temporarily rehabilitated by her ardor for Walter: It is he who now seems to be "the shining Prince" (p. 268). And, in many ways, he is. Walter is an utterly engaging and decent man, possessed of conventional virtues and gifts in implausible abundance. He is a self-educated gentleman scholar, whose book on Assyriology, written as a kind of avocation, immediately earns him the offer of an Oxford professorship. He is courageous; it is he who thrashes Klein and rescues Yetta. He is, in short, another heir to the line of romance heroes, the outsized outsider, rather like Eugene Harden in *The Cage*.

However, Bullard has elaborated Walter's gifts and invented his study of the "Haktite" language not merely to prove his miraculous talent, but also to testify to his fundamental distance from Yetta and her concerns. He is sympathetic to the left, to the workers, to the immigrants: His sheer intelligence demands that he notice the profound corruption of American society. But, finally, Walter represents the irrelevant aristocrat, the beneficiary of the system he professes to despise. He is "the shining Prince" indeed – in the full sinister sense of the phrase, suggesting a politics as reactionary if less floridly threatening as the manifest bestiality of Harry Klein.

Consequently, unlike Eugene Harden, Walter Longman does not command *Comrade Yetta*'s final allegiance. The novel, and its heroine, turn to Isadore Braun, undersized, physically unattractive, a Jewish man of the working class. (Yetta falls in love with Isadore while she is nursing him through a serious case of typhoid – a detail of the plot that insists on Isadore's antiromantic function.) And, after four years of marriage, Yetta continues to work as Isadore's partner on the *Clarion* in the service of the cause. Thus, the matchmaking that occupies a considerable portion of the novel's pages can be seen as Bullard's effort to absorb romance into politics, rather than the other way around. Even Yetta's two children, who are invested with generous quantities of saccharine sentimentality, are dedicated to political utility: "They've given Socialism a new meaning," Yetta exults to Isadore. They've "brought it all nearer, made it more intimate and personal, more closely woven into myself. [We] were used to the tenements, they'd ceased to impress us – till the babies came. . . . the thought of all the millions of babies in the slums has become the very corner-stone of my thinking. It's for them. We've just got to win Socialism for the babies!" (p. 445).

Yet if the sentimentality and matchmaking are channeled into ideology, they remain sentimentality and matchmaking nonetheless. The concluding events are inevitably indecisive in their implications, as Bullard gropes to articulate an alternative to the derangements he has systematically exposed in the novel's first half. The problem has its familiar roots in the limits of language and the limits of fictional forms. An abbreviated and startling illustration of the dilemma occurs in the novel's climactic scene, the moment at which Yetta detaches herself from her love for Walter. The emotional battle she is engaged in represents, as we have seen, an ideological allegory – the movement away from the evasions of romance and toward the demands of reality. Yet this turning point is costumed by the narrator in the full, shopworn regalia of romance, the very language that the novel has repeatedly indicted: "The Enemy [her need for Walter's love] made a desperate assault – surprised her with her visor up, her sword in its sheath, her shield hanging useless on her back" (p. 348).

Given its context, this is a remarkable statement. The point of the narrator's declaration is precisely to mark the essential transformation of Yetta's consciousness: She is about to defy the old stereotypes of love bequeathed by tradition and embodied in her attachment to Walter; she is about to dedicate herself to work and socialism. Yet the announcement is given in all the stylized language of romance itself. The disjunction between style and substance here is only apparent. In fact, the passage strikingly predicts what we have already seen of the novel's actual outcome.

Yetta is not Walter's wife, but she is Isadore's. And if she remains his working partner, the partnership is still defined by a traditional inequality. This is made clear as early on as their honeymoon, when Yetta discovers her "real delight in the new experience of cooking a meal for her man, in washing and mending his clothes" (p. 424). Thus *Comrade Yetta*'s divided mind: The novel stands poised uneasily between conflicting perspectives. Bullard's sexual politics lead at once away from and back toward the cultural assumptions he has struggled to surmount. The circle of paradox is virtually complete: Yetta's devotion to equality leads rather to her personal success, and that in turn leads to her eager subordination as wife and mother.

Talk of "princes" and "shields" is one index to the tentative nature of political ideas in *Comrade Yetta*. Another is the periodic insertion of the unfocused antinomianism, which so often serves as a receptacle for American dissent, into the socialist argument. Early in the novel, for example, Yetta is given a list of "socialist" books to read, first among them Thoreau's *Essays*. On the flyleaf is inscribed: "Thoreau lived before Socialism commenced. But I don't think any of the modern writers have bettered 'On the Duty of Civic Disobedience' " (p. 198). Only a "socialism" of such modest theoretical sophistication as America's before World War I could conceive of Thoreau in this way. It is, furthermore, an apt if accidental irony that Bullard doesn't even get Thoreau's title right. Thoreau, after all, is not really being invoked here as a thinker, socialist or otherwise, but as a vague symbol of morally righteous self-sufficiency. Karl Marx, on the other hand, whose name we might expect to find in such a list, is not mentioned.

Much later, a peculiar scene in the office of the *Clarion* economically captures this dimension of *Comrade Yetta*'s confusion over ideological authority. Aging Mary Ames, the paper's bookkeeper, is dividing up the week's salary money, which, as always, is short. The entire staff, reporters, typesetters, editors, and clerks, gather round Mary and amiably decide who will get what ("to each according to his need," and so forth). The prodigies of generosity these men and women engage in elicit this tribute from good-hearted Mary Ames (the only nonsocialist in the room): "I don't know much about Socialism . . . I ain't educated like you young people; I haven't read very much. Keeping books all day is all my eyes are good for. But I just know it's right. If it wasn't the real thing, there'd never be a paper like this" (pp. 399–400).

Though Bullard undoubtedly planned this vignette as a high compliment to his socialists, and though it may even have historical sources, the uses the scene is put to turn it into a tacit admission of analytic defeat. The inference of political legitimacy from personal integrity is charming but irrelevant to the dialectical task Bullard has been engaged in for four hundred pages. Interestingly, in *Comrade Yetta,* as we have seen, Bullard was capable of disentangling Walter Longman's politics from his virtues. But in offering his own creed, Bullard falls – inevitably, it seems – into an altogether personal appeal.

It should be clear that Arthur Bullard's socialist accomplishments in *Comrade Yetta* are several and significant: He hands up a shrewd and powerful indictment against capitalist institutions; he renders the working class, without condescension, as both humane and increasingly conscious; he illuminates at least some of the specific hardships of women; he articulates, albeit interruptedly, a socialist alternative. Yet in the end, *Comrade Yetta*'s intermittent antinomianism conspires with its residual romanticism to obscure its ideological statement. In this, the novel is representative. American literary socialism, even as it rebelled against the formulas through which the imagination of its time encoded its conservatism and nostalgia, was captive to the vocabulary, the forms, perhaps even the epistemology of that imagination. For the socialists Teller and Bullard, no less than for the progressive Phillips, the critique of American culture's prevailing values reveals at least as much of unwitting dependence as of conscious dissent.

In *John Barleycorn* (1913), his autobiographical tract on the evils of drink, Jack London wrote of the "White Logic" that had come to torment him. After suffering without sleep through whole nights, he would fall into the vivid hallucination that he had divided into two people, with two conflicting personalities. One was a diabolic figure who made sport of him and his humanity; the other was a reformed version of himself, faithful to humble virtues and common decency.[28] As any reader of his biography and stories knows, London's nightmare was no more than a bizarre, alcoholic caricature of the fundamental structure of his whole life and art. He was *always* divided against himself, often into more parts than two.

Indeed, Jack London so completely exemplifies the paradoxes we have been discussing that he practically disappears beneath his contradictions. At one time or another, and often simultaneously, he adopted just about every code, creed, fad, and system of his time, from materialism to social Darwinism to imperialism to vegetarianism to socialism to Nietzschean individualism. And any notion he adopted he professed with passionate enthusiasm; distinctions, despite his endless talk of "logic," were not in his line.

His deep compassion for the poor and the victims of capitalism was real enough (it had its source in his own youth's hardships), but it was matched by his contempt for weakness of any kind. His vision of a more humane society coexisted with his breathless adulation of violence and white male supremacy. His continuous appeals to science were almost always couched in the language of primitivism. His shifting combinations of Darwin and Kipling, Nietzsche and Marx, make no sense at all, but derive with almost touching directness from his own experience and ambitions. Yet the hodgepodge of his "synthesis" provides a fair reflection of the heterogeneous currents surging against each other in turn-of-the-century America. His productivity was mammoth (he had written nearly fifty books by the time he died at age forty), and his popularity has been spectacular (in his own lifetime, and since his death in 1916, more copies of his books have been printed and sold around the world than of any other writer of this period). Those facts, along with the encyclopedic cacophony of his ideas, identify him as a representative figure: significant far beyond his provable artistic or intellectual achievement because he carried so many of the conflicted tendencies of his time to superlative excess.

Above all, London was the epitome of the romantic socialist. Devoted to adventure and hypnotized by the dream of success, he was also the most widely noticed socialist propagandist of the early twentieth century.[29] His anti-utopian novel, *The Iron Heel* (1906), dramatized the depravities of capitalism in language that even many socialists found overheated. His lectures and pamphlets reached hundreds of thousands, a phenomenon that his more rigorous but less colorful comrades observed with combined envy, admiration, and bemusement. President of the Intercollegiate Socialist Society, he was a fine orator, and the speeches he gave to large audiences all over the nation were apocalyptic in their fervor.

There are, he announced, seven million socialists around the industrial world, and they have declared war on capitalism and its lords. "We want all that you possess. We will be content with nothing less than all that you possess. We want in our hands the reins of power and the destiny of mankind." World capitalism was doomed, either to electoral or to a more violent extinction. He opened a lecture before a huge crowd in New York's Grand Central Palace in January 1906 by telling of an exchange of letters he had just had. "I received a letter the other day. It was from a man in Arizona. It began, 'Dear Comrade.' It ended, 'Yours for the Revolution.' I replied to the letter, and my letter began, 'Dear Comrade.' It ended, 'Yours for the Revolution.' "[30]

The word "revolution" punctuated the speech with a regularity that may seem to us theatrical (and it surely was) but that the audience found "stunning" (the word is Upton Sinclair's, as he recollected the scene a decade later in his obituary notice "About Jack London," in *The Masses*).[31] "The revolution is a fact. It is here now. Seven million revolutionists, organized, working day and night, are preaching the revolution – that passionate gospel, the Brotherhood of Man."[32]

Recall that this evangelical prophet of socialist fire and brimstone traveled from one lecture to another in advanced capitalist style, ensconced in a Pullman berth and attended by a Korean valet. Recall, too, that if the overt purpose of his incendiary lecture tour was to raise the consciousness of America, it was equally important to London as camouflage for his liaison with Charmian Kitteridge, shortly to become his second wife.[33]

These contradictory inclinations all find expression in Jack London's fictions, sometimes alternately, sometimes all at once. *The Call of the Wild* (1902), for example, which made him rich, and *White Fang* (1906), which made him richer, can be read as London's respective idealizations of individualism and socialism.[34] *The Sea-Wolf* (1904) glorifies physical strength and anarchic self-sufficiency while at the same time trying hard to disapprove of them. Wolf Larsen possesses both London's own nickname and most of London's admiration, but the civilized Humphrey Van Weyden ultimately beats Larsen at his own game (and gets the girl as well). Larsen's talk of laws of behavior beyond good and evil, and Van Weyden's protestations on behalf of love and fair play, constitute a debate that recurs throughout London's fictions and anticipates the divided selves of his "White Logic."

London always felt the need to encircle an issue from all sides at once, be the consequences what they might for his coherence. "The Dream of Debs" (1914) offers a small example from among his overtly political stories. A fantasy set in the future United States, the tale describes a successful nationwide general strike (the event Debs dreamed of). In their conversations with each other, the confessions of the assorted plutocratic targets of the strike reveal how justly retributive it is, and reveal as well London's sympathy for the exploited workers, who are finally taking their proper revenge. Yet the whole story is told from the viewpoint of a rich capitalist who also commands a measure of London's sympathy and who survives the bloodshed to point to what appears to be his author's moral: "The tyranny of organized labor is getting beyond endurance. Something must be done."[35]

What in a more mature or subtle mind might offer evidence of an ongoing dialectic seems mere schizophrenia in that of Jack London. Another of his political stories, "South of the Slot" (1914), illustrates the issue with particular clarity. The main character is one Freddie Drummond, a personally and politically conservative professor of sociology at the University of California. Drummond has gained his reputation with a book called *The Unskilled Laborer,* hailed by industrial leaders of all ranks as "a splendid reply to the literature of discontent," bought in boxes full by the Manufacturers' Association. London doesn't disclose the details of the book's thesis, but he doesn't have to. It is an industrial version of plantation literature: a tribute at once to the rectitude of the system, to the benevolent masters who own it, and to the happy workingmen who fuel its engines with their lives. London describes *The Unskilled Laborer,* with heavy-handed irony, as being "almost as immoral as the far-famed and notorious *Message to Garcia,* while in its pernicious preachment of thrift and content it ran *Mrs. Wiggs of the Cabbage Patch* a close second."[36] Drummond gathers materials for his books by disguising himself as a worker, Bill Totts, and living and laboring in the slums and factories of San Francisco (the region of the title's geography, south of the railway-cable slot dividing the city).

As time goes on, Drummond finds himself spending more and more time as Totts, living a life as worker denied to the professor, and possessed increasingly of a workingman's consciousness. Drummond and Totts "were two totally different creatures. The desires and tastes and impulses of each ran counter to the other's" (p. 198). The bifurcation in this politicized Jeckyll and Hyde fable is complete, and it reaches from the trivial to the profound. Drummond is solemn and reserved,

Totts humorously gregarious. Drummond doen't dance; Totts "never missed the nights at the various dancing clubs, such as The Magnolia, The Western Star, and The Elite" (p. 198). Drummond is an influential voice for orthodoxy and reaction; Totts moves ever leftward, acquiring the nickname "Big Bill" (a toast to Bill Haywood of the IWW) and soon appearing regularly in the front lines of each strike. Totts's "hatred for a scab even exceeded that of the average loyal union man" (pp. 198–199). Inevitably, each of Drummond's two selves is provided by London with a symmetrically suitable woman. Drummond's fiancée is the rich, bloodless, college-educated Catherine Van Vorst, who "possessed an inhibition equal" to his own (p. 203). Totts falls in love with "royal-bodied," exuberant Mary Condon, the president of the International Glove Workers' Union No. 974 (p. 200).

In the story's last scene, Drummond and Catherine find themselves accidently in the middle of a violent battle between a group of strikers and the San Francisco police. They watch the bloody proceedings for a few minutes with apparent detachment, but in fact, "looking out of Freddie Drummond's eyes was Bill Totts, and somewhere behind those eyes, battling for control of their mutual body, were Freddie Drummond, the sane and conservative sociologist, and Bill Totts, the class-conscious and bellicose union working man" (p. 208). As the riot before him begins to swing in favor of the police, the inner struggle is won by Totts: He emits "an unearthly and uncultured yell" (p. 208), leaps into the fray, and single-handedly overpowers the entire police force. He is last seen walking down Third Street with Mary Condon, disappearing "into the labor ghetto" (p. 210).

The outcome is irrelevant. The real significance of "South of the Slot" is its rendition of a man divided to the point of self-parody. Upton Sinclair's sly judgment that his friend Jack London couldn't decide whether he wanted to be a revolutionary or a landed gentleman is no more than a pale statement of the case. The full statement was given by London himself, repeatedly in his fictions, and climactically in the novel *Martin Eden* (1909).

Autobiographical in dozens of its details, *Martin Eden* offers Jack London's apotheosized self-portrait, a figure at the farthest edge of romance. Martin Eden, from the prelapsarian perfection connoted by his name to his stupendous intellectual and physical power, is London's man as superman; he is, in his own words, one of "Carlyle's battle-scarred giants who will not be kept down."[37] The plot of the novel, such as it is, consists of Martin's successive and irresistible triumphs over all those who would keep him down. He moves, godlike, from one challenge to another, proving unmatchable in everything he puts his hands to, from street fighting to poetry to philosophy. He recog-

nizes his own immense superiority early in his life, and he spends most
of the novel peering contemptuously down on the rest of mankind
from his high Nietzschean fastness. His suicide, a tragic forecast of
London's own death seven years later, results as much from irritated
boredom as from anything else.

In nothing did London so clearly reveal his self-division as in the
suprising political significance he attached to Martin Eden's suicide. In
April 1910, he wrote that the novel had been widely "accepted as an
indictment of socialism," which was a misreading. "Had Martin Eden
been a socialist he would not have died," London added.[38] Again, not
long before his death, London made a note for a "Socialist biography.
Martin Eden and *Sea Wolf,* attacks on Nietzshen [sic] philosophy, which
even the socialists missed the point of."[39]

The most interesting thing about these comments is that what they
describe is simply not what *Martin Eden* shows us. No matter what Jack
London may have wanted his correspondents (or himself) to believe in
retrospect, the burden of his allegiance in *Martin Eden* lies with the
heroic and alienated individual and not with any version of socialism.
Martin's several speeches on the subject of socialism are consistent with
each other, and any one can stand for all. In this one, he is denouncing
his host and the guest of honor at a dinner party: "I mean to tell you
that I am not suffering from the microbe of socialism. I mean to tell
you that it is you who are suffering from the emasculating ravages of
that same microbe. As for me, I am an inveterate opponent of socialism
just as I am an inveterate opponent of your own mongrel democracy.
. . . I am a reactionary. . . .I look only to the strong man, the man on
horseback" (pp. 296–297). The strident urgency of the metaphors, as
always in London's work, is a symptom of his own engagement with
the attitude expressed here.

It is probably true that if Martin Eden had "been a socialist he would
not have died," but London's distinction is jesuitical. If Martin Eden
had been a socialist, he would not have been the character conceived by
London in this book. In any case, to suggest that Martin's individualism fails to save his life is by no means also to assent to a socialist
alternative. The most that can be argued for a coherent socialist position
in London's thought is that he regarded socialism as an unhappy means
to the higher end of a reestablished individualism. This is, for example,
the explicit proposal of one of the characters in London's late, unfin-
ished adventure, *The Assassination Bureau, Ltd.*: "Liberty, unrestricted
by man-made law, cannot be gained except by evolution through a
stage of excessive man-made law that will well-nigh reduce us all to
automatons – the socialistic stage, of course. But I, for one, would
never care to live in the socialist state. It would be maddening!"[40]

One capable student of London's life recently argued that "from 1896 when Jack London joined the socialist ranks until he resigned from the Socialist Party in 1916 . . . he remained a committed socialist."[41] But it was a peculiar and ambiguous form of socialism. On the other hand, as we have seen, the "socialism" envisioned by the American imagination was itself often peculiar and even more often ambiguous. And to claim the existence of a socialist norm among all the competing sects would be a simplification. Perhaps, therefore, for our purposes, enumerating Jack London's ideological limitations is less important than remembering how seriously he was taken by so many men and women of his own generation. "Imagination in him," wrote one worshipful contemporary, "generates the strong, the pictorial and the heroic as inevitably as the sun and soil bring forth oak and sequoia. Notwithstanding this virility of fancy, Jack London is prone to regard his storytelling as so much needful effort toward a more vital and august end – the social redemption of the race."[42] This estimate was typical. And to make such a judgment of Jack London, regardless of the critical limits it exposes, is to tell us much about the American society in which London played so celebrated a role.

THE HARBOR

Though it was Ernest Poole's first novel, *The Harbor* (1915) became one of the most widely reviewed and discussed works of its time. Notes, comments, and essays, some of considerable length, appeared on both sides of the Atlantic. The New York *Times* called *The Harbor* "the best American novel that has appeared in many a long day." *The New Republic* termed the novel an "epic." *The Outlook,* the sometime mouthpiece of Rooseveltian strenuousnes, reviewed Poole's book along with two others under the heading "Three Novels of Unrest." *The Harbor,* said *Outlook*'s writer, "has a far greater claim on the attention of readers than most novels." *Book News Monthly* called the book "one of the more significant novels of the year."[43] And so on, in *The Dial, The Nation, North American Review, The Spectator, Atlantic Monthly,* and a dozen other journals. *The Harbor* was numbered among the ten best-selling books of its year. Its author's celebrity was assured; Poole's second novel, *His Family,* won the first Pulitzer Prize awarded in fiction, in 1917.

Writing in 1936, Joseph Freeman called *The Harbor* "a high point in radical fiction."[44] Twenty years later, Lewis Mumford recalled the "special place" *The Harbor* claimed in the imagination of American intellectuals just before the war.[45] And ten years after that, John Hart

judged Poole's book to be simply the "best socialist novel of that pre–
World War I era."[46]

Yet in spite of its original reception, in spite of its contemporary
influence, and in spite of Poole's long and productive subsequent career
(he continued writing until his death in 1950), *The Harbor* and its author
were both quickly forgotten in the years after the First World War. The
occasional partisan, such as Joseph Freeman, kept Poole's novel in
mind. But the evidence offered by Alfred Kazin's *On Native Grounds*
(1942) is surely more significant. The intersections between literature
and society are of great interest to Kazin, but neither Poole nor *The
Harbor* is ever mentioned in Kazin's large and immensely well-informed
study.

A thorough inquest into *The Harbor*'s disappearance from America's
consciousness lies beyond our scope. Such an inquiry, however, if we
undertook it, would begin and end with the First World War. Though
the war, as we have seen, was only the last in a long chain of causes that
made the dreams of an American socialism impossible, the guns of
1914–1918 ensured that the demolition of those dreams was complete,
and permanent. *The Harbor* was published just a few months after the
war began, thus guaranteeing that "the best" of the socialist novels
would also be the last. But the irony of Poole's timing is more definitive than mere coincidence. The book was initially completed and accepted for publication in 1914. When the war broke out, Poole re-
trieved his manuscript and rewrote its ending to take account of the
new crisis. With a desperately contrived ebullience, Poole's hero predicts that the war will make the triumph of transatlantic socialism inevitable: The "furnace of war" will consume the old civilization and
forge the brotherhood of all workers. In fact, of course, history had an
altogether contrary outcome in store. And thus, in welcoming the war,
the affirmation with which *The Harbor* ends proved an epitaph, at once
to Poole's novel and to the movement it celebrated.

Yet even if the war had not overtaken Poole and his allegiance, *The
Harbor* reveals much about the failure of American socialism. Indeed, the
novel virtually recapitulates both the aspirations and the limits of the
movement in the early twentieth century. Despite its integrity and its
quality, *The Harbor* flinches at the end from the most radical implications
of its own socialist logic. A novel of singular ideological energy, its
energy is eventually dissipated in a retreat from its own leading ideas.

The form of the book is the familiar one of education. The protaga-
nist-narrator, Bill (his last name is never given), tells the story of his
life, which is organized into a chronicle of his commitments. In the
novel's four books and four hundred pages, we watch Bill move further
and further left, from the devotion to romance of childhood, to the

aestheticism of early adulthood, through an adult dedication to reform that yields finally to a belief in "the people" and the socialist alternative.

The first third of the novel renders Poole's portrait of the young man as an artist. Bill grows up in a brownstone in Brooklyn Heights that looks down over the New York harbor, a place of endless activity, peopled by an ever-changing, exotic cast, a cornucopia of all the world's precious and needful things, a "strange and terrible" fairyland in the imagination of a seven-year-old boy.[47] Seething with its ships and noises and smells, its shifting, alien population, the harbor exists for young Bill not as a set of facts but as a provocation to romance and adventure. He yearns to be absorbed into its energy, its life and mystery; in the manner of excited children, his response is undifferentiated and uncritical.

As he grows older, from his teens on, Bill's relationship to the harbor modulates toward the specifically aesthetic. He fancies himself a writer, and he trains himself – first at Princeton and later in Paris – toward the goal of capturing the harbor as art. He travels, makes friends, observes the worlds of economics and politics, only with the hope of translating his experiences into fiction, of preparing himself for the epic encounter with the harbor. Bill's understanding of the men and women he meets is intendedly functional. He has at first no interest in evaluating the social or economic conditions of others, only in registering those conditions elegantly.

Early in the novel, Bill meets Joe Kramer, a slightly older, sophisticated radical; Kramer reappears intermittently, serving as Bill's teacher and model throughout the story (though never with more than partial success). In Paris, it is Joe Kramer who tries to argue Bill out of his aestheticism by denouncing it as superstitious and unreal: "Your religion is style, technique and form" (p. 90). Over the next few years, Bill yields to Kramer's instruction and example enough to move from detachment to partial engagement. He returns to New York and its harbor and finds himself being gradually drawn actively into its human problems. He becomes acquainted with an engineer named Dillon (the father of the woman he will marry later in the novel), and under Dillon's influence he shifts his moral allegiance in the direction of reform.

This transition is Bill's first major turning point, and Poole marks it by means of an elaborate symbolic tableau. Dillon's office occupies the entire top floor of the tallest building overlooking the harbor. After resisting Dillon's invitation for several months, Bill agrees to visit the engineer in his high workplace; the chapter in which he tells of that visit opens with Bill saying, "At last I went up to the tower" (p. 184).

The iconographic lineage of this structure lies, of course, in the romantic tradition. As a number of literary historians have shown, high

retreats such as Dillon's serve as recurring emblems of the artist's relation to society. Maurice Beebe, for example, traces what he calls the
"Ivory Tower Tradition" through nineteenth-century American and
European literature, from the doomed mansion of Roderick Usher to
the towers of Yeats and Stephen Daedalus. The artists in these towers,
priests of the religion of art, peer from their lookouts, "not so much *at*
the world as down upon it."[48]

A member of this aesthetic company, Bill climbs the tower in order
to look down on the world of the harbor. But those heights become
instead the scene of his conversion to the new religion of reform.
Where Joe Kramer's more radical tutelage had failed, Dillon transforms
Bill with his essentially progressive vision of efficiency. Dillon is a
masterful man, charged by the New York City government with re-
making the entire port. Dillon plans to turn the harbor into a smoothly
functioning, technologically sophisticated machine, whose multiplied
productivity will benefit all of New York's citizens, poor as well as
rich. Bill's adoption of this agenda is in part the result of his worshipful
personal response to the heroic engineer Dillon himself: "I told myself
that here was a big man, the first really big one I'd ever come close to"
(p. 149). Concerned now for the welfare of "the people," but skeptical
of their ability to improve their own lives, Bill accepts Dillon's hierarchical conception of reform. "I don't believe," Bill declares to Kramer,
that "the people can" change things themselves. "From what I've seen I
honestly don't believe they count. The fellows that count in a job like
this . . . are the efficient ones – . . . the fellows that have the brains and
that know to work – to use science, money, everything" (p. 196).

Thus, the distance from artist to engineer is not as great as it seemed at
first. Dillon's tower may be steel rather than ivory, but in his detached
and superior relationship to the society beneath him, in his idealizing
vision of the perfected world, in the specifically religious aura that sur-
rounds him, he resembles nothing so much as the artist he has putatively
replaced. Bill gives himself enthusiastically to the notion of a benevolently shaping mind behind the vast machine of the harbor. "By degrees I
made for myself a new god, and its name was Efficiency" (p. 188).

Following this declaration, Bill enumerates the gods that have preceded Efficiency, and in doing so he provides an abstract of the novel's
plot to this point.

> Here at last was a god that I felt could stand! I had made so many
> in years gone by, I had been making them all my life – from the
> first fearful idols [of childhood's imagining], the condors and the
> cannibals, to the kind old god of goodness in my mother's church
> and the radiant goddess of beauty and art over there in Paris. One

by one I had raised them up, and one by one the harbor had flowed in and dragged them down. But now . . . I had found and taken to myself a god that I felt sure of. No harbor could make it totter and fall. For it was armed with science, its feet stood firm on mechnical laws and in its head were all the brains of all the strong men at the top. (Pp. 188–189)

In each and all of its parts, this is the confession of Progressive faith. Above all, Bill's new religion holds out the promise of order. Early in the novel, the harbor is defined as a symbol for the whole of American life, especially in its tumultuous disorder. "The rest of the country was like one colossal harbor, changing, heaving, seething" (p. 27). By taming the harbor, Dillon symbolically places all of the chaotic motion of the United States under the domination of his enlarged reason.

Dillon's definition of the new port figuratively reaches to this implication: A "port [is a] complicated industrial organ, the heart of a country's circulation, pumping in and out its millions of tons of traffic as quickly and cheaply as possible. But it's got to be done for us all in a plan instead of each for himself in a blind struggling chaos" (p. 186). In this self-celebrating vision, the commercial becomes the organic (the "heart" of the circulation), and rational plans imposed from the top miraculously supersede the Social Darwinian contest.

In the same speech, Dillon declares: "That's efficiency, scientific management or just plain engineering, whatever you want to call it" (p. 186). His specific reference to "scientific management" invokes the widely influential prewar movement bearing that name. Frederick W. Taylor, the most famous of the Progressive engineers, published his landmark book, *The Principles of Scientific Management,* in 1911. The cosmopolitan, amiable, visionary Dillon is not modeled very directly on the parochial, splenetic, near-sighted Taylor. Rather, Dillon is Taylor's apotheosis, as his universalized application of scientific management expands the time-and-motion studies of Taylorism into a creative, global system. Poverty will be eliminated and justice established, not by the interference of governments or the zeal of crusaders or the people united. Instead, social progress will follow naturally from intelligent business practice and technological innovation.

Thorstein Veblen famously contrasted producers and profiteers, insisting that engineers were of higher social utility than bankers.[49] Taylor, unsurprisingly, made the same distinction: "He would often contrast finance and manufacturing, as if they were competing and irreconcilable functions. To Taylor a firm was run either by financiers or engineers. The former might make a profit but little else."[50] Dillon's engineering becomes a metaphor for progress itself. It is so redemptively spacious that it justifies, indeed absorbs, the money that lies behind it. In the middle sections of *The Harbor,* Wall Street is proposed as the ally rather than the enemy of humanity. Capitalism and technology march together at the head of the army of progress.[51]

This is the divinity that Bill reveres at the age of twenty-five; the second half of *The Harbor* records his rejection of this god and his gradual embrace of socialism. For several years, Bill remains the loyal progressive: humane and meliorist in sentiment, friendly toward big business, suspicious of radicals, and contemptuous of "the masses." Married to Dillon's daughter Eleanore, Bill makes a lucrative career out of journalism by writing profiles of America's most sucessful men: presidents of huge industrial corporations, millionaire speculators in money and real estate. "I liked these men," admits Bill to himself; "I liked to enthuse over all the big things they were doing. And still true to my efficiency god, the immense importance of getting things done loomed so high in my view of life as to overshadow everything else" (p. 213).

In part because of Joe Kramer's continued example and exhortation, in part because of his own irrepressible dissatisfaction with the reformist program of the engineers, in largest part because of his growing acquaintance with the workers and the poor of New York, Bill moves away from his god Efficiency. The turning point is commemorated in another symbolically expressive scene, a tableau constructed precisely in symmetrical opposition to Bill's earlier ascent of Dillon's tower. He descends into the hold of a ship in the harbor and for a few hours shares the lives of the coal stokers who tend the veessel's huge furnaces. The lurid darkness, lit by leaping tongues of flame; the soul-melting heat; the blinding, choking dust and dirt; the enormous physical danger; the wounding and frequent death: It is all, to be sure, a consciously "literary" moment, the journey to the underworld of epic, the risky voyage to hell and back. But if it is stylized, the episode is also vigorously written and affecting. Deep in the burning steel prison of the ship's bottom, literally beneath the surface of the harbor upon which he had been content earlier to look down, Bill experiences his decisive insight. His place is with the people and the conditions below, not with those high above.

Shortly after this reversal, the radical union leader Jim Marsh enters the book to take charge of a general strike in the port of New York. (Marsh represents Poole's fictionalized homage to two men, IWW leader Bill Haywood and Michael Donnelly of the Butcher's Union.) To Marsh, the harbor is every bit as central an American symbol as it is to Dillon, but it does not signify the benevolence of well-organized machinery. Rather, weaving together both statistics and anecdotes in a rousing speech, Marsh "pictured a harbor of slaves, over-burdened slaves, driven into fierce revolt" (p. 273).

The remainder of the novel's Book III is given over to that revolt, a long and vivid reportorial account of the strike. Bill insists that this strike is an action undertaken out of genuinely radical motives, not to achieve improvements in wages or working conditions but to pull down the existing structure and replace it with the army of labor. Ultimately, after a series of temporary victories, the workers lose, the strike is broken, and Dillon's world of hierarchical force reasserts itself. But by that time Bill's transformation is complete; a bond of solidarity links him to the union and its revolutionary agenda. Though sympathetic, he had initially seen in the strike only unfocused energy. By the end of the strike, in spite of its failure, he detects the emergence of order, the assertion of collective will, the appearance of a spontaneous design.

At the end of the third book, Bill rehearses again his litany of religions, this time declaring his new – and final – commitment, to the people: "The last of my gods, Efficiency, whose feet had stood firm on mechanical laws and in whose head were all the brains of all the big men at the top, had now come tottering crashing down. And in its place a huge new god, whose feet stood deep in poverty and in whose head were all the dreams of all the toilers of the earth, had called to me with one deep voice, with one tremendous burning passion for the freedom of mankind" (p. 351).

Needless to say, conservatives such as neohumanist Paul Elmer More, who reviewed *The Harbor* in *The Unpopular Review*, were by turns amused and appalled by talk like this. More conceded that Poole's book "is a faithful echo of the currents of thought sweeping over a large portion of the world."[52] More went on to ridicule both the idols of efficiency and the people, on behalf of "individual life as a thing . . . valuable in itself and worthy of cultivation," and he instances Saint Bernard in his cloister as the happy man.

Saint Bernard is a splendidly antithetical figure to the Bill of the latter part of *The Harbor*. Contemplative, detached, committed to a transcendent divinity, he embodies values that the novel systematically repudiates. Above all, individualism, with its overtones of alienation and egotism, gives way to an absorption in humanity. Joe Kramer had predicted Bill's metamorphosis early in the story, in words that Bill recalls at the height of the strike.

When you see the crowd, in a strike like this, loosen up and show all it could be if it had the chance – this sight is so big it blots you out – you sink – you melt into the crowd.

Something like that happened to me. I had seen the multitudes "loosen up." I had felt myself melt into the crowd. (P. 311)

As we have seen, the novel's final chapters consist in large measure of
Bill's meditation on the coming of the war, whose guns he professed to
believe would realize "the dreams of the toilers." Yet, a second look at
Bill's celebration of those dreams suggests that like most of the American socialist visions that preceded it, this one too is inherently untenable
and internally self-defeating. We have observed that the form of *The
Harbor* is essentially that of an education. In it, Ernest Poole went far
toward adopting both the idea and the implications of socialism, further
certainly than most other significant American novelists. But the final
lesson Bill learns proves not to be socialist after all. At virtually the last
moment, Poole undertakes a retreat from the socialist creed he had
worked so hard to verify.

For Bill at last disassociates himself from *all* dogmas, socialism
among them. He adopts the familiar accents of pragmatism, abruptly
dismantling the ideological perspective that the entire novel had seemingly endeavored to establish. The antidoctrinal attitude toward which
Bill has moved in the last few pages of the novel is most spaciously
delineated by a minor character, an unnamed English novelist introduced into the book for the sole purpose of making this thematic
announcement.

> "I told him," says Bill, "how all my life I had been raising up
> gods to worship, and how the harbor had flowed silently in be-
> neath, undermining each one and bringing it down."
> "It seems to have such a habit of changing," I ended, "that it
> won't let a fellow stop."
> "Lucky people," he answered, smiling, "to have found that
> out so soon – to have had all this modern life condensed . . . into
> your harbor before your eyes – and to have discovered, while
> you are still young, that life is growth and growth is change.
> . . . a man if he's to be vital at all must give up the idea of any
> fixed creed." (P. 377)

So, at the last, all specific programs, including those of socialism, are
replaced by what might be called a pragmatic vitalism, an adaptable
immersion in the organic changefulness of life.[53] The directionless élan
of the Englishman's sentiments will deflect Bill from translating his
genuine sympathies for "the people" into any concrete platform or,
indeed, into any particular principles.

This is the conception and mood that dominate the concluding paragraphs of the story. In the immigrant faces on a crowded street Bill
still sees "a giant slowly born" (p. 386). But where he had recently
seen socialism as the future toward which this giant would march,
now he can foresee only change. The future seems altogether enig-

matic to him, and he contemplates it passively. In the mournful horn of the ship rising from the foggy harbor Bill hears a voice, preaching a near-mystical celebration of "life": "Make way for me. Make way, all you little men. Make way, all you habits and all you institutions, all you little creeds and gods. For I am the start of the voyage . . . I am always starting out and always bearing you along! For I am your molder, I am strong – I am a surprise, I am a shock – I am a dazzling passion of hope . . . I am reality – I am life! I am the book that has no end!" (p. 387).

The diffuseness of the sentiment is matched by the studied exuberance of its expression, and the tired religio-aesthetic trope of the last line suggests that Saint Bernard is not so antithetical a figure after all.

The resolution of *The Harbor* opposes an ironic rebuke to the novel's putative purposes. Poole apparently regarded the book's structure as linear and its concluding hymns to chaos as a mature insight. In his autobiography, written a quarter-century later, he nonchalantly defined the "theme" of the novel as "the challenge of change."[54] In fact, however, there is something circular and even regressive about the intellectual outcome of the book. Bill's apolitical collapse into the unfocused forces of change carries him unintendedly back to his childhood, to his fantasies of merging into the adventure and excitement of the harbor's "strange and terrible" wonderland.

The Harbor is a novel whose intentions we know: Ernest Poole was as designedly pro-socialist in his book as David Parry was the opposite in *The Scarlet Empire.* Part of the significance of *The Harbor,* then, lies precisely in the extent to which its clear purpose is obscured in the execution. Poole is led, almost it seems in spite of himself, into counterstatement, an oddly American combination of mysticism and pragmatism in which the energy of a directed political action is dissipated.

It is ironic, given Frank Norris's methodically antisocialist proclivities, that *The Harbor* resembles no other novel so clearly, in broad outline at least, as *The Octopus:* the elaborated epic devices, including the omnicompetent central symbol (wheat, of course, in *The Octopus*); the vast and emblematically all-embracing geography; the movement from Art, to the People, to a quietist-mystical acquiescence in Force or Life. The perceptible similarities between these apparently antagonistic works, the one near the beginning and the other at the end of our period, contain and perhaps even define the limits of what is possible in the ideological fiction of early twentieth-century America.

Irving Howe proposed that international socialism, in spite of its decisive prewar failure, can claim a number of substantial achievements: It "placed upon the historical agenda the idea of human liberation; it

brought to unprecedented intensity the vision of a secular utopia; it
enabled masses of previously mute workers to enter the arena of
history."[55] But beyond this, at least in America, socialism could not
go – an outcome whose imagainative evidence we have sampled in the
preceding pages.

Ours is the nation, after all, that could completely miss the point of
the one authentic and influential socialist novel produced in these years.
The Jungle is a book *not* undermined by romance, or deflected into
conciliation, or distracted by mysticism; and if its embrace of socialism
is "impulsive and awkward,"[56] it remains nonetheless intact.[57] The
irony of its misreading is exquisite. Upton Sinclair wrote *The Jungle* as
a cry of anguish on behalf of the literally millions of Americans being
pulverized in the nation's political-industrial machine; as a denunciation
of the systemic alliance between justice and capitalism that legalized
inhumanity; and as a call to socialist arms. What the American public
noticed was the unhygienic processing of its meat. Sinclair demanded a
revolution; he got the Food and Drug Administration instead.

Chapter 5

On being black: Booker T. Washington, W. E. B. Du Bois, and others

BOOKER T. WASHINGTON

The wisdom in this matter is altogether received. The formula in which Booker T. Washington comes to us originated with Du Bois at the turn of the century, and it has found renewed expression in the literature and symbols of each succeeding generation. "Old Buckethead" is Ralph Ellison's cruel caricature in *Invisible Man:* a slighting reference to Washington's most famous speech, with its call to southern blacks and whites to cast down their respective buckets where they were. Dudley Randall gives us his version of the formula in the poem "Booker T. and W. E. B.":

> "It seems to me," said Booker T.,
> "That all you folks have missed the boat
> Who shout about the right to vote
> And spend vain days and sleepless nights
> In uproar over civil rights.
> Just keep your mouth shut, do not grouse,
> But work, and save, and buy a house."
>
> "I don't agree," said W.E.B. . . .[1]

Perhaps the most convincingly damning of the Washington portraits emerges in the unlettered but wise soliloquies of Nate Shaw:

They gave that man piles of money to run this school business here in the state of Alabama. But I wouldn't boost Booker Washington today up to everything that was industrious and right. Why? He was a nigger of this state and well known and everything, but here's what his trouble was, to a great extent: he didn't feel for and didn't respect his race of people enough to go rock bottom with em. He leaned too much on the white people that

controlled the money – lookin out for what was his worth, that's
what he was lookin for. He was a big man, he had authority . . .
he had a political pull any way he turned and he was pullin for
Booker Washington. He wanted his people to do this, that, and
the other, but he never did get to the roots of our troubles. . . .
Yet and still the veil was over the nigger's eyes. Booker Washington didn't try to pull that veil away like he shoulda done.[2]

Irreverent and even flippant as they are, these estimates of Booker T.
Washington have much to commend them. Washington's climb up,
triumphant beyond calculation in his own view, was by any standard
extraordinary. But it was marked and indeed was made possible by a
commitment to conciliation and self-abnegation so intense as to document to his critics a fundamental confusion between means and ends.
According to men like Du Bois and W. M. Trotter, Washington served
only himself and his own advancement, and willfully cooperated in
obstructing the progress of the mass of black people. First in his pugnacious review of *Up from Slavery*,[3] and shortly after in the well-known
essay "Of Mr. Booker T. Washington and Others," Du Bois announced that the ideological battle had been joined. The essay itemizes
the destructive, threefold outcome of Washington's program: the acceptance of disfranchisement, the submission to civic inferiority, and the
depreciation of any education for blacks save industrial training.

Washington's avoidance of quarrels with white America was so pain-
staking that whatever controversy he did cause was inadvertent and
seemed to take him by surprise. The most famous instance was surely
the celebrated lunch with Theodore Roosevelt in October 1901. Since
the racism of recent years has at least become subtler, it is instructive to
recall that this meal had a volcanic effect on national politics. The event
is best told, and its impact for our purposes best assessed, by Rosevelt's
friend, the journalist Arthur Wallace Dunn. Dunn called the affair "a
sensation": "For days it was one of the most widely discussed subjects
in the country. In the southern states the President was universally
condemned by public men and in the press."[4] Dunn thought it would
prove an expensive lunch for Roosevelt, and told him so. "It was," he
explained to the president:

a great shock to that element which was about to launch a white
man's Republican party in the South. I had an opportunity to
observe the effect of the Booker Washington episode in communities where there was quite a large negro population. In Mary-
land, many Democrats had left the party on the silver issue,
and . . . about determined to remain in the [Republican] party.
But the Booker Washington luncheon completely upset them.

The Democrats who had remained steadfast jeered them and talked about "nigger equality." It drove many of them back to Democracy. (P. 358)

But more significant for our purposes than the electrifying meal itself is the fact that neither Washington nor Roosevelt intended it to happen. As the exasperated Roosevelt explained to Dunn: "I'll tell you how it happened, and I told him to come in and have lunch while we continued our talk. That was all there was to it" (pp. 358–359).

So Washington's most incendiary gesture of racial self-assertion turns out to have been an afterthought, and not even his own but his host's. Washington's personal response, here as in similar situations when white celebrities regarded him with any respect, was some degree or other of embarrassment. Thus are all the climactic moments of his life tinged with ironies he didn't recognize.

Both Washington and his critics read in such encounters the meaning of his career; but where Washington finds his achievement and his authority documented (after all, Roosevelt did not have lunch with any other black leader), Du Bois and others find his authority, indeed his authenticity, decisively denied.

These competing perspectives are enabled by a recurring pattern in Washington's greatly successful autobiography:

I saw two of my young mistresses [writes Washington, recalling an episode from his youth as a slave] eating ginger-cakes, in the yard. At that time those cakes seemed to me to be absolutely the most tempting and desirable things that I had ever seen; and I then and there resolved that, if I ever got free, the height of my ambition would be reached if I could get to the point where I could secure and eat ginger-cakes.[5]

Washington's rhetorical strategy here is to suggest by contrast the dimensions of his ultimate accomplishment: such modest beginnings yielding eventually to such remarkable conclusions. His critics, on the other hand, would find those ginger-cakes portentous: always to be satisfied with trifling prizes, with the superfluities allowed him by white culture.

Washington's first hat, which he consciously elaborates into a symbol of his progress, finally reveals itself as emblematic beyond his design. The passage is worth citing in full, both because of what it reveals of Washington's conception of himself and because it summarizes much of the tone and point of view of the entire book. With no money for a "store hat," Washington's mother made one for him by sewing two pieces of "homespun" together.

The lesson that my mother taught me in this has always remained with me, and I have tried as best I could to teach it to others. I have always felt proud, whenever I think of the incident, that my mother had strength of character enough not to be led into the temptation of seeming to be that which she was not – of trying to impress my schoolmates and others with the fact that she was able to buy me a "store hat" when she was not. I have always felt proud that she refused to go into debt for that which she did not have the money to pay for. Since that time I have owned many kinds of caps and hats, but never one of which I have felt so proud as of the cap made of two pieces of cloth sewed together by my mother. I have noted the fact, but without satisfaction, I need not add, that several of the boys who began their careers with "store hats" and who were my schoolmates and used to join in the sport that was made of me because I had only a "homespun" cap, have ended their careers in the penitentiary, while others are not able now to buy any kind of hat. (Pp. 33–34)

This paragraph is virtually synoptic of *Up from Slavery*. There is, to begin with, the sentimental image of woman as the repository of unflinching integrity, along with the singularly unbookish view of education. Throughout *Up from Slavery*, Washington repeatedly adduces episodes outside of classrooms as more educational than lectures and texts. To be sure, a characteristically American and specifically Emersonian accent can be heard in some of these pronouncements: "There is no education which one can get from books and costly apparatus that is equal to that which can be gotten from contact with great men and women" (p. 55). Be that as it may, Washington is everywhere prepared, as in this tale of his home-made hat, to subordinate the speculative to the practical and the abstract to the concrete.

Note also the recurrence of the word "proud" in the passage. Washington's pride is anchored paradoxically in humility; but, of course, it is equally true to say that his humility fuels his pride. The passage offers simultaneously a sermon against uppityness and a complacent assertion of self. That double perspective is linked to the divided time scheme that defines Washington's point of view here and throughout the book: "I have owned many hats since." On another page, in which he recounts having slept under a sidewalk in Richmond, Washington tells within a sentence or two of a great reception held in that city in his honor years later. When he writes of his difficulties as a young waiter, he quickly adds how often he has since eaten in the same restaurant as a guest. Always the later success is superimposed upon the earlier trial, as in the anecdote of the hat, and failure is transformed instantly into success. (Thus, though the book is organized altogether chronologically, the structure is actually less successive and more "spatial" than it appears.)

The final sentence of Washington's recollection of his first hat extends the contrast between past and present into a self-serving contrast between Washington and his youthful companions: "Several of the boys who began their careers with 'store hats' . . . have ended their careers in the penitentiary, while others are not able now to buy any kind of hat." A massively egocentric teleology is embodied in these anonymous imprisoned and impoverished others. This reduction of the people around him to object lessons declaring his own significance is typical of Washington's stance in *Up from Slavery*. It is also among the more sinister constiuents of his legacy from Christianity. Washington's reiterated Christian commitment sounds like nothing more than convenient and conventional piety; his voice comes to us in relentlessly secular tones. But the paranoid shape of the moral epistemology in *Up from Slavery* is essentially identical to what we find in the more persuasively religious transactions of earlier American autobiography, especially those of the New England Calvinists.

Washington's mocking classmates are the lineal if unwitting descendants of the "proud and very profane yonge man, one of the sea-men," who continually taunted William Bradford and his companions aboard the Mayflower two and a half centuries earlier. The "hauty" young man "would allway be contemning the poore people in their sicknes . . . and did not let to tell them, that he hoped to help to cast halfe of them overboard before they came to their journeys end. . . . But it plased God before they came halfe seas over, to smite this yonge man with a greevous disease, of which he dyed in a desperate maner. . . . Thus his curses light on his owne head."[6]

Washington's tone is no less grimly smug than Bradford's. Though not conscious of the logic, Washington is ratifying his own covenant with success in part by insisting on the failure of other blacks. To Du Bois and others, the intimations of racial infidelity, though implicit, were inescapable.

Correlatively, at the same time that Washington's self-approval is implicated in his disapproval of blacks, the limits of his identity are located in his approval by whites. Like so many victims of ideological oppression, Washington affirmed the system that denied his own integrity.

Du Bois, the analyst of black "two-ness," posits Washington's success as deriving precisely from his "singleness of vision and thorough oneness with his age."[7] Thus, episodes that seemed to his critics symptoms of moral exhaustion symbolize to Washington the dawn of a robustly new and well-ordered day. Among the speakers on the day of

President McKinley's visit to Tuskegee was Secretary of the Navy John Long, who baldly announced, "The problem [of race relations] has been solved" (p. 309). The solution to America's racial nightmare consisted, in Long's diapason, in "a picture . . . which should be put upon canvas with the pictures of Washington and Lincoln . . . a most dramatic picture. . . . The President of the United States standing on this platform, on one side the Governor of Alabama, on the other, completing the trinity, a representative of a race only a few years ago in bondage . . ." Such a picture, Du Bois would have rejoined, was emphatically not a solution nor even the sign of one; rather it was a gesture, and a gesture of capitulation to boot. It summarized nothing more edifying than Washington's self-deluding collaboration with his own adversaries. Washington's "one-ness" with the economic and moral imperatives of American culture had, of course, a specifically racial outcome, in Du Bois's view. It compelled Washington to permit himself to be absorbed into a racism so malign as to have done him the fundamental indignity of denying him a name.

Washington glances at the decisive link between name and identity, but with an oddly detached tone. Describing the days immediately following emancipation, he writes: "In some way a feeling got among the colored people that it was far from proper for them to bear the surname of their former owners, and a great many of them took other surnames" (p. 23). A few pages later, he adds, with a quiet pride that stops inexplicably far short of outrage: "I think there are not many men in our country who have had the privilege of naming themselves in the way that I have" (p. 35). These passages are moving, as much in their philosophical opacity as in the undeniable victory they signalize. The victory was real. Self-naming constitutes a quasi-divine act of self-creation, an existential triumph of unexampled proportions. Yet Washington's address to this climactic event is oblique almost to the vanishing point. Two generations later, Ralph Ellison would discern in the "hidden names" of Negroes their entire complex fate: the etymology of "Brown" and "White" is written in blood.[8] For Washington, on the other hand, the issue hardly transcends the puzzling: "In some way a feeling got among the coloured people." And his sole interest lies in narrating his own name's story, a story revealing his "privilege."

Which brings us back to the anonymous young men who laughed at Washington's boyhood hat. They are absolutely representative of blacks in *Up from Slavery* by virtue of their namelessness. Aside from his wives and one or two other people (T. Thomas Fortune, for example), Washington names practically none of the literally hundreds of blacks who move through the pages of his tale. The names – the identities – belong almost without exception to whites. William McKinley. Postmaster

General Charles E. Smith. John Addison Porter, secretary to the president. Charles W. Hare of Tuskegee. James Wilson, Secretary of Agriculture. President Charles W. Eliot of Harvard. Massachusetts Governor Roger Wolcott. Henry Cabot Lodge. West Virginia Governor George W. Atkinson. Herman Smith, mayor of Charleston. New York Governor Benjamin Odell, Jr. Andrew Carnegie. Samuel Armstrong. Susan B. Anthony. Queen Victoria. This list is immense, and altogether white. Blacks have become the invisible men and women of Booker T. Washington's world.

Washington's own estimate of his perceptions and of the significance of his career was, needless to say, rather different. For him, accommodation was a tactic, not a goal. In ways that his middle-class adversaries could only misunderstand, Washington was not a theoretician but a survivor. This fact, more than anything else, shapes his vision of race and progress. The gospel is work, and Washington preaches it with undivided zeal: "Nothing ever comes to one, that is worth having, except as a result of hard work" (p. 188). The large numbers of Tuskegee students are kept out of mischief, Washington explains, because they are "kept busy." And he appends an outline of daily work that echoes, deliberately or not, Benjamin Franklin's famous schedule:

> 5 am., rising bell; 5.50 a.m., warning breakfast bell; 6 a.m., breakfast bell; 6.20 a.m., breakfast over; 6.20 to 6.50 a.m., rooms are cleaned; 6.50 work bell; 7.30, morning study hour; 8.20, morning school bell; 8.25, inspection of young men's toilet in ranks; 8.40, devotional exercises in chapel; 8.55, "five minutes with the daily news"; 9 a.m., class work begins; 12, class work closes; 12.15 p.m., dinner; 1 p.m., work bell; 1.30 p.m., class work begins; 3.30 p.m., class work ends; 5.30 p.m., bell to "knock off" work; 6 p.m., supper; 7.10 p.m., evening prayers; 7.30 p.m., evening study hour; 8.45 p.m., evening study hour closes; 9.20 p.m., warning retiring bell; 9.30 p.m., retiring bell.

The roster is fussy to the point of compulsion or self-parody; but it provides Washington with a vehicle for defining black worth in detailed terms of the prevailing ideology. The sixteen-and-a-half-hour day doesn't include so much as a hint of leisure or play or unvocational culture.

Though extreme in its severity, the schedule is typical of the book. The predominating tone of *Up from Slavery* is its daunting seriousness: As Washington's day was not lightened by recreation, so his book never lapses into humor or elegance. Inarguably high stakes were being contested in a struggle that allowed no distractions. Tuskegee's students construct their own furniture and build their own buildings because they have to, and because such tasks enable them to prove their self-reliance. Even though "at present" (i.e., 1900) much could be bought, Washington's educational principles require the manufacturing to continue; and another version of progress is manifested: "The workmanship has so improved that little fault can be found with the articles now" (p. 174).

To put this in the context of the widespread contemporary phenomenon we are recalling from time to time, what Washington is describing is an unself-conscious arts and crafts movement – or better, an arts and crafts countermovement – exactly opposite in its intentions to those of the contemporary American disciples of Ruskin and Morris. Washington's students are not a group of bourgeois intelligentsia trying to capture an ersatz "folk" identity. They are, rather, the folk itself trying earnestly to become bourgeois.

The ubiquitous hallmark of Washington's world, as the Franklinish schedule that regulates it implies, is materialism. The ever-growing number of buildings on the Tuskegee campus, the value of the plant, the volume of contributions, the size of the student body and staff – these are the relevant indices. Like all progressives, Washington's interest directed itself to the quantifiable sums of achievement. Like all progressives, too, Washington drew his strength from his tenacious collaboration with the assumptions of his time.

Yet perhaps it is time to propose – gingerly – a subversive hypothesis: that Washington's conformity to the presumed primacy of material values evinced a realism beyond special pleading, a substance beyond opportunism. An analogy might be illuminating.

In the later nineteenth century, and well into the twentieth, assorted conflicting theories were elaborated to isolate one or another characteristic as chiefly responsible for the evolutionary ascent of humans above their predecessors. The great majority of anthropologists, especially in the English-speaking world, insisted upon the primacy of an enlarging brain. Stephen Jay Gould quotes this observation made by the English anthropologist G. E. Smith in the 1920s: "It was not the adoption of the erect attitude or the invention of articulate language that made man from an ape, but the gradual perfecting of a brain and the slow building of a mental structure."[9] Since there was no evidence at all for any of the major hypotheses – an enlarging brain, speech, an upright posture – Gould proposes that the nearly universal preference for the first of these theories directly exposes the cultural biases of nineteenth- and twentieth-century society: the traditional notion that humanity is identical with its rationality. The unsupported but widely held doctrine of cerebral primacy illustrates the vigor with which traditional opinion encumbers innovation.

Instead of presenting itself as a preeminent question for reserach, the evolutionary sequence was virtually obscured behind a curtain of partiality and was dealt with axiomatically.

Our interest here is with one of the few exceptions to this generalization. In 1876, Friedrich Engels wrote an essay entitled "The Part Played by Labour in the Transition from Ape to Man." (The essay was not published until 1896, after Engels's death.) The essay is significant both for its rejection of an assumed cerebral primacy and for its postulation of work as a critical evolutionary mechanism. Engels hypothesizes the descent of apes from the trees, followed by the adoption of a "more and more erect gait."[10] The hands were freed for toolmaking and labor, *after* which came increased intellect and speech. Thus the hand, not the brain, impels evolutionary progress.

The idealist prejudice in philosophy and politics so dominated nineteenth-century intellectual life that a manual-materialist counterproposal such as Engels's was condemned to a priori defeat. Engels himself accurately predicted that defeat when he wrote that even apolitical and materialist scientists automatically ascribe "all merit for the swift advance of civilization . . . to the mind, to the development and activity of the brain. Men became accumstomed to explain their actions from their thoughts, instead of from their needs."[11]

I do not intend by this glance at Engels's evolutionary theorizing to suggest any direct connection between Engels and Washington, nor to insinuate any likeness between their political ideas. (Washington was of course a tireless champion of capitalism and an equally hard-working opponent of labor unions.) Taken analogically, though, Engels's opinions might justify such a speculation as this. Without access to the terminology, Washington is proposing a sociology that recapitulates Marxist biology. Economic base precedes and indeed provides much of the substance of ideological superstructure, and economics in turn is based on the hand. When, in the Atlanta Exposition address, Washington asked blacks to "draw the line between the superficial and the substantial, the ornamental gewgaws of life and the useful" (p. 220), he was not merely and necessaarily rationalizing his assent to the permanent exclusion of blacks from the worlds of culture. He was, rather, subordinating those worlds of culture to the world of economics.

Note that the Atlanta address, despite the legendary obsequiousness of its tone, includes more than one explicit demand for ultimate equality: "It is important and right that all privileges of the law be ours" (pp. 223–224). Washington, who had spent the first years of his life as a commodity, understood that law is the creature of power, and in America specifically of financial power. Never in American history was this truth more nakedly evident than in the years around the turn of the century. Booker T. Washington had no need to reach this insight analytically; it was virtually the sum of his birthright.

The thoroughly modest thesis of this excursion has been to suggest that vantage points other than that of Du Bois might afford alternative assessments of Washington's ideology. One such vantage point is that of August Meier, in *Negro Thought in America, 1880–1915*. Conceding the limits of Washington's public efforts toward black liberation, Meier argues with some cogency for Washington's more strenuous work behind the scenes. His correspondence shows a long, losing struggle against the lily-white Republicans and a good deal of quiet financial support for court cases brought to preserve the Negro franchise throughout the South. According to Meier, Washington "was surreptitiously engaged in undermining the American race system by a direct attack upon disfranchisement and segregation."[12]

Whatever their varying estimates of its quality, the quintessentially American cast of Washington's mind is the central fact on which he and his critics could agree. They could also agree on his energetically American optimism. As the progress of his race will replicate the past evolutionary history of mankind, so his own story encapsulates the future progress of his race. Thus, despite his repeated protestations of modesty, Washington emerges from the pages of his autobiography as far more than exemplary: He becomes a central historical figure. Sacvan Bercovitch has provided the superlatively useful term that best captures the reach of Washington's self-authored significance: *Up from Slavery* is a text in the genre of "auto-American-biography." Bercovitch derives the phrase from Cotton Mather's hagiographical portrait of John Winthrop in Mather's *Magnalia Christi Americana*. As it is rendered in the *Magnalia*, Winthrop's career is transformed into both saint's life and national epic. Winthrop at once embodies the personal virtues attendant upon election and resumes the story of the whole elected community. In him secular and sacred history are joined.[13]

Unaware of the references, Washington in *Up from Slavery* plays Mather to his own latter-day black Winthrop. Acting on his belief in America's post-Christian design of salvation (a design derived in some measure from that of Winthrop's Puritans but emptied of its transcendent focus), seeing his people as covenanted and journeying, relying on the instrument of learning, Booker T. Washington has his symbolic reference – as Winthrop had his, two and a half centuries earlier – in the figure of Moses. Even more exactly than Winthrop, who led his people into a wilderness, Washington would lead his people out of one. There is, thus, far more at work than miscellaneous self-congratulation when Washington quotes correspondent James Creelman's account of his Atlanta speech, which appeared in the New York *World;* "While President Cleveland was waiting at Gray Gables today, to send the electric spark that started the machinery of the Atlanta Exposition, a Negro Moses stood before a great audience . . . and delivered an oration that marks a new epoch in the history of the south" (p. 238).

The typological self-portraits of the Puritans have become one of the commonplaces of recent criticism. American black people were equally compulsive typologists, though their accomplishment has been treated less extensively. The subversive political purposes to which they put the Christiantity imposed upon them were ingenious and multiform. The enslavement in Egypt, the years of exile and wandering in the desert, the Babylonian captivity, the destruction of temple and homeland: All these antetypical events found a far more convincing typological fulfillment in the experiences of American blacks than in those of any other group, and certainly more than those of the regionally dominant Puritans.

This transformation of religious materials was more patently relevant before the abolition of slavery. Washington himself recalls the approach of emancipation in a tone of unusual, sprightly irony:

> Most of the verses of the plantation songs had some reference to freedom. True, they had sung those same verses before, but they had been careful to explain that the "freedom" in these songs referred to the next world, and had no connection with life in this world. Now they gradually threw off the mask; and were not afraid to let it be known that the "freedom" in their songs meant freedom of the body in this world. (Pp. 19–20)

Blacks, in other words, rediscovered the aboriginal revolutionary energy of Christianity, focusing through its powerful images their quite worldly millennial expectations.

Du Bois offers the same reading of the signification of "freedom" in the hymns of antebellum blacks; but the details of his analysis expose rather his distance from Washington than any resemblance to him. Following his customary practice, Du Bois casts his reconstruction of black Christianity in historical terms. He sees Christianity as having initially reinforced the hegemony of white masters by inculcating "doctrines of passive submission" (p. 199). As a good many students of oppression before and after him have done, Du Bois found in Christianity a sublimely efficacious slave morality, a system that transformed weakness into virtue and pacified its adherents with promises of joy beyond the grave. Thus did religion collaborate with power and buttress economic strength with an ideology: Blacks assented to a system of values that insisted on their own degradation.

Out of this and against it arose "the class of free Negroes," free that is to say both intellectually and politically, for whom "Freedom became a real thing and not a dream." It was, according to Du Bois, the free Negro who instilled the desire for liberty in "the black millions still in bondage" (p. 200) and who identified "Negro religion . . . with the dream of Abolition." In other words, what appears in Washington's acount as a spontaneous redefinition of "freedom" by the enslaved blacks themselves is explained by Du Bois in terms of leadership. Resident in these utterly different conceptions, to be sure, are symmetrically opposed self-portraits.

Further, though Washington and Du Bois alike perceived Emancipation as having had an apocalyptic significance – "a literal Coming of the Lord," in Du Bois's phrase – the two diverge immediately in assessing the generations that followed. For Du Bois, it had been a long era of retreat and disillusion: "Joyed and bewildered" by his liberation, the former slave "stood awaiting new wonders till the inevitable Age of Reaction swept over the nation and brought the crisis of to-day" (p. 201). For Washington, the years had been marked by progress, and testimonials to that effect punctuate his writings. In *Up from Slavery,* perhaps most memorably, he interprets the "demise" of the Klan as symptomatic. "To-day there are no such organizations in the South, and the fact that such ever existed is almost forgotten by both races. There are few places in the South now where public sentiment would permit such organizations to exist" (p. 79).

The essential meaning of black history in America lies for Washington in such melioristic contrasts as this. Injustice, reduced to a memory, in any case contained the seeds of its own reformation. Most important, the structure that animates the story of black America is identical with the structure of Washington's own life. From the perspective of this awareness, Washington's thoroughgoing blindness to the humiliating realities of black life at the turn of the century can be seen as something more than the simple result of calculated dishonesty at the service of self-aggrandizement. More complexly, Washington interlinked his own fate with that of his race so intimately that his personal success *required* a commensurate collective success. The connection is virtually syllogistic; as in all syllogisms, the premise contains its conclusion and evidence is superogatory. Racial progress is for Washington a crucial and needed act of self-delusion, because his career is made legitimate not as the tale of an exceptional man but – whether paradoxically or not – as the narrative of the ultimately representative man. Hence, conditions must be getting better. If they were not, if indeed they should actually get worse, then Washington's personal gains would constitute an affront rather than a portent of hope.

IN WHITE AMERICA

The Nigger, a once-popular but now totally forgotten melodrama by
Edward Sheldon, offers a quite different version – in part because it is a
white version – of the racial dialectic being explored in these pages.
Produced at the New Theater in New York in 1909, and published in
1910, *The Nigger* possesses only modest dramatic values but considerable thematic interest. Sterling Brown, in a survey he made half a century ago of white plays about blacks, called *The Nigger* "the most
ambitious" of such works and suggests that it takes "the problem"
more seriously than the exploitative average.[14] In fact, Sheldon offers a
white view of blacks that is at once generous in its intentions and
potentially more liberating than Washington's, yet at the same time
more inescapably steeped in the bigotry of racial stereotypes.

The action of the play is in three acts; the place is the South, the time
is "now." Act I takes place at twilight at "Morrow's Rest." The first
act comprises two consecutive events. In the beginning of the act, the
lovely Georgiana Byrd refuses the repeated marriage offers of Clifton
Noyes, the rich, coarse owner of the region's largest industry, a liquor
distillery. Noyes's other purpose in his visit is to offer the governor-
ship, on behalf of the state's businessmen, to his host, Philip Morrow,
who is also the sheriff of the county. (He is also Noyes's cousin and
Georgiana's preferred suitor.) Immediately after the exposition of this
romantic-political plot, the black tenant of Morrow's Rest, a young
man named Joe White, appears: He is the terrified fugitive from a lynch
mob. Clinging to the skirts of his mother, the old servant Jinny, White
confesses that he did commit the savage rape for which he is being
pursued, but he pleads for protection from Morrow. Morrow regards
White as a "black beast";[15] he is, however, a defender of law against
mob rule. Therefore he tries to get White safely to jail. He fails, and the
act ends with the sounds of an off-stage lynching: "Amid a far-away
roar of voices and savage cheers, comes a long scream of agony and
terror. Jinny, without a sound, slowly crumbles away into a shapeless
heap on the ground" (stage directions, p. 99). Though Morrow rebukes
himself for White's death, Georgiana consoles him, saying to him as the
curtain falls, "Aftah all, he's – well, he's only a negro" (p. 100).

The second act takes place a few months later and is set in the office
of now Governor Morrow. A race riot, common in these years in
northern and especially in southern cities, is heard in full career off-
stage. (Though the play's city and state are never specified, the riot's
details link it most closely to the 1906 riot in Atlanta.) The instigators,
according to the governor's secretary, are drunken whites: "This
ba'-room riffraff – dam' em! . . . it makes a man ashamed of his race t'

see such things go on!" (p. 112). Because of the connection between liquor and violence, Governor Morrow, who had run a "wet" campaign, has resolved to support prohibition in his state. (Georgia, the first southern state to legislate prohibition, did so in 1908; Alabama and Mississippi followed in 1909.) Morrow's decision, defended by the play as rational, of course enrages distillery-owner Noyes. Noyes comes to the governor's office to contest the decision, and in the course of the argument he produces documentary evidence that Morrow's grandmother was black. Noyes summarizes the consequences: "What I'm tellin' you is not only that yo' gran'-mothah was a niggah, Phil, but that yo' a niggah, too" (pp. 147–148). Noyes's deal is that the governor will veto the prohibition law and Noyes will suppress his evidence. Otherwise, the "newly-black" Morrow will lose his job; his property; his fiancée, Georgiana; and probably his life. The governor refuses Noyes's offer, and the consequences begin to follow immediately. When Morrow tells Georgiana the truth of his genealogy, she falls into what the stage directions call "a paroxysm of nervous horror" (p. 193). The act closes with the arrival of the state militia to put down the riot.

The final act consists principally of conversations between Morrow and Senator Thomas Long, a prohibitionist also possessed of moderate racial views (views, indeed, by the standard of the other characters, that are downright radical). "The White Niggah," Morrow has called him, "the man that has da'kies at his dinah-table" (p. 38). In spite of what he now knows about his own lineage, Morrow continues to argue a reductive white supremacist line. The "niggah's not a man," Morrow tells Long, "he's an animal – he's an African savage – all teeth an' claws – it's monkey blood he's got in him, an' you can't evah change it" (p. 212).

Against this vulgar but (as we shall see) by no means idiosyncratic position, Senator Long appeals: "Young fellah, don't say wo'ds like them, not even t' yo'self. They'ah wicked, an' what's mo', they ain't true! Ev'ry niggah's a man. You an' me have had mo' time t' push ahead – that's the only diff'rence between us! We're all men an' we're all doin' the same thing – stumblin' an' fallin' t'gethah, on our jou'ney t' God" (pp. 212–213). Prompted by Long's persuasion, but moved primarily by his loyalty to the racist fictions he takes for truth, Morrow chooses to announce his race publicly, to declare himself black, rather than to bargain for escape. The play gives him a splendidly opportune setting in which to do so when the militia arrives after settling the riot. The final act ends with the governor calling for quiet as he prepares to address the assembled soldiers and citizens. The preposterous but inevitable tragedy that will follow, in which Governor Morrow, owner of Morrow's Rest, will be transformed into "Niggah Morrow," a less-than-man without position or property, need not be shown.

Many years ago, in a survey of turn-of-the-century American theater, Joseph Wood Krutch identified Edward Sheldon as one of the handful of "serious" playwrights of the period, one of those "who made a cautious effort to treat themes which had some relation to contemporary life."[16] Sheldon's seriousness is documented by the very plot of *The Nigger*. He achieves an almost Faulknerian sense of futility and waste in the revelation of Philip Morrow's mixed blood, and through Morrow he captures something of the South's corporate commitment to self-destruction. It is Morrow who early in the play denounces miscegenation: "If we want t' keep our blood clean, we've got to know that *white's white an' black's black* – an' mixin' 'em's damnation!" (p. 33). And it is Morrow who marches off to one sort of certain death or other at the play's close by remaining faithful to the barbarism that will now impale him.

Morrow's function as an emblematic figure is made clear not only in the patent irony of his fate but even more vividly in his response to it. From the moment that he admits the truth of Noyes's charge, Morrow exemplifies the full dimensions of the ideological prison in which he and his society are sealed. Not for an instant does he consider redefining the racist stereotypes that have suddenly been turned against him in a bizarre reversal. Rather, he instantly redefines himself, away from humanity.

Morrow has been presented throughout the play as a specimen of the best the South has to offer: courageous, honest, a success in business and politics whose integrity has remained intact. But Sheldon's point is to demonstrate that in a society based on the premises of the American South, the best is necessarily corrupted by the worst. More, Sheldon intends to suggest that the very categories of moral value are evasive when measured against the institutionalized crime of racism that forms their setting. When, in a perverse version of *deus ex machina*, Morrow becomes "the nigger" of the title and chooses to pay the great price of his own beliefs, his abrupt transformation represents the South's revenge on itself for the evils of racism. Thus does Sheldon use stereotypes with shrewd malice to explode the pretenses of the society that is built upon them.

Yet the play is ultimately as interesting for the stereotypes it accepts and trades on as for those it denies. It is Sheldon's simultaneous resistance to and complicity with the prevailing racial mythology that makes him especially relevant here. To put it summarily: Only four blacks actually appear in *The Nigger,* and all of them are either demeaning or degraded images. Simms, Morrow's butler, is a small role, a thoroughly comic character, a descendent of the minstrel clowns and an ancestor of Step 'n Fetchit, with bulging eyes and exaggerated gestures of deference. Jinny, Morrow's "mammy," is a sentimentally positive character, but a figure of complete helplessness and ineptitude. The third black in the play is Joe White, the rapist. In the words of Morrow's deputy sheriff, just before White's entrance: "It's a niggah, suh, – the usual crime" (p. 60). The crime is admitted and particularly vicious; White's victim has died. The pathos of Mamie Willis's violated, broken body justifies Joe White's death, a justification prepared for in White's entry on stage, in cowering flight from the pursuing posse: He is, according to Sheldon's stage directions, "a huge, very black young African . . . a horrible picture of bestial fear" (p. 79). Through Joe White, the entire doubled lie of black carnality and black bestiality receives uncontested expression in the play.

As we have seen, Sheldon's ability to transcend the most simple-minded of the one-dimensional racial conceptions of his time is embedded in the action of the play. And, through the oratory of Senator Long, Sheldon evinces larger sympathy for the possible humanity of blacks than will be found in other works of the period that deal in the same plot and imagery. The defaced images of blacks with which white writers have typically satisfied themselves can be grouped into familiar stereotypical categories. In "Negro Character as Seen by White Authors," his important synoptic essay of 1933, Sterling Brown sketched out a half-dozen or so of these categories.[17] Probably the most recurrent stereotype in the years after the turn of the century, and probably the most destructive, portrays the Negro as a beast. Thomas Dixon's *The Clansman* (1905) is the most celebrated example, with its sustained caricature of the animal-like Gus. Charles Carroll's *The Negro a Beast* (1900), a notorious pseudoscientific "demonstration" of the same point, has on the title page: "All Scientific Investigation of the Subject Proves the Negro to Be An Ape. The Reasoner of the Age, the Revelator of the Century! The Bible As It Is! The Negro and His Relations to the Human Family! The Negro a beast, but created with articulate speech, and hands, that he may be of service to his master – the White Man."

The ugly stereotype lurks everywhere in the literature of this period. A famous item in the bibliography of muckraking offers an example chilling in its casualness. Judge Ben Lindsey of Colorado made a career and a national reputation for probity out of his administration of juvenile justice, his opposition to child labor, his support for women's rights. Lincoln Steffens wrote about him in an article called "The Just Judge." After years of fighting corruption in his state, he decided to expose it. Aided by the writer Harvey O'Higgins, Lindsey in 1909 published a sensational series called "The Beast and the Jungle" in *Everybody's* magazine. The "beast" of the title was corruption. Yet, in describing a particularly violent election night, in which a black deputy sheriff was murdered, Lindsey reapplies the metaphor: "I went over to the Negro. The murder that had been bought and paid for, lay at my feet. His mute eyes were wide open; a puzzled frown puckered his black forehead that was wrinkled like an ape's. He lay there . . . with this sort of dumb question staring at me from his poor, bestial, bewildered face."[18]

In 1910, the same year *The Nigger* was published, the British critic and translator William Archer published *Through Afro-America,* the record of his several weeks of travel across the South in search of answers to the questions of race. Archer's chapters are brief, and by the third one this professedly disinterested observer is mouthing – in detail – the white party line on black bestiality, identifying it specifically as a post–Civil War phenomenon. In other words, the enslaved Negro was not only contented but good: Freedom is the source of bestiality. As Archer puts it, after commenting admiringly on the "touchingly beautiful" conduct of the slaves during the war, when wives and children were safely left under black protection: "But what matters the admission that the malignant and bestial negro did not exist forty years ago, if it has to be admitted in the same breath that he exists to-day?"[19]

Sheldon's effort to understand the reality of black experience is obviously much larger than Dixon's or Carroll's or Archer's; it is larger than those of most of his white literary contemporaries. Sheldon's sympathy finally exhausts itself, however, in pity (at best) and (at worst) in assent to the cruel racial misconceptions of his time. An altogether plausible reading of the play's logic would locate Philip Morrow's tragedy not in his suicidal enslavement to racial myths but simply in his blackness. Senator Long may preach the equality of black and white, but Joe White is a rapist and a murderer. And the play makes it quite clear that White deserves precisely what he gets; beastliness demands lynching. This, too, is a vital part of the racist equation that *The Nigger* ratifies.

In *The Negro: The Southerner's Problem* (1904), Thomas Nelson Page, one of the prominent apologists for inequality and segregation, summarized the well-worn case for lynching as a response to rape. Lynching, argued Page, is justified, "for it has its roots deep in the basic passions of humanity; the determination to put an end to the ravishing of their women by an inferior race. . . . A crusade has been preached against lynching, even as far as England; but none has been attempted against the ravishing and tearing to pieces of white women and children."[20] "Think what it means," implores the visitor William Archer, "to have this nightmare constantly present to the mind of every woman and girl in the community."[21]

Each act of lynching (and there are estimated to have been over one hundred per year in the period between 1900 and the First World War) signified far more than a particularly unspeakable act of violence against its victim. Lynching was a bloody reminder – renewed at the rate of one every three days – to the entire American black population of the double system of American law. Lynching both memorialized and sustained the subordination of justice to white hatred; it verified the fundamental impotence of blacks by removing all of them from the protections of due process. Lynching signalized at its most virulent the contamination of the American judicial system. The apartheid world of Jim Crow, which was reaching a perfected state of minute detail during these years, possessed in lynching its implicit enforcement mechanism (Plate 6).

Several years before *The Nigger*'s production, the two major politicians of the era, Theodore Roosevelt and William Jennings Bryan, linked lynching and rape in a ludicrously blind gesture of evenhandedness. Agreeing with a speech of Roosevelt's, Bryan wrote:

> The president is also to be commended for having coupled a denunciation of rape with a condemnation of lynching. Too many cry out against the lawless punishment without saying anything about the horrible crime which arouses the anger of the people. If some of the enthusiasm that is spent passing resolutions denouncing mob law was employed in condemning the unspeakable bestiality that provokes summary punishment there would be fewer instances of mob law.[22]

Of course Bryan, Roosevelt, and even Sheldon, for that matter, need to be heard in the context of their time, a time in which any number of worse attitudes were possible. Consider Tom Watson, who delivered himself of this numbingly perverse declaration in 1914: "Lynch law is a good sign. It shows that a sense of justice lives among the people."[23] For a man like Tom Watson, the character Joe White is simply evidence of what he already knows, a paranoid nightmare come to flesh-and-blood life onstage. (The irony embraced in black Joe White's being played by a white actor in blackface would, needless to say, have been altogether lost on Watson.)

If Joe White is the most gruesomely obvious stereotypical portrait in *The Nigger*, he is neither the most provocative nor the most problematic. Another of the recurring images Sterling Brown analyzes in his essay on Negro character is that of "the tragic mulatto," and this of course is Philip Morrow's role in the play. In a society even microscopically more humane than turn-of-the-century America, the mulatto might have taken symbolic shape as a consolatory or conciliatory figure. In a society more fully dedicated to simple truth, the mulatto might at least have been accepted as proof of black humanity. Instead,

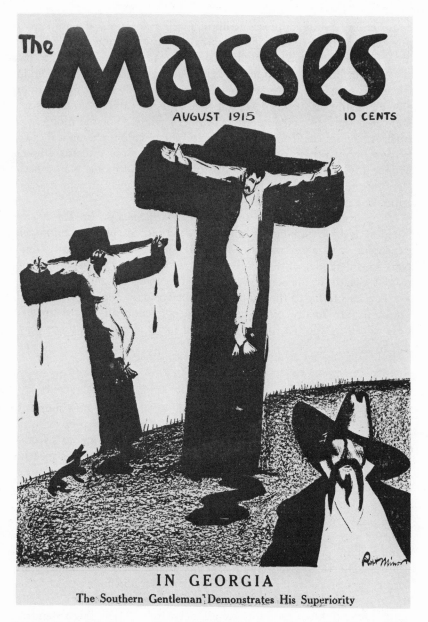

IN GEORGIA

The Southern Gentleman Demonstrates His Superiority

PLATE 6. Robert Minor's cover drawing for the August 1915 issue of *The Masses*. (Courtesy of the Tamiment Library, New York University.)

begotten by white oppression upon black subjection, the mulatto is portrayed as the product of a hierarchically divided inheritance: "From his white blood come his intellectual strivings, his unwillingness to be a slave; from his Negro blood come his baser emotional urges, his indolence, his savagery."[24] As we shall see, the allegedly scientific apparatus erected in support of this deception was immense; and by no means was it created only by self-interested southern whites. For the moment, it suffices to note the irony that despite all the pseudomathematical calculations of quantities of white and black blood, the mulatto remains irrevocably a "nigger"; one figure of Otherness among many in the elaborate turn-of-the-century American morality play in which a self-appointed native nation confronts its adversaries.

My purpose here is not to indict Edward Sheldon or *The Nigger*. Sheldon was an intelligent, inquisitive writer; his play, a serious engagement with a set of serious topics. He was by no construction a conscious defender of the southern society he rendered. His significance resides exactly in his status as an observer who brought more than an average sensitivity to the problems he analyzed in *The Nigger*. That his questions are finally overwhelmed by conventionally racist answers only confirms the hegemonic power of racial ideology in these years.

SCIENCE AND RACE

More than perhaps anyone in this period, W. E. B. Du Bois sought to batter down the walls of stereotype and caste and segregation with the engines of science. He would defeat the premises of America's second slavery with truth, systematically arrived at. Repeatedly in his speeches and essays of these years, Du Bois announces his commitment to this agenda, and in so doing he reveals as well his intellectual conformity with progressive assumptions. In 1898, Du Bois read a long paper, "The Study of the Negro Problems," before the American Academy of Political and Social Science. In that paper, which constituted as much a statement of personal principles as a manifesto for his academic colleagues, Du Bois elaborates a double theme: "The sole aim of any society is to settle its problems in accordance with its highest ideals, and the only rational method of accomplishing this is to study those problems in the light of the best scientific research."[25] That high standard, complained Du Bois, had rarely been met in the investigation of race, though the problems of race surely made up one of America's most troubling and baffling concerns. Studies of the Negro, Du Bois argued, had been deficient because they had been incomplete, unsystematic, and uncritical. Undoubtedly having in mind his own accomplishment in

The Philadelphia Negro (1899), Du Bois demands that henceforth the investigation of black life be guided by the "simple aim" of science: "the discovery of truth."[26]

Years later in 1938, on his seventieth birthday, Du Bois looked back over his whole career. In his fourth decade, the years 1898 to 1908, he himself discerned especially his allegiance to science. "The Negro problem," he thought then, "called for systematic investigation and intelligence. The world was thinking wrong about races because it did not know. The ultimate evil was ignorance and its child, stupidity. The cure for it was knowledge based on study."[27]

A grimly ironic trap lay in wait for the confident Du Bois. The history of science in these years was not to unfold along the path of accelerating liberation he foresaw. On the contrary, science inscribed a profoundly dialectical trajectory, a sustained contest between revolution and reaction. Gertrude Himmelfarb, after tracing the immense but divided impact of Darwin upon the intellectual life of Europe and America, terms the outcome "the conservative revolution."[28] Himmelfarb's fine phrase can be applied more generally, indeed to the entire collection of transactions between science and American society from the turn of the century to the First World War.

Undeniably, the theoretical and technical achievements of science, both large and small, comprise some of the most genuinely revolutionary changes on the American scene in the early twentieth century. In Chapter 1, I quoted Mark Sullivan's breathless estimate of the consequences of scientific and technological advances for daily life. It was, Sullivan said, like a "fairy story," like living "in the Arabian Nights Tales." Frank L. Baum made much the same claim when he compared the Oz he had invented invidiously to the more exciting "great outside world" of the early 1900s.[29]

The sciences of society, on the other hand, told no "fairy story." Or, perhaps more precisely, they retold the sinister fairy tales of white supremacy and racial hierarchy. Then, as now, social-scientific ideology – with important exceptions – tended to ratify the needs of concentrated capital and the prejudices of public opinion. Progressives might eagerly follow the forward march of scientific thought, they might view themselves as the natural legatees of science, they might adopt such of its strategies and methods as they could. But they could not prevent the power and prestige of science from being captured by a hundred manifest quackeries, among them most tragically a pseudo-scientifically strengthened, reactionary racism.[30]

The first years of the twentieth century witnessed a cascade of xenophobic and antidemocratic diatribes against the races and ethnic groups of Europe and Asia. Many of these outbursts carried the cachet of academic authorship. As quite a few of them made explicitly clear, their assaults on the inferior other peoples beyond the pale were most devastatingly applicable to blacks. One of the early documents in the debate over immigration restriction, "European Peasants as Immigrants," was written by the dean of the Lawrence Scientific School at Harvard University, Nathaniel S. Shaler. In Shaler's authoritative view, the Anglo-Saxon race may be taken as the norm of evolutionary perfection and Negroes as the corresponding norm of baseness.[31]

Franz Boas, of course, was the preeminent and noble exception. In essays such as "Race Problems in America";[32] in his report–ignored in the event–to the Dillingham Commission; in his service at Du Bois's request on the advisory board of The Encyclopedia of the Negro; in his book, The Mind of Primitive Man, published in 1911; Boas labored with energy and humanity against theories of racial supremacy.

Against Boas was ranged not only ignorance but much of the learned and literate communities as well. High authority in support of the lowest racial slander was not far to seek. In the latter part of the nineteenth century, the influential Darwinian popularizer Ernst Haeckel published Anthropogenie, illustrated with an engraving of an "evolutionary tree," on the branches of which sit the four highest prehuman creatures: chimpanzee, gorilla, orangutan, and Negro. The enemy, Du Bois's optimism notwithstanding, was more sinister than mere stupidity; black humanity was repudiated by a viciously misdirected intelligence.

A representative statement was to be found in the Encyclopedia Britannica.[33] The Britannica served (then more than later) as the most widely consulted repository of scientific consensus. An opinion appearing in the Britannica carried a considerable authority. The articles under the heading "Negro" that appear in the encyclopedia's successive editions therefore have a conspicuously "reliable" character. The ninth edition of the Britannica was published during the years 1875 to 1889. Because the tenth edition, published 1902–1903, was not a full-scale revision but consisted only of the issuing of supplementary volumes, the ninth edition's opinions remained ubiquitously unamended until the publication of the eleventh edition, in 1910–1911.

The thesis of A. H. Keane's essay on the Negro in the ninth edition is straightforward and uncluttered:

> Wherever found in a comparatively pure state, as on the coast of Guinea, in the Gaboon, along the lower Zambesi, and in the Bennua and Shari basins, the African aborigines present almost a greater uniformity of physical and moral type than any of the other great divisions of mankind. By the nearly unanimous consent of anthropologists this type occupies at the same time the

lowest position in the evolutionary scale, thus affording the best material for comparative study of the highest anthropoids and the human species.[34]

Keane's opinions, and his magisterial self-assurance, are less alarming in themselves than in their thoroughly representative nature: He was right in associating his mumbo jumbo with "the nearly unanimous consent of anthropologists."

Keane goes on to buttress his thesis in a familiarly "scientific" way: He enumerates fourteen separate points in which the Negro is said to differ anatomically or physiologically from the Caucasian. Such differences, needless to say, constitute *ipso facto* proof of black inferiority. Keane's itemized inventory of black difference consists of: (1) the abnormal length of the arm; (2) prognathism, or protrusion of the jaws "(index number of facial angle about 70, as compared with the Caucasian 82)"; (3) weight of brain, as indicating cranial capacity, 35 ounces "(highest gorilla, 20, average European, 45)"; (4) full black eye; (5) short, flat snub nose; (6) thick protruding lips; (7) high and prominent cheek bones; (8) exceedingly thick cranium, "enabling the Negro to butt with the head and resist blows which would inevitably break any ordinary European's skull"; (9) correspondingly weak lower limbs, with a somewhat prehensile great toe; (10) complexion deep brown or blackish, and in some cases even distinctly black; (11) short, black hair, "distinctly woolly, not merely frizzly, as Prichard supposed on insufficient evidence"; (12) thick skin, "cool, soft, and velvety to the touch, mostly hairless, and emitting a peculiarly rancid odor, compared by Pruner Bey to that of the buck goat"; (13) frame of medium height; (14) the cranial sutures, which close earlier in the Negro than in other races.

How would Du Bois, or anyone else eager to find in the potent new sciences the instruments of human liberation, even begin to reply to this? Keane's racism is arrayed in all of science's impressive trappings – the massings of measurements, the latinate terminology, the learned citations, the appeal to authoritative consensus. Du Bois had appealed only for the "simple truth" that science would discover. He asked that America's blacks and whites submit their racial struggle to the arbitration of scientific inquiry. Keane's essay provides the bitterly ironic reply.

The word "revolution" has a complex history as an English political term, but it begins indisputably to denote change or alteration in the commonwealth only in the early seventeenth century.[35] The original meaning of the word, of course, now overshadowed, was in astronomy: the turning of the planets in their orbits. The crucial moment in the history of the word corresponds to a great juncture in Western intellectual history. The publication of *De Revolutionibus Orbium Coelestium* in 1543 marks the moment at which the word "revolution" exploded its specialized definition and became the commanding trope and dominant idea of the modern age.

Keane's pseudoscientific denigration of black humanity is the whimper in which that explosion subsides. Scandalously on public show here is the custom of social science to ingratiate itself with prevailing opinion. After all, in his own view Keane was only cementing with scientific precision the inferences of common sense. What seems to us in retrospect self-evident superstition seemed to him and his contemporaries equivalently self-evident truth.[36] The disfiguring images of blacks we have been reviewing throughout this chapter are, let us not forget, deeply rooted in Western culture. In *White over Black*, Winthrop Jordan produced a controversial book. Whatever the merits of his analysis, his research codified beyond all doubt the virtually axiomatic insistence of European whites, in particular Anglo-Saxon whites, on the subhumanity of blacks. The axiom preceded any actual encounter between Europe and Africa. The Manichaean symbolism at the very core of Western civilization – the conception of blackness as the omnicompetent sign of all evil, the correlative alliance of whiteness with good, and the logical deduction that perpetual enmity must exist between the two – doomed black people before they physically entered onto the stage of European-American history.[37]

BETWEEN BLACK AND WHITE

The domination of black stereotypes over American consciousness is most incontrovertibly and most tragically proved by their ability to elicit the assent of some of their victims. I have from time to time in these pages made reference to Gramsci's notion of ideological hegemony. Gramsci used this term to delineate what he took to be his Marxist insight into the phenomenon he watched at work among large numbers of proletarians who conformed their values to those of their masters. By analogy, the phrase is perhaps also appropriate here to describe that desperate condition beyond tactical accommodation in which blacks in indeterminable numbers internalized values that turned on the axis of their own self-debasement. Of the literary documents relevant to this issue from the turn of the century, the caricatures of blacks regularly created by Paul Laurence Dunbar in his dialect verse come readily to mind.[38]

The three novels of Charles Waddell Chesnutt have routinely been accused of ratifying this sort of black false consciousness.[39] In fact, Chesnutt's novels reveal a far more complex world of attitudes. His characters typically occupy a border region between black and white, divided in mind and sometimes in allegiance, confronting the question of personal identity at an elemental level. If, to cite Richard Wright's resonant epigram, the Negro is America's metaphor, that function was never more manifest than in the early twentieth-century ambiguity dramatized in Chesnutt's fiction.

The House behind the Cedars (1900) was Chesnutt's first novel and is probably his best. The title summarizes Chesnutt's attentive concern, in all his tales and novels as well as in his own life, with place. (It is an unsurprising concern for any American black, and even less surprising for a black born in Cleveland before the Civil War who found himself living in North Carolina during Reconstruction and the early compromise years.) The house that stands hidden behind its screen of cedars on a small-town North Carolina street in the late 1860s, detached from any commerce with either the black or the white communities, is immediately established as a potent symbol of isolation. Living in the house are Mis' Molly Walden, the aging, light-colored mulatto who was once the mistress of one of the town's prominent white men, and her white-colored, late-teenaged daughter, Rena. The novel opens with the return to the house of Molly's elder child, John. Under the name John Warwick, he has spent the past few years passing for white in South Carolina. There, by virtue of his exceptional talents, his personal appeal, and his racial disguise, John Warwick has climbed easily toward success in the familiar Alger manner. His rise has been signalized by his marriage to a white woman, soon deceased, who has left him both her modest fortune and a son.

Warwick returns by night, in order that he remain unseen and unremembered by his native town. He proposes to take his sister back to South Carolina with him, to care for his son, to share in his success, to pass into the white world with him, and eventually to find an eligible and affluent white mate. Moving forward from that premise, the novel's thirty-three chapters trace primarily two large movements. In the first half of the book, the Warwick scheme matures quickly and fully, and Rena is soon the fiancée of George Tryon, a white lawyer of extensive means and still greater prospects. The novel's second half tells the consequences of Tryon's discovery of Rena's secret: his instant repudiation of her and her subsequent life as a teacher in a small black school. There she is pursued by her employer, the lascivious black superintendent of schools Jeff Wain, and by the repentant and ardent Tryon. The book concludes with Rena fleeing from both men and losing her way in a swamp. She falls unconscious and dies shortly after she is found. Her body is brought back home to her mother's house behind the cedars by a loyal, dark-skinned neighbor named Frank, who has for years kept his love for Rena hidden.

The House behind the Cedars carries a much more conflicted thematic burden than its reputation would suggest. It is, to begin with, true (though it is only a part of the novel's truth) that some of the black characters articulate without much complication an antiblack racist ideology. The black teenager Plato, to give an example from the minor characters, is "proud of the fact that he had once belonged to Mars Geo'ge" Tryon.[40] He is, in fact, prouder of that than of anything else about himself, and he continues to behave accordingly. Mis' Molly goes a step further and thinks of herself as actually human in proportion as she is white. Her circle of acquaintance does not extend to people of decidedly dark color. The narrator introduces a party Mis' Molly presides over by clarifying for the less-informed reader the distinction at the center of her sociology:

> All people of mixed blood were called "mulattoes" in North Carolina. There were dark mulattoes and bright mulattoes. Mis' Molly's guests were mostly of the bright class, most of them more than half white, and few of them less. In Mis' Molly's small circle, straight hair was the only palliative of a dark complexion. (P. 188)

She did not, we are told, "sympathize greatly with the new era opened up for the emancipated slaves"; indeed, since the war's outcome had diminished her own circumstances, she often "sighed for the old days, because to her they had been the good days" (p. 144). It is correct, though anachronistic and irrelevant, to call Mis' Molly's attitude accommodationist and her consciousness false. It would also be wrong to refuse the small understanding needed to trace the links of the chain that bind her prejudices to her material fate. In any case, it would deform the novel substantially to identify her opinion with Chesnutt's. The novel's moral judgments, to remark on only one subject, in no way conform to Molly's racial hierarchy: The book's splendid heroine is the light-skinned Rena; the most sinister character, Wain, is a mulatto of middle hue; and Frank, the worthiest of all the story's figures, is also its darkest.

Yet there are elements of ideological capitulation in the book, which reveal themselves in Chesnutt's treatment of the major character, John Warwick. What takes the form in Mis' Molly's case of a doubly ironic racial-moral blindness appears in Warwick as cold-blooded calculation. At least as far as his thoughts are revealed to us, Warwick is troubled by his racial masquerade for only one reason, and that has nothing to do with any faintest hint of failed allegiances or existential anguish. John Warwick intends to go far, and he has observed that blacks do not. Race therefore has become for him a matter of tactics rather than identity; the agonizing questions associated with passing are cut loose in his mind from their political and ethical implications and float eerily in a seemingly neutral sea of detachable strategy and planning.

John Warwick views his racial heritage, then, as a handicap to be surmounted, in the manner of a bad eye or leg, and not as (even potentially) a fundamental element in a robustly equal humanity. Warwick is oblivious to the devastating irony of his choice. Booker T. Washington, we saw earlier, offered an oddly casual recollection of the self-naming that took place widely among American blacks after Emancipation. The former John Walden has gone a step further, manufacturing for himself not only a name but a new race and, perforce, a new history. More precisely, since his history cannot be made "white," he has denied to himself a historical existence altogether. Herein lies the tragic irony: His act of self-creation is simultaneously an act of self-destruction.

To apply different but converging terms, Warwick embodies, with the solidity of allegory, the farthest reach of the cultural schizophrenia that has been this chapter's concern. I use the term, to be sure, in an analogic rather than in a clinical sense. Whether Warwick consciously considers his sundered state or doesn't is just about beside the point. Like the house behind the cedars, Warwick is caught between two worlds; and, as he would be an inhabitant in both, he finds a home in neither.

Chesnutt appears to admire Warwick for his decision to pass as white. He speaks, at least, of Warwick's "great courage" (p. 116), his transcendence through subterfuge of the stereotype of Negro cowardice. In proportion to that admiration, Chesnutt lays himself justly open to the charge of collaborating with the enemy. But again, while true, this is but a portion of the novel's truth. Chesnutt's most sustained admiration is reserved neither for John Warwick nor for his sister when they are passing for white in the first part of the novel, but for Rena after her secret has been revealed. When the shock of the discovery has subsided, her brother proposes that they simply try again – move farther away, to the North this time, and carry off the concealment successfully. Rena refuses. At first her motives are unclear, even to herself. In part she acts not for racial reasons but out of loyalty toward her mother, reinforced by a religious guilt. As her life among black people proceeds, however, she grows toward them, and her decision finally rises to the level of conscious allegiance:

Her early training had not directed her thoughts to the darker people with whose fate her own was bound up so closely, but rather away from them. She had been taught to despise them, because they were not so white as she was, and had been slaves while she was free. Her life in her brother's home, by removing her from immediate contact with them, had given her a different point of view – one which emphasized their shortcomings, and thereby made vastly clearer to her the gulf that separated them from the new world in which she lived; so that when misfortune threw her back upon them, the reaction brought her nearer than before. Where once she had seemed able to escape from them, they were now, it appeared, her inalienable race. (Pp. 174–175)

The House behind the Cedars, in other words, is only in smaller part a novel about passing at all. In larger part, it is about *not* passing. Despite the opportunity and the shameful absence, at this time and in this place, of any other realistic escape from the unmerited punishment that follows from the unearned "guilt" of blackness, Rena chooses her race. Chesnutt measures her fate to the inch: The "taint of black blood was the unpardonable sin . . . more far-reaching in its consequences than any blood-curdling crime" (p. 116; clauses rearranged). If the absurd, in a quite technical sense, involves the radical separation of cause and effect, then, as Richard Wright and others have often suggested, American blacks lived intimately with the reality of absurdity long before the term was available to define it.

The vocabulary that *was* at Chesnutt's disposal, and which he used by turns mindlessly and with considerable sophistication, was that of romance. I do not mean merely the conventions of the romance genre, which Chesnutt indulges in to a fare-thee-well – the rhythm of jeopardy and escape, accompanied by countless coincidences; the melodramatic villain and heroine; the heroine's "beautiful death" at the finale. The prevalence of these devices, indeed, has obscured Chesnutt's ultimate transcendence of them, his shrewd use of romance as a satiric weapon against the same society in which his protagonist John Warwick is losing himself.

The fifth chapter of the novel describes the annual tournament sponsored by the Clarence, South Carolina, Social Club:

The influence of Walter Scott was strong upon the old South. The South before the war was essentially feudal, and Scott's novels of chivalry appealed forcefully to the feudal heart. During the month preceding the Clarence tournament, the local bookseller had closed out his entire stock of "Ivanhoe," consisting of five copies, and had taken orders for seven copies more. The tournament scene in this popular novel furnished the model after which these bloodless imitations of the ancient passages-at-arms were conducted. (Pp. 42–43)

Significantly, the tournament comprises our first glimpse of the white civilization John Warwick has successfully penetrated. The elaborate game is not merely an episode: It is an emblematic tableau. Chesnutt's target, here and throughout the novel, is the wholesale substitution of fantasy for reality in the culture of the American South. Myriad interlocking levels of pretense and sham are exposed in the book. Post–Civil War southern white society is imitating the forms of the antebellum culture. In turn, the prewar culture, though built on a far stronger economic base, imitated the chivalric modes and models of Walter Scott's romances. But Scott's work, let us remember, a fountainhead of the slither of the pandemic medieval revival, retailed one sentimentalized imitation of medieval life after another. *Ivanhoe* has roughly the same relation to historical reality as Tom Sawyer's "A-rabs."

If this whirligig of pretense had had indifferent human consequences, then it would have provoked only amusement. On the contrary, the toll in life and spirit was enormous. Entangled in the web of white fantasy, providing the expropriated and grotesquely manipulated "reality" upon which the fictions fed, were American's blacks. Stretched on the twinned rack of economic and legal tyranny, black men and women had even the fact of their identity torn from them. Here is South Carolina race law, quoted by Chesnutt in the novel:

"The term mulatto . . . is not invariably applicable to every mixture of African blood with the European, nor is one having all the features of a white to be ranked with the degraded class designated by the laws of this State as persons of color, because of some remote taint of the Negro race. Juries would probably be justified in holding a person to be white in whom the admixture of African blood did not exceed one eighth. And even where color or feature are doubtful, it is a question for the jury to decide by reputation, by reception into society, and by their exercise of the privileges of the white man, as well as by admixture of blood." (P. 154)

This is a world more fantastic than Scott's, and far more sinister in its power to shape human beings into the stuff of its self-serving fictions. At the innermost of the circles of pretense stand two figures: John Warwick, who has chosen the ultimate pretense of imitating a three- or fourfold imitation, and his sister Rena, who refuses. As Chesnutt has told us, hers is not the path of escape from doom. Rena's choice is the entry to whatever possibilities of self-realization may have survived the contamination of America's racist disease. Her death, whatever its genealogy in melodrama, signifies nothing less than Chesnutt's inability to imagine black freedom.

W. E. B. DU BOIS

Throughout these pages, W. E. B. Du Bois has appeared as a comparative standard, a relatively fixed term in the debate over racial definition being conducted by both blacks and whites in the early twentieth century. So he saw himself and so, in large measure, do we still see him. Yet, whatever its broad accuracy, such a perception of Du Bois tends to ignore fundamental elements in his personality and work, and tends therefore to obscure his more complex reality. Du Bois did not discover the "twoness" of American blacks by sweeping the telescope of his genius across the night sky of somebody *else's* experience: Du Bois knew of the divided mind of the black because it was his own.

> The Negro is a sort of seventh son, born with a veil, and gifted with second-sight in this American world, – a world which yields him no true self-consciousness, but only lets him see himself through the revelation of the other worlds. It is a peculiar sensation, this double-consciousness, this sense of always looking at one's self through the eyes of others, of measuring one's soul by the tape of a world that looks on in amused contempt and pity. One ever feels his twoness, – an American, a Negro; two souls, two thoughts, two unreconciled strivings; two warring ideals in one dark body, whose dogged strength alone keeps it from being torn asunder.[41]

The resolution Du Bois hopes for is integrative – "to merge his double self into a better and truer self" – but not deferentially so. Opposite equals advance toward the merging Du Bois foresees (or wants to foresee): The Negro "would not Africanize America, for America has too much to teach the world and Africa. He would not bleach his Negro soul in a flood of white Americanism, for he knows that Negro blood has a message for the world. He simply wishes to make it possible for a man to be both a Negro and an American" (p. 3).

While its basic theme is doubleness, the voices and tones of *The Souls of Black Folk* are many. Du Bois masterfully combines statistical data, anecdotes, analysis, and oracular lyricism. His book is at once personal testament and solemn prophecy, a dirge for the bloody past of American chances lost and a polemical forecast of the doomed future white bigotry has earned. In its adumbration of the role of the "talented tenth," in its evocation of the indomitable will of ordinary black citizens, and in the example of its own wisdom, *The Souls of Black Folk* is also, if less resolutely, a hymn envisioning the humane new day that could fall to the grasp of an America willing to exchange its hegemonic prejudices for common sense.[42]

The social and political turmoil of the early 1900s only propels the divided mind of American blacks into starker polarities: "The worlds within and without the Veil of Color are changing, and changing rapidly, but not at the same rate, not in the same way; and this must produce a peculiar wrenching of the soul, a peculiar sense of doubt and bewilderment" (p. 202). Du Bois's personal bewilderment was caused, to put it summarily, by the failure of history in his lifetime to go forward. Despite the promises of law and constitution, despite the educational and economic achievements of blacks during their single generation of freedom, the American South had become little more than an armed and organized system for intimidating blacks, and the American North had been reduced to bored collaboration. As Charles Crowe phrases it: "The retreat from Reconstruction . . . reached a nadir in the Progressive era."[43]

For a man like Du Bois, who sought for the black community not individual concessions but equality of opportunity as a matter of right, who did not demand a more comfortable second-class status but recognition as a member of the one class of American humanity, the facts of segregation and disfranchisement and harassment stretched his nerve to its breaking point every waking moment of his life. And for Du Bois in particular, with his Ph.D. from Harvard and his postdoctoral study in Germany, his lengthy list of publications and his gigantic command of Western literary and philosophical culture, sitting in the Jim Crow car and bearing the discourtesy of illiterate Georgia crackers must have seemed quite simply lunatic. He must often have wondered whether he waked or slept. Eventually, we know, Du Bois would resolve his intellectual struggle by accepting a fairly dogmatic Marxism and his personal struggle by leaving the country.

But those resolutions lie beyond the years of our concern. In the early twentieth century, W. E. B. Du Bois's life and thought take on the pattern of a fierce search, an odyssey that leads to a long series of differing hypotheses, some of them overlapping, some complementary, some contradictory. In *The Souls of Black Folk,* for example, he derides socialism as "cheap and dangerous" (p. 151); in 1910 he joins the Socialist Party, only to resign in 1912. At the turn of the century, in *The Souls of Black Folk* and elsewhere, he calls for the leadership of the talented tenth; by the end of the decade, that call would become muted. Correlatively, Du Bois's conception of the black nation would emerge with growing clarity during those years. In the years around 1900, as we have seen, Du Bois declares his passionate belief in the liberating efficacy of science; that belief would become attenuated by disillusioning experience over the next few years. When the First World War commences, Du Bois supports it; but within a few years he is savagely interpreting the war as a monstrous proof of the white world's conspiracy against blacks.[44]

When Du Bois speaks of "the writhing of the age translated into black," his own conflicted striving provides the preeminent example. Viewing his world simultaneously as sociologist and Jeremiah, committed to both materialism and the transcendent spirit, locating historical causality alternately in politics and economics, demanding at once integration and the separate identity of the black people, a middle-class intellectual proud to "sit with Shakespeare" and equally proud to pronounce his blackness, Du Bois in these years proves himself "the epitome," in August Meier's phrase, of "the paradoxes in American Negro thought."[45]

Darkwater (1920) is a collection of essays, poems, fiction, and autobiographical sketches going back as far as 1904 and transcribing Du Bois's external and internal debates in the years between the beginning of the Niagara Movement and the close of the war. The book, in some ways the sequel to *The Souls of Black Folk,* has been termed the most reliable guide to Du Bois's intellectual probings in these years. It bears witness to the several different grounds on which he sought to base his answer to poverty, to the oppression of both blacks and women, to the economic injustices of capitalism. *Darkwater* captures the powerful threefold tension that agitated Du Bois in the early twentieth century: the triangle formed by socialism, black nationalism, and liberal idealism.[46]

Du Bois's first novel, *The Quest of the Silver Fleece* (1911), also provides exceptional insight into the ambivalence that both energized and frustrated him. Indeed, *The Quest* so thoroughly combines realism and romance, naturalism and sentimental melodrama, documentary verisimilitude and allegory, scholarship and mysticism, that it may usefully be taken as paradigmatic of Du Bois's inner dialectic in these years.

Although the number of white and black characters in this long novel is large, *The Quest* is principally the story of two young Alabama blacks, Bles Alwyn and Zora. The opening chapter is significant both for its title, "Dreams," which initiates a motif to which we shall return, and because it introduces the hero Bles as a young man leaving home to start his adult career with education. Bles temporarily loses his way in a swamp, a decisively symbolic swamp in which he briefly encounters the wildly beautiful Zora, who lives in a sordid cabin in the wilderness with her mother, Elspeth. Elspeth is a grotesque figure out of Gothic: "Short, broad, black and wrinkled, with yellow fangs, red hanging lips and wicked eyes."[47] Elspeth inhabits the swamp and represents its values: lawlessness, decay, rank sensuality, all intensified by hints of actual witchcraft.

For much of its length, *The Quest of the Silver Fleece* tells of the much-troubled romance of Bles and Zora. It tells as well of Bles's efforts to make a career in Washington, D.C., and of Zora's striving to transform the swamp, to clear and drain and cultivate it and turn its sinister fecundity to productive purposes. Out of the rich soil of the swamp will come cotton, not just a commodity in this novel but a symbol of hope and progress, the "silver fleece," with both its sources and its terminus in epic and myth.

> The cry of the naked was sweeping the world. From the peasant toiling in Russia, the lady lolling in London, the chieftain burning in Africa, and the Esquimaux freezing in Alaska; from long lines of hungry men, from patient, sad-eyed women, from old folk and creeping children went up the cry, "Clothes, clothes!" Far away the wide black land that belts the South . . . the dense black land sensed the cry and heard the cry of answering life within the vast dark beast. All that dark earth heaved in mighty travail with the bursting bolls of the cotton. (P. 54)[48]

Around Bles and Zora, Du Bois constructs a detailed, sometimes cumbersome plot, involving greedy whites of both the genteel Old South and the pushing New North; schemes to corner the cotton market and to buy and sell legislation and high offices; accommodating middle-class Washington blacks, whose lives are spent in self-denying imitation of white society ("black white people," they are called [p. 240]); all of this acted out in settings that range from Alabama to New York. The rich and politically powerful whites, abetted by collaborationist blacks and by the hegemony of custom and ideology and law, labor to manipulate both Bles and Zora, to exploit their talents and in the end to destroy them and through them the emerging black consciousness they signify. These countless adversaries represent Force, the oppressions of past and present, the failure of both black individualism and of the structures of cooperation within the victimized black community that would allow an equal fight.

The realism of the novel resides primarily in its rendering of these agents of oppression and of the damage they inflict. One of Du Bois's chief strengths as a writer of both fiction and nonfiction consisted in his ability to make vivid the landscapes of human suffering. *The Quest of the Silver Fleece* is filled with brief vignettes and long scenes devoted to

such landscapes. The degradations of peonage under the crop-lien system, the daily physical violence and verbal insults, the humiliation of
white-owned justice, the decline into despair or self-loathing: This is
the South of the turn of the century for blacks, and it is the fate that
must lie waiting for Bles and Zora.

That their destiny is different, that their doom hovers over them only
to be lifted suddenly at the novel's close, that they end the book with
their lives, integrity, and prospects all intact, discloses accurately one
dimension of Du Bois's ambivalence. He disposes of his hero and heroine as he would wish for them, and as their merits would deserve,
rather than as his unflinching analysis of their plight would demand.
This outcome is worth exploring in a little more detail.

More than a love story, *The Quest* has the contours of a familiar
success story – indeed, of two parallel success stories. Where the other
characters are built to human scale, both Bles and Zora are figures out
of romance, bigger than life, gifted with an overplus of talent, courage,
and grace. Their first labor together, surreptitiously clearing a couple of
acres of the swamp and planting cotton, succeeds beyond all expectation: The crop is more abundant and of finer quality than any other in
the region. When a misunderstanding divides them during the book's
middle chapters, the pattern of outsized success continues.

Bles goes to Washington, establishes himself directly as the finest
orator in America, and single-handedly swings the presidential election
to the Republicans by keeping the black vote in line. He does so because he believes in Lincoln's party; but his efforts are conformable to
less sincere white maneuvering, and he finds himself rewarded with the
promise of nomination to the job of treasurer of the United States, a
post higher than any previously held by an American black. Always
subordinating personal advancement to honor, however, he chooses to
sacrifice the appointment when he learns of a piece of Republican racial
perfidy. Moving to the predictable rhythms of romance, he returns to
Alabama, apparently but only momentarily ruined.

There he rejoins Zora. Without his knowledge, since he left her Zora
has spent most of her time as a lady's maid to the wife of a powerful
Washington politician. She has educated herself, has watched invisibly
over and actually assisted Bles's own short career, and has now returned with a clear vision of the mission she will undertake to lead the
black people out of their bondage.

Zora had been given ten thousand dollars by her former mistress
when she resigned from service (the first of a long chain of implausible
events that propels the book's conclusion). With that money she buys
the swamp. She gathers an army of blacks to buy and work parcels of
the land, recruiting them by magnificent preaching at Sunday worship

meetings. She organizes the division and clearing of the land, the establishment of a communitarian society, the building of a school and an infirmary. She successfully defends her title to the property in court, acting as her own lawyer. She devises a strategy to outwit an enraged and drunken white mob that descends on the community. And, in the novel's last chapter, she reaps the double harvest of her victory. First, she learns that Colonel Cresswell, a former slaveowner, an unreconstructed bigot throughout the novel, and Zora's most malevolent enemy, has repented at his death and has left two hundred thousand dollars and his plantation to help the good work. And second, Zora proposes marriage to Bles.

Zora is indeed, as she is called, a "wonder-woman" (p. 421), her success "a superhuman miracle" (p. 400). What Zora is manifestly *not*, for better or worse, is the credible protagonist of the realistic novel whose virtually naturalist premises Du Bois has spent several hundred pages elaborating. Multiplied coincidences and improbabilities are needed to snatch an unlikely happy ending out of the vise of this book's logic. Together, these benign but gratuitous twists and turns split the novel in two. Or, to use a different figure, Du Bois grafts the consolatory but ungainly blossom of a fairy tale ending onto the unsightly but robust stalk of actuality. Recall the title of the first chapter, "Dreams." Much of the novel's thematic dissonance is compressed into Du Bois's divided response to that word. On the one hand, *The Quest of the Silver Fleece,* like everything else Du Bois ever wrote, declares an interdiction against dreams, dreams that arise from and lead to idleness and a retreat from the tasks of the world. Every bit as strongly as Booker T. Washington, Du Bois was dedicated to the ethic of hard work, and dreams are an impediment to labor. On the other hand, dreams can provide imagery that makes the purposes of work concrete.

Zora's triumph is Du Bois's dream. Evading causal logic on behalf of symbolic gesture, Zora is Du Bois's vision of the journey's end, a vision made more poignant than strong by its transparent implausibility.

Aside from the generally inspiriting notion of the black nation's rise, two issues in particular are knit together in Zora's achievement. First, through Zora, Du Bois continues his debate with Washington over the right definition of education. Washington's arguments – sometimes parodies of them – are scattered across the pages of *The Quest*; significantly, they are spoken without exception by white racists. Equally significantly, Du Bois's ideal of a liberal education tied to self-realization and public service is articulated by a Miss Smith, one of those northern white schoolma'ams who came South after the Civil War and whom Du Bois warmly admired. "I want," says she with heat to a small group of bigoted whites, "to make these children full-fledged men and women, strong, self-reliant, honest, without any 'ifs' and 'ands' to their development" (p. 177).

Given voice by Miss Smith, the Du Boisean ideal is embodied in Zora, who begins the novel unable to read or write and who at the end is presiding over a flourishing school. She takes Bles for a tour, concluding with her own study. She points to a shelf of books she calls "my university" (p. 399). Bles scans the titles: "Plato's Republic, Gorky's 'Comrades,' a Cyclopedia of Agriculture, Balzac's novels, Spencer's 'First Principles,' Tennyson's Poems." Whatever particular gloss might be attached to each of these titles as an entry to the novel's themes, Du Bois's general intention is plain: Zora commands a cross section of liberal culture. Manual labor, straightforward practical work, has its valuable place, but it is outnumbered by poetry and fiction and philosophy. Zora's own multiple accomplishments, as a farmer, a manager, a lawyer, and even a military tactician, collaborate to "prove" Du Bois's conception of education.

The second issue brought to a conclusion in Zora's achievement is religious. Throughout the book, Zora is associated with religious images and language. When she and Bles are working in the swamp in the early chapters, he builds her a small tree hut of vines and branches. The sole decoration is "a little picture in blue and gold of Bouguereau's Madonna" (p. 97). Much later, a madonna also hangs on a wall of Zora's study, near her "university." Most significantly, Zora's mission to her people is conceived by her in religious terms: She has experienced a "resurrection," a "conversion," not to Christ but to the black people. She has found "the Way," in solidarity with her black fellows (pp. 296–297). She refers to this as her "calling."

The vocabulary of Zora's exertions, in short, is a displaced religious discourse. As we have seen, she recruits her army of owner-laborers by preaching her new gospel in churches, and as she does so she literally outpreaches the congregation's minister, a Reverend Jones. Jones unsuccessfully exhorts the black people to content themselves with Christian self-abnegation and humility. Du Bois's purposes in translating Christian language and action are several. He wants, first, to talk his people out of their debilitating allegiance to the slave ideology imposed on them by whites. In addition, he wants to invest his alternative revelation with the same mythic energy and dignity as the conventional religion it will replace. Against Christianity's oppressive campaign to turn blacks white, Du Bois opposes the subversive strategy of turning a secularized Christianity black.

Zora first appears in *The Quest* as a near-apparition, as a figure in Bles Alwyn's dream in the swamp. In the final chapter, set in the spring, she is sitting "in the transformed swamp – now a swamp in name only – beneath the great oak, dreaming. And what she dreamed there in the golden day she dared not formulate even to her own soul" (p. 426). Zora's apotheosis is the dream that Du Bois dared, but only in the guise of fiction, to formulate. It is a vision, not a program nor even a fully convincing statement. But its false starts and internal inconsistencies, its evident ambivalence and tensions, reveal Du Bois's personal struggle to discover what could be affirmed, and they stand for the almost insurmountable obstacles confronting American black people in the early twentieth century.

Chapter 6

Woman's place:
Edith Wharton and others

The struggle for the right to vote occupied the center of feminist attention in the early years of the twentieth century. Though efforts of women to secure this fundamental entitlement can be traced back several generations before 1900, the Nineteenth Amendment was not ratified until 1920. The early twentieth century witnessed the climactic episodes in the campaign, as the suffrage movement, according to its leading historian, "came of age" in the years 1906–1913.[1] Susan B. Anthony's death in 1906 culminated a decade of mounting suffragist frustration. Only a handful of state suffrage referenda had been conducted in those years, and all had been unsuccessful. The federal amendment was making no progress. Politicians at all levels, President Roosevelt among them, met the demands of women with courteous indifference, amused contempt, or worse.

The decade following Anthony's death, however, though it contained almost as many reversals as victories, brought women near the brink of success. More effective leaders emerged, among them Harriet Stanton Blatch, Alice Paul, and Carrie Chapman Catt; if Catt's National Suffrage Association and Paul's more militant Congressional Union (later The Woman's Party) treated each other disputatiously, their combined effect was nonetheless powerful. A number of state referenda were won. The Progressive Party, headed by now ex-president Roosevelt, included a woman suffrage plank in its 1912 presidential platform. Interest in the federal amendment was revived, and the measure was finally passed (in part, to be sure, as a consequence of the First World War), on January 10, 1918. The vote was 274 to 136, barely the required two-thirds majority.

Despite the forecasts of some supporters of woman suffrage, America's electoral politics absorbed the new voters with apparent serenity. If men voting alone could elect Grant and Hayes in turn, women voting with men would elect Coolidge and Hoover. Perhaps the failure of the Nineteenth Amendment to inaugurate an electoral millennium explains the inclination of some historians, women as well as men, to underrate the significance of the suffrage movement. The franchise was in fact of the most profound importance: Its denial had for centuries epitomized America's repudiation of the adulthood, the dignity, and the power of women. If winning the vote has proved only a chapter in the history of equal rights, it is an altogether critical chapter.

In addition to the immense efforts women devoted to the suffrage movement, the list of other political and social battles they waged in the early years of the century is impressively long. And though some of the issues they contested were of preeminent or even exclusive interest to women, others reached to the conditions of society as a whole. The General Federation of Women's Clubs, for example, founded in 1890, had one million members by 1912. More important, the federation's emphasis shifted during those years, from the organized contemplation of high culture to an increasingly articulate concern with social reform. Mrs. Sarah Platt Decker, elected president of the federation in 1904, summarized the organization's changed agenda in the irony of her presidential address: "Ladies . . . I have an important piece of news for you. Dante is dead. He has been dead for several centuries and I think it is time that we dropped the study of his inferno and turned attention to our own."[2]

Acting as individuals but more often in increasingly effective groups, relying by turns on moral suasion, economic pressure, and legislative lobbying, women intervened in America's public life. Child and woman labor, pure food and drugs, education, penology, rehabilitation – these were some of the principal questions to which women turned their energies. The National Consumers League, founded in 1899, attempted to educate consumers about the facts of female employment in retail stores and to persuade consumers to patronize shops listed on the league's "White List." The Women's Trade Union League was formed in Boston in 1903 to provide what organized labor's men (specifically, the American Federation of Labor) would not: a unionized mechanism for improving women's working conditions. The first significant strike by working women was the walkout by shirtwaist workers in New York City and Philadelphia in September 1909.[3]

Aside from their kaleidoscopic activities in these various public arenas during the early 1900s, the speeches and pamphlets and books produced by women on their own behalf constituted a sustained reappraisal of the role of women in American society. Elizabeth Cady Stanton's *Woman's Bible,* for example, whose two volumes appeared in 1895 and 1898, analyzed in detail the pervasive misogyny of the Old Testament.

The Bible teaches that woman brought sin and death into the
world, that she precipitated the fall of the race, that she was
arraigned before the judgment seat of Heaven, tried, condemned
and sentenced. Marriage for her was to be a condition of bondage,
maternity a period of suffering and anguish, and in silence and
subjection, she was to play the role of a dependent on man's
bounty for all her material wants, and for all the information she
might desire on the vital questions of the hour, she was com-
manded to ask her husband at home. Here is the Bible position of
woman briefly summed up. (P. I, p. 7)

Stanton's self-appointed, herculean task was to debunk the allegedly
divine authorization of male supremacy by ridiculing its biblical source.
But the constellation of myths surrounding woman's place dies hard, as
Margaret Sanger also found when, a few years later, she commenced
her career of birth control education and advocacy. Her landmark pam-
phlet, *Family Limitation* (1917), is directed to working-class women. In
it, Sanger appeals to working women to consult their own economic
and sexual interests in the matter of conception: "Don't be over sentimental in this important phase of hygiene. The inevitable fact is that
unless you prevent the male sperm from entering the womb, you are
going to become pregnant. Women of the working class, especially
wage workers, should not have more than two children at most."[4]
Stanton on religion; Sanger on sexuality; Elizabeth Otley, Helen
Sumner, and Mary Conyngton on labor: These and many others made
important contributions to the changing understanding of women.[5]
    Of all the polemics and essays in theory to appear around the turn of
the century, one of the most far-reaching in its scope, and for many
years one of the most influential, was *Women and Economics* (1898), by
Charlotte Perkins Gilman. Poet, novelist, sociologist, and sexual theoretician, she was ranked by Carrie Chapman Catt as the leading feminist thinker of her generation. More recently, Alice Rossi asserted
the same claim: Rossi calls Gilman the "leading intellectual in the
woman's movement during the first two decades of the twentieth
century."[6]
    Women and Economics is an exhaustive inventory of the evils inflicted
upon women, and upon society as a whole, by the patriarchal, andro-
centric traditions that define what Gilman calls the "sexuo-economic
relation." Written from approximately the perspective of Lester Ward's
Reform Darwinist sociology, Gilman's book lays out an unsystematic,
impatient, repetitive, but cumulatively stunning indictment of contemporary attitudes and behavior. Gilman's demand is for the complete
emancipation of women. Particular reforms – in voting laws, in wages,

in education–Gilman considers desirable but insufficient. As women
are totally subjected, so must they be totally liberated.

The chief instrument of female oppression, according to Gilman, is
motherhood: not the biological activity, of course, but the idealized
institution, what Gilman calls "matriolatry."[7] She rehearses at length
the virtually sacrosanct conception of motherhood that dominates her
culture, but she interprets that sanctity to be at bottom a matter of
economic and political expediency for men. Women have been defined
by their sex-function alone, leaving to men an uncontested mastery
over all the machinery of public life in exchange for an occasional
sentimental gesture toward motherhood. Ironically, in Gilman's view,
the systematic exclusion of women from most of the events and places
of life not only victimizes the women, it makes them utterly inadequate
in the one job left to them.

> The human mother does less for her young, both absolutely and
> proportionately, than any kind of mother on earth. She does not
> obtain food for them, nor covering, nor shelter, nor protection,
> nor defence. She does not educate them beyond the personal hab-
> its required in the family circle and in her limited range of social
> life. The necessary knowledge of the world, so indispensable to
> every human being, she cannot give, because she does not possess
> it. (P. 189)

In short, women, who are ruthlessly prohibited from contact with just
about all branches of human activity outside the home, are unable to
educate their children into knowledge and experience. This is what Gilman means, too, by her designedly shocking assertion that human
motherhood is inferior to that of animals: "Human motherhood is more
pathological than any other, more morbid, defective, irregular, diseased.
Human childhood is similarly pathological. We, as animals, are very
inferior animals in this particular" (p. 181). The culturally imposed definition of human maternity is a lopsided, destructive caricature.

At the core of this deranged overspecialization of women into a
single function lies, as Gilman's title proposes, the economic opportunism of men. It is the "economic position of woman which makes her
what she is. If men were so placed it would have the same effect. Not
the sex-relation, but the economic relation of the sexes, has so tangled
the skein of human life" (p. 333). The economically dependent woman
has no more freedom than has a bird in a cage or a flower in a pot. The
labor of her life is to wait upon the people and things that crowd her
habitat.

Gilman pursues her economic insight to its most sensational conclusion in her comparison of marriage and prostitution.

> From the odalisque with the most bracelets to the debutante with the most bouquets, the relation still holds good, – woman's economic profit comes through the power of sex-attraction.
>
> When we confront this fact boldly and plainly in the open market of vice, we are sick with horror. When we see the same economic relation made permanent, established by law, sanctioned and sanctified by religion, covered with flowers and incense and all accumulated sentiment, we think it innocent, lovely and right. The transient trade we think evil. The bargain for life we think good. But the biological effect remains the same. (Pp. 63–64)

As a further consequence of the "sexuo-economic" reality of marriage, the loathing of the "good" woman for the "bad" is not actually a moral response at all. According to Gilman, it is rather "the hatred of the trade-unionist for 'scab labor.'" The prostitute "offers the same goods – though of inferior quality, to be sure – for a far less price" (pp. 110, 109). The tone is scalding but deliberated.

Gilman's analysis of the crimes committed upon women by custom and power is dramatic, unblinking, often brilliant. Her corollary demand is that women be acknowledged as the equals of men, and, perhaps, following the gynecocentric theories of Lester Ward, even as their superiors. Yet the professed ground of that superiority reveals Gilman's divided response to the cultural stereotypes she confronts: She acquiesces in the premise of sexually determined roles. Gilman is a committed naturalist, and one of the lessons she felt she had learned from nature was that a significant degree of functional differentiation by gender exists. The specialization required of women by American culture may be crudely excessive, but some specialization there must be. "Certain psychic attributes," for instance, "are manifested by either sex. The intensity of the maternal passion is a sex-distinction as much as the lion's mane or the stag's horns." Tendencies and instincts, no less than physical appearance, are sexually determined.

> The belligerence and dominance of the male is a sex-distinction: the modesty and timidity of the female is a sex-distinction. The tendency to "sit" is a sex-distinction of the hen: the tendency to "strut" is a sex-distinction of the cock. The tendency to fight is a sex-distinction of males in general: the tendency to protect and provide for, is a sex-distinction of females in general. (P. 41)

Gilman's gynecocentricism follows from her judgment that the female "sex-distinctions" are self-evidently superior, that providing is of greater social utility than fighting. Gilman maintained these convictions and elaborated them repeatedly in later books. "The whole feminine attitude toward life differs essentially from the masculine, because of women's superior adaptation to the service of others." Women are superior to men as a matter "of principle. On the one hand, the male principle of struggle, conflict, and competition, the results of which make our 'economic problems.' On the other, the female principle of growth, of culture, of applying services and nourishment in order to produce improvement."[8]

Here is the paradox: In her struggle against the inequities of her time, Gilman arms herself with a conception of sexual identity perilously similar to the stereotypes in which she and other women are imprisoned. It may indeed be that in some higher evolutionary human state (a utopian "Herland," for instance) the obvious superiority of service to self-indulgence, of nurturance to acquisition, of cooperation to competition, will be ratified. But to assent, in 1900, to the notion of a "natural" female tendency toward service and nourishment is obviously if willy-nilly to choose domesticity and privacy for women, while abandoning all the vulgar and inferior but nonetheless dominant fields of getting and spending to men.

Charlotte Perkins Gilman saw further and more clearly than most of her contemporaries into the realities of sexual oppression at the turn of the century. Her own transcendence of the ideology that sanctified the oppression was only partial; but this is predictable and instructive. Her sociology, her vocabulary, even her mode of dissent came to her from the culture that conspired against her. And the material causes of American sexual inequality were changing at a glacial rate. Though women were entering the work force in unprecedented numbers in the early 1900s, the greater upsurge in female employment – and the expansion in the kinds of jobs open to women – would occur during and after the First World War.[9] In the absence of substantial economic opportunity, many women ultimately adopted the hegemonic definition of their place. This is what Gilman calls "the heavy legacy of the years behind, – the innumerable weak and little women, with the aspirations of an affectionate guinea pig."[10] Women who revolted against the role often found themselves confronting a bleak vista of frustration and self-doubt, opposed by women as well as by men. It is, says Gilman, "the crowning imbecility of history, – the banded opposition of some women to the advance of the others" (p. 168).

Thus, Gilman would not have been surprised by the formation, in 1911 in New York City, of the National Association Opposed to Woman's Suffrage. This was a woman's organization, headed by Mrs. Arthur M. Dodge. The "banded opposition" Gilman refers to continued, of course, through the period we are considering. In 1916, Winifred

Kirkland published "The Joys of Being a Woman," which celebrates the status quo and eschews political action for women altogether.[11] In the same year and journal, Mrs. S. P. Ravenel published "The Eternal Feminine," another deeply conservative statement: opposed to political engagement, opposed to change, suspicious even of education for women.[12]

Gilman was and remained the tenacious opponent of women like these; yet to say this is to simplify the situation. For the basis upon which Kirkland condescends to current feminism is her allegation of women's superiority to men, whereas Ravenel rests her argument against change on the "essential" domesticity of women. Though they are turned to completely different purposes, these positions, as we have just seen, resemble Gilman's own.

The dialectic disclosed by *Women and Economics,* as it simultaneously repudiates and embraces prevailing norms, provides an unintended commentary on the career of Gilman's friend and more famous contemporary, Jane Addams. For several decades, Addams not only proved herself a person of high ambition and accomplishment, she achieved a nearly legendary stature. She was perhaps the most prominent woman of her time; she was consultant to presidents; she seconded Theodore Roosevelt's nomination at the 1912 Progressive convention; she was saluted by William James as the quintessential American.[13] The settlement house movement, of which her Hull House was the prototypical example, was no merely marginal or cosmetic response to the dislocations and sufferings of the urban poor. As Allen F. Davis shows in his meticulous study, settlement houses played a major role in the entire turn-of-the-century urban reform movement.[14] Addams herself once claimed that the settlement houses transformed a generation of young Americans from philanthropists into reformers;[15] Davis, among others, agrees.

Yet the paradox is once again plain. The settlement house translates to a larger context exactly the virtues traditionally associated with women's roles in the family. The values of domesticity are writ large and institutionalized in the settlement. Hull House, bustling and active and effective as it may have been, was a "feminine" organization; it enabled women to deal with their traditional constituents (the hungry and the sick, children in trouble) and to carry out their familiar tasks (feeding, nursing, caring). Interestingly, the goals of Hull House, as enunciated by its founders, were couched in high Progressive generalizations and were in no obvious way circumscribed by gender. Jane Addams and her colleagues intended to "provide a center for a higher civic and social life; to institute and maintain educational and philanthropic enterprises; and to investigate and improve the conditions in the industrial districts of Chicago."[16] Despite these broad and abstract claims, the settlement house clearly represented a compromise with the predominating conceptions of "woman's place." Hull House permitted Jane Addams a life of immense productivity – a life actually quite radical in the quantity of its public accomplishments – that at the same time did not threaten received images of women. In an odd but unsurprising way, in fact, Addams's career reinforced the stereotypes by presenting them on so large a scale.

Not only Jane Addams but Lillian Wald, and others, tended rather readily, even automatically, to trace their strategies back to their special, feminine instincts. They believed that they were possessed, as women, of a heightened sensitivity to the injustices of society and of an inherent sympathy for society's victims. But, as the most probing student of Jane Addams's life observes, "to base one's social criticism upon the idea that feminine intuition could both diagnose and direct social change was to tie one's identity as a social critic to acquiescence in the traditional stereotype of women."[17]

Three writers in particular dramatize in their fictions the divided mind of turn-of-the-century American women. Kate Chopin, Ellen Glasgow, and Edith Wharton each in her distinctive way weaves the debate we have been exploring into the fabric of her novels.

THE AWAKENING

Throughout the novel, the voices of dissent are powerful but inarticulate. On the first of her nights recorded in the book, Edna Pontellier is awakened from sleep by her obtusely ordinary husband, Léonce. In less than a minute, he is asleep, leaving her – "by that time thoroughly awake" – to spend the rest of the night weeping.[18] Not far away she hears "the everlasting voice of the sea," mournful like her own, and like her own unable to translate the discovery of unhappiness into the particularity of language. Edna "could not have told why she was crying." She is seized by "an indescribable oppression, which seemed to generate in some unfamiliar part of her consciousness"; she is filled with "vague anguish." Her grief is a shadow, a mist, a mood.

In the course of the book, Edna's despair remains undetected by most of those she deals with, and it remains incomprehensible to those who know of it. To them, her situation is a good, even enviable, one. Unlike so many of her contemporaries in and outside of fiction – unlike Carrie Meeber, Maggie Johnson, Lily Bart, and the millions of women they signify – Edna has been treated rather gently in the struggle for existence. Affluent, young, and attractive, the mistress of a substantial home, the mother of two healthy sons, the wife of "the best husband in the world" (p. 9), possessed of modest artistic ability, Edna seems deliberately constructed to test at their most comfortable limits the possibilities of fulfillment for a woman in turn-of-the-century America.

The outcome of Chopin's experiment is as tragic as it is inevitable. Edna's fate closes in on her in several simultaneous ways, all of which follow from the major premise of sexual relations that governs her society's logic. According to that premise, everything will be permitted to Edna except what she desires and needs: self-sufficiency, self-realization, self-definition. Her husband's first glance reduces her to "a valuable piece of personal property" (p. 4), and that inescapable proprietary fact commands not only her roles in the novel but her identity. Like the gorgeously colored caged bird that, as the book opens, cries over and over "*Allez-vous en! Allez-vous en!*" (p. 3), Edna's acts of defiance leave the material and moral walls around her intact. Her final choice, her only choice, is death.

Edna's suicide has been variously interpreted as triumphant or defeated, heroic or cowardly, declarative or evasive. Chopin's description saturates the moment in the rhythmic wetness of passion, and the explicit language of rebirth suggests that a profound existential act of self-creation is imminent. Edna feels, as she steps into the sea, "like some new-born creature, opening its eyes in a familiar world that it had never known" (p. 113).

But rebirth is ultimately regressive, and a striking pattern of regression dominates this entire last scene. As Edna swims far out, she remembers the bluegrass meadow of her childhood, her father's voice and her sister's, and the barking of an old dog. Finally she hears the clanging spurs of the cavalry officer, the man who stirred her earliest sexual excitement. In other words, Edna's rebirth is at best inconclusive and at worst secures more strongly the trap that holds her fast. Her last moments lead only (but necessarily) back to the images of her own childhood illusions. The stifled yearning of the adult woman after an unapproachable freedom leads backward and downward; her longings betray themselves in desperate nostalgia. The irony is harsh and patent. Those adolescent scenes represent events in an inexorable history – Edna's history as a woman – and their recapitulation serves to exclude even the dimmest outlines of an alternative story for her.

Those remembered scenes are specifically adolescent as well in their embodiment of the transience of potentiality and the pretense of freedom. As Edna's consciousness dissolves into those images, then, the irony resides not at all in any contrast between her recollected happiness and her present despair, but rather in the emptiness of what she recalls and in the unbreakable causal and imaginative links between her past and her present.

Thus memory annuls self-creation. The caged bird of the novel's first chapter is matched symmetrically by a "bird with a broken wing," which appears over the sea in the final scene, "reeling, fluttering, circling disabled down, down to the water" (p. 113).

A number of readers have understood Edna's death as signaling Chopin's collapse – whether witting or not – into the received sentimental moral conventions of her time. The wage of sin is, after all, death, especially for a sexually transgressing woman, and even more especially for a woman of means who chooses to vacate her well-upholstered niche. According to this view of the novel, Edna's death subverts the book's sustained and sympathetic engagement with her change and growth. Consequently, this ending diminishes Edna's stature and perforce reduces the significance of her rebellion.[19]

This is intelligent but it misses the point. The diminishment implicated in the final scene does not result directly from Edna's death; it follows rather from her motives, from the structure of her choice as Chopin renders the final moments of her consciousness. Furthermore, the disabling limits that Edna's last scene discloses are not at all inconsistent with what we have learned of her to that point. On the contrary, what we know of her and of the society she inhabits – the Creole society and American society more generally – leads with rigorous finality to her suicide and to the specific images linked together at that instant.

Rather than encapsulating a concession by Kate Chopin to the pressures of orthodoxy, Edna's death actually dramatizes a tough-minded recognition. Edna's dissent from the sexual ideology of her milieu is necessarily partial. Though it is genuinely subversive, Edna's assault on her sexual prison is narrowed, ultimately frustrated, by her own acceptance of what she rejects. Sexuality forms the limit of her awakening; and while the novel labors intermittently to argue that sexual awakening provides in turn both the cause and the symbol of a more general agenda of liberation, the effort proves at last impossible. Edna's glimpses of freedom remain glimpses only, opposed, obscured, and denied by the absence of an enabling vocabulary.

The most synoptic definition Edna herself offers of her awakening occurs in a conversation with Dr. Mandelet following the birth of Adèle Ratignolle's child.

> "Nature [says the doctor] "takes no account of moral consequences, of arbitrary conditions which we create, and which we feel obliged to maintain at any cost.
>
> "Yes" [Edna responds]. "The years that are gone seem like

dreams – if one might go on sleeping and dreaming – but to wake
up and find – oh! well! perhaps it is better to wake up after all,
even to suffer, rather than to remain a dupe to illusions all one's
life." (P. 110)

Edna embraces reality with courage; yet the details of her declaration
disclose something of the dilemma in which she still remains. "To
find . . ." precisely what? Edna defines neither the illusions from which
she recoils nor the conception of herself that is to follow her release
from them. She does not define these things because she cannot; and the
rest of the novel in a sense merely tracks the fatal consequences of that
inability.

When Edna decides to move into the small house around the corner
from her husband's home, she makes her most calculated gesture of
independence. As she explains her decision to Mlle. Reisz (who, significantly, was "neither surprised nor especially interested" [p. 79]), Edna
offers a number of almost miscellaneous reasons. The little house looks
"cozy, so inviting and restful"; the big house is too much trouble to
keep up, is staffed by too many servants; the little house can be paid for
with her own money. "I know I shall like it," she says finally; I shall
"like the feeling of freedom and independence." Edna's words not only
exactly capture her moral achievement. They also and unintendedly
predict her eventual defeat: She will like the *feeling* of freedom. Beyond
the immersion in such feelings she cannot go. Thus, Mlle. Reisz speaks
with authority when she objects, "Your reason is not yet clear to me."
The narrative continues: "Neither was it quite clear to Edna herself"
(p. 80); and though Edna soon resolves a motive out of her uncertainty – she has determined "never again to belong to another than
herself" (p. 80) – it will not prove adequate to the tests she is to face.

The little house into which Edna moves only emphasizes the limits of
her affirmation: It is so small she calls it a "pigeon house." An unde-
signed but substantial likeness joins Edna's tiny house down the street
from her husband's with Thoreau's cabin, jerry-built on fourteen acres
of land borrowed from his friend Emerson. Both dwellings have been
taken as architectural emblems of self-sufficiency and independence.
And both Thoreau and Chopin's heroine are playing for high, indeed
for mortal, stakes. But the two buildings signify more impressively the
deeply marginal, almost utterly ceremonial quality of their occupants'
dissent. Thoreau, insulated by family and friends from any serious
venturing, carries his laundry into Concord each weekend for his aunt
to wash. Edna, attended by a servant or two, and sustained by a small
legacy and gambling winnings, settles down to paint.

That Edna is forced into an essentially peripheral gesture subtracts not at all from the heroism of her refusal. It simply ratifies the impossibility of her escape from the ideological prison of her time and place. Like other American dissidents, Edna stands baffled and alone, casting defiant but finally puzzled glances toward the impermeable wall of hegemonic custom and belief.

Thus, even at its most fully developed, Edna's consciousness of self remains fragmentary. Accordingly, though she resolves never to belong to another than herself, the exhilaration of that declaration soon fades. She finds "the old ennui overtaking her; the helplessness which so often assailed her" (p. 88). She flees for relief to a vision of "the presence of the beloved one," Robert. Thus again, though she tells Robert himself, "I am no longer one of Mr. Pontellier's possessions. . . . I give myself where I choose" (pp. 106–107), her imagination invariably summons up the young man's countenance as the object of her freedom. "She could picture" – this right after her conversation with Dr. Mandelet about her triumph over illusions – "no greater bliss on earth than the possession of the beloved one" (p. 110). This is significant on at least two counts. First, however casually the word "possession" may have been used here, it discloses the limits of Edna's understanding of love. As she has been a possession, so she would possess. Not, let us be clear about this, out of any conscious design, certainly not out of any purpose of vindication, much less retribution. Rather, Edna uses the languages of love and ownership synonymously because the only definition of love she has ever known is congruent with possession. But second, and more important, Edna's recurrent imaginative reversion to Robert documents exactly her ideological impoverishment, and thus it portends her eventual defeat. Put briefly, Edna's death memorializes the impossibility of her autonomy. The assorted roles that suffocate her are also the exclusive sources of her identity. Though her dilemma in many ways resembles that of earlier and later American heroes, at its roots she is the victim of her sex. As a woman, she is denied access even to the sustained illusion of freedom.

A passage quite early in the novel offers a prophetic comment on Edna's entire career. Adèle Ratignolle is being introduced, and of her the narrator says: "There are no words to describe her save the old ones that have served so often to picture heroine of romance and the fair lady of our dreams" (p. 10). For the "mother-women," that is to say, for the women like Adèle who serenely adopt both the behavior and the consciousness decreed by traditional codes, a full vocabulary exists. Whatever its falsity, its banality ("heroine," "fair lady"), its actual inhumanity, it nonetheless ensures the solidity of a stable, orderly arrangement of social affirmation. For Edna, on the other hand, who would reconstruct the codes to ground social norms upon her

own spontaneity, the commensurate vocabulary does not exist; nor
can she invent it. Its absence is the measure of Edna's failure, of her
society's crime against women, and of Kate Chopin's strength as a
truth-teller.

VIRGINIA

Ellen Glasgow's portrait of a lady in *Virginia* (1913) rather remarkably
complements Kate Chopin's in *The Awakening*. What Edna Pontellier
refuses, Virginia Pendleton not only accepts but incarnates. Virginia is
the perfected ideal of southern womanhood, formed to submit and
doing so eagerly, at peace only in her several subordinate roles as
daughter, wife, and above all mother. She is Chopin's "mother-
woman" in poignant apotheosis, whose only joy comes from self-sacrifice and whose self-assertion reaches only to the willfull extinction of
her own identity. *Virginia* is a big book, and it follows its heroine
through a quarter-century of her life: from the single-minded, tremu-
lous expectancy of her girlhood, through the raptures of her early married years and the supreme felicity of her childbearing and -rearing, to
the loneliness of her middle age, left behind by her children, who find
her and her beliefs obsolete, and abandoned by her husband, who finds
her simply dull. Through it all, she remains loyal to the self-destructive
principles she has been taught.

Edna Pontellier pays with her life for contemplating the overthrow of
the traditional sexual codes that Virginia tenaciously defends. Patheti-
cally, the price exacted from Virginia for her orthodoxy may be higher:
a long, living death unalloyed by any hope. At the end of the book, she
has a piercing vision of "the dreadful weeks that would run on into the
dreadful years. Silent, gray, and endless, they stretched ahead of her,
and through them all she saw herself, a little hopeless figure, moving
toward the death which she had not had the courage to die."[20] Virginia
will survive, but only as a memorial to her own despair and to the fatal
consequences of her allegiances.

Glasgow's double theme in *Virginia* joins what she several times calls
the "evasive idealism" of turn-of-the-century southern society with the
human wastage such evasiveness brings. The first of the novel's three
parts is called "The Dream," and the first chapter in that part is "The
System." The words "dream" and "system" may seem at first discor-
dant, taken as they are from the vocabularies, respectively, of romance
and naturalism. But in this book, in the fictional city of Dinwiddie,
Virginia, in the years just before and after 1900, the two terms and their
connotations not only coexist, they converge and coincide. *Virginia* is a

roman expérimental, an extended study of the determining power of
romantic illusion: The system *is* the dream.

Though most of the novel is told from Virginia Pendleton's point of
view, the opening chapter is given over mainly and appropriately to a
sketch of her teacher, Miss Priscilla Batte, proprietress and sole instruc-
tor of the Dinwiddie Academy for Young Ladies. Miss Batte embodies
the ideals she inculcates: She is possessed of an innocence that experience cannot harm or even touch, "for it was the product of a courage
that feared nothing except opinions." Armed with the formidable weapons of prejudice and illusion, the equable and overweight Miss Batte
incorporates southern civilization itself: "Just as the town had battled
for a principle without understanding it, so she was capable of dying
for an idea, but not of conceiving one" (p. 11). Finding most of life
distasteful, this is a society that, like its emblematic educator Miss
Batte, chooses neither to grumble about actuality nor to change it but
to ignore it altogether. Virginia's father, for example, the Reverend
Gabriel Pendleton, is a man who had "never in his life seen things as
they are. . . . To reach his mind, impressions of persons or objects had
first to pass through a refining atmosphere in which all baser substances
were destroyed, and no fact had ever penetrated this medium except in
the flattering disguise of a sentiment" (pp. 31–32). Gabriel's life is
devoted to "embellishing" actuality. He had married at twenty a
woman "only less ignorant of the world than himself," an idealist who
shared his cherished conviction that "to acknowledge an evil is in a
manner to countenance its existence." Like Miss Batte, the Pendletons
too represent a society that clings to the belief "that a pretty sham has a
more intimate relation to reality than has an ugly truth" (p. 32).

The collective southern commitment to sightlessness seemed to Glasgow downright pathological. The three Pendletons are capable of looking directly at an overladen and straining mule, sore and bloody from
injuries and the lash, without seeing it. "What they beheld . . . was the
most interesting street in the world, filled with the most interesting
people, who drove happy animals that enjoyed their servitude and
needed the sound of the lash to add cheer and liveliness to their la-
bours" (p. 60).

For Glasgow, especially in the novels she wrote before the First
World War, southern culture distinguishes itself above all by the subordination of fact to idealizing vision; actuality is annihilated in the green
shade of consolatory dream. In the relatively early novel *The Deliverance* (1904), Glasgow shaped her complaint about southern mythmaking into a startling image: the blind and paralyzed Mrs. Blake, whose
family conspires to surround her for two decades with the benevolent
fiction that the South won the Civil War. The illusion they create for

her to live in is furnished elaborately with details, including the invented names of a succession of Confederate presidents.

Early in the nineteenth century, Emerson had called America's beset-
ting disease "ophthalmia": a failure of sight. But the metaphor he had
in mind came nowhere in his own experience so perilously close to
literal reality as it does in the world of Ellen Glasgow's fiction. "The
Sabbath calm, so heavy that an axe could have scarcely dispelled it,
filled the curving streets and the square gardens like an invisible fog; a
fog that dulled the brain and weighed down the eyelids" (p. 122) – the
very atmosphere of Dinwiddie interrupts sight.

Virginina Pendleton is the choicest product of this world. "To look
at her was to think inevitably of love. For that end, obedient to the
powers of Life, the centuries had formed and coloured her, as they had
formed and coloured the wild-rose with its whorl of delicate petals"
(p. 95). She has running through her veins the blood of generations of
pious ministers and angelic, self-sacrificing women, and she has offered
"as little resistance as some exquisite plastic material" (p. 21) to the
elders and teachers who have molded her. The entire purpose of her
education, like "that of every other well-born and well-bred Southern
woman of her day, was . . . to solidify the forces of mind into the
inherited mould of fixed beliefs" (p. 20).

Virginia's dedication to love epitomizes the evasions of her culture.
She is flatly incapable of seeing a fact uncolored by an idealizing love. In a
chapter entitled "Her Inheritance," Glasgow describes Virginia's instant
infatuation with Oliver Treadwell, the man whom she will marry. At
the mere thought of him, "the Pendleton blood in her rose in a fierce
rebellion against all that was ugly and sordid in existence" (p. 42).

Virginia is a woman of intelligence, courage, and strength. Even
through the blindfold of blood and training she can detect shadows of
what is being denied her because of her sex. At a party early in the
book, for example, she looks out across the faces of the dancing girls
and feels the suspense in which all their lives are being held. "Was that a
woman's life, after all? Never to be able to go out and fight for what
one wanted? Always to sit at home and wait, without moving a foot or
lifting a hand toward happiness! Never to dare gallantly! Never even to
suffer openly! Always to will in secret, always to hope in secret . . ."
(p. 138). But at that moment, her beloved Oliver arrives, and Virginia's
half-formulated discontent collapses into the satisfactions of traditional
courtship. By the eve of her marriage, she is happily submerged in
Dinwiddie's sexual culture; no ripples disturb the quiet pool of her
devotion to love. "What could make her happier than the knowledge
that she must surrender her will to Oliver's from the day of her wedding until the day of her death? She embraced her circumscribed lot

with a passion that glorified its limitations" (p. 184). The woman's fate
of subordination and suspense, which a few months earlier had momentarily clouded her contentment, becomes now the very source of
her joy. "She ecstatically pictured herself in the immemorial attitude of
woman."

> She saw herself waiting–waiting happily–but always waiting.
> She imagined the thrilling expectancy of the morning waiting for
> him to come home to his dinner; the hushed expectancy of the
> evening waiting for him to come home to his supper; the blissful
> expectancy of hoping he might be early; the painful expectancy of
> fearing he might be late. (P. 186)

For two-thirds of the novel, this is Virginia's choice. Hers is a life given
to the routine performance of ordinary domestic tasks, carried out in
pinched obscurity and in the service of provincial and disabling ideals.
Yet it is also a life–such is the intensity of Glasgow's concern with it–
that approximates the scale of heroism and tragedy. Almost everyone in
the book is more active than she–not only all the men, but many of the
women as well. But she clings so ferociously to her passivity, she
extinguishes herself with such fixity of will, that she appears to us more
purposeful in her denials than do the others in their demands.

To a more searching extent than she is usually given credit for, Ellen
Glasgow has provided in *Virginia* a serious appraisal of the condition of
women. She understands that the issue is power, that the "historical
dogma of the supplementary being of woman" (p. 279), which is
shared in by every member of the society, including its women, is
nothing more complicated than a creed rationalizing the exploitation of
one half of humanity by the other. After one of Virginia's characteristic
acts of submission to her husband, Glasgow generalizes to "the instinct" of woman "to adjust her personality to the changing desires of
the man she loves" (p. 294), and then she appends this parenthesis: "this
instinct older than civilization, rooted in tragedy, and existing by right
of an unconquerable necessity." Each of these clauses might serve as a
chapter heading in a volume of sexual history. They summarize the
grim lesson that Virginia Pendleton Treadwell and Glasgow's other
women have had to learn, and they cast a different, darker light over
the comedy of Miss Batte.

Apparently neutral and even banal statements expand with sinister
significance in the setting of such awareness, as when Virginia confesses
to a friend, "I was made just to be a wife and mother, and nothing else"
(p. 408). Glasgow said that as a young woman, she read and reread *The
Origin of Species* until she knew every page of it; and she frequently
proposed the relevance of that book to an analysis of her fiction.[21] But

Darwin has little to do with the particular self-sacrifices and adaptations of Virginia Pendleton Treadwell. In assenting to her own inferiority, in denying herself the possibility of an existence grounded on mutuality or equality, in surviving by means of self-abnegation, Virginia responds tragically but coherently to the ideological limits of her time and place. The "system," to return to the language of the novel's first pages, may be a highly developed engine of oppression, the "dream" may be a nightmare, but for Virginia they are reality, and they offer her the happiness of martyrdom.

Glasgow's tone in *Virginia* is more complex than mere contempt for the evasions and deceits built into the structure of southern society. She is also affectionate toward the men and women who live in that society, and her affection encompasses not only pity for the victims, among them Virginia, but a more energetic admiration as well. The Reverend Gabriel Pendleton, for example, who is unable to see even a fact except in the consoling disguise of a sentiment, is somehow capable of rising to a necessary courage. At sixty-five, he dies of the heart attack he chooses to risk by fighting off a gang of white thugs who are harassing a young black man. He had fought bravely in the war, decades earlier, and the imagery of those days is superimposed on the present:

> Spinning round on the three of them he struck out with all his strength, while there floated before him the face of a man he had killed in his first charge at Manassas. The old fury, the old triumph, the old blood-stained splendor returned to him. He smelt the smoke again, he heard the boom of the cannon, the long, sobbing rattle of musketry, and the thought stabbed through him, "God forgive me for loving a fight!" (P. 347)

The effect of this juxtaposition is not ironic. On the contrary. Here, Glasgow comes fairly close to exploiting the sentimentality of the "lost cause" that she elsewhere scorned. In any case, her point is to prove that some strength and virtue remain in the hearts of these seeming ghosts, even if attenuated almost to the vanishing point by a generation of pretense. Thus, Glasgow's satire against the South's "inheritance" confronts her occasional claims for the still-living promise buried under the culture's more visible futility.[22]

Furthermore, Glasgow's attack on the customs and beliefs of the Old South is also complicated by her equally vigorous dissent from the future. The disappearing smoke of Civil War battlefields is yielding to the thickening smoke of factories, prophetic of the South's spiritual as well as economic future, its loss as much for worse as for better of the past. Oliver's father, Cyrus Treadwell, the richest man in Dinwiddie, with a fortune based on railroads and industry, serves as Glasgow's representative of the New South. And Cyrus is a caricature, a one-dimensional near-monster, empty of human warmth, indifferently tyrannical to wife, children, and dependents both domestic and commercial, devoted only to business and to acquisition. He had, we are told, "never stopped to think about anything except the absorbing problem of how to make something out of nothing. Everything else, even his marriage, had made merely a superficial impression on him" (pp. 76–77). Long before the first Snopes descended on Yoknapatawpha to make his first sharp deal, Glasgow had anatomized the moral type. "Success . . . had controlled his thoughts and even his impulses so completely for years that he had come at last to resemble an animal less than he resembled a machine; even Nature . . . had punished him in the end by depriving him of the animal capacity for pleasure" (pp. 147–148). This is the future that Glasgow sees, and her recoil is savage.

EDITH WHARTON

From her earliest years, Edith Wharton was repelled by the protean changefulness that dominated not only the facts of America's late nineteenth-century life but American values as well. Her loyalty was always to stability and tradition. But hers was a vexed loyalty. For she not only recognized how much was frivolous and sordid in the traditional society around her, but she herself, as a writer and as a woman, was also in several specific ways the victim of traditional codes and customs. In her childhood completely, and throughout her life intermittently, Edith Wharton found her deepest intellectual and creative aspirations denied or denigrated because of her sex.

The pain she felt provoked her outrage at the traps of the conventional, but it was an outrage baffled by her even stronger, ineradicable revulsion from modernity. Edith Wharton's lifelong engagement with her society was marked by powerful ambivalence, a response reinforced by her unlikely success: She accomplished all that her environment conspired to deny her. In addition, that same environment afforded her as much nourishment as denial. She was simultaneously appalled by the shams of her class and contemptuous of classes beneath her. Except for fast cars, she was unnerved by novelty in any form; yet her own accomplishments, as well as the facts of her intimate life, were not more than marginally congruent with the conventional definitions of women and society she assented to.

A profoundly divided woman, Edith Wharton exhibits in her novels and tales a discriminating but deep sympathy for her victimized female characters, a sympathy anchored by her understanding of their fates as

women. Yet she is unable to delineate or even to imagine careers for
her heroines that do not end in disappointment, or despair, or death.
For, like most conservatives, Wharton imaged society as an organism;
and to such a conception, disruption anywhere in the system threatens
the disintegration of the entire culture. Since anarchy represented for
Wharton the worst of all possible outcomes – certainly worse than
death – restraint always declared itself a better strategy than reform,
and protest, no matter how vigorous, evaporated in caution.

In any case, though her life as Edith Newbold Jones and then as Mrs.
Edward Wharton brought punishments, it brought compensations, too:
among them money, leisure, status, travel, cultivated friends. When, in
A Backward Glance (1934), she came to recollect her life a few years
before its end, she itemized the rewards more spaciously than the frus-
trations. But there is a long distance between what she professed at last
to believe and what she had accomplished only by ignoring those beliefs. The resultant ironic tension shapes the design of her memoir more
surely than her intentions. Thus, the woman résuméd in *A Backward
Glance* emerges in an extraordinary but predictably conflicted self-
portrait. Looking into the mirror of memory is the much-published,
well-paid author, the shrewd entrepreneur, the divorced wife of one
man and passionate lover of at least one other, the widely traveled
adventurer whose journeys have taken her around the world and
through a war (and possessor of the rank of chevalier in the French
Legion of Honor for her work in that war), the unabashed confidante
and disputant of many of the leading writers and thinkers of her time.
Reflected in the mirror, however, is the distressed observer lamenting
the decline of domestic virtues, belittling the struggle of women toward
equal rights in the political and economic arenas, insisting on the preemptive importance of good behavior, and announcing that a woman's
place is not merely in the home but precisely in the kitchen. (It is a
matter of some doubt that Edith Wharton ever so much as saw the
inside of any of her several kitchens, except on tours of inspection.)

To be sure, *A Backward Glance* is the work of a woman of seventy,
and the book, like the author at that age, is crotchety and often unreliable in details. Nonetheless, the ideological commitments the memoir
announces, though etched with less subtlety than might have been the
case two or three decades earlier, constitute a fair rendering. Above all,
the reiterated allegiance to social stability, however much her career
stood proof against her own ideas, summarizes a commanding theme of
Edith Wharton's life.

On the other hand, the finality of Wharton's tone in the book – her
eagerness to endorse extravagantly almost anything that appears to prom-

ise "order" and to denounce its opposite with routine shrillness – is distinctive to her last decade and a half, the period following World War I. She suggests this altered tone herself in the first chapter of the memoir. Summoning up "Old New York," at best only palely imitative of the European social system from which it derived, Wharton concludes that it has taken on in retrospect an aura of serene coherence by contrast with what was waiting around the corner of the future. "Twenty years" earlier, she writes, she would have been among those who would have smiled at "the idea that time could transform a group of *bourgeois* colonials and their republican descendants into a sort of social aristocracy." Now, twenty years later, she consents to "the formative value of nearly three hundred years of social observance: the concerted living-up to long-established standards of honour, of education and manners. The value of duration is slowly asserting itself against the welter of change."[23]

Wharton's chronology here is by no means casual. The "twenty years" she refers to bring her and her reader back exactly to 1914, the outbreak of the Great War. Wharton is making a careful distinction here. The war did nothing to originate her affection for the idea of "social aristocracy." It merely made her more tolerant toward the version of aristocracy that may have existed around her in childhood. The additional and more important point of the passage is to pronounce Wharton's intolerance for any and all departures from the aristocratic norm.

Though the First World War overwhelmed Edith Wharton, as it did so many of her contemporaries, with its apocalyptic significance, it is important to define the precise nature of her response. The tidal wave of destruction to which she was a personal witness might have led her to question the strength, the integrity, the downright simple truth of cultures that proved to contain within themselves so much self-destructive violence. Instead, the war elicited from Wharton a redoubled feeling of patriotic fidelity to France and a rededicated belief in the primacy of tradition.

Immediately after the war, in 1919, she published *French Ways and Their Meaning,* an introduction and guide to France intended for American soldiers and visitors. In the course of her comments, she underscores the "lesson" that France might "teach" America:

> It was our English forebears who taught us to flout tradition and
> break away from their own great inheritance; France may teach us
> that, side by side with the qualities of enterprise and innovation
> that English blood has put in us, we should cultivate the sense of

continuity, that "sense of the past" which enriches the present and binds us up with the world's great stabilizing traditions of art and poetry and knowledge.[24]

Edith Wharton's flight from the machinery of anarchy thus embraces an inevitable flight from innovation altogether, and her embrace of stability and coherence becomes an embrace of the status quo. The First World War, then, presented itself to her as the most explosive and frightening attack in the still larger assault of modernity itself; the war is the symbol of the ubiquitous welter of change from which Wharton recoiled.

To make the same point the other way around: The war only ratified and strengthened what we might call her theology of continuity. An earlier book she wrote about France, lighter-hearted and less polemic than *French Ways,* gives to a version of Wharton's beliefs a combined aesthetic and political focus. *A Motor-Flight through France* (1908) is probably her most instructive travel book and is surely her most entertaining. Recording and reflecting on her drives near Paris, Wharton includes along the way as suggestive a statement as she would ever make concerning the moral implications of the "sense of continuity," and especially of its expression in manners:

> Never more vividly than in this Seine country does one feel the amenity of French manners, the long process of social adaptation which has produced so profound and general an intelligence of life. Everyone we passed on our way, from the canal-boatman to the white-capped baker's lad, from the *marchande des quatre saisons* to the white dog curled philosophically under her cart, from the pastry-cook putting a fresh plate of *brioches* in his appetising window to the curé's *bonne* who had just come out to drain the lettuce on the curé's doorstep . . . each had their established niche in life, the frankly avowed interests and preoccupations of their order, their pride in the smartness of the canal-boat, the seductions of the shop-window, the glaze of the *brioches,* the crispness of the lettuce. And this admirable fitting into the pattern, which seems almost as if it were a moral outcome of the universal French sense of form, has led the race to the happy, the momentous discovery that good manners are a short cut to one's goal, that they lubricate the wheels of life instead of obstructing them.[25]

The claims Wharton makes here reach far indeed. To begin with, manners are said to recapitulate history; the discerning observer of a nation's behavior at any present moment also comprehends that nation's whole social past. More significantly, manners and history reciprocally justify each other. Inserting for rhetorical purposes a glancing metaphorical reference to evolutionary meliorism, Wharton defines manners as "the long process of social adaptation." In other words, in a vaguely Spencerian way, Wharton shrewdly christens the most irreducibly arbitrary and artificial of human phenomena – manners – in the name of the organic and natural.

But the key to the passage occurs in the last sentence, where the evolutionary hypothesis is restated in explicitly ethical terms. The picturesque "fitting into the pattern" of the several obscure French citizens enumerated here discloses not just the social but the "moral outcome" of a sense of form. The whole conception of society toward which Edith Wharton consciously tended is compressed into this sentence. What detains us, however, is the almost alarming if unintended irony that the passage directs toward her own situation. That irony could be defined like this: Edith Wharton's reduction of the citizens of the Seine region to the colorful tiles in a human mosaic is a function and a revelation of class loyalty. The baker's helper, the merchant, the curé's maid are reduced to ornament, their "place" made permanent and their mobility denied, as we have seen, by an elliptically uttered law of nature. Yet Edith Wharton herself, by virtue not of class but of sex, lived her life as a member of a group threatened with a like diminishment to the decorative, the marginal, the picturesque. American women were denied power and individual identity – they were prohibited, in Henry Adam's vocabulary, from becoming either Venus or Virgin – and were permitted only to be ornamental. They were permitted to play for American society the consoling and utterly symbolic role that the people of the Seine country played for Wharton: to decorate the landscape of the status quo and to provide idealized images of community.

More than anything else, Edith Wharton's novels and tales record the lives of women trapped within just such limits. And the powerful feeling of ambivalence, which in the essays and travel books lies beneath a surface of assurance, moves altogether to the center of the fiction. By way of a familiar paradox, the disguises of fiction enabled Edith Wharton to address more forthrightly questions that in her other writings she worked with unconscious diligence to suppress. Without falling into the reductive vulgarity of mistaking art for autobiography, it is possible to understand the novels and stories she wrote between the turn of the century and the war as transcribing Wharton's sustained argument with herself, her restless search for values finally worth affirming.

One of the earliest chapters in that debate, "Souls Belated," is also a superb story by any measure. Included in Wharton's first collection of tales, *The Greater Inclination* (1899), "Souls Belated" describes the fate of Mrs. Lydia Tillotson, a woman who has left her wealthy husband and Fifth Avenue mansion in which they lived and has run off to Europe with a "promising" young writer named Gannett. After several months of traveling aimlessly in discreet and comfortable isolation, Lydia and Gannett have discovered that their undistracted intimacy exacts a cost. In particular Lydia, through whose consciousness most of the tale is told, finds herself poised agonizingly among the emotions of passion and anxiety, pride and doubt.

The opening section of the story is set on a train carrying the couple across northern Italy. They are alone in their first-class carriage, and sorry for it: "A shaft of sunlight struck across the dusty red velvet seats into Lydia's corner. Gannett did not notice it. He had returned to his *Revue de Paris,* and she had to rise and lower the shade of the farther window. Against the vast horizon of their leisure such incidents stood out sharply."[26] Over the landscape of their attachment looms a vague but daily more visible sense of dissatisfaction. On the heavily charged day of this first section, the decree announcing that Tillotson has divorced Lydia arrives, and this precipitates a crisis between the lovers.

Gannett's response is straightforward. He proposes that he and Lydia promptly marry and gradually reenter the circle of acquaintance from which their illicit status has exiled them. Lydia's response is far more complicated; tracing it is indeed what the story is about. Though she knows that the divorce was inevitable, she finds the fact of it unexpectedly painful. Her pain has nothing to do with the definitive loss of Tillotson. Rather, the divorce compels Lydia to define more closely what she has done, and to estimate more bluntly the value of her decision to leave her husband. "Nothing had mattered, in those first days of supreme deliverance, but the fact that she was free" (p. 86). However, the news of her divorce brings to sharp finality a realization that had begun taking dim shape the moment she left Tillotson: It was "not so much . . . that freedom released her from Tillotson as that it had given her to Gannett." Though she had been unhappy in her life as Mrs. Tillotson, she "had not left him until she met Gannett" (p. 86).

Lydia thus dramatizes the ironic limits of freedom for a woman who is ideologically captive to the sexual definitions of turn-of-the-century American society. Freedom can reach no further than identity, and female identity is derivative and dependent. Lydia's diminished view of the significance of her infidelity thus follows with remorseless, pathetic logic: "She had left her husband only to be with Gannett" (p. 89). The more radical assertion of self and freedom that she had hoped to make disintegrates under her own scrutiny.

This concession, however, is only the first of the ironies that "Souls

Belated" practices upon its heroine. The second, and more profound, has to do with Lydia's attitude toward the upper-class society from which she has fled. It is a foolish, fatuous society, in her judgment, a society in which,

> after dinner, the ladies compared the exorbitant charges of their children's teachers, and agreed that, even with the new duties on French clothes, it was cheaper in the end to get everything from Worth; while the husbands, over their cigars, lamented municipal corruption, and decided that the men to start a reform were those who had no private interests at stake. (P. 88)

Such people are the arbiters of both taste and morals, and are the unforgivably banal defenders of a system of values as trivial as themselves. These are the men and women Lydia has chosen to defy. The clarity of her gesture has been, as we have seen, obscured for her by the realization that she has given herself to one man in place of another. Nonetheless, infidelity is a familiar and adequately convincing act of rebellion against convention, and as rebellion Lydia defends it eloquently. She refuses Gannett's predictable offer of marriage, responding with what she calls in self-deprecation a "lecture on sociology." She delivers a long, passionate monologue in which she tries to explain to her obtuse lover that their marriage would put her integrity at far greater risk than their liaison:

> "We neither of us believe in the abstract 'sacredness' of marriage; we both know that no ceremony is needed to consecrate our love for each other; what object can we have in marrying, except the secret fear of each that the other may escape, or the secret longing to work our way back gradually . . . into the esteem of the people whose conventional morality we have always ridiculed and hated?" (Pp. 95–96)

Gannett is mystified by the deep feeling as well as the logic of Lydia's speech. For tritely chivalric reasons, he lets her have her way so far as to agree to settle into a fashionable Alpine resort with her rather than pressing his opinion that they travel directly on to Paris and be married.

The hotel at which they find themselves, the Bellosguardo, is only nominally in the charge of its proprietor, Monsieur Grossart. In fact, Lady Susan Condit thrones over the Bellosguardo, enforcing a rarefied atmosphere of almost unbreathably high propriety and distinction. She decides whom the inn's guests will and will not recognize, and she is, in the hushed words of an awed admirer, "very difficult . . . about new people. One might almost say that she disapproves of them beforehand, on principle" (p. 103). As Mrs. Gannett, Lydia is immediately accepted by Lady Susan and is drawn into a social group more or less identical in its demands and its denials to the one she has revolted against in America.

The story's crisis is provoked by Wharton's introduction of a woman in something like Lydia's own situation. Lydia is approached for help by the overdressed Mrs. Cope, who has notoriously eloped with the slightly younger Lord Trevenna. Mrs. Cope seeks Lydia's aid in holding on to Trevenna until her own divorce decree is secure. Working against her are the legions of Trevenna's aristocratic relatives. Mrs. Cope appeals to Lydia's compassion, but behind that appeal Wharton is implicitly testing Lydia's commitment to the antinomian principles she has ringingly declared. Surprised into a decision more automatic than reflective, Lydia immediately chooses solidarity with convention and its representatives against the transgressing woman.

This is the irony toward which Wharton had worked, and Lydia herself assesses it in excruciating detail when she explains her decision to Gannett:

> "Oh, do you see the full derision of it? These people – the very prototypes of the bores you took me away from, with the same fenced-in view of life, the same keep-off-the-grass morality, the same little cautious virtues and the same little frightened vices – well, I've clung to them, I've delighted in them, I've done my best to please them. . . . Respectability! It was the one thing in life that I was sure I didn't care about, and it's grown so precious to me that I've stolen it because I couldn't get it any other way. . . . I who used to fancy myself unconventional! I must have been born with a card-case in my hand." (P. 120)

Actually, this judgment is more candid than completely accurate. Whatever Lydia may think of herself, Edith Wharton is not interested in her as a mere hypocrite. Rather, Lydia represents the narrow constraints surrounding the imaginable freedom of women. Compelled all her life to accept the reality against which she consciously struggles, Lydia can only fail. She had "mechanically accepted" the hegemonic sexual ideology of her time; it "had become a matter of course" (p. 88). She is trapped by needs more fundamental than her will, desires to which she must yield at the very moment she knows them to be superficial and even destructive. Indeed, her knowledge only intensifies her self-condemnation.

The circumstances within which women must define themselves in Edith Wharton's world – the world of the American 1900s – condemn any vision of autonomy to frustration. Yet the vision in its turn rebukes assent to convention. Gannett, though he comprehends even less fully than Lydia the causes of her despair, starkly renders her fate when he thinks of her as "walking barefooted through a stony waste" (p. 127). She wanders in a maze of irreconcilable convictions, "a labyrinth of self-torture" (p. 123). These images are precise. Lydia's suffering is multiplied by a loneliness beyond isolation. She is not simply unable to discover or create a life for herself outside the boundaries of stereotypical femininity. Rather, at the core of Lydia's tragedy lies a much more fundamental calamity: She is doomed to yearn after what she despises.

In the tale's exceptionally moving final scene, Lydia acts out her fate in a wordless pantomine. Significantly, the point of view shifts away from Lydia and, for the only time in the story, joins Gannett. It is dawn, the morning after Lydia has suffered through her insight into her own character. Gannett hears her in her bedroom, moving quietly, as if not to waken him next door. A few moments later she appears in the garden before the hotel, visible to Gannett, who peers down at her from behind the shutters of his room. Lydia is dressed in a traveling cloak and carries a small suitcase. Gannett watches her walk down to the steamboat landing. She buys a ticket and sits down to wait for the early ferry, scheduled to leave in a few minutes and take its passengers across the lake, to the mainland, to train connections, to the larger world. Gannett makes no move either to stop her or to join her; though whether from respect for her independence or a failure of love or irresolution is not made clear. The boat arrives, but Lydia stands apart as the few other passengers cross the gangplank and board. The boat's bell begins to ring "querulously"; there is "a shriek of steam" (p. 128). She moves "waveringly" toward the gangplank, pauses, then begins to board: "Half-way down the short incline to the deck she stopped again; then she turned and ran back to the land. The gang-plank was drawn in, the bell ceased to ring, and the boat backed out into the lake. Lydia, with slow steps, was walking toward the garden." It is a consummate dramatic image of the inevitable defeat of a sensitive but powerless woman whose unsupported impulses toward liberation must end in self-imposed control.

Watching her from the hotel window, Gannett mechanically reaches for his Bradshaw and begins "looking out the trains to Paris" (p. 128). It is a moment of wrenching pathos, intensified by Wharton's careful manipulation of perspective. Our distance from Lydia reduces her scale, emphasizes the futility of her gesture, and insists on her failure. But all of these effects enlarge our sympathy as well. And the bewildered complacency of Gannett, through whose eyes we are observing the scene, multiplies even further our pity for the self-tortured woman he cannot understand.

Thirty years after she wrote it, Edith Wharton defended her choice of subject matter in *The House of Mirth* (1905), insisting that even a frivolous society could provide the setting for tragedy. The frantic posturing of turn-of-the-century New York's old and new money may seem to be humanly pointless motion, but it finds social and dramatic significance in what it destroys, in the human beings and moral values debased in the ruthless pursuit of luxury and show.[27] Above all, the society of *The House of Mirth* is ravaged by a confusion between means and ends: Forms, divided from purpose, are reduced to nothing but themselves. Ethical imperatives are diminished and at last absorbed into an incoherently freestanding obsession with propriety.

Yet Wharton's outrage against the shams she delineates is ultimately deflected by a powerful ambivalence. Though she abhors the premises of the world she explores, she also undercuts with mockery or pity whatever alternative social ideologies her novel contemplates. Thus, by the end of Lily Bart's life and story, Wharton's satire is reshaped into dialectic.

Wharton's contempt for the occupants of the house of mirth marks almost every page of the novel. If her intended point is to reveal the deformations caused by a frivolous devotion to appearances, then the evidence could be taken from the book almost at random, but the proof text may be the splendidly acid portrait of Lily Bart's aunt, Mrs. Peniston. A minor but thoroughly illuminating character, Mrs. Peniston virtually embodies the ethical dislocations of her society. In her case, manners stand in no discernible relation to morals: Manners have simply replaced morals altogether. Respectability, a sealed and self-regarding system, has supplanted humanity. "Mrs. Peniston had kept her imagination shrouded like the drawing-room furniture. She knew . . . that society was 'very much changed' . . . but the idea that any scandal could attach to a young girl's name . . . was so new to her that she was as much aghast as if she had been accused of leaving her carpets down all summer or of violating any of the other cardinal laws of housekeeping."[28] To Mrs. Peniston, the idea of immorality was as offensive "as a smell of cooking in the drawing-room" (p. 134).

The comic reductions captured in each of these comparisons express the essential reversal. Mrs. Peniston's grotesque failures of proportion are at the same time typical: She represents a whole society for which the outwardness of things has overtaken the inward.

The satire here is perfectly straightforward, but its implications deserve a moment's attention. Few writers in our literature were more interested in the connections between characters and their environments than Edith Wharton. Recall that her first book was not fiction at all but a guide to design, *The Decoration of Houses* (1897, written in collaboration with Ogden Cogman). Recall that her first novel, *The Valley of Decision* (1902), whatever its merits or demerits as a work of imagination, is taken up very largely with frequent and long and detailed re-creations of its eighteenth-century Italian scene. Recall, finally, the title of *The House of Mirth*. At the core of this novel's well-known naturalism lies Edith Wharton's conviction that personality depends largely upon circumstance. The fate that lies waiting for Lily Bart has announced itself, in a summary figure, as early as the novel's third page: "She was so evidently the victim of the civilization which had produced her that the links of her bracelet seemed like manacles chaining her to her fate" (p. 9).

This judgment reaches us from Lawrence Selden's point of view, but he quite obviously comprehends Lily's doom only dimly. Indeed, it is his inadequate grasp of what might be called this novel's materialist sociology that gives the lie to his rhetoric of liberation. Such as it is, Selden elaborates the book's only sustained definition of autonomy, and one hears in it familiar romantic and antinomian accents. Though Lily herself finds Selden's remarks appealing, both the vocabulary he chooses and the place in which he stands as he speaks suggest the irrelevance of what he says.

He identifies success with personal freedom. When Lily sensibly asks if he means freedom from worries, Selden replies impatiently: "From everything – from money, from poverty, from ease and anxiety, from all the material accidents. To keep a kind of republic of the spirit . . ." (pp. 72–73). The limits of Selden's conception expose themselves instantly in the self-consuming language in which he articulates it: freedom at once from money *and* poverty, from ease *and* anxiety. This is not an idea; it is, at best, talk. What is not trivial here is potentially ominous. That is, if a serious desire is being voiced in Selden's oxymorons, it envisions something like that yearning toward the denial of self that we saw recurring in the late fiction of Henry James.

In any case, as much as Selden's choice of words cripples his dissent, his authority is even more emphatically subverted by the setting of this conversation. He and Lily stand in a woods, and his appeal to her alleged self-sufficiency is enriched by its resonance with this most traditionally emblematic of American geographies. Lily has been refined almost out of existence and altogether out of freedom, Selden suggests, by a conspiring civilization. The trees and hills of their present retreat might recall her to an assertion of her "natural" self, and this in turn might give her the strength to break the mold of artifice in which she is confined.

Alas, the setting of Selden's rendezvous with Lily is indeed significant, but its meaning is flatly opposed to his intentions. As he seems to have forgotten, but Wharton has surely not, the woods he and Lily wander in are a part of Gus Trenor's suburban estate, Bellomont. The hills Selden climbs, the trees that shade him, the meadows he admires, have been paid for, measured, landscaped, and maintained by Trenor's fortune. This is one of the few scenes in *The House of Mirth* to take place outdoors. Yet, thematically, the woods of Bellomont serve to double rather than to contest the inescapable control of the society they embellish. Lily Bart and Edith Wharton both understand this; Selden's blithe ignorance of it measures to the inch his inadequacy (Plate 7).

Lily also understands that what is true for nature and for the decoration of houses is true for her as well. Lily Bart, shaped from her birth to treasure the gilded furnishings of her surroundings, is herself treasured only as a decorative object. In this are declared the most sinister dimensions of the social and moral incoherence embodied in Mrs. Peniston. In such an environment, Lily is of necessity alienated from whatever inner sources she might attempt to base her self-definition on. Her survival depends upon joining with all those around her and scrutinizing herself continuously from the outside.

Lily Bart is aware of the insults offered to her humanity by her society, and she struggles intermittently to escape them. But the truth of her situation annihilates her rebellion in the first moments of its emergence. She is doomed to grasp for what she despises, to desire what she knows is meretricious, and thus to assent to her own diminishment.

> She had learned by experience that she had neither the aptitude
> nor the moral constancy to remake her life on new lines . . . and
> let the world of luxury and pleasure sweep by her unregarded . . .
> Inherited tendencies had combined with early training to make her
> the highly specialized product she was: an organism as helpless
> out of its narrow range as the sea-anemone torn from the rock.
> She had been fashioned to adorn and delight. (P. 311)

Like Glasgow, Wharton encodes her heroine's fate in the specific terms of evolutionary biology. But this is little more than mannerism. For, again like Glasgow, Wharton only uses the quasiscientific formulas metaphorically, to further deepen the shades of an already dark insight into the oppression of women in this culture.

The several elements of Lily Bart's fate converge in the novel's central and most richly symbolic event, the *tableau vivant* staged by the Wellington Brys. The procession of women who precede Lily in this evening-long event serve to delay her own appearance and thus to heighten her effect; but that procession works thematically to assert that all women in this society are its victims, not Lily alone. Carry Fisher as a Goya, Mrs. van Alstyne as a Van Dyck, Miss Smedden as Titian's "Daughter," and many others march lightheartedly across the impro-

She turned on him a face softened but not disfigured by emotion.

PLATE 7. One of the A. B. Wenzell illustrations that accompanied the serialization of *The House of Mirth* in *Scribner's Magazine*. The meeting between Lily Bart and Lawrence Selden appeared in the March 1905 installment.

vised Bry stage, unwittingly affirming their own abasement, their reduction to delectable entertainment.

Lily appears last, and her *tableau* creates a sensation: "The unanimous
'Oh!' of the specatators was a tribute, not to the brushwork of Reynolds' 'Mrs. Lloyd' but to the flesh-and-blood loveliness of Lily Bart"
(p. 141). Wharton's further compliment is actually frightening in its
implications: "It was as though she had stepped, not out of, but into,
Reynolds' canvas" (p. 141). Though its overt tone is less portentous,
there is a chilling resemblance between this scene and that in which
Milly Theale confronts the Bronzino portrait in *The Wings of the Dove*.
In both scenes, a woman's life is being translated into aesthetic terms,
and identity is being submerged in an idealization that is coextensive
with negation.[29] Appropriately, the point of view at the moment of
Lily's "triumph" shifts to the staring, admiring crowd. At the rear of
that crowd, Selden, who sees more than he comprehends, realizes that
he is witnessing "the real Lily Bart" (p. 142). Typically, Selden misun-
derstands. He applauds the "reality" for its stunning beauty, and it is
only when he hears Ned Van Alstyne make a moderately salacious
comment that Selden reinterprets the episode, feeling in it "the whole
tragedy" of Lily's life. Selden has got it almost exactly wrong. The
tragedy of Lily's life is declared in her *tableau,* but it has nothing to do
with Ned Van Alstyne's response. Lily as Reynolds's *Mrs. Lloyd* has
reached a kind of negative apotheosis, a poignant proof of her dependent, derivative, and decorative existence. It is perhaps significant that
salon portraitists of the 1890s and early 1900s, among them Aman-Jean
and Blanche, heightened the idealization of their female subjects by
repeating the poses, costumes, and settings of well-known eighteenth-
century portraits. One thinks of Sargent's *The Acheson Sisters* (1902) or
Mrs. Huth Jackson (1907), with their allusions to Reynolds and Ingres,
respectively.[30]

Thus, Lily's presentation of herself may be seen as an act of multiple imitation. She is not only re-creating Reynolds, she is recalling
the imitative techniques of the painters of her own generation. Acting
as her own artist, she complies with the sexual commands of her
culture by sentimentalizing herself and by detaching herself from the
reality of an immediate context. In this way, her creation of herself is
simultaneously a symbolic act of self-extinction. The rest of the novel
merely chronicles the outcome predicted by this moment in Lily's life.
Hounded by the predators who inhabit the house of mirth, she yet
yearns to live among them. Taunted by the idealism of the republic of
the spirit, she is intuitively sure of its unreality and of the weakness of
its spokesman. Lily wanders through the half-chosen, half-imposed
turnings, the gratuitous reversals, and the blind alleys of her moral

maze. At the end of the path awaits death, the only release such a woman in such a setting can achieve.

A brief comment here on *Ethan Frome* (1911). This novel offers the most provocative transcript in the record of Wharton's debate between liberation and control to appear between *The House of Mirth* and *The Custom of the Country* (1913). The moral dialectic of the book is more elusive than critics have perceived. Wharton simultaneously affirms and denies the rigorous vestigial (or atavistic) puritanism embodied in Ethan. His personal integrity, fidelity, and self-sacrifice are undeniably heroic. But the same standards eventuate in the inhumane, repressive, and claustrophobic world in which Ethan Frome lives out his tragedy. And the end is unforgiving waste: Wharton holds out no vision of redeeming self-knowledge, or hope, or love, or even illusion. Rather, Wharton renders a landscape in which integrity creates its own trap.

In such stories as "Souls Belated" and *The House of Mirth*, Edith Wharton stands anxiously and ambivalently between two social worlds; in *Ethan Frome*, between two moral worlds. And, given her own assumptions as a novelist of manners, that is, the interpenetration of manners and morals, the two situations are, if not identical, closely linked.

The last chapter of *The Custom of the Country* opens with nine-year-old Paul Marvell's desultory tour of the immense Paris *hôtel* his mother and stepfather, Undine and Elmer Moffatt, have just bought. Though Paul has been a fairly prominent figure throughout the novel's second half, these few pages are the only ones told through his point of view. Wharton's use of Paul is shrewd.

To begin with, Wharton is employing Paul as a perspective device. As he wanders about the newly purchased *hôtel*, his small size multiplies the huge scale of the place. Wharton's purposes at the close of the novel include the persuasive rendering of Undine Spragg's almost unimaginable financial and material success, and she achieves that effect to a substantial degree simply by "shrinking" the point of view to that of a child. The vast hallways, high ceilings, huge furniture, and oversize paintings grow fantastically yet plausibly to almost immeasurable dimensions as they surround and loom over the small, sensitive boy.

Further, as he wanders to "all the rooms in turn,"[31] his main emotion is a loneliness exactly in proportion to the gigantic emptiness of his home, a sense of isolation as complete as the assorted spoils of several nations and centuries can devise. When he reaches Mr. Moffatt's rooms, Paul encounters a painting that sums up both the opulence of his setting and the sadness of his fate: "a single picture – the portrait of a boy in grey velvet – that interested Paul most of all. The boy's hand rested on the head of a big dog, and he looked infinitely noble and charming, and yet (in spite of the dog) so sad and lonely that he too might have come home that very day to a strange house in which none of his old things could be found" (p. 578).

In its own diminished mode, this encounter between the boy and the elegant portrait (surely by Van Dyck) that proclaims his sorrow rather resembles – to refer to the scene for the final time – Milly Theale's twinned shocks of elation and despair when she faces the Bronzino at Matcham. We have seen, in discussing *The House of Mirth*, Edith Wharton's resort to analogies of art in support of her themes. In a society such as hers, which has reduced both its women and its children to the status – at best – of ornament, these analogies are especially apt.

Paul's alienation from the innumerable and beautiful things around him constitutes a finely disconcerting emblem for the waste implied by his mother's career, as the echoing emptiness of the mansion summarizes the emptiness of her triumph. James's example again suggests itself: Undine's excess is revealed to us, at the last, through the eyes of an innocent, and the corruption we see appears the more vile therefore.

In addition, Paul is not merely an innocent, he is a victim, hurt and bewildered by his mother's rapacity, her single-minded campaign in pursuit of place and possession. Not only the Van Dyck, but the cascade of beautiful objects around him describes the limits of Paul's freedom and embodies as well the conviction of desolation that so deeply informs the novel's conclusion. Thus, Paul is attracted to the library, with its

> rows and rows of books, bound in dim browns and golds, and old faded reds as rich as velvet: they all looked as if they might have had stories in them as splendid as their bindings. But the bookcases were closed with gilt trellising, and when Paul reached up to open one, a servant told him that Mr. Moffatt's secretary kept them locked because the books were too valuable to be taken down. (Pp. 578–579)

This vignette not only dramatizes the transformation of culture into consumption, the subordination of the contents of books to their bindings, it also intensifies the poignance of Paul's isolation: "If he could have found a book anywhere – any kind of a book – he would have forgotten the long hours and the empty house" (p. 580). The shadow of Paul's dead father, Ralph Marvell, falls across this moment as well, that sensitive, ineffectual man whose bookish proclivities marked him out as incapable of surviving in the world of Undine Spragg.

Indeed, Edith Wharton multiplies the echoes in this scene. "*Hôtel*," French for mansion or great house, nonetheless inevitably places before us the English world "hotel," which in turn reminds us that the novel opened in the Hotel Stentorian and that Wharton's concern has been to anatomize American culture as characteristically a civilization of transience. Undine's third husband, Raymond de Chelles, captures all of his creator's outrage and despair when he denounces Undine for her demand that he sell his valuable tapestries:

> "You come among us from a country we don't know, and can't imagine, a country you care for so little that before you've been a day in ours you've forgotten the very house you were born in – if it wasn't torn down before you knew it! . . . you come from hotels as big as towns, and from towns as flimsy as paper, where the streets haven't had time to be named, and the buildings are demolished before they're dry, and the people are as proud of changing as we are to holding to what we have." (P. 545)

For Edith Wharton, as for Henry James, the hotel epitomizes the American character. I cited earlier James's bitterly comic question of whether "the hotel-spirit may not just *be* the American spirit most seeking and most finding itself."[32] Wharton could have written the lines herself.

That restless spirit is quintessentially Undine Spragg. Named appropriately for a cosmetic application her father once marketed, her name unintendedly but even more aptly recalls the fluid, ever-changing waves of the sea. She "could not help modelling herself on the last person she met" (p. 19). She rests only in the restlessness of change, she is possessed of an appetite made always hungrier by acquisition. Hotels are her home, and homes are transformed into mere hotels, moments only of pause for this supremely American spirit, seeking but never finding itself.

Which brings us back to Paul, in the novel's final chapter. For Paul is the latest and most pathetic casualty of his mother's rootless restlessness, and the one on whose behalf Wharton's readers are probably prepared to forgive least. Watching him wander adrift among Undine's gargantuan things, we remember that Paul himself has been reduced to a commodity by his mother's ambition: She had literally tried to sell him to his father. Cut off by her sex from dealing in the money markets of capitalism, Undine emerges as a plutocrat of the flesh, her own most often, her son's most perniciously.

It is, of course, fitting that the Saint Désert tapestries, which provoked the rupture between Undine and Chelles, should make their way in this final chapter to the walls of the Moffats' enormous house. More than anything else, more than their intrinsic beauty, or their historical dignity, or their financial worth, the tapestries had signified

Family: that "powerful and indivisible whole" (p. 513) to which individuals willingly subordinate themselves, whose stability and continuity is far more than the sum of its parts. Thus, the forsaken Paul and
his "French father's" misappropriated tapestries together represent the
disintegration of familial values under the tumultuous impact of Undine's modernity.

Significantly, in the novel's final scene, Paul sees the newly installed
tapestries and his newly returned mother at the same moment: "As he
reached the landing he saw the ballroom doors were open and all the
lustres lit. His mother and Mr. Moffatt stood in the middle of the
shining floor, looking up at the walls; and Paul's heart gave a wondering bound, for there, set in great gilt panels, were the tapestries that had
always hung in the gallery at Saint Désert" (p. 587).

Edith Wharton has worked deliberately toward the climactic irony of
Paul's joy, the "wondering bound" of his heart, and she sustains it with
equal deliberation: " 'Oh, mother, mother!' he burst out, feeling, between his mother's face and the others, hardly less familiar, on the
walls, that he was really at home again, and not in a strange house"
(p. 587). Needless to say, Paul is not at all at home; nor shall he ever
be. And the house he is in is and will remain altogether strange.

Paul has come to the landing from Mrs. Heeny's room. Her presence, too, propels the novel's conclusion back toward its opening; she
had initially appeared in the first chapter. Her large reticule full of
newspaper clippings is another measure of Undine's success. At the
beginning of the novel, playing the role of Undine's social guide, Mrs.
Heeny had documented the celebrity of others by producing one or
another torn scrap of journalistic evidence. In the novel's last chapter,
all of her clippings have a single subject, Undine herself.

"Just you look at these clippings," Mrs. Heeny commands Paul. "I
guess you'll find a lot in them about your Ma" (p. 582). And if not in
them, then nowhere, is Edith Wharton's point. Not merely because
Undine is too rapidly in motion to find time to tell Paul anything about
herself, though she is. Nor merely because she would lie, though she
would. Rather, more important, Mrs. Heeny's clippings, comic when
they are first introduced, have *become,* in a reductively sinister way,
whatever identity Undine has.[33] Surrounded throughout her story by
mirrors and reflecting surfaces, Undine takes her definition of herself
from what she sees around her. Despite the enormity of her vanity
(perhaps because of it), she exists exclusively for others: She *is* insofar as
she is perceived and *as* she is perceived. The newspaper accounts of her
are thus not a deforming caricature but a fair estimate of the caricature
she has become: a woman devoid of interiority, given substance only
by publicity.

"To have things had always seemed to her the first essential of existence" (p. 537). At its most engaged and intense, Undine's vision of
things unrolls "itself before her like the long triumph of an Asiatic
conqueror" (p. 538). Against Undine's indomitable materialism, Edith
Wharton opposes Ralph Marvell's idealism. And against her outward-
looking vision of a universe of things, Wharton opposes Ralph's in-
ward-looking gaze: toward "the world of wonders within him" (p. 75).
If Undine's moral geography consists of vistas crowded with objects,
Ralph's is symbolically comprised of the cave he discovered as a child:
"a secret inaccessible place with glaucous lights, mysterious murmurs,
and a single shaft of communication with the sky" (p. 76). Whereas
Undine lives a derivative, imitative life, dependent on brightly lit show
and filled with noise, Ralph's cave is an image of self-sufficiency, suffused in half-light, steeped in silence, and altogether suggestive of an
identity whose sources are interior.

But this contrast between Undine and Ralph, accurate as far as it
goes, misleads by going nowhere near far enough. For Undine is not
simply the grasping immoralist of a feminized Horatio Alger tale; she is
as well a complexly determined victim. And Ralph is not at the last a
traditional idealist in protest against the ravages of materialism but a
moral trifler whose small strength evaporates in the atmosphere of his
own passivity.

Consider again Ralph's cave. The emblem of his inward being, yes,
but the emblem as well of evasion. Wharton may or may not have had
Plato consciously in mind; in either case, Ralph's cave resembles that of
the *Republic*. It is a place from which the world's reality can be discerned only obscurely, in which any being outside the self is reduced to
the peripheral condition of shadow. Ralph is another in Wharton's long
gallery of American heroes whose conception of autonomy reveals itself
as coextensive with escape. Unable to act efficaciously upon the external world, Ralph contents himself with dissident gestures acted out
against a background of repeated ethical self-congratulation. Without
insisting on influence in either direction, Ralph resembles no one so
closely as his nearly exact contemporary, J. Alfred Prufrock. Like
Eliot's timid lover, Ralph lingers in his sea chamber until he is literally
drowned by the human voices of the twentieth century.

Continuously throughout the novel, Edith Wharton insists on the
inadequacy of Ralph's ideals. His poetry and sketches lie about unfin-
ished, evidence of his "desultory dabbling with life" (p. 75). It is only
partially the case that Ralph is unfitted for the broils of modern life
because of his sensitivity, though his sensitivity is real. The usually
astute Charles Bowen is inclined by his affection for Ralph to see his
friend's failures in these terms. Bowen casts his analysis in terms of the

sociology of power, the unequal contest between new and old: "poor
Ralph was a survival, and destined, as such, to go down in any conflict
with the rising forces" (p. 280). Such a judgment carries something of
Edith Wharton's conviction. So too do Ralph's own, rather more sar-
donic estimates include a measure of the truth, his feeling for instance
that the Dagonet attitude – the aristocratic inclinations of old New
York – has "as little bearing on life as the humors of a Restoration
comedy" (p. 311), or his view that he himself "seemed to be stumbling
about in his inherited prejudices like a modern man in medieval armor"
(p. 469). The echoes of Edith Wharton's sympathy – of her own abiding
conservatism – may be heard in Clare Van Degen's wistful remark to
Ralph, "Shall I tell you what I think, my dear? You and I are both
completely out of date" (pp. 445–446).

But Ralph represents something far more troubling than the lament-
able fate of antique virtue in a commercial world. The "small, cautious,
middle-class" ideals of what Ralph calls "aboriginal New York," ideals
he regards as "singularly coherent and respectable" (p. 74), prove upon
testing to be singularly inhumane; and though they *are* coherent and
altogether respectable, Ralph's adherence to them unintendedly exposes
the *trivial* strengths of the "Dagonet system." The "reverses and discriminations" of the Dagonet tradition that Ralph has proudly opposed
to the "limitless concessions" of the modern world are negative values
(pp. 305–306). Even at their best, they signify absence of one sort or
another.

Summarily stated, Ralph's proves to be an ethic not of decency but of
respectable conformity, not of compassion but of convention, not of
spontaneous generosity but of calculated propriety. An unmistakable
confusion over means and ends marks Ralph's values. Nowhere does
Wharton make this clearer than in the exquisite irony that at once
explains and condemns Ralph's failure to fight Undine for custody of
their son: "For Paul's sake," he had been told, "there must be no
scandal" (p. 437). We have already seen the consequences for Paul of his
father's weakness. Ralph's system proves to be built not on principles
but on "catchwords, the full and elaborate vocabulary of evasion: 'deli-
cacy,' 'pride,' 'personal dignity,' 'preferring not to know about such
things' . . ." (p. 436). These, then, are the moral limits of Ralph's cave:
willed ignorance disguised as superiority of feeling.

In an analogy of art – more specifically, of the artist – Claud Walsing-
ham Popple give appropriate expression to the ideals of Ralph's world.
Popple's artistic credentials are several, among them his unique ability
to "do pearls." He "always subordinated art to elegance"; he eliminated
the "messy" from his studio as completely as from his paintings; and,
finally, "it was often said, in praise of his work, that he was the only

artist who kept his studio tidy enough for a lady to sit to him in a new dress" (p. 187). The banality of Popple's mind matches the cosmetic irrelevance of his portraits. His talent lies in "idealizing flesh and realizing dress-fabrics" (p. 195). He paints, in other words, in the visual grammar of evasion. And, though Ralph despises him, he admits that Popple quite accurately expresses the ideals of the Dagonet-Marvell world (p. 72).

Edith Wharton, thus, stands poised – perhaps foiled – between contrasting but equivalently corrupt moral possibilities. On the one hand is Undine's world of appetite, indiscriminately ingesting everything in its path, on the other Ralph's world of passivity, fastidiously destructive in its omissions and bloodlessness.

Furthermore, though she virtually embodies the explosive new energies of her era, Undine is rendered a much more complex moral being than that sort of allegorical identification might imply. To begin with, like American heroines before and after her, she retains her innocence in spite of the most wordly experience. She seeks amusement, but she would have it coupled with respectability; and despite her divorce and her entry into the "fast" life of Paris, "her notion of amusement was hardly less innocent than when she had hung on the plumber's fence with Indiana Frusk" (p. 354).

Undine's innocence might be discounted as morally valueless, rather a predatory amorality commensurate with her total self-absorption than a genuine liberation from guilt. So also might be dismissed the "Apex puritanism which," we are told, "despite some odd accommodations and compliances, still carried its head so high in her" (p. 353). Nonetheless, judgments of this sort, appearing periodically throughout the novel, finally detach Undine from any one-dimensional moral identity. Her career implies conflicting but coexisting values.

Undine Spragg's dilemma as a character – which mirrors Edith Wharton's as an analyst – is contained most powerfully in the paradox that she is simultaneously the victim and the emblem of her society. Charles Bowen develops this view of Undine most expansively. He does so by placing her in the context of America's oppressive sexual beliefs, which, in turn, express the nation's deepest commercial commitments. America is a society, according to Bowen, in which "all the romantic values are reversed" (p. 207); its emotional center of gravity is not love, as in Europe, but business. "In America the real *crime passionel* is a 'big steal' " (p. 207). It is, says Bowen, as revenge against the indifference of their men that American women devote themselves so desperately to material things, to clothes and money and cars: "They pretend to themselves and each other that *that's* what really constitutes life" (p. 208). In their very acts of consumption, in short, these women are the most conspicuous ornaments in their culture. And, whatever their conscious feelings, they are victims. Bowen concludes his analysis with Undine: "She's a monstrously perfect result of the system: the completest proof of its triumph." Bowen is right, and so is Ralph a few chapters later when he proposes a version of Undine's fate to himself while trying to forgive her for neglecting Paul's birthday: "Poor Undine! She was what the gods had made her – a creature of skin-deep reactions, a mote in the beam of pleasure" (p. 224).

Ralph's pity for Undine is more than matched by his self-pity, as he begins to regard himself more and more rigorously as a victim. Typically, Wharton uses Ralph's art to comment on his circumstances: As he declines into despair, his proposed novel declines from heroism. "He no longer saw life on the heroic scale: he wanted to do something in which men should look no bigger than the insects they were" (p. 427). In short, Ralph would write a naturalist novel, trapping his characters in their diminished destinies much as Undine Spragg – in part through Ralph's complicity – has been trapped in hers.

There are glimpses of the heroic from time to time in *The Custom of the Country*, but they attach to Ralph's adversaries. Ralph himself says of Elmer Moffatt: "Jove, I wish I could put him in a book! There's something epic about him – a kind of epic effrontery" (p. 254). To be sure, the remark is a casual one; and it denies as much as it concedes. And, at the novel's end, the denial remains intact. By that time the sly and unscrupulous Moffatt has gathered the combined wealth of Midas and Morgan and Adam Verver; he has become the greatest of all the American collectors; his wedding presents to Undine have been enumerated ("a necklace and tiara of pigeon-blood rubies belonging to Queen Marie Antoinette, a million dollar cheque and a house in New York . . . which is an exact copy of the Pitti Palace"). Edith Wharton has created in Elmer Moffatt a grotesquely overblown parody of American success.

Yet, more significantly, Ralph's concessions to Elmer's epic stature remain intact through the novel's end as well. Moffatt is not a mere parody. The turn-of-the-century opinions of another novelist can specify Moffatt's role with greater precision. The essays collected by Frank Norris under the title *The Responsibilities of the Novelist* include several meditations on the possibilities for an American epic. (The book was published posthumously in 1903, a busy moment in the recurrent chase after that hoariest of American cultural hares, "the Great American Novel.") In the book's seventh essay, "The Frontier Gone at Last," Norris laments the closing of the West. The frontier had become an integral part of our conception of things: "It was romance," writes Norris, "the place of the poetry of the Great March."[34] After hundreds of years of real and imaginary westering, suddenly the frontier closed, and so, with an alarming simultaneity, did that further frontier, the Pacific. When the American navy entered Manila Bay, when the marines landed in China, "the Anglo-Saxon in his course of empire had circled the globe . . . and reached the starting point of his history" (p. 72). There was "no longer any West" (p. 72), save that of the barnstorming cowboy shows, which were not more than a collection of self-conscious, theatrical fakes.

Out of this imaginative bankruptcy emerges the new epic hero, the American businessman. With something very like Edith Wharton's mixture of awe and irony, Norris appoints the manufacturer as "the new warrior." A current Richard the Lion-Hearted would be "a leading representative of Amalgamated Steel" and, conversely, Andrew Carnegie, if he had been born earlier, would have been a Crusader (p. 74). It was Ralph Marvell, we recall, who had figured his own obsolescence by likening himself to a man stumbling about in his prejudices as in medieval armor. It is Elmer Moffatt, though, clad in no other armor than his nerve, who plays the heroic part in the modern romance of acquisition. The contrast with Ralph's inert irrelevance is pointed.

Furthermore, Moffatt is possessed of other virtues than courage, calculation, and good sense. He is meticulously honest, at least in those of his dealings that affect any of the main characters. He is actually interested in Paul and compassionate toward him, both before and after his marriage to Undine. In his dealings with Undine, he is nothing short of chivalric; there is no other word for it. He permits her to divorce him when he proves inconvenient to her; he maintains his silence about the secret for years; he pursues her like some questing knight of the grail; and he rejects her own "unrespectable" proposal, insisting on marriage.

Again, while there is undeniable parody in Elmer Moffatt's knighthood, as there is in the image of four-times-married Undine as grail, there is a measure of truth as well. They represent not merely what succeeds, but what lives. Virtually all the novel's vitality is reserved for them.

In addition, the destructiveness that they embody proves at last not exclusive to them at all: It proves in fact close kin (though of a different coloration) to the malevolence of their antagonists.

More than Ralph Marvell, it is Raymond de Chelles whose values seem to be most precisely antithetical to those of Elmer Moffatt. Ralph's claims for stability, tradition, and so on, are at best derivatively European and thus, as we have seen, are of more interest in documenting Ralph's alienation than in demonstrating the integrity of the ideals he professes. Chelles, on the other hand, is the more or less literal and organic product of the tradition Ralph reveres. Properly it is Chelles, in a passage cited earlier, who gives voice to the novel's most polemical assault on America's indulgence in energy, its commitment to mobility and transience, and who most eloquently defends the primacy of the family, of continuity, of history.

Yet ultimately, Undine is right about Chelles. If he represents his house, it also represents him; and when the novel's scene shifts to the aptly named estate of Saint Désert, "everything in the great empty house smelt of dampness" (p. 490). And not to Undine only. The predominating imagery of the château is of stagnation and decay. The house is populated by a handful of female Chelles dependents, motionless in their chairs, reduced to endless needlework, denied a share of the present or any reason for the future, denied an identity aside from their master's. The long, empty, unlit, unheated halls and galleries echo only with dim recollections. The entire estate is thickly encrusted with spiritual rust. Even more pointedly, the hypocrisy resident in the contrast between the Marquis de Chelles's rural propriety and his frequent absences to visit his Parisian mistress is richly distasteful.

The real lesson of Chelles, then, as it was of Ralph Marvell, is not the opposition of traditional ideals to modern vices but rather the revelation of a complementary corruption. Like the Dagonet system, but far more massively and inescapably, Chelles's tradition implicates the diminishment of the people it purports to enhance, and most particularly the diminishment of its women. *The Custom of the Country* may be a text in the delineation of the "international theme," an essay in comparative European and American manners and morals, but beneath that comparison lies the central, fundamental likeness: Both worlds agree in reducing women to the superfluity of ornament. As Edith Wharton knew, Undine Spragg's victimization, which is no figure of speech, has roots that reach deep and far: back in time and across the Atlantic, from twentieth-century New York to the medieval European ideology that Chelles continues to uphold.

This identifies another of Elmer Moffatt's virtues quite clearly. Bad as the bargain between him and Undine may be from some points of view, he is the only person in the novel who treats her more or less as an equal. It is possible to find in his equality, as one group of distinguished critics does, only Edith Wharton's lament: "Undine's career of marital wreckage . . . is paralleled by the buccaneering financial career of Elmer Moffatt. . . . The two careers combine like elements in a vast metaphor . . . about the deepest and the strangely similar forces – sex and business – at work to shake and transform the world of American society."[35] This is eloquently said, but it says a good deal too little. As I have tried to show, *The Custom of the Country* is a lament, but it reaches much further than Undine Spragg and Elmer Moffatt: It reaches to just about every character in the book, and to every social possibility those characters represent.[36]

Chapter 7

Building the past and the future: Ralph Adams Cram, Frank Lloyd Wright, and others

THE ECLECTICS AND THEIR ENEMIES

Half a century ago, when the young Henry-Russell Hitchcock and Philip Johnson published *The International Style: Architecture since 1922*, they invented the phrase that has labeled the predominant architectural movement of the twentieth century. The book was, of course, a landmark. Its passionately dogmatic argument on behalf of Gropius and Mies and Le Corbusier predicted and indeed did much to shape critical orthodoxy in the years that followed. Hitchcock and Johnson made two principal claims. The first was that architectural developments in the twenties were coherent and even unified. Thus architects were finally solving "the problem of establishing one dominant style, which the nineteenth century set itself in terms of alternative revivals."[1] The solution, the international style, replaced the cacophony of eclecticism with a rational harmony.

The second claim was a corollary. In the admiring opinion of Hitchcock and Johnson, the international style was much less an evolutionary outcome than a revolutionary answer to what had preceded it; it was new in an essential way. Consequently, celebrating the international style perforce required denouncing what had gone before as "an impasse of imitation and sterility" (p. 18). The entire architectural performance of the nineteenth century is rebuked in a dismissive paragraph:

> The nineteenth century failed to create a style of architecture because it was unable to achieve a genuine discipline of structure and of design in the terms of the day. The revived "styles" were but a decorative garment to architecture, not the internal principles according to which it lived and grew. On the whole the development of engineering in building went on regardless of the Classical or Medieval architectural forms which were borrowed from the past. Thus the chaos of eclecticism served to give the very idea

of style a bad name in the estimation of the first modern architects
of the end of the nineteenth and the beginning of the twentieth
century. (P. 18)

Hitchcock and Johnson called these first modern architects "half-mod-
ern." Men such as Peter Behrens, Otto Wagner, Auguste Perret, and
H. P. Berlage each "broke in his own way with the immediate past"
(p. 24), but none was able to forge out of that break a new stylistic
synthesis. The only twentieth-century American numbered in the com-
mendatory list is Frank Lloyd Wright: "Wagner, Behrens and Perret
lightened the solid massiveness of traditional architecture; Wright dyna-
mited it" (p. 26). The incendiary metaphor catches the authors' blithely
pugnacious assurance.

Aside from Wright, the American architectural scene in the early
years of the twentieth century seemed to Hitchcock and Johnson an
undifferentiated wasteland. The prewar years at their best made up a
period of "confused and contradictory experimentation" (p. 20). At
their worst – which was far more typical – those years merely continued
the revivalist excesses of the nineteenth century. Wright himself would
later call this period a time in which eclecticism created "one grand
rubbish heap of the acknowledged styles."[2]

Writing from the midst of those years, in 1902, the irascible Brooks
Adams reached much the same glum conclusion:

> A body of material produced during certain epochs is arbitrarily
> selected as worthy, and from this material architects are thought
> to be justified in borrowing whatever may suit their purpose, or
> strike their fancy, irrespective of the language their predecessors
> spoke, or the ideas which they conveyed. The arms of a pope
> may be used to adorn the front of a New England library, or the
> tomb of the Virgin for a booth at an international commercial
> exhibition.[3]

It may indeed have been the case, as Hitchcock repeated in another,
later book, that "the first quarter of the twentieth century was on the
whole rather a period of reaction in architectural design," but the simplifications of Adams's sarcasm and Hitchcock's disdain obscure several
important truths nonetheless.[4] To begin with, the backward-looking
architecture of the early twentieth century was never "arbitrary," at
least not in its own terms, nor was it casual in its choices. It produced a
whole series of distinctive styles, each competing with the others, and
each supported by more or less sophisticated appeals to history, to
society, to culture.

Classicism was the most ubiquitous of the revival styles – and was

therefore for decades after the First World War the particular target of
modernists. Several versions of classicism dominated American architecture in the early 1900s; the fury of its later repudiation was in proportion to its immense success. According to Lewis Mumford, from
1895 to 1915, "the white cloud of classicism hung poisonously over the
whole country."[5] But if classicism was covering much of the available
building land, it nonetheless shared American space with other historical movements that looked back to different antecedents. The most
important of these, to which we shall shortly return, was Gothic. The
Georgian Revival is another example, both in its neo-Adamesque and
neo-colonial modes. And the so-called Jacobean Revival, with its bay
windows, tall chimneys, brick walls, and strapwork, reached a boister-
ous climax in the dormitories of the University of Pennsylvania (Cope
and Stewardson, 1895).[6]

To some observers, the only twentieth-century buildings that seemed
to confess any alliance with the present or the future were the skyscrapers; the rest looked to the past. Many writers remarked on this
dichotomy, but it remained for Geroge Santayana, in "The Genteel
Tradition in American Philosophy" (1911), to meditate on the doubleness of architecture as the most fully realized symbol of America's
divided mind.

> One half of the American mind, that not occupied intensely in
> practical affairs, has remained, I will not say high-and-dry, but
> slightly becalmed; it has floated gently in the backwater, while,
> alongside, in invention and industry and social organization the
> other half of the mind was leaping down a sort of Niagara Rapids.
> This division may be found symbolized in American architecture:
> a neat reproduction of the colonial mansion – with some modern
> comforts introduced surreptitiously – stands beside the skyscraper.
> The American Will inhabits the skyscraper; the American Intellect
> inhabits the colonial mansion. The one is the sphere of the Ameri-
> can man; the other, at least predominantly, of the American
> woman. The one is all aggressive enterprise; the other is all gen-
> teel tradition.[7]

Of course, Santayana's "colonial mansion" is shorthand for a congeries
of American imitations. Ancient Greece and Rome, Renaissance Italy
and England, these were some of the idealized and therefore mystified
cultures whose architectural leavings were "selected as worthy," in
Brooks Adams's archly disapproving phrase, and copied in museums,
colleges, hospitals, statehouses, tombs, and post offices all over the
United States. From 1893 on, the imperial gesture, with its Roman

arches and ersatz Roman site planning, became the undeviating mark of government buildings.

It would be hard to overemphasize the distance between the buildings that were widely admired in the early 1900s (Boston's Public Library, New York's Pennsylvania Station, North Carolina's Biltmore, Washington, D.C.'s, Pan-American Union) and those that have found praise in subsequent generations (Sullivan's Wainwright Building in Saint Louis, Greene and Greene's Gamble House in Pasadena, Wright's Larkin Building in Buffalo). Discrepancies between the tastes of a period and the judgments of a later time are, to be sure, commonplace in the history of all the arts. Equally common is the compulsive moralism that fuels each act of revision. Nineteenth-century responses to the rise of realism in fiction and twentieth-century reactions to its alleged decline, nineteenth-century comments on impressionism and twentieth-century estimates of cubism and the other modern movements in painting— such debates addressed separably formal questions only briefly and half-heartedly. Typically, the battle over style has been fought with the weapons of moralizing rhetoric. Aesthetic adversaries may find each other technically inept or culturally misinformed, but incompetence is invariably held to be the key to underlying turpitude. Architecture, perhaps because it is the most intrusive and inescapable, the most communally significant, and simply the most expensive of the arts, has provoked a library of ideological analysis.

One of the early contributors to that library was Pugin. The central thesis of Pugin's *Contrasts* (1836) "is that there is a necessary connection between religious truth and architectural truth."[8] Pugin's goal was to abolish the authority of the Renaissance and to restore the primacy of Gothic by emphasizing the perfect link between Gothic and Christianity. He developed the same argument in his next book, *The True Principles of Pointed or Christian Architecture* (1841): "If we view pointed architecture in its true light as Christian art, as the faith itself is perfect, so are the principles on which it is founded."[9] Architectural values are putatively deduced from the values of faith.

Over the past century and a half, the terms of the discussion have of course been secularized. Nonetheless, a single polemic line clearly runs from Pugin to Ruskin to Frank Lloyd Wright to Nikolaus Pevsner and beyond: Loosen the meaning of "religion" to include morality (or some equivalently evocative abstraction) and the argument hardly varies. The architectural styles each writer defends may be and often are utterly opposed to each other, but the strategy of defense is identical on all sides—the invocation of values beyond formalism, "higher" values such as "nature" or "necessity" or "democracy" or "truth."

The turn of the century illustrates the pattern. To their contemporary opponents, the practitioners of America's several historical styles acted as accomplices in a conspiracy of social and political chicaneries. The mansions they built seemed to their critics – such as Henry James – to be monstrous bombast, vulgar celebrations of wealth and pseudoaristocratic pretension. Frank Lloyd Wright, writing in 1910, scourged America's expensive houses as "dubious tributes to English architecture. They are 'manors' cut open and embellished inside to suit the ignorant 'taste.' . . . The result . . . is a more or less pitiful mongrel. Painfully conscious of their lack of traditions, our powerful get-rich-quick citizens attempt to buy Tradition ready made and are dragged forward facing backwards."[10] Wright continued his tirade by ridiculing these ersatz historical houses as America's "most characteristic example of 'conspicuous waste.' " And, acknowledging his source, Wright ends by commanding his reader: "Read Thorstein Veblen" (p. 95).

The direction is well advised. In *The Theory of the Leisure Class* (1899), Veblen declared that the "pecuniary canons of taste" had been "especially effective in the development" of architecture. Buildings, even more than other artifacts, were designed under the "surveillance of expensiveness" and were therefore particularly well adapted "to the end of conspicuous waste." American houses present only "an endless variety of architectural distress and of suggestions of expensive discomfort."[11] Public institutions, too – schools and libraries, hospitals and asylums – find their usefulness dissipated in ostentation.

> Certain funds, for instance, may have been set apart as a foundation for a foundling asylum or a retreat for invalids. The diversion of expenditure to honorific waste in such cases is not uncommon enough to cause surprise or even raise a smile. An appreciable share of the funds is spent in the construction of an edifice faced with some aesthetically objectionable but expensive stone, covered with grotesque and incongruous details, and designed, in its battlemented walls and turrets and its massive portals and strategic approaches, to suggest certain barbaric methods of warfare. The interior of the structure shows the same pervasive guidance of the canons of conspicuous waste and predatory exploit. (P. 349)

Veblen's critique would become the commonplace opinion of architectural and social observers during the succeeding half-century. Seen in this hard light, America's turn-of-the-century buildings were actually worse than pretentious. The architecture of conspicuous consumption ignored and at last betrayed the several purposes it ought to have served.

It was also, from the overblown domestic fantasies of Richard Morris Hunt to the commercial Gothic of Cass Gilbert's Woolworth Building

(1913), at bottom un-American. For one thing, its government buildings exalted an imperialism that William James, Mark Twain, and others found sordidly undemocratic. But the government buildings were not alone in this. McKim, Mead, and White; Carrère and Hastings; Warren and Wetmore – all set out to magnify the grandeur of their projects for two interconnected purposes. They wanted to prove the munificence of their public and private patrons and at the same time declare the preeminence of their country. America had taken its place among the leading nations and required an architecture commensurate with its new station. Their detractors perceived an exquisite paradox in such work. Precisely because the styles were derived so obviously from European exemplars, they confessed continued American deference; and stylistic deference implied moral and spiritual inferiority as well.

Thus, nationalism played a significant role on both sides of the architectural debate. But given the recurring confusion in this country between patriotism and theology, which was never more evident than in the early twentieth century, the invocation of undefined but mystical "nationhood" is predictable. Frank Lloyd Wright, self-professed disciple of Whitman and Emerson, saw the rhetorical possibilities early on and seized them. He may not have cleared away the obscurities of "organic architecture" by calling it "the architecture of democracy," but he accomplished something more. He bathed his formal program in the saving waters of America's civil religion.

Wright lived long enough to see the eclipse of his eclectic adversaries. Indeed, modernist architectural ideology prevailed so decisively after World War I that the major historical architects came near to being forgotten except on their opponents' terms. Their work has been perceived and explained chiefly in reduction and parody. Lewis Mumford found a vivid figure of consensus when he trivialized eclectic architecture as nothing more than a sustained act of "pious submission to the dead."[12]

Needless to say, these men had a rather different notion of what they were up to. To begin with, they attacked their Victorian predecessors for committing the same crimes that they would later be accused of by the modernists. Appealing to integrity and common sense, they charged their predecessors with being philistines, commercial in their motives, mindless in their misunderstanding of architectural and social history. As a corollary, though the turn-of-the-century eclectics disagreed on many things, they agreed on the essential honesty of their own use of the past. They anticipated the accusation of copying, and they denied it. They saw themselves, as a recent critic reconstructs their thinking, "taking up forms of proven and mature beauty from the formal and vernacular architectures of the past and adapting them,

learnedly but with personal touches, to modern building programs."[13]
The adopted forms were felt to be appropriate because they corre-
sponded to a whole range of cultural associations, and they offered a
completely intelligible iconography of political and social signification.
Through the power of historical allusiveness, form followed the function of inserting the new buildings of a new world power into the
continuum of Western civilization.

Whatever the merits of the various eclectic ideologies, the more important conclusion to be drawn about them is that they reflected a
widely shared mode of using the past in the years before the First
World War. Joseph Wells, one of the first of McKim, Mead, and
White's talented young designers, offers a usefully abbreviated example. Wells regularly jotted in a notebook his observations on art and
society. His contemporaries might have contested his particular judgments, but they would have accepted his way of proceeding, his recapitulation of architectural styles, as a choice among historical "ideals."

> The classical ideal suggests clearness, simplicity, grandeur, order
> and philosophic calm – consequently it delights my soul. The med-
> ieval ideal suggests superstition, ignorance, vulgarity, restlessness,
> cruelty and religion – all of which fill my soul with horror and
> loathing. The Renaissance ideal suggests a fine and cultivated soci-
> ety, with its crowds of gay ladies and gentlemen devoted to the
> pleasures and elegances of life – which excites my admiration, but
> not my sympathy.[14]

Note that architecture is never even mentioned. The engagement consists of the fiercely reacting Wells on the one side and, on the other, a
litany of past eras distilled into a handful of evaluative adjectives. Buildings are merely the implied outcome.

RALPH ADAMS CRAM

Cultural context, along with what the eclectics took to be the meaning
of the past, guided architectural type. Formulas like those of Joseph
Wells seem to threaten mannerism and literal imitation. And strict
imitation did occur from time to time – most notoriously perhaps in
the ludicrous lath and plaster re-creation of the Parthenon in Nash-
ville, Tennessee (1896; rebuilt in concrete in the 1920s). Yet such
copying is rare. The more typical historical architect mastered and
then varied his selected style. He "studied all aspects of the style in
which he proposed to design not just the standard ornamental motifs,
but the scale, proportions, massing, colors, and textures."[15] Even the

most devotedly nostalgic of these men – and that may very well have been Ralph Adams Cram – objected to exact imitation. Cram labeled that kind of copying "archaeology," and he excluded it from architecture altogether. "Movie theatricalism" was his term for mere reproduction, as he claimed to search for the "essence" underneath details of design.[16]

The turn-of-the-century Gothic movement, which Cram served both as chief practitioner and indefatigable propagandist, was the third of America's Gothic revivals. The first, of the 1830s–1850s, had produced among other buildings Richard Upjohn's Christ Church in Binghamton, New York, and St. Mary's in Burlington, New Jersey. It was succeeded, in the 1870s, by the High Victorian extravagances of Frank Furness. The first major building of the third revival was probably Cram's All Saints Church in Ashmont, near Boston.

From the mid-1890s to the First World War, Gothic flourished in several fields of construction. Predictably, churches provided the most frequent Gothic commissions, but the style spread to other sorts of buildings as well. Bryn Mawr (designed by Cope and Stewardson in the 1890s) introduced "Collegiate Gothic" into the United States. A large number of early twentieth-century mansions – a genre that had hitherto found its models mainly in French châteaux (what Wright called "French millinery") – were built in a Gothic manner. Cram and Bertram Goodhue created a "military perpendicular" for West Point in 1903. And the Woolworth Building brought Gothic to an improbable commercial apotheosis. Rising to almost eight hundred feet, this "Cathedral of Commerce" looked rather like "a Gothic church seen in one of those distorting mirrors which exaggerate the vertical dimension."[17] For twenty years, it was the world's tallest building.

For Cram and his co-workers, as it had been for Pugin and Ruskin, and as it would be later for Le Corbusier and Mies, architectural choices were not only stylistic, but political and moral. Just a few years after Hitchcock and Johnson's *The International Style,* Cram, then in his seventies, published his autobiography, *My Life in Architecture* (1936). What the younger men saw as the remedy for architecture's imitative disease, Cram deplored as "the débâcle of contemporary modernistic art."[18] And the aesthetic débâcle had social roots; a deranged art reflected a corrupt society.

The jeremiad Cram preached in his old age merely repeated the opinions he had been delivering all his life, in a fair-sized list of speeches and articles and books. Frankly reactionary to a breathtaking extent, Cram embraced not only the forms of medieval architecture but the politics and religion those forms expressed. The enemy was the twinned plague of democracy and secularism. In Cram's dyspeptic view, the history of

the West since the fifteenth century was a chronicle of ineluctable decline, from idealism to materialism, from hero worship to "defiant
democracy," from aristocracy to a "fictitious social equality."[19] The
"riot of individualism," which prevailed especially in America, had
produced cultural blight in myriad and interconnected forms. For
Cram, realism, naturalism, impressionism, mammonism, eclecticism,
agnosticism, rationalism, democracy, and the competitive system were
all heads of the same beast.[20] A number of nineteenth-century figures
elicited Cram's admiration as "heroic truthtellers," among them D. G.
Rossetti and Cardinals Newman and Manning. Above all, Cram identified three men as his spiritual predecessors in the struggle for imagination and idealism: John Ruskin, William Morris, and Richard Wagner.
These were Cram's "prophets," who rejected "realism" in its various
forms and were therefore called "reactionists. Perhaps, like the word
'Gothic,' the name given in scorn may in a little time be held in
honour."[21]

Cram considered all English art from the time of Henry VIII ("Henry
the Demon") to the end of the nineteenth century to be degraded. By
1900 those centuries of degradation had led to what Cram pillories as
the aesthetic department store:

> "College Buildings? You will find a complete line of Greco-
> Georgian articles down the alley to the right. Yes, madam, great
> sale of slightly shopworn Romanesque remnants now going on:
> down-stairs, turn to the left. Post-offices? Certainly, an enor-
> mous stock with . . . accessories, all guaranteed real Renaissance:
> Tailoring department, second floor. No, madam, we do not
> carry any châteauesque Fifth Avenue palaces now; no call for
> them. M. Cartouche will fit you splendidly, however, if you
> desire quite the latest thing from Paris. . . ."[22]

And so on.

As this heavy-footed satire suggests, Cram, as much as his own
subsequent detractors, yearned for release from the jumble of eclectic
eccentricity. As one corollary, his analyses of earlier American architecture often pressed a resolutely "functional" thesis. He says, for example, of Jefferson:

> Like all amateurs, even those of the High Renaissance, he severed
> design and style from construction and function. Ionic porticoes,
> carefully worked out according to Vitruvius, were attached to
> clapboarded dwellings; Doric columns and entablatures fronted
> Protestant meetinghouses; and, all made of thin boards neatly
> fitted together, these became for a time the established mode.[23]

Sounding rather like Louis Sullivan, Cram claimed to believe that "a building must look like what it is," must "express visibly the energy that informs it"; but in his particular understanding of those loaded terms he meant that each building must "declare its spiritual and intellectual lineage through its architectural vesture."[24] Function has primacy, but function is the revelation of tradition.

For Cram, the solution to eclecticism was Gothic, precisely because it was the language of the Christian faith and was therefore continuous with the history of Western civilization. The forms of classicism, on the other hand, spoke rather of pre-Christian heathenism and post-Christian barbarism, of disruption and discontinuity, of what Cram repeatedly refers to as "the new paganism" of the Renaissance.[25] During the anti-Christian Renaissance, the retrieval of pre-Christian forms led to the architectural style "which, modified and elaborated by Paris, is now offered us for universal acceptance."[26]

In a comment on the Ecole des Beaux-Arts in his autobiography, Cram suggested something of the goals of his own, quite different architecture. The Ecole's "strength," he wrote, "lay not in its theory of style, but in its logical planning and its insistence on unity and integrity in every architectural scheme."[27] These, it can be assumed, are the qualities he associated with his own designs. At least in theory, Gothic was not for Cram a matter of detail or ornament or mannerism. Indeed, properly interpreted, Gothic was not a style at all but a spiritual attitude. For that reason, Cram refused in his writing and lecturing to concentrate his analyses on details. For that reason, too, Cram was able logically to liken European Gothic to the Buddhist temples of China and Korea and Japan. What made these disparate traditions similar – what made them all "Gothic" – was not style at all but the common expression of a religious ideal. The cathedrals of France and the temples of Japan testified equivalently to "the rising of a people out of barbarism, the development of the splendid virtues of heroism, sacrifice, chivalry and worship."[28]

Cram put his conception of Gothic in different terms when he defended it as a successfully "organic" architecture. What he called the "organic synthesis" of the Gothic church derives from the church's association with "the laws of life itself."[29] The organic metaphor was, of course, widely though differingly applied to building in this period, as the more familiar example of Frank Lloyd Wright attests. But Cram was not alone in trying to capture the authority of the "organic" for Gothic. The influential Montgomery Schuyler, surveying the Princeton campus in 1910, wrote that "the perennial utility of medieval architecture" derives from the fact that "it is not and never was an architecture of mere convention and tradtion, like the hieratic architecture of Egypt or like the Roman classic, from Vitruvius to this day. Throughout the thousand years through which it held sway and remained alive . . . it was an architecture of craftsmanship and not of formula; it was founded on the nature of things, and not on conventional assumptions."[30]

Cram's repeated attempts to generalize his ideological system explain his hostility to "archaeological" imitation. The Middle Ages hold out inspiration, "not because we believe that through faithful copying and slavish mimicry we may rebuild a fictitious but plausible simulacrum" of antique buildings, but because the general lesson of medieval architecture is "structural logic" and beauty. Consequently, modern Gothic would be "very different in its outward seeming" from that of the twelfth and thirteenth centuries.[31]

Despite all this talk of the differences between the new Gothic and the old, and the corresponding emphasis on inward spirit over outward manner, Cram's work is in fact a sustained act of scrupulous imitation. Just about all of Cram's buildings, not only the churches that were his major business but his designs for colleges and for West Point as well, bear the unmistakable stamp of scholarship and close visual study. The logic of Cram's ideology necessarily led him in this circle. As the chaos of twentieth-century architecture reflects the anarchy of modern society, so Gothic reflected the perfection of the medieval world. Conforming to the judgment of Pugin and other nineteenth-century medievalists, Cram decided that "the civilization of Medievalism was more nearly perfect than that of Athens, far nobler than that of Rome, and separated by the entire diameter of being from the repulsive barbarism of the High, or Pagan Renaissance."[32] Cram's meticulously derivative buildings document the scale of his despair over modern life. He has, without ever quite admitting it – perhaps without fully realizing it – reversed cause and effect. Where hundreds of years earlier the Gothic expressed the good society, now it would be the mechanism for re-creating it. Cram's nostalgic utopia consists, if I may, in a kind of medieval postmodernism, with the Catholic Church returned to its hegemony and with the political structures of feudalism reinstalled in their accustomed place.

How seriously is all this to be taken? Cram's biography is littered with the sometimes bizarre evidence of his lifelong efforts to replace the twentieth century with romanticized versions of the twelfth or thirteenth. In his twenties, for example, he organized a band of vaguely Catholic aesthetes into "The Order of the White Rose." The principal work of the group was writing and reading medieval-ish ballads, mourning the feast of Charles the Martyr, and singing Jacobite songs. "We were," Cram redundantly explained, "William Morris enough to hate industrialism."[33] Later, Cram founded and helped edit the magazine *Knight Errant,* and he wrote a blank verse drama on the Arthurian cycle called *Excalibur.* Later still, when he had earned the money to support his medieval imaginings, he called his hundred acres in Sudbury, Massachusetts, "Whitehall"; he built a chapel on the property and decorated it with the coat of arms he had designed for himself. He adopted Saint Benedict and William of Wyckham as his patrons.

If gestures like these escape lampoon, it is only through the defiant scope of their consistency. In any case, their significance for our purposes is twofold. They certify Cram's status as a near-archetypal figure of reaction in the dialectic we have been examining. And they explain Cram's architectural style much more eloquently than his articles and books can. The "old art" demands the "old life."[34] And thus, although he professed to disdain copying, Cram had to build in the old forms because he so urgently sought the reestablishment of the old order those forms ratified. Cram's circular logic redeems itself in the context of his apocalyptic agenda: An architecture must express its time, and Gothic will express the twentieth century once the twentieth century has renewed its commitment to the pre-Renaissance, pre-Reformation civilization of European Christendom.

Furthermore, Cram's wishes were father to his hopes. In that revolutionary year, 1905, he published an article in which he predicted that the twentieth century would be an era of "great spiritual awakening [and] expansion."[35] That year, we recall, was also the year of Henry James's return to the United States. Cram and James heard much the same sermons in the stones (and clapboards and bricks) of America, but Cram's response was a jeremiad in that strict and tonally divided sense we examined earlier.[36] Cram's wrath was moderated by pious expectation.

Gothic was the visual key, but Cram carefully discriminated Gothic into its several styles. Under the gigantic influence of Ruskin (whose work he began reading in his teens), Cram opened his Gothic quest in Venice. Though he would later migrate spiritually northward, Venice always remained for him, as it did for James, the preeminent city of civilization. Like James, too, Cram lamented Venice's twentieth-century decline, reading in its "reversal" a symbolic history of modernity.

Throughout his career, Cram experimented with versions of both Continental and English Gothic. His most characteristic work is based on English architecture of the early sixteenth century; his reasons for selecting this as the style most suitable for adaptation in the twentieth century follow with eccentric rigor from the rest of his views. According to Cram, the Gothic of Henry VII's reign, and of the first years of Henry VIII, was the supreme medieval achievement. The chapel of Henry VII at Westminster, the chapels at Windsor and Kings College and in Sherborne Abbey – in these structures could be seen "the root Gothic rising into a tree of wonderful beauty, blossoming with quite new flowers." But this style was never fully developed; it never, in Cram's words, "completed itself." In 1537, Henry VIII stamped it into extinction. The job of the modern Goth is one with his opportunity: "the gracious labor of trying to develop [this architecture] on the lines indicated by its fragmentary remains."[37] This may be the most fantastic formulation of the links between tradition and individual talent in our literature.

Two examples will illustrate the architectural practice that Cram's ideas supported. In 1913, ground was broken for the Swedenborgian Cathedral-Church of the New Jerusalem in Bryn Athyn, Pennsylvania. Disputes with the client, John Pitcairn, eventually led to Cram's departure, but he remained enthusiastic about the resulting group of buildings, regarding them as "a sort of epitome of English church-building from the earliest Norman to the latest Perpendicular; learned, scholarly, poetic; a real masterpiece of reminiscent yet creative art."[38] The central tower, evocative of the thirteenth and fourteenth centuries, rises with anachronistic assurance one hundred fifty feet above Montgomery County, just a couple of miles from Philadelphia. Attached to the main church are a council hall and tower on the south and a choir hall on the north, both derived from Romanesque antecedents (Plate 8).

What Cram probably admired about Bryn Athyn, even more than the completed buildings themselves, was the unusual process of construction. Along with other "Goths" on both sides of the Atlantic, Cram was devoted to the medieval guild (or to his imagined version of it). He deplored the specialization of modern construction, the distinction between artists and artisans, the separation of design from engineering. He sought what many medievalizing builders in these years sought, what Peter Davey, speaking more generally, called "a Ruskinian fusion of art and craft."[39] Something like this fusion was attempted at Bryn Athyn. A partisan account of the construction was published by the church authorities:

All the designers and craftsmen were carefully selected and brought together and grouped in workshops around the actual building, where they could give all their time and attention to the work growing from day to day before them. Thus the men worked together in the presence of the building and of each other under the guidance of those who planned. Thus all the workers could gain a sympathetic understanding of the part each one played with a view to producing work as beautiful as that done between the twelfth and fourteenth centuries.[40]

PLATE 8. The Cathedral-Church of the New Jerusalem in Bryn Athyn, Pennsylvania. (Courtesy of John M. Meyers.)

Cram tried the same sort of organization on a much larger scale when he took over (for a time) the building of the Cathedral of St. John the Divine in New York. His evaluation of both undertakings is perfectly expressed in the self-hypnotic prose of the Bryn Athyn publicists. Indeed, those glowing lines accurately sketch Cram's mystified conception of medieval work and workmen.

Princeton University offers a different but equally significant illustration of Cram's ideas. In 1909, in an action that suggestively recapitulates many of the themes we have been discussing in these chapters, the president of Princeton, Woodrow Wilson, appointed Ralph Adams Cram to the job of supervising architect of the university. Wilson, the self-professed enemy of entrenched privilege, decreed that his university would express its twentieth-century energy through the visual signs of feudalism.[41] Wilson would shortly move on, but Cram held his post until 1931. His assignment was to design some buildings of his own and to enforce a consistently Gothic style on all Princeton architecture. Of the several structures Cram built at Princeton (among them Campbell Hall and the University Chapel), he considered the Graduate College (Plate 9) the most important. It offered "the most spacious opportunity the office ever . . . had for working out its, by then, fully established ideas and principles in the matter of 'Collegiate Gothic' adapted to contemporary conditions."[42]

Ralph Adams Cram tried to transport the Middle Ages across the intervening centuries by sheer force. His life spanned decades in which a good many other Americans, in endlessly varying ways, tried to do the same thing. The Gothic was visible everywhere in American life throughout the nineteenth and early twentieth centuries. Architecture, literature in all genres, social theorizing, and community organizing all provide examples. In 1906, for instance, John La Farge looked back over his early schooling in the 1850s and recalled: "I was made or allowed to read anything which would bring up the beauty of the medieval ideal, and even out-of-the-way knowledge was shown me, so that at this date [ca. 1851] I was already far away from the eighteenth century and was being taught how wrong all sorts of things in art were which did not agree with the medieval."[43]

In the 1860s, to give another instance, Longfellow completed his translation of *The Divine Comedy*. As the translation progressed, he had sought and received advice from the members of the Dante Club, among whom were Charles Eliot Norton and James Russell Lowell. Lowell himself, in 1861, published "The Cathedral," 800 lines of verse that recall a visit to Chartres in a vaguely Wordsworthian way. Nineteenth-century American poetry was filled with medieval echoes and

PLATE 9. The refectory and tower, Princeton Graduate College. (Courtesy Wyman Hilscine.)

attitudinizing. It was a habit that continued through and beyond the First World War, reaching its last serious efflorescence in Edward Arlington Robinson's gigantic Arthurian narratives. If several generations of New England reiterated the fanciful standards of medievalism, as many generations of southern planter society tried to act them out.[44]

The years before World War I also make up the last half or so of America's arts and crafts movement, and many of the members and groups that took part adopted medieval styles. The Rose Valley Association, for example, founded in 1901 by the architect William Price and located in suburban Philadelphia, designed furniture of a generally medieval character.[45] More important, though, than matters of medieval style was the recognition throughout the movement of what participants took to be the medieval source of their activities.

The most formidable academic outcome of the American medieval revival was the founding of the Medieval Academy. The organizing meeting took place in Ralph Adams Cram's living room in 1925; Cram served as the academy's first clerk. Scholarship addressed the public more directly in the construction of The Cloisters in New York City in the twenties and thirties. These dates lie outside the scope of our study, but a brief pause is permissible since The Cloisters, in the sheer scale of the undertaking, may perhaps be taken as both the close and climax of the medieval revival in America.

In an address he delivered at Harvard in 1902, William James spoke of the American mind as divided between the contending parties of force and education.[46] The Cloisters grew out of an astonishing act of collaboration between the two. The millions of needed dollars came from John D. Rockefeller, Jr., the earnest heir to one of the greatest of the industrial fortunes. The design and direction were provided by some of the shrewdest scholars and cultural administrators of the time.[47] What Cram and other Goths attempted through imitation and paraphrase, The Cloisters' builders accomplished literally. Stone by stone, they dismantled a piece of the European Middle Ages, carried it to twentieth-century America, and re-erected it on a Manhattan hilltop.

With very few exceptions, the new Goths yearned for the Middle Ages because they imputed to those centuries the values they found absent in modern America: craftsmanship, simplicity, unity. At no time was this nostalgia more intense than in the years around 1900; and no one evoked this mystified past more colorfully or more convincingly than Henry Adams. As the *Education* was Adams's study in twentieth-century "multiplicity," so the earlier *Mont-Saint-Michel and Chartres* (1904) was his tribute to thirteenth-century "unity." Adams's pages kaleidoscopically blend medieval literature, philosophy, and architecture to substantiate his assertion that the Middle Ages were spiritually and therefore humanly richer than everything that followed, and most certainly richer than the early twentieth century. Above all the Virgin, at once the source and term of medieval energy, embraced the parts of the society and made it whole:

> Illusion for illusion – granting for the moment that Mary was an illusion – the Virgin Mother . . . repaid to her worshippers a larger return for their money than the capitalist has ever been able to get, at least in this world, from any other illusion of wealth which he has tried to make a source of pleasure and profit.[48]

Adams insisted that he had no more professional standing than a tourist. Given the size of his learning and the sharpness of his eye, however, he brought to the cathedrals much more than a tourist's baggage. His architectonic analyses, his literary criticism, his historical reconstructions, and his summaries of philosophical disputes are substantial and often fine. But *Mont-Saint-Michel* is, above all and at last, a book of witness to Adams's nostalgia and regret, and its intellectual details – like the ornaments of a Gothic church – are subordinated to an emotionally charged single vision. The results include passages of indulgently sentimental rhapsody. Sitting in Chartres through a long afternoon, Adams declares:

> One sees her personal presence on every side. Any one can feel it who will only consent to feel like a child. Sitting here any Sunday afternoon . . . one sense reacting upon another until sensation reaches the limit of its range – you, or any other lost soul, could, if you cared to look and listen, feel a sense beyond the human ready to reveal a sense divine. (P. 193)

The key is the doubled backward pull toward the purity and simplicity common to both one's own childhood and that of Western civilization as it existed in the Middle Ages.

One of Adams's most devoted readers was Ralph Adams Cram, by then a fellow of the American Institute of Architects (AIA). Two decades later, Cram recalled his first encounter with *Mont-Saint-Michel* as one of the "crucial and determining events" of his life.[49] This was not, of course, quite accurate. Adams's book did not determine so much as corroborate Cram's own convictions. Be that as it may, it was altogether fitting that the first publication of *Mont-Saint-Michel* (aside from a small private printing in 1904) was sponsored by the AIA at Cram's suggestion; even more appropriately, the edition contained an adulatory preface by Cram (Boston, 1913). Speaking for himself and for the other revivalists of his generation, Cram praised Adams for re-creating the "reality" of the thirteenth century: "its gaiety and lightheartedness, its youthful ardor and abounding action, its childlike simplicity and frankness, its normal and healthy and all-embracing devotion" (p. ix). It is difficult to imagine a more sentimental rendering of the Middle Ages or, by inference, a more complete retreat from the twentieth century.[50]

ALBERT KAHN

Despite Santayana's claims for it, the skyscraper was surely not the building type that most accurately anticipated the architecture of the new century. As the example of the Woolworth Building has already suggested, and as other examples would confirm, tall buildings were altogether susceptible of ornamental and literary treatment. It was rather in the utilitarian structures of industry that a new architecture emerged. The problems addressed and solved in America's multiplying factories and warehouses stimulated innovative approaches because they were not formulated as aesthetic issues. They were the problems of the new technologies: movement, speed, efficiency, storage, profit. To put it only a little too simply, the historical styles were not invoked because this kind of work was assumed to be outside stylistic considerations. To be sure, this pragmatic independence from precedent was soon translated into a term in the aesthetic debate. I have quoted Brooks Adams's ridicule, in 1902, of America's turn-of-the-century architecture. In the same place, Adams made an exception: "Our architecture, when dealing with iron and steel, with matter of fact factories, railway stations, and warehouses, is admirable. When it strives after an aesthetic ideal it is a failure; and, logically, it could be nothing but a failure, because it is unintelligent."[51]

Adams's admiration for America's industrial architecture was eventually rather widely shared. Russell Sturgis, originally a disciple of Ruskin, became an influential convert to "realistic design." He became an advocate of industrial architecture and published in 1904 a two-part account of "The Warehouse and the Factory in America." Sturgis implies the novelty of his subject by beginning with the question What is a warehouse? "Anything" he decides, "is either a warehouse or a factory which is devoted to the rougher kind of business enterprise." Such a building may be costly and well built, but it will be "the reverse of elegant. . . . [It] can hardly be minutely planned, with many refinements in the way of interesting arrangements, nor can it be the recipient of elaborate exterior decorative treatment. . . . The windows can hardly be grouped in extraordinary combinations – the external walls will put on the appearance of a tolerably square-edged, flat-topped box, nor will the external masses anywhere break out into porches or turrets."[52] Having offered this anticipatory glimpse of modernism's aesthetic of the unadorned box, Sturgis generalizes for himself by observing that "one sees in the treatment of these recent and very plain – very utilitarian – structures, a wholesome architectural influence" (p. 14). "There is something to be said," Sturgis concludes, "for the theory broached now and then by the persons not enamored of our present architecture of mere pretence, that the designers should be restrained to square masses and sharp corners and plain windows for twenty years to come – with sculpture denied them and all the bad architectural forms *tabu*. Then, it is thought by some, a chance for design rightly so-called, might be found in the very inability to misuse old forms."[53] Given Sturgis's background and the reach of his influence, his was an important statement of the case.

Peter Bonnett Wight was another ex-Ruskinian, with successful Gothic buildings to his credit, including Yale's School of Fine Arts. In 1910, Wight published an article called "Utilitarian Architecture at Chicago," in which he gave up his medieval commitment, embraced realistic design, and praised the warehouses of the Middle West. The admirable new utilitarian building is one, wrote Wight, "in which the

materials and workmanship are of good and lasting charcter, devoid of
all ornament, but relieved from monotony by the best dispositon of
its parts to express its function. Such a building . . . is always attractive by its good proportions alone."[54]

Note that the enthusiasm here is as narrow in scope as it is real. The
segregation of "utilitarian" architecture to a small range of "utilitarian"
structures prevailed through the prewar years. Factories and warehouses are the buildings that result from a desire to work out "practical
business propositions in the interest of those who have to pay the
bills."[55] In some ways, therefore, the more significant fact remains that
"no one yet seriously proposed that the new way should be applied
outside of industry to buildings intended for monumental sites or for
major civic or cultural purposes."[56] The vocabulary of industrial buildings might achieve piecemeal recognition as a real language instead of
untutored noises, but it was nevertheless still not a language spoken in
the politer regions of architecture.

This particular version of America's divided mind is illustrated with
dramatic clarity in the work of Albert Kahn. Kahn kept up a busy
practice for over half a century, until his death in 1942, but just about
all of his posthumous reputation has rested on his industrial buildings.
He worked principally in and around Detroit, and his industrial work
began in 1901. Kahn proved to be a shrewd and innovative architect,
and his influence was considerable. Starting in 1903, he built a series of
factories for the Packard Motor Car Company, and a dazzled contemporary magazine praised "the new style" of the work. "It is most
fitting that the automobile industry as the newest great industry of the
country should in its new factories add to the strength of the movement
toward rational working places."[57] In this journalist's view at least,
Kahn's stylistic choices did duty both as images of the new and as
symbols of the progressive. In 1905, in Building No. 10 of the Packard
plant, Kahn built Detroit's first reinforced concrete factory building.

Over the next decades, Kahn designed dozens of major industrial
projects, especially for the exponentially growing automobile industry.
The Packard buildings were followed by factories for Ford, Hudson,
Continental Motors, Chalmers Motor Car Company, Fisher Body, and
others. According to a recent admirer, the "practical problems" of
factory design appealed to Kahn: "Reconciling himself to the economic
necessity of eliminating historical ornament in industrial architecture,
he found aesthetic values in the forms engendered by new technologies
and functional considerations."[58]

This genre of Kahn's work achieved its most memorable statement in
his collaboration with Henry Ford. In 1911–1915, Ford developed and
perfected the first continuously moving assembly line. Only a handful

PLATE 10. Ford's Highland Park Plant, erected in 1909. (Courtesy of Albert Kahn Associates.)

of events in the years before World War I have cast a longer shadow across the subsequent history of the twentieth century. And the buildings of the legendary Highland Park Plant, in which Ford's employees worked, were designed by Albert Kahn (Plate 10).

Whatever "aesthetic values" Kahn may have discovered in his factory buildings, however, he kept them scrupulously divorced from the rest of his work. His houses and public buildings, his museums and libraries and offices are studies in the historic styles. He covered acres of suburban Detroit with Italian villas, medieval cottages, Tudor mansions, and colonial houses (Plate 11). His Detroit Athletic Club (1915) was derived from the palaces of Florence and Rome, and his Country Club of Detroit (1905) was Georgian. In the Detroit Public Library, in the buildings of the University of Michigan, the eclectic story was the same. In short, Kahn was leading two architectural lives, contributing influentially to a modern style and at the same time committed to the hierarchy and symbolism of the historic taste.

Of these two lives, he much preferred the latter. His admiration was for the past, and a comment he made about Charles McKim vibrates with self-defense: "I have little patience with those who claim his work is archaeology and not architecture. Indeed, he found his inspiration in the past, but he knew how to employ the best of the old to do service to the new. His was never slavish copyism but a judicious adaptation of

PLATE 11. The interior of the Horace E. Dodge house, Detroit, built in 1910 and no longer standing. (Courtesy of Albert Kahn Associates.)

established forms with plenty of his own individuality incorporated."[59] This was the universal creed of the eclectic, and Kahn made it his own. On another occasion, describing and justifying his own work, he declared: "If, in re-employing older forms and applying them to our newer problems, we have done wrong, then all architecture of the past is wrong, for all of it is but a development of what was done before."[60] Albert Kahn's architecture changed the landscape of twentieth-century America, perhaps as decisively as that of any other man. But, like so many of his contemporaries, he built the future in spite of himself and felt more comfortable in the past.

FRANK LLOYD WRIGHT

Wright's widely conceded status as "the greatest innovator of his generation" is a less simple matter than it seems.[61] For one thing, in a culture that would come increasingly to reverence novelty, a hint of paradox cuts across such assertions as Nikolaus Pevsner's, in 1936, that "Wright's position in 1903 was almost identical with that of the most advanced thinkers on the future of art and architecture today."[62] For another thing, the nature of Wright's innovation proved easier to announce than to pin down exactly. Did it lie in his "development of the principles of abstract design"?[63] In his commitment to "organic architecture"?[64] In his devotion to the "appropriate" use of materials?[65] Was it Wright who rediscovered the possibilities of architectural space? This is the view of many critics: "Whereas the Rationalists, such as Viollet-le-Duc, could conceive only of the *structure* of churches as providing the archetype for a new way of building, Wright took the *space;* and it is this which distinguishes Wright from the other great architects of his generation . . . as the first great architect of the twentieth century."[66]

As much as anything, Wright's identity as architectural pioneer, especially in the early estimates that most concern us here, was based on his identification with the machine. In the contest over the cultural significance of machinery, Wright repeatedly announced his adherence to the party of the technological future. His admirers often isolated this attitude in acclaiming Wright a prophet. When, for example, Pevsner congratulated Wright, in the passage quoted earlier, for the foresight and good sense of holding views "almost identical" to Pevsner's own, he had specifically in mind Wright's famous address "The Art and Craft of the Machine." With symbolic fitness, Wright first gave the speech at Jane Addams's Hull House on March 6, 1901. It was not reprinted in full for many years, but it was nevertheless quickly and widely recognized as a manifesto on behalf of the modern. The speech was obviously important to Wright himself. Thirty years later, when he was invited to deliver the Kahn Lectures at Princeton, he said that the first lecture would consist essentially of rereading "The Art and Craft of the Machine."

When the Kahn Lectures were published, E. Baldwin Smith provided a prefatory note in which from the first paragraph he fastened onto Wright's "modernity" and his fate as a rejected heroic innovator: "As early as 1903 [sic] at Hull House in Chicago, Frank Lloyd Wright challenged all Romantic efforts to escape from the realities of a modern machine world when he objected to the formation of a Society of Arts and Crafts to perpetuate the pseudo-medieval dreams of Morris and Ruskin, and he read a paper on 'The Art and Craft of the Machine.' He was voted down and has continued to be voted down in America."[67]

Wright intended his title as a defiant oxymoron. His 1901 audience was accustomed to taking the words "arts and crafts" and "machine" as self-evidently antithetical. For them, the separation between the terms measured to an inch the distance between past and future, between traditional aesthetic possibilities and the subartistic world of manufacturing and mass production. Wright's purpose was to obliterate that separation and that distance. His logic was apparently crisp to the point of syllogism. (Major:) Architecture has always expressed the fundamental reality of each age. (Minor:) The twentieth century is and will continue to be the age of the machine. (Conclusion:) Therefore, architecture must express the machine. Or, as Wright put it in one of the most familiar passages from the 1930 version of his speech:

> In this age of steel and steam the tools with which civilization's true record will be written are scientific thoughts made operative in iron and bronze and steel and in the plastic processes which characterize this age, all of which we call Machines. [New inventions and materials] have made our era the Machine Age – wherein locomotive engines, engines of industry, engines of light or engines of war or steamships take the place works of Art took in previous history. Today we have a Scientist or Inventor in place of a Shakespeare or a Dante.[68]

The machine will dominate the making of twentieth-century art because it will command the century itself.

Wright claimed that he did not merely resign himself to this outcome, he welcomed it. "The machine is capable of carrying to fruition high ideals in art – higher than the world has yet seen!"[69] According to Wright, the widespread aesthetic fear and loathing of the machine is understandable, but those are reactions only to what the machine has been and not to what it could be. The machine has been abused, and it has been the vehicle for abuse. Aesthetic reformers, Morris and

Ruskin for example, have rightly protested against the machine "because the sort of luxury which is born of greed had usurped it and made of it a terrible engine of enslavement, deluging the civilized world with a murderous ubiquity, which plainly enough was the damnation of . . . art and craft" (Hull House, p. 56). In short, the machine's aesthetic and human disrepute is chargeable to the immoral men who have exploited it.

Taken out of the hands of these "usurping vulgarians," the machine will not only "undo the mischief it has made." It will become the instrument of a genuine twentieth-century art, an American art. Wright's thesis here is strongly rooted in his politics. The machine is "the great forerunner of democracy"; it is therefore the critical juncture at which America's ideology and history converge. Wright often repeated his belief in the egalitarian implications of technology. "The machine is here to stay," he wrote in 1908. "It is the forerunner of the democracy that is our dearest hope."[70] This future appears so certain to Wright that his predictions often drift into one or another form of celebratory determinism. He prophesied, for example, that the new democratic age of benevolent machinery will arrive of "its own momentum" (Hull House, p. 56). And he asked, "Why will the American artist not see that human thought in our age is stripping off its old form and donning another?" (Princeton, p. 16). The power his contemporary James Joyce reserved to the artist was entrusted by Wright to machinery: "We may find [machines] to be the regenerator of the creative conscience in our America" (Princeton, p. 16). Wright was never given to understatement. But then, as we have seen, the heavy political and moral weight he attached to his aesthetic preferences had numerous precedents.

The tension between art and machinery dissolves conveniently when the machine is understood as a way to make art rather than as art's adversary. This reconciliation requires a fair amount of arbitrary redefinition and even wishful thinking, but Wright works hard to bring it off. Some of the most persuasive passages in both versions of "The Art and Craft of the Machine" are those in which Wright describes the technical advantages that machines offer to artists and architects working in different materials and at different scales. Quite simply, machines make all sorts of things possible that men laboring with hammers and chisels and saws could never accomplish. Wright talks about wood and marble and stone, terra cotta and metal. "The beauty of wood," he says, for example, "lies in its qualities as wood, strange as this may seem." And machines bring out those qualities, and preserve them, better than manual handling and treatment.

Even more significantly, machines put beauty democratically within the grasp of everyone. "Machines have . . . placed within reach of the designer a technique enabling him to realize the true nature of wood in his designs harmoniously with man's sense of beauty, satisfying his material needs with such extraordinary economy as to put this beauty of wood in use within the reach of every one" (Princeton, p. 17). (Recall that at about this same time, ca. 1900, the Austrian Josef Hoffman established the Wiener Werkstätte [Vienna workshop]. The workshops "continued the craft traditions of William Morris and the English arts and crafts movement, with the contradictory new feature that the machine was now accepted as a basic tool of the designer."[71])

Machines liberate artists from necessity as democracy liberates citizens from compulsion. The link here is surely more metaphorical than Wright allowed, but the association of ideas powerfully attracted him. It led him, as well, to defend the possibilities of the twentieth-century city against pastoral escapism. Like the machine itself, Wright concedes that the reality of modern urban life is more oppressive than free, more sordid than edifying. But again like the machine, the causes of urban misery are traceable to venal man.

"Go at nightfall," orders Wright, "to the top of our newest Skyscraper." Look down and see "the image of material man, at once his glory and his menace . . . this thing we call a City." Elaborating fantastically on analogies he learned principally from Sullivan, Wright sketches the city's portrait in melodramatically organic terms:

> Beneath you is the monster, stretching out into the far distance. High overhead hangs a stagnant pall, its fetid breath reddened with light from myriad eyes endlessly, everywhere blinking. Thousands of acres of cellular tissue outspread, enmeshed by an intricate network of veins and arteries radiating into the gloom. Circulating there with muffled ominous roar is the ceaseless activity to whose necessities it all conforms. This wondrous tissue is knit and knit again and inter-knit with a nervous system, marvelously effective and complete, with delicate filaments for hearing and knowing the pulse of its own organism. (Princeton, p. 13)

Wright continues in this remarkable fashion for several paragraphs, turning the man-made city into a living being and emphasizing the scale and power of the city-creature.

Wright insists that the city of 1900 is fearsome and inhumane only because, like the machines with which and of which it is built ("the tall modern office building is the machine pure and simple" [Hull House, p. 60]), the city's ideal possibilities have been perverted by human greed. The city of America's future, on the other hand, is both inevitable and utopian. "[We] ourselves are already become . . . some cooperative part" in the "vast machinery" of the city. The "texture" of that city, "this great Machine, is the warp upon which will be woven the woof and pattern of the Democracy we pray for" (Princeton, pp. 13, 14). Two generations later, Wright would still insist that the "dream of the free city is to establish democracy on a firmer basis."[72] These democratic developments will occur as the outcome of law – "law no less organic so far as we are concerned than the laws of the great solar universe. That universe, too, in a sense, is but an obedient machine" (Princeton, p. 14). So Wright's grand themes, of democracy and the organic, of art and the machine, assemble themselves in a quasimystical coherence. Everyone, Wright predicts, will eventually share the vision that moves him: both the workers who despise the machines that now exploit and kill them, and the artists who ignore machinery in favor of "the paths of the past."

Tracking errant turn-of-the-century architects down these past-leading paths is the other main preoccupation of "The Art and Craft of the Machine." Few of the eclectics' subsequent opponents attacked them with quite the same overwrought panache as Wright.

> We half believe in our artistic greatness . . . when we toss up a pantheon to the god of money in a night or two, or pile up a mammoth aggregation of Roman monuments, sarcophagi and Greek temples for a postoffice in a year or two. (Hull House, p. 61)

> On Michigan Avenue Montgomery Ward presents us with a nondescript Florentine Palace with a grand companile for a "Farmer Grocery" and it is . . . common . . . to find the giant stone Palladian "orders" overhanging plate glass shop fronts. (Princeton, p. 9)

What its proponents were smugly calling an "American Renaissance" Wright acidly dismissed as "the Renaissance of 'the ass in the lion's skin' " (Princeton, p. 9). The use of materials in disguised ways made him almost as angry as the invocation of historic styles. He was, for example, offended by the use of nonstructural stone to "cover" the steel skeleton of a tall building:

> Granite blocks, cut in the fashion of the followers of Phidias, [are] cunningly arranged about the steel beams and shafts, to look "real" – leaning heavily upon an inner skeleton of steel for support from floor to floor, which strains beneath the "reality" and would fain, I think, lie down to die of shame. (Hull House, p. 61)

Against all this back-looking, Wright counterposes the energy of his commitment to the future. He declaims the power of the new: "The new will weave for the necessities of mankind, which the Machine will have mastered, a robe of identity no less truthful, but more poetical, with a rational freedom made possible by the machine, beside which the art of old will be as the sweet, plaintive wail of the pipe to the outpouring of the full orchestra" (Hull House, p. 62). Rather like Emerson calling for the poet of the new American democracy, Wright summons the artist equal to the demands of the new age of machinery: "This Machine Age is suffering for the artist who accepts, works, and sings as he works, with the joy of the *here* and *now!*" (Hull House, p. 63, Wright's emphasis). Emerson found his poet in Whitman; Wright, by self-sufficient contrast, found his artist in Wright.

Though he had already passed into his thirties by the turn of the century, Wright would outlive the period we are interested in by more than four decades. By 1900, he had achieved considerably more success than either he or his disciples would later recall. He was by no means, especially in the years from 1901 to 1910, the lonely hero of later mythmaking.[73] His commissions gave him a good many chances to build according to his ideas.

Of the buildings he designed in the early years of the century, the one that later seemed to him to best exemplify his welcoming response to the machine age was the Larkin Building in Buffalo (1904; demolished 1950). In his *Autobiography,* Wright looks back on the Larkin Building as "the first emphatic protestant in architecture, [the first] protest against the tide of meaningless elaboration sweeping the United States."[74] The Larkin Building made architecture "genuine" by affirming "the new Order of this Machine Age." It expressed "power directly applied to purpose," and thus resembled the ocean liner, the plane, and the car (p. 175).

It was certainly a remarkable building (Plates 12 and 13). The outside was a slab; the inside was organized around a bold but humane central court. From its statement of space to its furnishings (many of them designed by Wright) to the disposition of its technologies (plumbing, ventilation, lighting), the Larkin Building expressed something new and undeniably important. Shortly after it went up, *The Architectural Review* (U.S.) clamorously if rather vaguely insisted on the Larkin Building's achievement: ". . . about as fine a piece of original and effective composition as one could expect to find. This sort of thing is absolutely in the line of creative architecture."[75] Sixty years later – and, sadly, twenty years after the building was torn down – Vincent Scully, Jr., went further: "Here structure and space, function and mechanical means, the demands of the inside and those of the outside were integrated perhaps more completely than in any other building ever built in America."[76]

The Larkin Building was one of Wright's many efforts to affirm "the

PLATE 12. Exterior view of the Larkin Building, Buffalo. (Courtesy of the Frank Lloyd Wright Foundation.)

joy of the here and now." His houses in the Prairie Style were others. What Ezra Pound demanded of the new century's poets Wright tried to accomplish in three dimensions – he made it new. His buildings were the evidence, and his subsequent esteem was the verdict. The publication in Germany of the Wasmuth Portfolio (1910–1911) brought Wright to the eager attention of young architects all over Europe. Sev-

PLATE 13. Interior view of the Larkin Building, Buffalo. (Courtesy of the Frank Lloyd Wright Foundation.)

eral of the makers of modernism, among them Gropius and Mies, felt Wright's influence.

This is the conception of Wright that he endorsed himself: the single-minded prophet who turned the face of architecture toward the twentieth century, who guided culture's steps away from the paths that beckoned toward the past, who memorialized the hope of the technological future and the primacy of the common man's democracy in wood and concrete and stone. Such a sketch has a certain undeniable verve. It also suffers, however, from several defects, the chief of which is that it is no more than half true. While he did much to shape the aesthetic attitudes of the new century, and while he greeted the future with exuberant optimism, Wright simultaneously clung with both hands to the several pasts of childhood, of nineteenth-century America, and of the European tradition. The abstract quality of his design may, for example, have had its source in the Froebel blocks of his preschool experience. But he lingered over those blocks in his later backward glances with far more affection than the explanation required. Nostalgia for his rural boyhood permeates many of the passages in his various memoirs. "I saw it all," he wrote of the first Taliesin, "and planted it all and laid the foundation of the herd, flocks, stable and fowls as I laid the foundation of the house. All these items of livelihood came back – improved – from boyhood."[77] Such references to his childhood and to his "beloved" rural Wisconsin are common in Wright.

On the other hand, with the exception of his deference to Sullivan, Wright consistently did his best to conceal or minimize his connections with the architectural past. Yet his links and even his indebtedness to the traditions he denied were substantial. The pivotal lecture we looked at earlier, "The Art and Craft of the Machine," provides an interesting illustration and an entry into this topic.

The general purpose of Wright's altogether inaccurate statement that the speech he read under that title in 1930 was the same one he had read three decades earlier was to obliterate and then reconstruct history. The more particular history he worked hardest to erase and rewrite was his relationship to his nineteenth-century predecessors, specifically Ruskin and Morris. In the 1930 version, Ruskin and Morris appear infrequently, and only as the enemy. In the middle of his blast at eclecticism, for example, Wright says that students "are taught in the name of John Ruskin and William Morris to shun and despise the essential tool of their age" (Princeton, p. 11).

In 1901, on the contrary, Ruskin and Morris are invoked at the outset, as admirable figures: "All artists love and honor William Morris. He did the best in his time for art and will live in history as the

great socialist, together with Ruskin, the great moralist." Morris repudiated the machine, as we have seen, only because its humane possibilities were obscure in his generation. It was not yet "apparent to William
Morris, the grand democrat, that the machine was the great forerunner
of democracy" (Hull House, p. 56). What Wright pictured in 1930 as
his rejection of Morris and Ruskin was in fact more like the tension
between different but kindred spirits. In 1901 at least, Wright didn't so
much abandon Ruskin and Morris as attempt to translate their aesthetic
and moral creed into his own later age and his own terms. Because so
many subsequent historians accepted Wright's 1930 portrait of his turn-
of-the-century ideas, his inventions have worked a good deal of mischief. That question, however, lies outside our scope, except insofar as
it directs us to study the issue of Wright's antecedents with special care.
Clearly, Wright's response to his European predecessors was complex
and ambivalent. This is particularly the case with Ruskin.

Certainly the differences between Wright and Ruskin are not far to
seek. Perhaps most fundamentally, if Wright's architectural aesthetic
centered on the creation of space, Ruskin's was absorbed in ornament
and detail. Where Wright spoke of the inside volume *becoming* the architectural outside, Ruskin subordinated structure as well as space to the
surfaces he most cared for.[78]

Nonetheless, in their descriptions of the social role of the architect, and
in the ideological assumptions they bring to architecture, Ruskin and
Wright sometimes offer quite similar notions. Most critics would not go
as far as John D. Rosenberg, who calls Wright Ruskin's "disciple," but
many would concede a vital connection.[79] Rosenberg's major thesis is
that Ruskin and Wright shared the same "cardinal principle," their mutual commitment to "the organic" foundation of architecture. Though
Ruskin's use of the metaphor is no easier to define than Wright's, what
both men intended to convey was "the dependence of all vital and beautiful design on Organic Form. Ruskin," Rosenberg concludes, "is Frank
Lloyd Wright's link to the Romantic tradition" that lies behind both of
them (p. 71).

Furthermore, it was this understanding of what they admired as
"natural" that led to the transformation of both Ruskin's and Wright's
quite different stylistic preferences into similar moralistic imperatives.
In a word, what wasn't acceptable was immediately "unnatural." Dividing houses or churches or office towers between the categories of
natural and unnatural is of course, on the face of it, an absurdity. Be
that as it may, Ruskin and Wright not only agreed on this logic, they
sometimes agreed upon particular judgments as well. So, for instance,
both abhorred the Renaissance. Wright regarded the Renaissance as a
"debased" and "degenerate" period of art. Not being authentically "or-

ganic," the Renaissance was also unable to develop naturally; it was "scholastic." Wright does indeed sound here like one of Ruskin's American disciples, as he does also when he embraces the Middle Ages as the alternative to the Renaissance. The alleged "freedom" bequeathed to men by the Renaissance encouraged them only to "mar the more genuine art of the Middle Ages past repair. One cannot go into the beautiful medieval edifices . . . marred in this later period without hatred of the word Renaissance growing in his soul."[80]

Wright goes a long step further than preferring medieval over Renaissance buildings. He suggests that America return to "the Gothic spirit": "I suggest that a revival, not of the Gothic style but of the Gothic spirit, is needed in the Art and Architecture of the modern life of the world."[81] If this sounds more than a little like the ideological program of Ralph Adams Cram and his fellow Goths, so be it. Vincent Scully, Jr., at one point refers to Wright as "a Gothic-Revival phenomenon after all."[82] Whether this goes too far or not, Wright's regular invocation of "the Gothic spirit" documents the tenacious hold the myth of the Middle Ages had on his imagination. Indeed, that phrase "the Gothic spirit" lay near the center of Wright's ideas in the early years of the century. We have already observed the sleight of hand through which Wright accepted the machine only by turning it into its opposite, by pretending that machinery was what happened to nature in the twentieth century.

> A home is a machine to live in.
> The human body is a machine to be worked by will.
> A tree is a machine to bear fruit.
> A plant is a machine to bear flowers and seeds.[83]

Wright works a similar trick with Gothic. If "the modern" means "the machine," and the machine means "the organic," and the organic is "the Gothic," then the Gothic – at the close of this extraordinary chain – becomes the modern: "I have called this modern feeling for the Organic-character of form and treatment 'the Gothic spirit.' "[84]

Statements such as these suggest that Wright's alleged iconoclasm is better interpreted as a complex (and often frankly confused) dialectic between past and present. A professed populist who did much of his most characteristic work for the suburban rich, a champion of the city who lived most of his life in rural isolation, a pioneer suffused in nostalgia, Wright's contradictions are at once more interesting than his simplified later version of himself and a rendering as well of the divisions of the early twentieth century.

Chapter 8

Innovation and nostalgia:
Charles Ives

If the early years of the twentieth century produced a genuinely representative figure, that figure was probably Charles Ives. Especially in his most productive years, from the late 1890s to World War I, Ives experienced the paradoxes of American culture with unmatched intensity. Both his life and his music took shape dialectically, as Ives simultaneously disputed and affirmed the prevailing cultural assumptions of his time.

Perhaps it was his solitariness that permitted the antagonistic crosscurrents of his generation to develop in him to such a state of conflicted maturity. In any case, Ives's solitude is the starting point for any consideration of his biography or his work; he was surely the most isolated artist of his time. The bedrock commonplace of romanticism renders the artist as a supremely alienated figure, locked away by choice or public indifference or both, in some ivory tower of the imagination. This is one of the enduring myths near the center of developments in all the arts from the late eighteenth century to the present. Ives exemplified this conception totally, almost to the point of parody.

Most artists, whatever the degree of their apparent idiosyncracy, and whatever the hostility of the larger public, find at least a small group of supporters, a handful of admirers, who provide consolation and perhaps even understanding. But for many years, Ives had literally no professional response to his music except rejection and no auditors at all aside from his remarkable and sympathetic wife, Harmony.

Years later, Ives could comment on his aesthetic exile with a kind of detached humor. In the "Postface to 114 Songs," he wrote of that collection that it "stands now, if it stands for anything, as a kind of 'buffer state' – an opportunity for evading a question somewhat embarrassing to answer: 'Why do you write so much——which no one ever sees?' " (to which is appended in the first draft of the manuscript: "[most of our friends are too polite to add – 'ever hears?']"). "There are several good reasons, none of which are worth recording."[1]

In small part, Ives's problem was in his medium. Poems and novels, paintings and sculpture, no matter how bizarre they may seem, are accessible without mediation in a way that the notations of music are not. Far more than even plays, which are only fully realized in performance but which survive nicely and communicate something of themselves as texts, music unplayed and unheard is virtually stripped of being. During the most creative decades of his life, Ives's music was almost never performed. And when it did receive informal hearing – when for example Ives would play over some piece at the piano for a conductor or a musician – the results were almost without exception disastrous. He tells of the visit to his West Redding home by a famous violinist, "a typical hard-boiled, narrow-minded, conceited, prima donna solo violinist with a reputation due to his coming to this country from Germany with Anton Seidl as concert master." This "professor" began to play the first movement of the First Violin Sonata but quit after less than a page; he stalked out of Ives's music room, saying over and over, "This cannot be played." Then, in an unforgivable combination of gesture and metaphor, the violinst clapped his hands over his ears and announced: "When you get awfully indigestible food in your stomach that distresses you, you can get rid of it. But I cannot get those horrible sounds out of my ears with a dose of oil."[2] Ives may have found some of this funny in retrospect, but such judgments had to be alarming and even humiliating, even to a person of Ives's self-reliance. In the event, the first public performance of an orchestral work took place in 1927, several years after Ives had stopped composing. Eugene Goossens conducted two movements from the Fourth Symphony in New York in that year.

Ives had been warned by his father, the bandleader and chief musician in Danbury, Connecticut, that a career seriously devoted to music was impossible in America. George Ives, from everything that his son Charles and other sources reveal about him, was an unusually imaginative man. Charles may have yielded to an excess of filial piety when he said, "If I have done anything good in music it was, first, because of my father," but the father certainly taught the son a good deal.[3] George gave Charles rigorous instruction on half a dozen instruments, including piano, organ, violin, and cornet, as well as in sight-reading and counterpoint. More important, George was an indefatigable maker of musical experiments, many of which appear in some form in Charles's music. He built several instruments (including a modified piano) for producing quarter tones. He positioned his brass and wind players on church tops and village greens. He wouuld have his family sing a popular song like "Sewanee River" in the key of E-flat while he played piano accompaniment in the key of C: "This was to stretch our ears and strengthen our musical minds, so that they could use and translate things that might be used and translated . . . more than they had been."[4]

It is not clear that George Ives was acting on any very detailed theoretical agenda when he sent two bands marching past each other playing different songs in different keys. Or when he stood in the rain through the better part of a night listening to the sounds made by church bells in the storm. (It was his inability to imitate those sounds on a conventional piano that led to the construction of one of his quarter-tone contraptions.[5]) Charles Ives would develop a more elaborate and well-informed aesthetic program than his father, but what actuated both of them to a considerable extent was impatience with the limits imposed by musical conventions and curiosity, an irrepressible itch to hear what would happen if new sounds were combined in new ways. "Father had a kind of natural interest in sounds of every kind, known or unknown, measured as such or not."[6] Charles Ives passionately shared that interest in sounds; he would go on to create more of them than any composer had before.

Charles received the most formal part of his musical education at Yale College. His teacher was the recently appointed Horatio Parker, a man almost as conventional in his teaching as George Ives had been eccentric. Many years later, when Charles Ives was scribbling the furious notes that would be found among his papers after his death, he was still justifying himself against the scolding academic shade of Parker. But more than himself, Ives was repeatedly driven to defend his father from Parker: "Parker was a composer and widely known, and Father was not a composer and little known – but from every other standpoint I should say that Father was by far the greater man."[7]

According to Ives, Parker was shackled to the conventions of the nineteenth century and "the German tradition." (Since a quantity of Parker's music survives, including the once-popular *Hora Novissima,* Ives's opinion is readily confirmable.) Ives includes a vignette that

> shows the differences between Father's and Parker's ways of thinking. In the beginning of Freshman year, and getting assigned to classes, Parker asked me to bring him whatever manuscripts I had written (pieces, etc.). Among them, a song, *At Parting* – in it, some unresolved dissonances, one ending on a [high] E♭ ([in the] key [of] G major), and stops there unresolved. Parker said, "There's no excuse for that – an E♭ way up there and stopping, and the nearest D♮ way down two octaves." – etc. I told Father what Parker said, and Father said, "Tell Parker that every dissonance doesn't have to resolve, if it doesn't happen to feel like it,

any more than every horse should have to have its tail bobbed just because it's the prevailing fashion."[8]

This is engagingly earthy, and it is witty: Dissonance is defended by means of a doubled figure of speech, in which sound is first personified (it doesn't have to do what it doesn't want to do) and then yoked with a horse's tail in an outrageous conceit. George Ives's own rhetoric here is a species of unresolved dissonance, a winking gesture *épater le bourgeois*. It is also, at bottom, a political rather than a specifically musical statement. Geoge Ives argues for his son's music exclusively in the vocabulary of democracy, in the language of free choice and equality and transcendental oneness. (For Parker, a horse's tail would be only a horse's tail.) Not a word of separable technical analysis intrudes on George Ives's rebuke of the aristocratic European conventions Parker represents. But then it was the very notion of music as a self-contained system of convention that both Iveses rejected.

When Charles Ives appraises his adversaries, such as Parker, in the sprawling, inelegant pages of his *Memos,* his tone is typically belligerent, frequently overheated. Some of his fiercest estimates, however, occur (as in his music) in the silences of ironic juxtaposition: "After the first two or three weeks in Freshman year, I didn't bother [Parker] with any of the experimental ideas that Father had been willing for me to think about, discuss, and try out. Father died in October 1894, during my Freshman year."[9] Ives adds no further comment, but the emotions telescoped into the adjacence and sequence of those two sentences are palpable. More was at stake than the sudden transition from childhood to adulthood and the loss of a beloved parent – though these were calamitous events. Through an eerie coincidence, George Ives had been "replaced" by Horatio Parker. Charles was abruptly deprived of the musical encouragement, the downright indulgence he had been receiving; he was confronted instead with the grim, censorious stare of musical Authority, a stare that would face him reprovingly for fully thirty years.

At some deeply implicit level, then, the simultaneous death of George Ives and the emergence of Horatio Parker enacted a symbolic tableau: the triumph of constraint over freedom, of negation over plenitude. Ives "did not bother [Parker] much after the first few months (but occasionally all the same)." Parker was "seldom mean"; he would merely glance at a couple of measures of, say, a fugue of four keys and "hand it back with a smile." Another time, he joked about "hogging all the keys at one meal."[10] Parker's casual arrogance obliquely but officially condemned the musical ideals of both Iveses as aberrations and their experiments as mere eccentricity. It is as if, at the end of George

Ives's life and the beginning of Charles's maturity, the son found the father's failure and marginality ratified. It is almost, to go one step further, as if Parker – the collection of established prohibitions that Parker represented – were *responsible* for George Ives's death.

After that first, decisive month at Yale, Ives behaved with enough musical docility to graduate with a C average and a bachelor of music in 1898. With the poignant example of his father's life and death before him, Charles seems never even to have considered music as a career. In the summer of his commencement he moved to "Poverty Flat" (317 West 58th Street) in New York City, an apartment inhabited by a half-dozen Yale graduates, and he began working for the Mutual Life Insurance Company. The following spring he was transferred to the Raymond Agency, where he met Julian Myrick. It was with Myrick, first at Raymond and later in their own agency, that Ives created the hugely successful partnership that would continue through Ives's retirement in 1930. (Ives became far less active in the business after his illness in 1918.)

The Ives & Myrick Agency was for a time the largest life insurance agency in New York and on several occasions did a larger monthly business than any other in the country. Whatever might have been his reluctance, Ives was a superb businessman. Myrick recalled years later:

> "I had to do with the applications that came in – process them – and he had to do with handling the agents. . . . And so we divided that part of the work, not only in the Raymond Agency, but later on in life. . . . He never did any direct selling, but he was a very good trainer of agents, and taught them how to sell. . . . He made the balls for other people to throw. . . . He had a great conception of the life insurance business, and what it could do and should do, and had a very powerful way of expressing it."[11]

Appropriately, perhaps, Ives's first published literary work was a booklet he wrote to train insurance agents, *The Amount to Carry – Measuring the Prospect* (1912). This became something of a classic in its field, often reprinted, its advice becoming the common knowledge of the business. Estate planning was Ives's invention; Henry Cowell and Sidney Cowell tell of meeting an insurance lawyer in 1953 who described estate insurance as an idea devised "by a famous insurance man of a past generation named Charles Ives." This man was astonished to hear that Ives wrote music.[12]

This sort of anecdote is one way of measuring Ives's success. Another is Myrick's financial summary of the partnership: "In our first year of business we paid for $1,800,000 and in the last, 1929, $48 millions. In the 21 years we were partners in the firm of Ives and Myrick, we put in force some $450 millions of new business."[13]

The two decades of Ives's immense busyness and success in insurance were the same decades of his major productivity as a composer. A list of just a few of his datable compositions gives some idea of what he accomplished. The Second Symphony was written in 1901, as was the first movement of the First Piano Sonata. *Four Ragtime Pieces* followed in 1902, and *Autumn* (later adapted as the first movement of the Second Violin Sonata), in 1903. *Thanksgiving* was sketched and then finished in 1904, and the Three-Page Sonata and *Country Band March* in 1905. *Halloween* was written in 1906, as was *In the Cage* (later incorporated into the *Set for Theatre Orchestra*). The first and second sections of the Second Violin Sonata were completed in 1907. The fifth movement of the First Piano Sonata, along with at least a portion of *Browning,* was composed in 1908. In 1909 (the year Ives & Myrick was established), Ives wrote the first movement of the *First Orchestral Set* and a sketch of *Washington's Birthday.* The Fourth Symphony was started in 1910. In 1911, Ives sketched the second movement of the Second String Quartet; started *The Fourth of July;* finished *Hawthorne;* and conceived the idea of the *Concord* Sonata. The next year saw *The Saint-Gaudens* and the completion of *Emerson.* In 1913, Ives arranged *The New River* for voice and piano. The fourth movement of the Fourth Symphony was finished in 1914, along with *The Alcotts.* (On the Fourth of July, 1914, Yale University conferred the honorary degree of Doctor of Music on 49-year-old Jan Sibelius; Horatio Parker was presenter.) Ives completed *Thoreau* in 1915 and *At the River* in 1916. Then, although he would live for another four decades, Ives's composing ended. The coronary he suffered on October 1, 1918, seems to have followed rather than to have caused this ending.

In the compositions listed here, and in the many others of these years, Ives virtually created modern music singlehandedly – though neither he nor anyone else knew it. Atonality (most of Ives's major work is at least intermittently atonal), block forms and free forms, tone clusters, aleatory passages, polymeters, polyrhythms, polytonality, even a kind of serial composition: All these were employed by Ives before they appeared elsewhere in music. He did not, of course, have the terminology, but he invented the methods and devices. His "Scrapbook" comments on *In the Cage* (1906) illustrate the wry amusement with which Ives later "learned" what he had accomplished. In that piece, diatonic and whole-tone components are juxtaposed, and no tonal center is established. Ives writes that "technically this piece is but a study of how chords of 4ths and 5ths may throw melodies away from a set tonality. . . . The principal thing in this movement is to show that a song does not necessarily have to be in one key to make musical sense. To make music in no particular key has a nice name nowadays—'atonality.' "[14]

In 1949, Ives gave a rare interview, to Howard Taubman of the New York *Times*. Taubman pointed out that Ives had anticipated all the technical explorations of later, more quickly famous twentieth-century composers. Ives responded characteristically: "That's not my fault."[15] Whether it pleased him or not, Ives had to live long to hear this sort of congratulation; indeed, he outlived his own creativity by a long generation. In the creative years, his artistic isolation was so extreme and lasted so long that when his pieces were finally publicly performed, critics and audiences heard "new" music that had in fact been written a quarter-century and more earlier. Ironically, although this chronology was not secret, it was repeatedly ignored, and Ives was routinely interpreted as the disciple of one or another European modernist whose work he had never seen or heard. As Ives told anyone who would listen, he attended few concerts of any kind and heard no European modern music until 1919 or 1920. (In one of those years, he says, he heard "a part of *Firebird*" and found it "morbid and monotonous."[16]) By that time, most of his own work was finished.

It "is interesting (and perhaps funny) to know that I . . . have been influenced by one Hindemith (a nice German boy) who really didn't start to compose until about 1920 . . . several years after I had completed all my (good or bad) music, which Aunt Hale says is influenced by Hindemith."[17]

The mirage of European influence upon Ives's work is just part of a compound irony. His complete anonymity also ensured that he would have no more effect on contemporary composers than they had on him. Despite his enormous musical production, Ives was not an influence nor even a progenitor but a prototype discovered after the fact. It is as if Ives and the rest of twentieth-century music were developing in parallel but distant worlds, aesthetic landscapes of likeness that actually touched at no point.

All his music, as Ives so often reminded the listeners and correspondents who later became interested in it, was written on weekends, at night, on occasional holidays, even on the train commuting to work. Thus, Ives became the financial success his father never was, but only by sequestering his music in the private corners and crannies of his day. He escaped marginality, but only by confining his music to the literal margins of his own life. His doubleness seems, as we look back on it, utter: in public the shrewd, acquisitive, law-abiding entrepreneur; in private the anarchic, defiant craftsman. Prominent in business, he was invisible as a musician.

Yet Ives himself, while he would accept the facts, would reject the tone of this sketch of his divided life. If his corporate career caused him any discomfort, he rarely confessed it. His satiric humor tended to come in broad bursts, and he would occasionally include business among his targets. A page of the manuscript of the *Holidays* Symphony includes this versified sarcasm in Ives's handwriting:

> He doesn't know much,
> *But* – he thinks he knows a lot.
> Oh, *doesn't* he think he knows an awful lot!
> But – what he knows everybody knows,
> And what he doesn't know everybody knows too.
> And when it comes to talkin',
> He's there with both his jaws,
> An' the sounds you hear are the sounds you hear
> When crows get going their 'caws';
> Yes – he's a busy, buzzin' business man,
> Talkin' glib and continual . . .[18]

Even this heavy-footed broadside is about as amiable as it is hostile. And Ives's more typical comments on business are a good deal more amiable than that. In an important letter to Henry Bellaman he insisted:

> I have experienced a great fulness of life in business. The fabric of existence weaves itself whole. You cannot set an art off in the corner and hope for it to have vitality, reality and substance. There can be nothing *exclusive* about a substantial art. It comes directly out of the heart of experience of life and thinking about life and living life.[19]

In his own view, in others words, the forces operating on Ives's life tended not toward schizophrenia but toward synthesis and wholeness. In an altogether different way from Roosevelt,[20] Ives, too, claimed to have realized a version of the venerable dream of integrating the *vita activa* and the *vita contemplativa*. His was a particularly modern and American version: "My work in music helped my business and work in business helped my music."

The serenity of this declaration depends upon a prior assumption, Ives's idealization of business itself. Given his own experiences, it is not surprising that Ives should compare the domains of business and music invidiously: "It is my impression that there is more open-mindedness and willingness to examine carefully the premises underlying a new or unfamiliar thing, in the world of business than in the world of music." This settles one or two scores, and it was probably a fair judgment as well. Ives goes much further, however, testifying not merely to the

ingenuity of business, or its capacity for innovation, but its high transcendental virtue: "It is not even uncommon in business intercourse to
sense a reflection of a philosophy – a depth of something fine – akin to a
strong sense of beauty in art. To assume that business is a material
process, and only that, is to undervalue the average mind and heart. To
an insurance man there *is* an 'average man' and he is humanity." As
Ives rendered it, the American musical establishment in the early years
of the twentieth century was not only derivative and timid, it was not
even musical: It was inartistic. Such art as can be found expresses itself
in business instead. Ives's remarkable identification of philosophy, art,
and business is the apotheosis of what Santayana referred to as America's idealistic materialism. This moralized conception of commerce
looks quaint today, but its roots can be traced from the turn-of-the-
century magazine *Success,* through Franklin, to Cotton Mather's *Bonifa-
cius*. Ives is merely continuing the custom of sanctifying the practical, of
insisting that the pragmatic and the real are near allies, as against the
airiness of detached metaphysics and the cloistered irrelevance of academic culture.

So, Ives's reverential attitude toward business is closely tied to his
high regard for the "common man." The equation of the common man
with "humanity" is the most recurrent thesis in all the published and
unpublished prose Ives wrote over forty years. Ives more often wrote
about politics and society than about music, and even his essays on
music usually resolve themselves fairly quickly into political statements,
and typically along these lines. The wisdom of the majority, the benevolence of democracy, the superior virtues of the average citizen –
these were the tenets of Ives's exuberant Americanism. "The majority –
the people – will [soon] need no intermediary. Governments will pass
from the representative to the direct."[21] Humanity's innate virtues are
corrupted by "unnatural institutions."[22] The following directive to insurance agents empahsizes the connections between business and the
people: "If you can't make your prospect like you or your policy, make
him like Life Insurance anyway. Knock some BIG ideas into his mind.
Every man wants to be independent and have his family independent.
That's the spirit of America and of humans in general."[23]

Ives's longest essay, "The Majority," is a tub-thumping, celebratory
hymn to the people, the common man, progress. "The day of
leaders . . . is gradually closing – the people are beginning to lead themselves – the public store is being opened; the Common Heart, the
Over-Soul and the Universal Mind are coming into their own."[24] If
Emerson is the ancestor of these capitalized protestations, the politics of
Ives's own generation often provides a more current vocabulary. The
text accompanying *The Masses* (1915) includes these lines:

The Masses! The Masses! The Masses have toiled,
Behold the works of the World!
The Masses are thinking,
Whence comes the thought of the World!
The Masses are singing, are singing, singing,
Whence comes the Song of the World![25]

Ives's miscellaneous egalitarian enthusiasms have been labeled "Progressive."[26] In fact, however, Ives shared only a little of progressivisms's faith in technocratic planning, bureaucratic reform, the ascendance of managers, and the supremacy of efficiency. (He did invoke "science" from time to time on behalf of his insurance schemes.) Rather, Ives's antihierarchical impulses and his dedication to direct democracy, his belief in the unmanaged people, identify his thought as a latter-day version of populism. The people as leader. In his famous "Suggestion for a Twentieth Amendment," Ives supported the electoral devices of initiative and referendum, two favored goals of Progressive reformers, but his endorsement was coextensive with his redefinition of both terms toward populist significations. Whereas the conventional understanding of these notions restricts the people's ballot to occasional interventions, Ives proposed that the voters regularly and routinely make policy of all sorts. If the government were run on the lines Ives suggested, Congress would become merely "the clerical machine of the people," and the president would be reduced to the nation's "executive head clerk."[27]

Ives's devotion to "the people" seems to have forged the link, in his own imagination, between his musical and business careers. A kind of actuarial mysticism informed his conception of insurance: security for all the people, not just the economic elite, in a system of shared risk and mutual benefits, built on what Ives actually called the "divine" law of averages.[28] Similarly, the common man creates both the material and the norm of Ives's music. Ives claimed to have the average citizen in mind as his judge when he wrote. Further, he constructed his music out of quotation, and while he occasionally quotes the European masters (Beethoven in particular), by far the largest number of references are to the music of the people: folk tunes, popular songs and ballads, above all hymns. Such music, and especially the old hymns as they were actually sung in the nineteenth-century country churches, elicit all Ives's admiration. Performed by ill-sorted choirs accompanied by half-trained organists, the old hymns were not "nice" (one of Ives's reverberant cuss words), but they were real, and true. Discord and substance were one; pedestrian standards of beauty were transcended by intensity, and especially by sincerity. The old hymns had "a truer ring than many of those groove-made, even-measured, monotonous, non-rhythmed, indoor-smelling, priest-taught, academic, English or non-English hymns (and anthems) – well-written, well-harmonized things, well-voice-led, well-counterpointed, and well O.K.'d."[29]

Comments such as this appear frequently in Ives's writing. Remembered amateur performances contributed heavily to his composition and theory. Furthermore, Ives's populist affirmations reached out to include his conception of the performance of his music as well. Conductors and players are regularly given options: instrumentation for certain parts is given in alternative forms; different scorings are given for some choral works; omissions are suggested. Performers are to decide whether or not to add the flute in "Thoreau." The cadenza at the center of *Over the Pavements* (1913) is to be played at the performer's discretion: "To play or not to play? If played, to be played as not a nice one – but EVENLY, Precise and unmusical as possible!"[30]

Ives's attitude toward the performance of his music is startling for its time. The freedom Ives allows to musicians is, as H. W. Hitchkock observes, "prophetic of the stance of a John Cage."[31] More important, the options Ives offers, and the conception of music they imply, follow logically from his most basic beliefs. The "people," in addition to serving as the inspiration and the subject of Ives's music, also provide models of performance. Their playing of a song or hymn or march would vary dramatically each time they attempted it – no matter how hard they tried to get it "right." Ives does more than accept this variability: He endorses it as a value higher than accuracy, and in doing so he reverses centuries of musical presupposition. He is searching for a way to ensure the triumph of the spontaneous over the habitual, of independence over convention. He is carrying his contempt for the "groove-made" and "indoor-smelling" and "academic" and "priest-taught" from the design of music into its performance as well.

An agenda of this sort has limits, to be sure. If some of Ives's music is to be performed in discretionary ways, most of it is not. Indeed, stories of Ives's endless troubles with copyists who routinely corrected his apparently "wrong" notes are legendary. He insisted on his own choices, when he made them. Typically, in fact, the seemingly wrong notes Ives wrote also spring from the band concerts he remembered from his childhood. Ives would painstakingly score the note some amateur horn player or oboist had hit, decades earlier, by mistake. Those discords pay retrospective tribute to the common man as musician, as the alternative scorings offer the parallel prospective compliment. In either case, Ives's philosophical point remains intact. His faith in the musicians who would play his compositions – a faith strong enough to survive countless disappointments – derived from the same egalitarian sources as the music itself.

The academicians and priests who periodically propel Ives into sputtering outrage are, of course, the musical equivalents of political leaders. Both classes try to get between the people and their own instinctive truth. Despite their efforts, the common man is emerging as his own leader, and Ives commemorates that evolution in his music. He goes even further when, in a fervor of Whitmanesque soothsaying, he predicts that the common man will become not merely his own leader but his own bard as well: "The instinctive and progressive interest of every man in art, we are willing to affirm with no qualification, will go on and on, ever fulfilling hopes, ever building new ones, ever opening new horizons, until the day will come when every man while digging his potatoes will breathe his own epics, his own symphonies (operas, if he likes it)."[32]

Predictably, given Ives's preference for the defiantly ordinary, the chief citizen of his musical-political utopia is digging potatoes. The image is also an abbreviated index to the significant pastoral dimension of his thought and music. His sketch of the future is obviously at bottom a glancing version of nostalgia. So too his notion of government by endless universal ballot resembles a gigantically multiplied New England town meeting. *The Majority,* completed just a couple of years after the 1920 census had declared that more of the U.S. population now lived in cities than in rural settings, includes in its final pages a glorification of the farmer as the most essential and most "natural" of citizens. As a corollary, the city is made the target of routine pastoral invective: "Perhaps city life is itself an unessential. Perhaps it is caused nowadays more by curiosity than necessity – the restless, nervous curiosity of men that Thoreau may have had in mind when he said that rubbing elbows together does not necessarily bring minds closer together."[33]

Actually, this invective is not quite routine: To suggest that people in twentieth-century America live in cities out of "curiosity" is to approach novelty of a bizarre kind. And, since Ives's great business success depended absolutely on the city – and on that aggregate, actuarial behavior that he elsewhere claimed to consider "divine" – his revulsion from the urban crowd is illogical as well as flatly ungenerous.

No matter. Backward-looking pastoral longing is among the prime determinants of Ives's art, perhaps the single most conclusive one. For Ives, as for so many of his countrymen before and since, the pastoral entwined itself with the patriotic; the theme is loss, and the tones are those of the jeremiad: The "seed of 1776 [has] gone soft." The reason is "commercialism, with its influence tending toward mechanization and standardized processes of mind and life (making breakfast and death a little too easy)."[34] The words Ives wrote for *The Ruined River* (1911) are characteristic:

> Down the river comes a noise!
> It is not the sound of rolling waters
> It's only the sounds of Man
> Dancing halls and tambourine
> Phonograph and gasoline
> Human beings gone machine
> ta-ra-ra-BOOM-de-ay
> KILLED is the blare of the hunting horn
> The River Gods are gone . . .[35]

Honegger would write a famous orchestral piece that imitated the sounds of the railroad train (*Pacific 231*), and other modernists would celebrate machinery as assorted as farm implements and airplanes. For Ives, machines were usually the enemy, and "human beings gone machine" the cause of his lamenting. Predictably, Ives's pantheon was inhabited by eighteenth- and nineteenth-century figures, by Washington and Jefferson, by Thoreau and Lincoln, above all by Emerson.

"He was," Ives wrote of Emerson, "a born radical, as are all true conservatives."[36] Perhaps. In any case, Ives, for his part, like almost all American radicals, was in equal measure conservative. Consequently, the most discernible fact about his music is that its technical innovations, which catapulted his work forward one or even two generations, serve an emotional and ideological alliance with the past.[37] His musical experiments shape themselves more often than not into efforts of restoration. His songs and sonatas and symphonies are attempts to recover the past: America's past generally, and specifically Ives's own past as a boy in small-town New England.

This is the interlinked, nostalgia program behind virtually everything Ives wrote. *Essays before a Sonata,* written to accompany the *Concord Sonata* (1915), has chapters on each of the figures who give their names to the music's four sections: "Emerson," "Hawthorne," "The Alcotts," and "Thoreau." Ives's homage to the Concord masters is sometimes diverted into scarcely disguised exercises in self-defense. Thus, his plea on behalf of Emerson's style is surely to be taken as a justification for his own music as well: "Nature dislikes to explain as much as to repeat. It is conceivable that what is unified form to the author, or composer, may of necessity be formless to his audience. . . . Initial coherence today may be dullness tomorrow."[38]

Ives works hard in his essay to trace the analogy between his music and Emerson's prose; his effort is a measure of the significance the connection had for him. He placed himself consciously in the role of disciple, searching for an adequate musical expression for Emerson's message, the "revelation of the soul of humanity knocking at the door of the divine mysteries, radiant in the faith that it *will* be opened – and ·' human become the divine!"[39] The "Emerson" section of *Concord* is ₁ves's passionate effort to give musical voice to the oracular insight of his master.

Similarly, the other three sections of *Concord* are programmatic responses to their several subjects. Ives has less to say about Hawthorne and the Alcotts. Hawthorne, writes Ives, was "dripping wet with the supernatural";[40] the music his name gives title to is intended to re-create a sense of his "wilder, fantastical adventures into the half child-like, half fairy-like phantasmal realms." The "Hawthorne" section, in Ives's deliberately vexed formulation, is "music about something that never will happen, or something else that is not." Of "The Alcotts" Ives writes that "we won't try to reconcile this section with much besides 'the memory of the home under the elms – the Scotch songs and the family hymns that were sung at the end of each day."[41] As always in Ives, celebration and nostalgia are linked.

Among his Concord subjects, Ives surely felt the greatest reverence for Emerson, but he approached Thoreau with a more initmate fellow-feeling. If Emerson was Ives's chief oracle, Thoreau was more accessible to his imagination as a man and personality. Ives was Emerson's disciple, but Thoreau's comrade. "You," Ives writes in defending Thoreau from the likes of James Russell Lowell and Mark Van Doren, "you know your Thoreau – but not my Thoreau – that reassuring and true friend, who stood by me one 'low' day, when the sun had gone down, long, long before sunset."[42] What Ives calls "the program" for the "Thoreau" section of *Concord* consists in Thoreau's "thought on an autumn day of Indian summer at Walden." And, for two pages, Ives narrates in detail the progress of Thoreau's thoughts and moods on that day, the sequence of restlessness and meditation, of observation and introspection.

Ives's music, then, whatever its innovative discordancy, was placed at the service of a meticulously reconstructed past. One of the people Ives discussed his music with was his young nephew, Brewster. Years later, in 1969, Brewster recalled the composition of the *Concord* Sonata. "He illustrated what he was attempting to do by reading passages from Emerson, the Alcotts, Hawthorne, and Thoreau and then playing passages after he had read them to convince me that the music was expressing the words of the author. . . . He showed me how with quarter-tones the means of expression could be multiplied in almost a geometrical fashion."[43]

What was true for *Concord* was true for Ives's music generally. Whether summoning Lincoln, "the great commoner," or a Yale–Harvard football game, or anti-abolitionist riots in Boston, or a horse-drawn delivery wagon, or church bells across a river, Ives's chief faculty was memory. Consider this explanation of the technique of "Thanksgiving," the fourth movement of the *Holidays* Symphony (Plate 14):

> Dissonances . . . had a good excuse for being, and in the final analysis a religious excuse, because in the stern outward life of the old settlers, pioneers and Puritans, there was a life generally of inward beauty, but with a rather harsh exterior. And the Puritan "no-compromise" with mellow colors and bodily ease gives a natural reason for trying tonal and uneven off-counterpoints and combinations which would be and sound of sterner things – which single minor or major triads or German-made counterpoint did not . . . come up to.[44]

Atonality itself, in other words, and not just the quotations from patriotic and religious tunes, is a mechanism for reaching toward the past. As Ives originally conceived of the *Holidays* Symphony, in 1905, each movement was to be "based on something of the memory that a man has of his boy holidays, rather than any present-day program of such."[45] Even his instrumentation might declare Ives's attempt to duplicate the past. He explained the ill-assorted groups of instruments he put together in his "theater orchestras" by referring them to the small-town groups he had seen and heard as a boy. The "average theatre orchestra of some years ago" was made up of what was available in a given village on a given evening. The orchestra "depended somewhat on what players and instruments happened to be around."[46]

Referring in particular to Edward Bellamy's *Looking Backward* and its multitudinous utopian progeny, Max Fisch describes the American turn of the century as a period "whose backward looks were for the sake of forward looks."[47] In fact, however, the situation was at least equally the opposite, as the "case" of Charles Ives reveals. Like so many of his contemporaries, Ives looked toward tomorrow only "for the sake" of his commitment to a vision of yesterday.

So, to return to the important example of the *Holidays* Symphony, Ives insisted that its experimental appearance should not obscure his nostalgic intentions. The movements of the symphony are pastoral pictures, not "abstract music." They are "pictures in music of common events in the lives of common people (that is, of fine people), mostly of the rural communities. That's all there is to it. There is not artistic purpose, no message."[48]

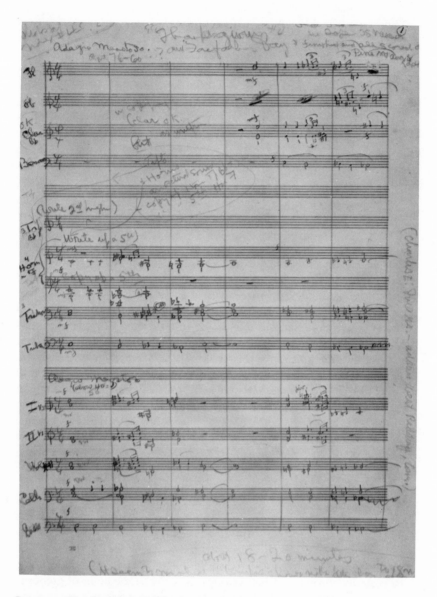

PLATE 14. The first page of "Thanksgiving," in Charles Ives's hand. (Courtesy of the Music Library, Yale University.)

There may have been no artistic purpose, but there was of course "message" in abundance. At the core of Ives's dissonant nostalgia lies his assent to a cluster of reactionary values that virtually prohibited him from directly engaging music in or for itself. Indeed, Ives's "innovative nostalgia" appears paradoxical only until its anguished but exquisite logic discloses itself.[49] Ives was shaped by a culture that rejected the intrinsic value of serious music and certainly rejected music as a suitable career for a man. Music was ornamental, marginal; the set of talents associated with it was compatible with the station of women. Music became manly only insofar as it subordinated itself to rugged ideological affirmations, preferably of a patriotic sort. Lying like a shadow across the years of Ives's musical development was the irony of his father's career: George Ives's moment of unqualified success occurred when, at the age of seventeen, he served as leader of what was regarded as the best Union band in the Civil War.

Serious music – embodied in the symphonies and sonatas of the eighteenth- and nineteenth-century European tradition – was simply not a permissible vocation for a man. Ives was obviously victimized by this attitude, but he made it his own as well. It was, in fact, this sexual-political conviction, far more than his often-discussed transcendentalism, that shaped Ives's musical beliefs. His vocabulary as he talked about music and musicians was strikingly and relentlessly sexual. He refers constantly throughout the *Memos* to the "ladies of both sexes" who can only tolerate an "emasculated" music. These "ladies" include the critics, for example "Aunt" Philip Hale and the "Rollos" who hide behind "their silk skirts."[50] A familiar anecdote recalls Ives's attendance at a Town Hall concert in January 1931. When the audience hissed at Carl Ruggles's *Men and Mountains,* Ives jumped up and shouted at the loudest offender: "You god damn sissy . . . when you hear strong masculine music like this, get up and use your ears like a man." If, according to a passage cited earlier, the abstract cause of America's decline is commercialization, the concrete effect is that America "is losing her manhood" (*sic*). America is being taken over by "nice Lizzies" both male and female, "cautious old gals . . . the ladybirds." The Puritans "weren't soft . . . weren't effeminate."[51]

Repeatedly throughout his writings, literally to the point of preoccupation, Ives denounces the "emasculation" of American culture. One symptom of that condition is the popularity of the European classics, themselves written mainly by "sissies." Ives on Chopin: "One just naturally thinks of him with a skirt on." And "Richy Wagner" was merely "a woman passing as a man." American ears haven't been stretched; the concert stages are dominated by Europeans playing "effeminate," "unmasculine" European music – "an emasculated art making money." And on and on. "Hasn't music always been too much an emasculated art? Mozart etc. helped." "The American ear has become a Soft-Static Co. (Limited), and the Gabrilowitsches et al, have got the money and coll[ected] the ladies smiles."[52]

Sociologically, to be sure, Ives is simply reflecting the facts of the case. By 1900, American culture had long since been feminized. The consumers of belles lettres, classical music, and most poetry were women – middle-class women, by and large, of polite though limited artistic accomplishment themselves, and custodians of norms of propriety that spanned aesthetics and etiquette. Relegating women to such peripheral domains permitted the men who manipulated them to have it several ways at once: to trivialize cultural achievement and interest by driving it into domesticity; to distract the attention of the women who were being locked out of the centers of political and economic power; to define the "real" meaning of America in terms of aggressive, escapist, determinedly anti-aesthetic masculinity.[53]

It was this kind of attitude, and not simply an adventurous spirit, that Ives absorbed from his father's instruction; the *Memos* give glimpses of this. When George Ives had his son do chromatic scales, he ordered each interval to be a minor ninth. "If you must play a chromatic scale, play it like a man." More than Emerson's individualism, or the universalism of the transcendentalist creed, or the patriotic appeal of the Founding Fathers, or even the twinned lures of pastoral and childhood, it was Ives's corrosive commitments to America's deep double hostility – to art and to women – that fixed the definition of his cultural politics. He had to write an American and a "manly music," to vindicate his dedication to the most suspiciously feminine of all the arts, and the one still most in thrall to Europe.

This is the more fundamental sense in which Ives's innovations point backward. They are his means, in the years of turmoil around the turn of the century, of ratifying traditional assumptions. Ironically, the values he thus affirmed included those that simultaneously circumscribed his own art within deforming conceptions. Understood aright, Ives's nostalgia was at last more sinister than picturesque, more tragic than celebratory. He must have found his emotional situation at least intermittently untenable. The conflict he waged within himself drove him periodically to deny altogether that he was writing music in any recognizable sense. "My God!" he declared in a famous polemical passage, "what has sound got to do with music!"

The waiter brings the only fresh egg he has, but the man at breakfast sends it back because it doesn't fit his eggcup. Why can't music go out in the same way it comes into a man, without having to crawl over a fence of sounds, thoraxes, catguts, wire, wood, and brass? Consecutive fifths are as harmless as blue laws compared with the relentless tyranny of the "media." The instrument! – there is the perennial difficulty – there is music's limitation. . . . That music must be heard is not essential – what it *sounds* like may not be what it *is*.[54]

What Ives often hints at elsewhere is here made explicit: his alienation from his own art. A story Ives tells about his father indicates that, once again, George Ives originated his son's attitude. A " 'nice' young man asked Father how he could stand to hear old John Bell [a member of George Ives's choir] singing – off-key, no voice, bellowing; father: 'Watch him closely and reverently, look into his face and hear the music of the ages. Don't pay too much attention to the sounds – for if you do you may miss the music.'"[55] Ives's opposition between music and its sounds is often, rather casually, glossed by appeal to the pale platonism of his transcendental ideas. It is better understood as an unwitting cry of anguish, the intendedly defiant but inescapably defeated lament of a man at war with himself, a man who had to annihilate his own artistic identity in order to preserve it.

Frank Rossiter, in his superb biography of Ives, suggests that cultural historians find it difficult to relate the composer to the avant-garde movements in the arts in the early twentieth century.[56] On the contrary. The casual coincidence of technical experimentation – often leading to explosive originality of form – with some reactionary ideology or other describes not only Ives's music but the work of the makers of modernism as well. In literature, for example, Lawrence and Henry James, Yeats and Eliot, Hemingway and Faulkner, above all Pound, took much of the energy for their formal explorations from their passionate devotion to varieties of reaction and nostalgia. Pound's example is of course scandalous: such a powerful contempt for the vulgarity of "the age" that it spilled over into a revulsion from humanity. Pound's yearning after archaic systems of order was so compelling to him that it fused into a worship of sheer force. The defender of accurate letters became the apologist for fascism and a barbarous anti-Semitism. Pound was not alone in the temptation he felt to take a part in the world of political events; a good many artists have hoped to remake reality through transliterations of their vision. That Pound ended by becoming only the morally suicidal tool of an especially noxious tyranny offers a signal comment on the limits of imagination.

If Pound's case presents itself as an enflamed, tragic caricature, it is nonetheless true to ideological tendencies visible across much of modernism's achievement. One fairly common analysis of this phenomenon was recently reformulated by Terry Eagleton: "In the absence of a genuinely revolutionary art, only a radical conservatism, hostile like Marxism to the withered values of liberal bourgeois society, could produce the most significant literature."[57] This makes its own shrill demands on history, but it captures at least a part of the dialectic that shaped early twentieth-century culture. Eliot's famous declaration of the late twenties – that he was in literature a classicist, in religion an Anglo-Catholic, and in politics a royalist – is more than a refined version of Pound's excess, to be sure, but it discloses some of the same inclinations (especially if the shocking word "royalist" is taken seriously, as it should be).

On its surface, Ives's ideology appears to distinguish itself, and sharply, from that of Pound and Eliot and the rest. In lines cited earlier, Ives located himself solidly on the side of the people; he as firmly opposed himself to the leaders and men on horseback and assorted messianic over-reachers who were to litter the ground of literature and then of reality in the first third of this century. Where Pound welcomed the advent of Mussolini, Ives celebrated the emergence of the common man. Yet, as we have seen, the assumptions underlying Ives's manifest politics had a distinct reactionary flavor of their own. And his insistence on the preeminence of a certain kind of primitive masculinity, his fascination with toughness and strength, brought him closer to modernism's adoration of force than his populism might predict.

The debate in Ives between primitivism and progress also resembles to some extent the tensions and fate of the futurist branch of Italian modernist painting. Unlike Ives and the literary modernists, futurism turned its back systematically on the past. Yet, in their adulation of the machine, the futurists – Filippo Marinetti, Umberto Boccioni, Giacomo Balla, and Gino Severini – were merely genuflecting before the newly refurbished shrine of atavistic power. They tried to turn their canvases into the speed and energy they admired in technology; and then they marched off to join in the war that several of them hymned as the ultimate expression of the new man-made civilization.[58] They were, in one tragic sense, right; and Boccioni, the best painter among them, died in the proof. Among those that survived, Marinetti, the inventor of the movement, and several others lived long enough to become minor spokesmen for fascism. Once again the future meets the past.[59]

The songs Americans listened to while they were ignoring Ives in the early years of the century were a chaos of themes and subjects. The music was, by turns, patriotic ("I'm a Yankee Doodle Dandy," 1906), subversive ("Dump the Bosses off Your Backs," 1907), rural ("In the Good Old Summer Time," 1902), urban ("Give My Regards to Broad-

way," 1905), sentimental ("A Bird in a Gilded Cage," 1900), downright mawkish ("All Aboard for Blanket Bay," 1910), romantic ("Let
Me Call You Sweetheart," 1910), cynical ("I Wonder Who's Kissing
Her Now," 1909), topical ("Meet Me in St. Louis," 1904), mythmaking ("Casey Jones," 1909), nostalgic ("School Days," 1907), suggestive
("I'd Like to See a Little More of You," 1906), and ethnically insulting
("Coon, Coon, Coon, I Wish My Color Would Fade," 1900). Heterogeneous as they are in tone and attitude, what these songs all have in
common is technical conservatism; and this in turn is what divides all of
them from the music of Ives. It is also what divides Ives – then and
now – from the audience of common men and women he longed for.
He predicted that "the day will come when every man while digging
his own potatoes will breathe his own epics, his own symphonies (operas, if he likes it)." Ives's forecast, needless to say, has so far proven
more than a little optimistic. As far as we can tell, the number of
opera-breathing potato diggers has not markedly increased over the
past half-century. Nor even has "every man" taken up the musical
cause of his champion, Charles Ives. Thus, a powerful irony has embraced Ives's hopes. When acceptance was finally offered him, it came
not from "the people," but precisely from the professional musicians
and the academicians whose predecessors had tormented his creative
years. Today, those professionals – the descendants of "Rollo" and
"Aunt" Hale – acclaim Ives as the major composer America has produced. The common man, on the other hand, remains indifferent to
Ives when he is not hostile. If he is uncommon enough to form alliances
with serious music at all, he is still loyal to the same set of nineteenth-
century composers Ives struggled to break away from. The phenome-
nal growth of the recording industry, from its major commercial beginnings in 1900 to the present, has merely reaffirmed old loyalties.

   For every listener who has even heard a composition by Ives, how
many are familiar with much of the work of, say, Tchaikovsky, whom
Ives described as "the great Russian weeper"? Or Chopin ("pretty
soft")? Or "the easy-made Haydn"? It is only a slight overstatement to
estimate that Ives remains almost as unknown in his apotheosis as he
was in his long years of obscurity. He once complained that "beauty in
music is too often confused with something that lets the ears lie back in
an easy chair."[60] A half-century later, the ears of most concertgoers are
still resting comfortably.

Chapter 9

Realism and modernism:
John Sloan, Alfred Stieglitz, and others

Fragments of two conversations, to begin with. In both of them, American painters, after inspecting the new art of Paris, confidently enlist on the losing side of the twentieth century's cultural debate. The first occurred in John Sloan's 23rd Street kitchen in November 1908. Robert Henri had just returned from France, filled with opinions about paintings and people, which he hurried to share with Sloan over dinner. The only record of the conversation is a sentence in Sloan's diary: Henri "spoke of the strange freaks of the Salon d'Automne in Paris, says that the Eight exhibition was much more notable."[1]

A few months earlier, Mary Cassatt had paid a call on Gertrude Stein at 27, rue de Fleurus. Cassatt glanced at the pictures, many of them by the same painters who were about to offend Henri, and she fled. She announced to the friend who had brought her: "I have never in my life seen so many dreadful paintings in one place; I have never in my life seen so many dreadful people gathered together and I want to be taken home at once."[2]

These two episodes exemplify a cultural truth: In painting (as in science), there was a revolution going on in the first two decades of the twentieth century, but its victories were not being won in America. It was in Europe, in the years before World War I, that modernism was invented and reinvented in all its startling variety: expressionism, cubism, fauvism, constructivism, and the other movements. The art works and attitudes "spawned in the intellectual ferment of this pivotal era [gave] modernist art . . . its quintessential forms."[3] Picasso and Matisse most spectacularly, but along with them so many others, Braque, Gris, Brancusi, Rouault, Marc, and Munch, established the grammar and indeed defined the very vocabulary of the dominant twentieth-century visual culture.

Some of the American painters and sculptors who traveled to Europe in the prewar years, like Cassatt and Henri, responded to all this activity with bewilderment or anger. Others did demonstrate a "willingness to experiment with . . . the major 'isms,' " but their involvement was usually halting or partial and their contributions marginal.[4] Maurice Prendergast took up Cézanne's cause as early as 1898; and Alfred Maurer was adopting fauvism by 1905. But the effects of such connections were typically tentative. Maurice Sterne, for example, "went no further than Cézanne and Gaugin, and [Samuel] Halpert no further than Picasso's Pink Period."[5] Only the painters who made up the Stieglitz group–John Marin, Marsden Hartley, Arthur Dove, and a few others–along with a handful of independents, made a significant exception to this generalization.

In short, the new styles were a European affair. Although they were not widely known to American artists or to the public until after 1913, they inevitably create a retrospective context in which the American paintings look all the more quaint and provincial. Needless to say, many of those same Americans did not quite see it this way, and they were right to this important extent: A spirit of revolt was abroad in the early years of twentieth-century American painting. If it took less decisive shape than in Europe, it may thus illustrate more clearly the divided mind of the culture whose visual record it has left us.

"THE NINE"

In fact, not just one but a series of quite different rebellions broke out. They had in common only an enemy, the Academy. Younger painters of all inclinations conceived of the Academy as the repository of an outworn and deadening system. John Sloan heckled "old Sir Caspar Purdon Clarke," director (briefly) of the Metropolitan Museum, as "the stupidest judge of painting in power today."[6] Clarke was "fossiliferous," and the satire could be enlarged to cover the Academy itself: an oversized, lumbering relic of the aesthetic age of dinosaurs, spiritually extinct but inexplicably still moving. The Academy's huge bulk blotted out the twentieth-century sun and provoked the outrage of a good many artists who were otherwise dissimilar. One critic summed up the prevailing standards as a combination of "polite genre and washed out aestheticism."[7] That sounds more editorial than descriptive, but it is coolly temperate compared with Lloyd Goodrich's downright indignation:

> In the opening years of this century American art was dominated by an academic idealism which ignored the realities of American life. Our artists shunned the crude American scene; in their work there was no thirst of our gigantic material growth, the great

flood of immigration, the growing social conflicts, or the life of the great mass of the people.

The only "city" in American painting was Fifth Avenue, and the tone was "sunny."[8]

Van Wyck Brooks regarded academic art as the principal creation of the genteel tradition. Brooks recalled with admiration George Luks's formulation of his aesthetic mission as "slapping down pretty art."[9] And Everett Shinn agreed. He said that he and Glackens and Sloan and the rest had no program: They "were against the monocle pictures at the Academy, that was all."[10]

Rather like the eclectic architects we examined in an earlier chapter, "the academic" has survived principally in the detractions of its opponents. Its advocates are now mostly forgotten. John C. Van Dyke was one such spokesman. My title for this section is a coinage, of course, a small pun intended to recall those numerological American art movements, the Eight and the Ten. My number comes from Van Dyke's table of contents in *American Painting and Its Tradition,* in which nine men are listed. Among them, they purportedly comprise the major figures of "the period in American painting dating, generally, from about 1878 to, say, 1915. That period has practically closed."[11] Van Dyke concedes that the nine "were by no means the whole count [but] they were certainly representative of the movement, and their works speak for almost every phase of it." They "wrought in a common spirit, making an epoch in art history and leaving a tradition" (p. vi).

Who are the nine who have made such a new and coherent movement? In Van Dyke's roughly chronological order: George Innes, Alexander H. Wyant, Homer Martin, Winslow Homer, John La Farge, James Abbott McNeill Whistler, William Merritt Chase, John W. Alexander, and John Singer Sargent. The list is not an embarrassment, either to Van Dyke or to American painting. Indeed, several of the choices still seem plausible. Even Whistler, however, makes only a partial exception to the homogeneity Van Dyke aimed to codify. The pictures produced by most of these nine painters tend to be reasonably decorous in subject matter, representational and idealizing, and familiar in technique. From our point of view, the list is most notable for its absences: not merely all the Eight and the original Ten, but George Bellows and Cassatt, and especially Albert Pinkham Ryder and Thomas Eakins.[12]

Van Dyke also saw a great absence in his list, but of a quite different sort. For him, the true significance of his painters lay not so much in what these men achieved as in what they did not, and could not. They are the major American figures, but they are, according to Van Dyke, a group of relatively small stature. The key, as it has also seemed to so many other critics of American culture in so many other generations, lies in the absence of a tradition. America has little painting to show because it has so little cultural history, so little tradition. We are in the company, again, of Henry James, for whom Americans are "the disinherited of Art! We're condemned to be superficial! We're excluded from the magic circle! The soil of American perception is a poor little barren artificial deposit."[13] It was a theme renewed at the turn of the century by Barrett Wendell, in his *Literary History of America* (1900), and by Van Wyck Brooks in his first book, *The Wine of the Puritans* (1909).

In John Van Dyke's terse restatement of the idea, "Out of nothing nothing comes" (p. 11). No amount of skill or training can succeed without the addition of "a something that has been more or less inherited" (p. 13). Of his nine painters, the one who came closest to possessing the artistic background of a European was La Farge, a circumstance that prompts Van Dyke to ask rhetorically: "Is that why he is now placed as the one Olympian of the period?" (p. 15). According to Van Dyke, the tradition that eight of the nine lacked, and that even La Farge entered into imperfectly, is more or less synonymous with the academic, since "the academies are usually the custodians and conservers of it" (p. 15).

To which Sloan would have replied with his definition of the Academy: "an organization of Cads and Demi-Cads, with soft brains and pointed beards."[14]

Sloan and his friends reserved some of their choicest hostility for Kenyon Cox. Sloan would sometimes call him "K. Kox" and refer to him as one of those "pink and white idiots."[15] There are significant sexual undertones here that I shall return to later. For now, I quote Sloan's unkind comments to introduce Cox, perhaps America's most ferocious adversary of modernist painting. Three years after the exhibition of the Eight, and two years before the Armory Show, Cox spelled out the details of his antimodernist creed in a set of lectures published under the title *The Classic Point of View* (1911). "The primary business of painting," Cox insisted, "is to create a beautiful surface, beautifully divided into interesting shapes, enlivened with noble lines, varied with lovely and harmonious colors."[16] Confident appeals of this sort, the litany of the noble, the harmonious, the lovely, permeate the book. It is an attitude that drifts easily and often into moralizing. Cox's aesthetic has at its center the virtues—jointly painterly and social—of order, clarity, and control. The classic spirit, according to Cox, resides "above all" in "the love of permanence and of continuity." It demands that art behave in a "fine and noble way," with "disciplined emotion and [with] individuality restrained by law."

The classic spirit "strives for the essential rather than the accidental, the eternal rather than the momentary – loves impersonality more than personality, and feels more power in the orderly succession of the hours and the seasons than in the violence of earthquake or of storm" (p. 4). Here is realism, but in that earlier, medieval sense, the doctrine that universals have a real and objective existence. In the rather altered environment of 1911, Cox's flight toward the eternal and the essential serves to detach the artist from the exigencies of modern reality.

Finally and unsurprisingly, Cox asserts that the classic spirit "loves to steep itself in tradition. It would have each new work connect itself in the mind of him who sees it with all the noble and lovely works of the past" (p. 4). Fidelity to the past is coextensive with the proper limits of imagination. Even more than the more famous proponents of the twentieth-century neoclassic ideal (for example, Eliot), and even perhaps more than his contemporary Ralph Adams Cram, Cox subordinates individual talent to tradition.

But such a difference between Cram and Cox is only of degree. The more fundamental connection is one of instructive likeness. Though he fancied himself a classicist, and is talking about painting, Cox's claims are more or less identical with those that the Goth Cram made for architecture. *The Classic Point of View* is another of those many documents in which the aesthetic finds its rationale in ethical terms. Such documents, as we saw in an earlier chapter, tend to be virtually interchangeable, despite the tremendously different styles they defend.

This resemblance is in turn derived from a shared assumption. Like other moralizing aestheticians, Cox and Cram both insist that the "spirit" they revere – whether it is classic or Gothic – is separable from particular forms of expression. In passages cited earlier (Chapter 7), Cram proposed that modern Gothic would be "very different in its outward seeming" from that of the Middle Ages; he rebuked "slavish mimicry" and "faithful copying." Similarly, Cox claimed that the "Classic Spirit . . . has little to do with the so-called 'classic school' founded by Jacques Louis David" (p. 5).

However, if Cox resembles Cram in decrying mere imitation, his paintings, like Cram's buildings, present themselves as blatantly imitative. A glance at his mural-like painting *Venice* will suffice to make the point (Plate 15). What looks to us like a combination of theatrical posturing, sentimentality, obsolete literary reference, anachronistic allegorizing, and trivial motif expressed for Cox a noble mixture of idealism and representation. Edwin Howland Blashfield's *Washington Laying Down His Commission* (Plate 16) is a rather similar work, and Cox's praise of it undoubtedly makes the case that he wanted to press for his own painting: "Washington, in blue and buff, seems naturally enough placed amid the half-medieval, half-ancient, costumes of the symbolical

PLATE 15. Kenyon Cox, *Venice*. (By permission of the Bowdoin college Museum of Art, Brunswick, Maine.)

PLATE 16. Edwin Howland Blashfield, *Washington Laying Down His Commission,* in the Baltimore County Court House.

figures about him. They are all removed from the present . . . and seem equally to belong to an ideal world. The effect of the whole is sumptuously decorative, while the larger implications of the story to be told are much more clearly expressed than they could be by a realistic representation" (p. 76). Mechanical and derivative in composition, historical, anecdotal, and narrative in subject, routinely idealizing in attitude, and simpering in tone: It is almost as if Blashfield had deliberately intended his painting as a defiantly complete catalogue of all the practices modernism would reject.[17]

Given Cox's enthusiasm for such a picture, and his more general theoretical program, it is not difficult to hypothesize how he would react to the radically new art of Paris. There "seems to me . . . to be a vast amount of mere charlatanism among the Neo-Impressionists, and an even larger amount of sheer madness." Cox means madness in a literal rather than metaphorical sense, as he goes on to insist (never letting mere facts stand in his polemic way): "Van Gogh cut off his own ear when he failed to kill his friend Gaugin with a razor; Toulouse-Lautrec had a keeper; several others committed suicide or died in asylums." The special anger Cox directs against cubism unguards his fear that the future belongs to Picasso: "We have even had compositions in which the human figure is represented by a series of triangles and a portrait is symbolized by an arrangement of cubes, and we have critics writing books and articles to prove that this is the real and vital art, the 'art of the future' " (pp. 20–21).

So it goes, throughout the book. The grotesquerie of modern art derives from its practitioners' "desire of noteriety," which leads them to inflict their "rabid self-exploitation" upon the public (pp. 150–151). In one of the few places where Cox attempts to deal with modernism analytically and not merely adverbially, he traces many of its problems back to Puvis: "The latest aberrations of modern art [are] an attempt to carry still farther what Puvis had already carried too far: to bring about the entire disassociation of abstract line and mass from representation" (p. 149).

As an alternative to contemporary European painting, Cox emphatically did not turn to the American tradition. For him, as for John Van Dyke and so many other influential critics, the very phrase "American tradition" is an oxymoron: On this side of the Atlantic Cox sees only a few primitive objects scattered across an aesthetic wasteland. Though there were numerous exceptions, and though talk of the high promise of American art has a long nineteenth-century history, nevertheless educated taste at the turn of the century remained loyal to older European standards and models, and critical judgment reinforced the buying habits of collectors. Through "the 1890's [and surely later] it was socially acceptable for Americans to talk only of European painters."[18] Isabella Stewart Gardner's offer of almost $200,000 for Gainsborough's *Blue Boy* is a notorious example, but the whole collecting career of J. P. Morgan is a more important one. The same Caspar Clarke whom John Sloan reviled, after he arrived in New York in 1905 and surveyed the Metropolitan's collections, observed that "Americans appear to be concerned with the art of every land save that of America."[19] To the highbrows, America itself was lowbrow.

There were, however, Americans deeply concerned with American art, painters who were trying to grasp the nettle of commonplace

American experience and shape it into a visual statement at once vernacular and significant. What Ives had tried to do for music and Dreiser
for literature, they would attempt in painting. In 1905, even as Caspar
Clarke reaffirmed their nonexistence, they were assembling in New
York and planning their assault on the citadels of gentility.

JOHN SLOAN AND THE EIGHT

"What infinite use," Theodore Roosevelt exclaimed, "Dante would
have made of the Bowery. . . . The Bowery is one of the great highways of humanity, a highway of seething life, of varied interest, of fun,
of work, of sordid and terrible tragedy; and it is haunted by demons as
evil as any that stalk through the pages of the *Inferno*." According to
Roosevelt, Whitman was the only writer America had produced who
had "dared to use the Bowery – that is, use anything that was striking
and vividly typical of the humanity around him."[20] This was Roosevelt's answer to the charge that nothing was available on the American
scene to engage a serious artist.

Taking the Bowery in both its literal and extended senses – "anything
that was striking and vividly typical of . . . humanity" – John Sloan
would have agreed. He recorded in his diary a walk through the Bowery with Albert Ullman, and he added this apostrophe: "the Bowery –
that name! so romantic to the youth of towns in the U.S."[21] It was
romantic to Sloan, too, a place not only of evil and tragedy but of
nobility and comedy as well; in short, a place in which to discover all of
life. And it was therefore a suitable artistic subject.

This conviction was at the heart of the Eight's realist revolt, and it
defined both their significance and their eventual relegation to the
shorter chapters of art history. Theirs was a concern primarily with
new subject matter, not with new technique. They reacted against gentility by redirecting a relatively traditional method toward people and
scenes previously excluded by genteel norms. To be sure, their technique was not academic in the most routine or insipid sense: They
handled pigments with apparent carelessness, their brush strokes were
often broad, their compositions were sometimes deliberately ungainly,
they left their surfaces rough. Nonetheless, if either triumph or scandal
attached to the work of the new realists, it centered on what they
painted, not how: dirty streets; threadbare interiors; eccentric, even
disreputable people. What the *Globe*'s critic had to say about a show of
Bellows in 1907 might have been applied to the others as well, particularly Sloan and Luks: "A more dreary and unhealthy lot we have sel-

dom seen. [We searched in vain for] a bit of beauty, of hope, of optimism [and we departed] with a sense of oppression." To the *Globe,* such paintings were "like some depressing dream, best forgotten."[22]

A squeamish response only confirmed Sloan and the other realists in what they were doing. They conceived of their art as defiantly American, not merely in its settings but in the democratic impulse that guided its choices. Sloan and his comrades were committed to the American people at their most ordinary and to visual plain speaking. Decades after the turn of the century, Sloan felt obliged to insist on the importance of what he and his friends had done. "There is so much talk today about the American Scene," Sloan wrote in 1939. "As though it had been discovered in the last decade! If anyone started this painting of the American scene it was our gang of newspaper men: Glackens, Luks, Shinn and myself. . . . But we didn't really start it. What about Homer, Eakins, and lesser men?"[23] Sloan could have gone a step further. Though the idea would have startled John Van Dyke and bewildered Kenyon Cox, the new realists were heirs and exemplars of the oldest and most conspicuous tradition in American painting.

As realists, they were also legatees of Puritanism's history of demands upon painting. Puritanism encouraged realism both because realism seems not to lie and because realism "ignores the sensuous, material elegance of the great tradition."[24] Furthermore, the Eight derived their epistemology from Puritanism through the mediation of nineteenth-century transcendentalism. The Puritans attended to the created world because it was a system of sacred signs. Every object or event, however familiar or obscure, each hailstorm or snake, sunset or tree, might provide a glimpse into the design of God. Generations later, the transcendental descendants of the Puritans preached a wholly different but wholly allied doctrine, one that might be called secular sacramentalism. The world remained revelatory for them, too, but it disclosed a post-Christian spiritual reality: the higher laws and unity of nature, and the correspondences between humanity and the rest of the created world. Emerson and Thoreau scrutinized the physical world as studiously as Cotton and Shepard, and they read lessons of equivalent universality.

In the work of John Sloan and his colleagues, the tradition comes near to its climax and close. The world of the commonplace has become central, and it signifies essentially itself: its irreducible concreteness and sufficiency. Look at the laundry that fills the center of Sloan's *Woman's Work* (1911; Plate 17). It would be possible, presumably, to read a metaphysical lesson or a particular political position into this scene, but it would also be meretricious. The painting might be a protest against poverty or, specifically, against the servile domestic limits of a poor woman's life; after all, the linens and shirts dominate the woman in the

PLATE 17. John Sloan, *Woman's Work,* 1911. (By permission of the Cleveland Museum of Art, Gift of Amelia Elizabeth White.)

composition. Yet the laundry is cheerfully bright, and the entire scene is suffused in tranquil sunshine; perhaps Sloan meant not to protest but to affirm the woman's homely but vital tasks. In fact, the painting resists all such translations. Sloan's title, *Woman's Work,* is neither demonstrably ironic nor sentimental. It is descriptive, intending neither theme nor narrative but an image. The woman, the tenement windows and fire escapes, above all that line of clothes, are simply there.

This elemental factuality is more often evident in Sloan's work than in that of the other realists. To generalize rather broadly: Luks typically embedded his characters and scenes in theatricality and sentiment; Henri rarely abandoned a style of European elegance; Glackens relied upon a derivative impressionism; and Shinn usually glamorized what he painted. More than the others, Sloan tried to give a straightforward account of the streets through which he walked and the backyards over which he looked from his own rear window. Michelangelo objected that his Dutch contemporaries merely painted what they saw. Sloan would have accepted the complaint for himself, with thanks.

Whatever the particular differences among them in their painting, the Eight held a set of ideas more or less in common. "I am not interested in . . . art as art," said Henri. "I am interested in life."[25] And again, "What we need is more sense of the wonder of life and less of this business of picture-making."[26] What such an attitude can lead to, and sometimes did, is an art that luxuriates in its inferiority to reality. It can even collapse into an art that seems to resent its own existence. "Art— my slats!" George Luks famously declared. "Guts! Guts! Life! Life!"[27] Here is the apotheosis of America's predilection for the "real."

Harold Rosenberg offers a shrewd comment on talk of this sort, but it doesn't go quite far enough. "In practice," Rosenberg writes, " 'reality,' as an alternative to art has been less an anti-art program than a social slogan. It may call for the abandonment of art; actually, it anticipates a renewal of art through raising substance above form."[28] Notwithstanding the relative justice of this observation, it silences those voices – some of them from the period we are studying – that actually did look forward to the eradication of art. Consider these two examples. Van Wyck Brooks, in his article on Vernon Lee (1911), propounded as a radically hopeful prophecy a future without art, because art is the expression of men who are not normal, who are not able to live their ideas.[29] A reality well ordered enough would obviate the cause and the need for art.

Emma Goldman started from quite different premises but wound up reaching much the same conclusion: "After the revolution, when classes were abolished, there would be no real need for art, [because] life would then be in itself an all-satisfying mountain of beauty and happiness."[30]

Neither John Sloan nor any of the other painters we are concerned with here went this far. But they were so eager to separate themselves from the idea of art as frivolous or ornamental that they regularly drifted into fulminations against art itself. Always their appeal was to life and reality, not to art. William Carlos Williams, running his finger across the American grain, would soon declare: "No ideas but in things." He spoke for Henri and Sloan, too.

What we have seen in the case of Ives occurs again in the lives of Sloan and the other realists. They were produced by a culture that trivialized and even stigmatized their artistic calling. America's interconnected ideologies of democracy and utility cast both the adequacy and the function of their work into doubt. What they required was a rationale beyond mere aestheticism that would justify their art and legitimize their careers as artists. Again like Ives, they worried that their artistic vocations might raise the question of their masculinity. They had to make "an attempt – necessary only in America – to prove that painting was a job for real men."[31] They could, without much anxiety, behave like citizens or journalists, or like laborers or politicians; but they could behave like artists only in that perilously American way that comes close to extinguishing itself.

In the early years of the century, Sloan often joined Luks and Henri in praising Life at the expense of Art. To give just one example, he complained that a Philadelphia friend had some valuable opinions but "not enough centering of the mind on an important idea about Life – rather than Art."[32]

Sloan wrote that in 1906. In the years preceding and following that date, both his ideas and his art went through a process of substantial change and adjustment. His early career, like that of many of his colleagues, was journalistic, and he first gained wide recognition for his superb drawings in the decorative poster style (Plate 18). He produced a large number of elegant, sometimes aristocratic magazine covers and Sunday feature illustrations, as well as full-page word and picture puzzles in an art nouveau manner (Plate 19). Within a few years, under the particular influence of Henri, Sloan had become a practitioner of the new realism. The September 7, 1901, edition of the New York *Times* announced, in its "Philadelphia Art Notes" column, that Sloan was "at work upon a series of studies of city scenes which will appear in the Fall exhibitions. Mr. Sloan is a believer in the capabilities of the modern American city for artistic work."[33]

After Sloan moved to New York in 1904, his city scenes multiplied, eventually making up an encyclopedic record of the new century's urban experience. Sloan never worked quickly (the more facile Henri said that "Sloan" was the past participle of "slow"), but he worked steadily, painting and drawing an extraordinary range of city events and personalities. A hairdresser in her shop window; children playing in Washington Park; a peculiar dust storm on Fifth Avenue; prostitutes walking on 30th Street; an election night crowd in Herald Square (Plate 20); a

PLATE 18. John Sloan, *Night on the Boardwalk,* from the July 8, 1894, Philadelphia *Inquirer.*
(By permission of the Delaware Art Museum, John Sloan Collection.)

PLATE 19. John Sloan, "Snake Charmer Puzzle," from the May 5, 1901, Philadelphia *Press*. The reader is invited to find the man playing the flute for the dancer. (By permission of the Delaware Art Museum, John Sloan Collection.)

Chinese restaurant; families sleeping through a hot summer night on tenement roofs; a well-dressed couple buying flowers from a vendor; young women getting ready for bed or drying their hair; the exteriors of the Haymarket and Carmine theaters; McSorley's Ale House: All of these people and places are documented in Sloan's prewar work. In

PLATE 20. John Sloan, *Election Night in Herald Square*, 1907. (By permission of the Memorial Art Gallery of the

1905–1906, Sloan produced a series of ten etchings of New York City's high and low life, and he offered them to dealers as a set (Plate 21 reproduces one). Both in concept and in execution, what Sloan had created was unique for American art. But he sold just two sets, and he had four etchings from a third set returned to him from an exhibition as too vulgar. It was just one of Sloan's many rejections by exhibitions and their judges.

Juried exhibitions were the principal instrument through which academic taste promoted its own interests and inhibited alternative points of view. As one historian puts it: "Annual exhibitions by this august institution [the Academy] only rarely featured paintings or sculptures that violated the rules of good taste that the juries . . . knew by heart (and by purse)."[34] Inevitably, in a pattern that goes back through the American and European nineteenth century, a differently conceived exhibition became as well the principal means of dissent. Sloan's diary entries for March and April 1907 include a series of laconic notes, understated out of all proportion to their eventual importance:

> March 18. Some talk after dinner [with Henri and Luks] of an exhibition of certain men's work. The time seems to be quite ripe for such a show. April 4. After dinner I went to a meeting at Henri's to talk over a possible exhibition of the "crowd's" work next year. Henri, Luks, Davies, Glackens, Sloan and Lawson were present.[35]

On February 1, 1908, after months of discussion and planning, the Eight opened their landmark exhibition at the Macbeth Gallery in New York. Newspaper columns and Sloan's diary both attest to the interest the event stirred up. Perhaps most important, the crowds were good. "The thing is a splendid success," Sloan decided a week after the opening. "Three hundred people were coming in every hour, about eighty-five constantly in two small galleries." Sloan complained about some of the press notices – "The Tribune . . . advised us to go and take an academic course, then come out and paint pictures" – but in fact the show attracted a good deal of favorable comment. According to Sloan, Arthur Davies regarded the exhibit as "an epoch," and Davies wasn't far wrong.[36] No single event ended the Academy's hegemony over visual taste, but the exhibition of the Eight, whether taken as cause or as symbol, marked the turning point.

If Sloan's own testimony is reliable, the years around the Macbeth show were as significant for his politics as for his art. It was in 1908, partly under the tutelage of his much more politically active wife, Dolly (and perhaps in part to please her), that Sloan began to move toward

socialism. The journey took only a few months, which is sudden and rather remarkable, since Sloan was in his mid-thirties and had evinced practically no political interest at all until this time. Sloan commenced his diary in 1906; in the first couple of years, his tone is uniformly apolitical. His descriptions of the slums, for example, verge dangerously close to the picturesque, and he has virtually nothing to say about local or national politics. Even the few political events he records are typically detached from their ideological significance. For example, in August of 1906, William Jennings Bryan delivered a speech in Madison Square. Sloan attended, not to hear Bryan but to take a look at the crowds. Of Bryan himself, Sloan says only and ironically: "He seems to be the Democratic nominee for President in 1907 or is it 1908? I dunno."[37] The "I dunno" may be a pose, but whether Sloan actually knew or not, he certainly didn't care.

When the local elections of 1907 occurred, Sloan included a long entry in his diary, but it has nothing to do with the contest itself or its outcome (no one is even mentioned by name). Rather, Sloan walked among the crowds, noting and enjoying their noise and disorder: "saw the noisy trumpet blowers, confetti throwers. . . . A good humorous crowd, so dense in places that it was impossible to control one's movement. A big election bonfire on Seventh Avenue with a policeman trying to keep its creators from adding fuel. They would creep through the dense crowd, and when he was busy, over the heads a barrel or box would sail into the flames."[38] A week later Sloan recalled the scene, but only because he had decided to turn a part of it into a painting (see Plate 20, *Election Night in Herald Square*).

Within a year, Sloan's attitudes changed. He greeted the election of Taft with a bitter denunciation of Republican "rottenness": "The cancerous growth is to have four more years." Sloan's shift was not immediately leftward. It was in fact in no particular direction save that of an implicit pragmatism: "I'm not a Democrat, I am of no party. I'm for change – for the operating knife when a party rots in power."[39] Nevertheless, from about this point on, politically engaged comments multiply across Sloan's pages; by 1909, he was identifying himself with socialism. "Read the platform of the Socialist Party," he wrote on May 21, "on which Debs ran last fall. Can't understand why the workers of the country were so disinterested or intimidated as not to vote en masse for these principles."[40] By June, Sloan had become assured of his own conversion and was busy trying to proselytize others. He tried to talk a workman who came to the apartment into socialism but failed, because the man was "of the contented sort." There may be a subterranean irony in the fact that this unnamed worker had come to deliver the canvases of the Eight after their New-ark exhibition.[41]

In 1910, and again a few years later, Sloan ran unsuccessfully for the New York Assembly on the Socialist ticket. Though he lost by a wide margin in 1910, the Socialists did well both in New York and nation-ally; Sloan's election night commentary was exuberant. "The Socialist vote in New York City is nearly doubled in the last two years! Returns from S.P. in the rest of the country are of course slow [but] Victor Berger of Milwaukee is the *first Socialist* to go to *Congress*. (In ten years there will be fifty Socialists in Congress.) . . . met [Rollin] Kirby on the street and went with him to his studio. He is foetid with conserva-tism. Says he don't see why I – how any artist – could be interested in Socialism. I told him that no man could do good work and *not* be."[42] All of this from the painter who just three years earlier had seen noth-ing in an election night rally except an opportunity for a crowd scene.

Sloan's changing politics brought changes in his art as well. His city subjects, for example, began to assume an altered significance for him. Where the tenements had once seemed to him merely visual objects, he now worried about the economic exploitation they proved. Yet Sloan was always more opinionated than systematic in his thinking, and more humanitarian than rigorous in his socialism. His sympathy for New York's poor mingled frequently with outrage after 1908, but his confi-dence in the socialist alternative was never robust. He continued to insist that he was "rather more interested in the human beings them-selves than in . . . schemes for betterment," and he even professed to worry that the people would be less "interesting when they are all comfortable and happy."[43]

Sloan was ambivalent about the relation between ideology and imagi-nation, and the distance between his politics and his own art tended to vary. Years later, in 1939, he tried to recapture summarily something of his thinking in the early years of the century. "There is . . . much talk today about socially-conscious painting. My old work was uncon-sciously very much so, especially before I became a Socialist. After that I felt that such a thing should not be put into painting and I reserved it for my etching."[44] This seems an odd distinction until one recalls that the egalitarian and progressive Sloan maintained an old-fashioned alle-giance to the notion that artistic forms are arrayed in a hierarchy; ideas appropriate to the pen and ink of drawings and mass reproduction might be forbidden to the medium of oil painting. Thus, the patient, documentary realism of Sloan's painting *Woman's Work* coincides al-most to the hour with sharply pointed editorial drawings for the social-ist *Call* and *The Coming Nation*.

THE MASSES

Whatever the merits of Sloan's logic, he did produce a huge number of political cartoons, some of which have to be counted among his best work.[45] In particular, the sixty or so drawings he contributed to *The Masses* over his four years of association with the magazine are undeniably some of the most impressive illustrations ever produced in America. In Henry May's reverent but accurate estimate, the drawings that Sloan published in *The Masses* spoke in "the language of Daumier."[46] Sloan's work was by turns angry and funny, blunt and sly. No two or three examples will be typical, but they will have to suffice. His image of the National Association of Manufacturers as a nude mountain of flesh is a stereotype, but revivified and embellished with witty details: the tattoo, with the American flag serving as a pirate's banner, and the ludicrously misplaced winged sandals (Plate 22). "Spreading the Joys of Civilization" is a broadly satiric indictment of imperialism (Plate 23), and "Before Her Makers and Her Judge" (Plate 24) tells something of the truth about prostitution.

Perhaps the most famous of Sloan's drawings for *The Masses* was also his angriest, "The Ludlow Massacre" (Plate 25), in bloody red. Sloan's response to the murder of Colorado's miners' wives and children by Rockefeller thugs is simple in its violence and yet oblique in its point of view. The focus is not exclusively on the victims. Instead, Sloan concentrates the energy of the composition on the retributive vengeance of the workers. The drawing's explosive sentimentality is thus apocalyptic in its theme. Mourning is absorbed into revolution.

Art at the service of revolution: This is what *The Masses* was up to, at least some of the time. Arturo Giovanitti, of the Industrial Workers of the World, put the proposition with a vigorous mixing of metaphors. *The Masses,* he wrote, "is the recording secretary of the Revolution. . . . It is NOT meant as a foray of unruly truant children trying to sneak into the rich orchards of literature and art. It is an earnest and living thing, a battle call, a shout of defiance, a blazing torch running madly through the night to set afire the powder magazines of the world."[47] The tone of this is revealing in its accusatory defensiveness, of course. From the vantage point of Giovanitti's high Wobbly seriousness, the behavior of some of *The Masses'* staff and contributors apparently seemed insufficiently single-minded – on the order of childish truancy.

And so it was. *The Masses* published hundreds of straightforward socialist essays, interviews, and biographical sketches. But the magazine also published much that was more ill-assorted, a great many articles,

If that keeps on itching back here, I'll have to scratch.

PLATE 22. John Sloan, "National Association of Manufacturers," from the October 1913 issue of *The Masses*. (Courtesy of the Tamiment Library, New York University.)

poems, stories, and cartoons that were only miscellaneously subversive. And much of the material was downright apolitical, socially irrelevant, or just fun. The statement of editorial purpose first printed in the February 1913 issue declared that this was "A REVOLUTIONARY AND NOT A REFORM MAGAZINE," but it immediately went on to add that it was

PLATE 23. John Sloan, "Spreading the Joys of Civilization," from the January 1914 issue of *The Masses*. (Courtesy of the Tamiment Library, New York University.)

A MAGAZINE WITH A SENSE OF HUMOR AND NO RE-
SPECT FOR THE RESPECTABLE: FRANK, ARROGANT,
IMPERTINENT, SEARCHING FOR THE TRUE CAUSES: A
MAGAZINE DIRECTED AGAINST RIGIDITY AND
DOGMA WHEREVER IT IS FOUND: PRINTING WHAT IS
TOO NAKED OR TRUE FOR A MONEY-MAKING PRESS:
A MAGAZINE WHOSE FINAL POLICY IS TO DO AS IT
PLEASES AND CONCILIATE NOBODY, NOT EVEN ITS
READERS.

This discloses a good deal more *spretzatura* than socialist orthodoxy and it hints (reliably) at the magazine's typically American willingness to go "wherever" its dissenting instincts led.

PLATE 24. John Sloan, "Before Her Makers and Her Judge," from the August 1913 issue of *The Masses*. (Courtesy of the Tamiment Library, New York University.)

Max Eastman drafted this paragraph, basing it on a suggestion of John Reed. This much in the statement proved unexceptionally true: *The Masses* never joined "the money-making press." Subscriptions, newsstand sales, and advertisements from companies such as the Commonwealth Co-Operative Association of Reading, Pennsylvania (makers of the Karl Marx five-cent cigar), could not keep the magazine solvent. Eastman's tireless and effective fundraising covered most of the deficits, but this created an irony of its own. Years later, he recalled soliciting an initial donation of two thousand dollars from Mrs. O. H. P. Belmont, divorced wife of W. K. Vanderbilt, which was then matched by one thousand dollars from Mrs. Belmont's dinner guest, the novelist John Fox, Jr.

> Thus our super-revolutionary magazine owed its send-off to a leader of New York's 400 – to the fortune of old Public-be-Damned Vanderbilt, in fact – and to a southern gentleman with as much interest in proletarian revolution as I had in polo ponies.[48]

If *The Masses* was not consistently "REVOLUTIONARY," it was relentless and often brave in its advocacy of "TRUE CAUSES" (or at least unpopular ones). On four or five questions in particular the magazine was a strong voice for justice and humanity. Feminism, for ex-

PLATE 25. John Sloan, "The Ludlow Massacre," the cover of the June 1914 issue of *The Masses*. (Courtesy of the Tamiment Library, New York University.)

ample, was the subject of many essays, and if the tone was sometimes
flippant, such subjects as the relationship of prostitution to capitalism
and the urgent need for brith control received repeated and unflinching
analysis.

The control of news by the pro-business Associated Press led to several famous Art Young cartoons and a series of law suits. The management of information, as *The Masses* understood, would prove decisive in
the struggle for the future. Floyd Dell wrote that "if the Associated Press
proves powerful enough – as it may, for it is the biggest political force we
have – to silence [its critics], we may as well forget all about the New
Haven Railroad, and the Telephone Trust, and the Standard Oil Trust,
and the Steel Trust, and the Money Trust, and every other problem of
combination that confronts us, for they are little or nothing by comparison with a sovereign control of true knowledge."[49]

Eastman's editorial policy promised that *The Masses* would conciliate
nobody, not even its own readers. As if to prove the honesty of that
boast, the magazine undertook a long and savage campaign against
organized religion and the churches. The entire December 1913 issue
was given over (as a caustic Christmas offering) to an attack on the
Christian churches. The graphics included an Art Young poster announcing that "Jesus Christ, the Workingman of Nazareth," would
speak on "The Right of Labor" at Brotherhood Hall. "He stirreth up
the people," reads Young's caption, thus distinguishing, in the manner
of so many radicals and socialists, between Christ and the corrupt
Christianity that used his name. Another cartoon, "Their Last Supper,"
by Maurice Becker, pictures a roomful of puffy-faced clerics munching
through twenty-dollar-a-plate dinners at the Episcopal Convention. A
life-size image of the crucified Christ looms censoriously over the proceedings. Among the essays in the issue is an obviously satirical series
of news dispatches datelined Jerusalem, "a.u.c. 783," with this as the
first of several banner headlines:

RIOTS OF UNEMPLOYED IN JUDEA CONTINUE
  JESUS OF NAZARETH LEADS HOBO
  ARMY ON JERUSALEM.

Other major issues, too, were frequently found in *The Masses'* table
of contents: the depredations of the criminal justice system, bigotry
against blacks, America's imperialism and its fondness for repressive
foreign regimes. Above all, *The Masses* stood against militarism and
war. Month after month, as Europe and then America marched resolutely toward conflagration, the magazine vainly cried halt. In the
event, however, the war proved to be the rock on which *The Masses*
itself and many of its causes foundered.

A year before the end, in 1916, John Sloan had resigned from the
editorial board in a dispute with Eastman and Young over artistic control. Sloan and some of the other artists wanted freedom from doctrinal
direction. They were rather handily defeated. "To me, " Young had
shouted, "this magazine exists for socialism . . . anybody who doesn't
believe in a socialist policy, so far as I go, can get out!"[50]

Young's hectoring certitude was actually hedged around by a double
irony. First, despite its putative commitment to Debsian socialism, *The
Masses* represented at bottom another version of nineteenth-century
American radicalism: the individual speaking on behalf of the individual
against the power and authority of the state. The radicalism of *The
Masses,* in Irving Howe's acute reconstruction of it,

> signified a stance – one could not quite speak of it as a politics – of
> individual defiance and rectitude, little concerned because little
> involved with the complexities of society. The radicalism of nine-
> teenth-century New England had been a radicalism of individual
> declaration far more than of collective action; and while Eastman
> and his friends were indeed connected with a movement, the So-
> cialist Party of Debs, in essential spirit they were intellectual free-
> booters, more concerned with speaking out than speaking to.
> They swore by Marx, but behind them could still be heard the
> voices of Thoreau and Wendell Phillips.[51]

A further qualification might be useful. If the makers of *The Masses* had
trouble taking their socialism straight (and with straight faces), they
were typical of American socialists. As I have had several occasions to
suggest in earlier chapters, socialism was transformed into something
more and less than its Marxian prototype when it migrated from Europe; it was translated into something recognizably American. In any
case, whether it was because of the idiosyncrasies of the magazine's staff
or because of the peculiar shape and flavor of American socialism, Art
Young's claims for the "socialist policy" of *The Masses* were feebly
supported by the facts. As with so many other would-be revolutionaries among their contemporaries, the women and men of *The Masses*
professed a romanticized politics of the future that actually derived its
substance and its form from the past.

Young's statement is ironic in a second way, which can be illumi-
nated by a résumé of Marx's theory of alienation. As Adam Schaff
explicates it, the concept of alienation refers to "the estrangement of
products of human activity, as a result of which these products come
to dominate their makers."[52] Schaff has in mind principally the material products of technology, and that narrow construction would
have a fruitful analytic applicability to our period. These were the

years in which some observers felt, as Henry Adams did, that mankind was finding itself driven by the machines it thought to drive.
We have traced the debate over machinery periodically through these
pages.

The Marxian concept of alienation, however, has a broader signification as well. Lee Benson has called it "a credible upper-range theory of
human behavior"; what he means by the term "upper-range" is that the
concept of alienation "comprehends, and can be specified so as to apply
effectively to, a very wide range of phenomena in all societies."[53] It can
certainly be applied effectively to the ultimate ironic fate of *The Masses*
in American cultural history. Years after it closed down, Max Eastman
tried to assess the magazine's influence:

> The long-time result of our pictorial revolt, it seems to me, was
> to introduce into commercial journalism some of the subtler val-
> ues of creative art. This change, at least, has taken place, and *The
> Masses* led the way. . . . The pictorial revolution for which *The
> Masses* artists worked without pay turned out to be one of the
> most profitable innovations in the history of journalism. At least
> that is my view, and I take no credit for this innovation except as
> a willing pupil. The central force in putting it through was John
> Sloan.[54]

Sloan himself said much the same thing: "*The Masses* set a pace and had
an influence on all periodicals after that."[55] In a word, *The Masses*
achieved a twentieth-century "look." Neither Eastman nor Sloan seems
to hear the confession he is making. What they are describing is a
pattern that would become increasingly familiar during the American
twentieth century. The radical protest evaporates, leaving behind a visual form that is turned into a profit by the established commercial
system. Social protest–magazine art, peace symbols, love beads, blue
jeans–becomes pop culture and kitsch couture. *The Masses* touched the
future after all, but only through the bouncy artwork of *The New
Yorker*.

ALFRED STIEGLITZ AND THE AVANT-GARDE

The significance of the Armory Show, according to John McCoubrey,
had actually more to do with "its impact upon public taste than [with]
its influence upon professional practice."[56] Harold Rosenberg made the
same point more categorically, declaring that the show was indeed a
"Great Event," but not in American art. Rather, it advanced American

art education and appreciation: It caused "the coming into being of the Vanguard Audience."[57] The distinction McCoubrey and Rosenberg propose is typically neglected, and the Armory Show has been accepted precisely as an event – the major event – in American art history. A number of influential textbooks have fixed and codified the show as the turning point in the entire development of American painting. Barbara Rose, for example, called her sumptuously illustrated folio volume *American Painting: The Twentieth Century* (1970), but the first chapter is entitled "The Armory Show and Its Aftermath." Her point is that whatever preceded the Armory Show can be designated as nineteenth-century work.

The show itself, officially the Independent Exhibition of the American Association of Painters and Sculptors, opened on February 17, 1913, in the cavernous 69th Regiment Armory in New York. Two-thirds of the 1,200 works of art were American, but these were not the reason for the show's notorious success. The American work served – unintendedly – as "pre-modernist" foils to the astonishing art of Europe. Gaugin, van Gogh, Cézanne, Redon, Kandinsky, Vlaminck were all represented, as were Picasso, Braque, and Picabia. What attracted most attention – curiosity, admiration, ridicule – was a group of paintings by Matisse and, of course, Duchamps's *Nude Descending a Staircase*. (The *Nude* may be the only painting in art history known primarily for the exhibition in which it appeared.)

Quite a few of the early notices were favorable, or at least polite, but the abuse the show provoked was more colorful and has lingered longer. Royal Cortissoz denounces the "flatly impossible pictures and statues" in the show as "impudence," a "dreary business."[58] The New York *Times* ran a full-page interview with Kenyon Cox, who the paper confided was "recognized both here and abroad as being in the lonely forerank of American art." Cox wearily allowed that the show raised only one question: "Are these men the victims of auto suggestion or are they charlatans fooling the public?" Cox answered his own question by declaring that the cubists and futurists "simply abolish the art of painting." Matisse's work he described as "the drawings of a nasty boy."[59] John Sloan's rebuke was much more good-natured, taking the form of a cartoon in *The Masses* depicting the adventures of a "cubic man" (Plate 26).

Theodore Roosevelt also attended the show. He came on March 4, perhaps to prove as publicly as possible how little he was interested in the inauguration of Woodrow Wilson that day. He coined the phrase "the lunatic fringe" to describe the painters whose work he saw, dismissed them as "extremists," likened them to P. T. Barnum in their

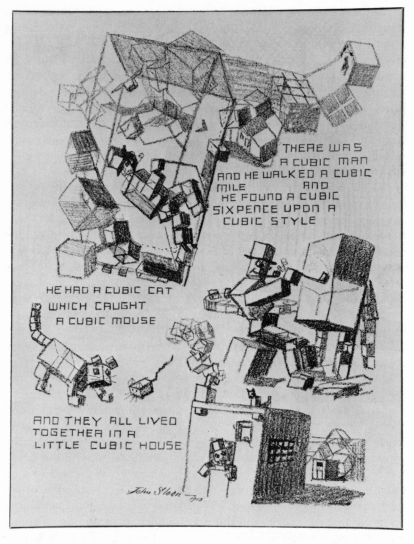

THERE WAS
A CUBIC MAN
AND HE WALKED A CUBIC
MILE   AND
HE FOUND A CUBIC
SIXPENCE UPON A
CUBIC STYLE

HE HAD A CUBIC CAT
WHICH CAUGHT
A CUBIC MOUSE

AND THEY ALL LIVED
TOGETHER IN A
LITTLE CUBIC HOUSE

A slight attack of third dementia brought on by excessive study of the much-talked of cubist pictures in the international exhibition at New York.

PLATE 26. John Sloan, "The Cubic Man," from the April 1913 issue of *The Masses.* (Courtesy of the Tamiment Library, New York University.)

skill at parting fools from their money, and compared their paintings invidiously with a Navajo rug in his bathroom. Withal, he also confessed that he felt the urgency and energy of the new art.[60]

If the art of Paris seemed to break as suddenly over the American public as an unpredicted tidal wave, that was because most Americans had not been frequenting Alfred Stieglitz's Little Galleries. From as early as 1908, Stieglitz had been mounting small exhibitions at "291" whose cumulative foresight would be difficult to overestimate. In April 1908, Stieglitz organized the first Matisse show outside France. ("Here was the work of a new man, with new ideas," proclaimed *Camera Work* of Matisse, "a very anarchist, it seemed, in art."[61]) The first U.S. exhibition of Toulouse-Lautrec, a group of thirty lithographs, was presented December 1909–January 1910. Cézanne's watercolors were shown in March 1911; and in March and April of that same year, eighty-three drawings and watercolors of Picasso were exhibited. An extraordinary list. Stieglitz also planned to show Gaugin and van Gogh in 1912, but those exhibitions did not take place.

Stieglitz was consulted by the organizers of the Armory Show, but he played little direct part in it. He nonetheless felt within his rights to appropriate it symbolically, to see it as vindicating five years of his own activities. He wrote to a friend that "the Big International Exhibition . . . was really the outcome of the work going on at '291' for many years."[62] That seems just. William Innes Homer has written a meticulously documented book to prove Stieglitz's claim; indeed, to prove the larger contention that from "1908 to 1913 . . . Stieglitz and his colleagues were virtually alone in the production and encouragement of advant-garde artistic currents in America."[63] If either Stieglitz or Homer over-reaches, it is only by a little. Recent scholarship has been recovering and reassessing more of the American modernist background, but Stieglitz's particular place has been left almost untouched. Abraham Davidson, for example, in his survey *Early American Modernist Painting: 1910–1935,* ranges far beyond "291" but acknowledges that the prewar American avant-garde was nurtured principally by Stieglitz. Davidson offers 1910 as a usable date to mark the beginnings of American modernist painting:

> That was the year of Arthur G. Dove's first nonobjective paintings, of Max Weber's nudes based on Picasso's Iberian figures, and of Morgan Russell's first still lifes done in the manner of Cézanne's. It was the year before Marsden Hartley's first landscapes in an Analytical Cubist style; two years after Patrick Henry Bruce's luminous still lifes and landscapes based on the paintings of Matisse, with whom he had studied in 1908; and three years

after Alfred H. Maurer's first broadly brushed, brightly colored landscapes.[64]

Notice how many of the people and movements enumerated here were linked in one way or another with "291." Hartley, Maurer, and Dove, for instance, were all included in Stieglitz's "Younger American Painters" show in 1910.

What Sloan and the realists sought in new subject matter the modernists, both those associated with "291" and others, sought in form. Their manifest differences should not obscure a fundamental commonality: They had all undertaken to find alternatives to the visual status quo. Sloan and his colleagues were not stylistically radical; nonetheless, their ideas about art and about "the teaching and exhibition of art were truly progressive and helped to foster the emergence of the avant-garde in America."[65] Similarly, Stieglitz's rhetoric was often cast in a vocabulary of dissent that was identical to that of Henri and Sloan: "I hate tradition for tradition's sake; – I hate the half-alive; I hate anything that isn't real. . . . as I grow older a hatred . . . against customs, traditions, superstitions, etc., is growing fast and strong."[66]

All these people, whether realist or modernist, wanted to "make it new," though they adopted widely differing strategies to do so. In addition, and affecting some members of all the artistic groups, there was a desire to bring painting into the twentieth century by making it "scientific." Hardesty Maratta, for example, devised a system of colors, a mathematically calculated palette that John Sloan, among others, took up around 1909. Canadian Jay Hambidge lectured on "dynamic symmetry," first in a 10th Street bar and then, after the war, at Harvard and Yale. In 1907, Denman Ross published *A Theory of Pure Design,* a zany but important prophetic book filled with dots and lines and assorted abstract shapes, all glossed with fervidly dogmatic commentary on the degree to which each line or shape succeeds in expressing harmony, balance, and rhythm. Any page to which the book falls open offers an illustration:

 In this case we have a series of straight lines with a constant and equal change of direction to the right, combined with a regular diminution of measures in the length of the lines, this in the terms of an arithmetical progression. The movement is in the direction of concentration and it is distinctly marked in its measures.

The movement is therefore rhythmical.[67]

Or this:

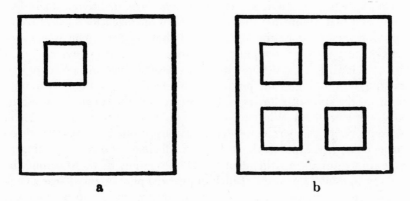

a   b

Arrangement "a" is less orderly than arrangement "b," so I have acted wisely in adding the outer outlines.[68]

Ross sounds impossibly mechanical in excerpts like these, but his commitment to a scientific method and to the primacy of design over representation in visual art made him a notable avant-garde theoretician in the years before the war. He was, in fact, in Barbara Rose's opinion, the "most advanced aesthetician" of his time, influencing Roger Fry among others.[69]

Science – more precisely, technology – was at the center of another cultural debate that stretched across the early years of the twentieth century, one in which Stieglitz was also a major figure. For three years, from its opening until 1908, "291" was devoted to exhibitions of photography; the Little Galleries were originally established to provide a headquarters for the members of the Photo-Secession. The self-appointed task of these women and men was to defend photography as an art, to chart an aesthetics that could incorporate photography as securely as painting.

When Stieglitz returned to the United States from Europe in 1890, he found virtually no one who took the artistic potential of photography seriously. Countless photographs were being taken, but they fell under just two headings: They were either the documentary devices used by ethnographers and other social scientists to record their subjects or they were the subartistic memorabilia of amateurs. Stieglitz, working indefatigably as photographer, impresario, and editor, labored successfully to change that.

The aesthetic course he and his associates traced across the prewar years recapitulates in yet another form the dialectic that has concerned us through these pages. The artistic theory that Stieglitz brought from Europe, and that dominated the early years of his magazine *Camera Work*, was one version or another of "pictorial photography." This was a conception that vividly exemplifies the process by means of which a new reality is initially accepted only insofar as it is redefined and absorbed into existing terminologies and points of view. Pictorial photography frankly imitated the style of painters highly esteemed in the late nineteenth century, among them Whistler, Corot, and members of the Barbizon School. Photographers aimed at atmospheric effects similar to those achieved by soft brushwork. In a word, adherents of pictorial photography argued for the artistic identity of photography by transforming the photograph into a painting. Much of pictorial photography "was a conscious emulation of pictures made by the brush, the pencil, or the etcher's burin. Because of the general criticism that photography was made by a machine, the pictorialists felt compelled to prove that their work was similar to those graphic arts done by the hand."[70] Historical and genre scenes, sentimental subjects of all kinds, soft focus and hazy atmosphere: The "new" artistic photography tended to look a lot like the "old" academic painting. Thus, a paradox, which Jonathan Green summarizes: "The art Stieglitz showed at '291' was dramatically different in style and intent from the work of the Photo-Secessionists. While the Photo-Secession prints look backward in time to 'the beauties of former art expressions,' the new art seemed unequivocally modern."[71]

By 1906, Joseph Keiley, one of Stieglitz's assistants on *Camera Work* and a founding member of Photo-Secession, could announce that "the real battle for the recognition of pictorial photography is over. The chief purpose for which the Photo-Secession was established has been accomplished – the serious recognition of photography as an additional medium of pictorial expression."[72] The battle was won, however, on terms that would eventually prove unacceptable. The pictorialists used physical and chemical manipulation to deny the integral properties of their own medium. Their attitude led to techniques that were "not unlike those industrial processes of the same period which sought to make cast-iron or machine carved wood appear hand-made."[73] The next step for artistic photography required insights analogous to those Frank Lloyd Wright was bringing to the nature of materials and the uses of machines. As late as 1910, both the prose and the photographs in *Camera Work* were marked by much fin-de-siècle sighing and moody elegance. Any number of the pictures Stieglitz so painstakingly reproduced in the magazine, both his own and those of other craftsmen, illustrate the outcome (Plates 27 and 28).

On the other hand, Stieglitz, though he produced a good many at-

PLATE 27. Gertrude Käsebier, "Portrait–Miss N.," a photograph of Evelyn Nesbit, appeared in the first issue of *Camera Work,* January 1903. (Copyright © 1973, courtesy of Aperture, Inc., as published in *Camera Work: A Critical Anthology,* Aperture, Millerton, 1973.)

PLATE 28. Alfred Stieglitz, "Katherine," appeared in the twelfth issue of *Camera Work,*
October 1905. (Copyright © 1973, courtesy of Aperture, Inc., as published in *Camera
Work: A Critical Anthology,* Aperture, Millerton, 1973.)

mospheric and pictorial photographs himself, was always also interested in the possibilities of "straight" photography. As early as 1901,
the astute critic Charles Caffin said of Stieglitz that he was "by conviction and instinct an exponent of the 'straight' photograph working
chiefly in the open air, with rapid exposures, leaving his models to pose

themselves, and relying for results upon means strictly photographic."[74] "The Steerage," taken in 1907 (Plate 29), which Stieglitz treasured as his favorite photograph, illustrates what Caffin calls his "strictly photographic" technique. Furthermore, if Stieglitz's much later reconstruction of the scene and of his response to it is to be accepted, the picture also illustrates his preoccupation with photographic form:

> A round straw hat, the funnel leaning left, the stairway leaning right, the white draw-bridge with its railings made of circular chains – white suspenders crossing the back of a man in the steerage below, round shapes of iron machinery, a mast cutting into the sky, making a triangular shape. I stood spellbound for a while, looking and looking. Could I photograph what I felt, looking and looking and still looking? I saw shapes related to each other. I saw a picture of shapes.[75]

Cézanne visits Ellis Island. Stieglitz would have us believe that he apprehended his highly charged human subject matter in purely formal terms. In fact, though the picture is wonderfully composed, it continues to move us after the better part of a century in large measure because of the tale it tells. Coincidentally taken in the midst of immigration's peak year, "The Steerage" leads us by way of its interesting shapes and angles into a world. It makes its demands through its evocation of what we take to have been reality.

"The Steerage" foretells photography's aesthetic path. After the epochal Albright exhibition of 1910, the proponents of "straight" photography moved decisively into command of the medium's aesthetic ideology. Fittingly, the final issue of *Camera Work* featured the ideas and pictures of the brilliant young photographer Paul Strand. Strand's subject was New York, not in the diaphonous mists of the pictorialists but in its unrelenting harshness and anonymous danger. Here were New York's people, starkly revealing the reality of the underside of modern urban life.[76] Strand's "Blind Woman" (Plate 30) is a powerful, unnerving image, antithetical in every conceivable technical and thematic way to Gertrude Käsebier's portrait of Miss N., published in *Camera Work's* first issue (Plate 27). This work of Strand's, wrote Stieglitz in homage, "is pure. It is direct. It does not rely upon tricks of process. . . . It is brutally direct. Devoid of *flim-flam.* . . . These photographs are the direct expression of today."[77]

Notice where we have arrived. In denying a contrived "artistry" as a means of securing photography's aesthetic place, Stieglitz invokes an American commitment to "the real" that closely resembles that of John Sloan. No flimflam. Photography itself, however, had already provided examples of "brutally direct" representations of modern life, devoid of

PLATE 29. Alfred Stieglitz, "The Steerage," 1907. (Photogravure from *Camera Work,* no. 36, 1911, Collection, The Museum of Modern Art, New York, Gift of Alfred Stieglitz.)

tricks. Strand learned to make photographs in an extracurricular course at the Ethical Culture School; his teacher was Lewis Hine. No one knows how many pictures Hine took in his thirty-five years of work; perhaps forty thousand. He did not in the beginning think of himself as an artist nor of his photographs as art objects.[78] Yet the phrases Strand

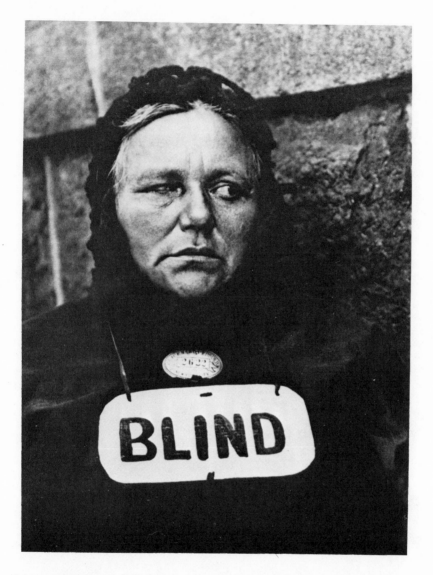

PLATE 30. Paul Strand, "Blind Woman," appeared in the last issue of *Camera Work,* no. 49/50, June 1917. (Copyright © 1973, courtesy of Aperture, Inc., as published in *Camera Work: A Critical Anthology,* Aperture, Millerton, 1973.)

PLATE 31. Lewis Hine, "Carolina Cotton Mill," 1908. (Gelatin-silver print on masonite, 10½ × 13½. Foundation of Photo League Collection. The Museum of Modern Art, New York. Purchase. Reprinted by permission.)

used to describe himself could be applied to Hine as well. The photographer, Strand wrote in 1917, must maintain "a real respect for the thing in front of him. . . . It is in the organization of this objectivity that the photographer's point of view toward life enters in."[79] Hine would have accepted Strand's elegantly formulated definition of the photographer's task as the organization of the objectivity before him, but he would have done so only on the condition that objectivity not be misunderstood as neutrality. Hine was committed to his subject matter, and its objectivity spoke social and ethical truths.

Hine's several great projects – Ellis Island (1905, 1926), the Pittsburgh Survey (1907–1910), the five thousand photographs of his child labor study (1909–1915) – contain some of the most moving and memorable images produced by anyone in the early twentieth century (Plate 31). It required a photographic aesthetic larger and more humane than the one that prevailed at the turn of the century to embrace Hine's stunning work. It was Stieglitz, whose *Camera Work* would have denied Hine's artistic claims in 1903 or 1904, who articulated the broader alternative in 1917. Here, then, is the somewhat ironic outcome of the aesthetic debate we have been tracing: The circle closes, as modernism becomes realism.

A concluding note: Before Hine in time, if inferior in talent, was Jacob Riis. *How the Other Half Lives* (1890) included forty or so of Riis's photographs, and the book's impact was partly the result of these striking documentary illustrations. Technology being at that date what it was, however, only some of the photographs were reproduced as halftones, and these are of generally poor quality. The other pictures are drawings based on Riis's camera work; some of them are signed "Kenyon Cox, 1889, after photograph."

Chapter 10

A glimpse into the twenty-first century: Emma Goldman

In the 1630s, when the English-speaking community had barely gained a foothold on the stony New England coast, Anne Hutchinson shook the foundations of the new colony by insisting on the superiority of her conscience to the rules of her governors. Her punishment was neither swift nor edifying, but it was sure and severe. She was harassed, interrogated, tried, and eventually condemned to exile.

Hutchinson's case was considered profoundly important at the time, and it has remained green in the national memory for centuries. With good reason. Hutchinson's trial and sentence signified far more than the suppression of a defiant female by a squinty-eyed, muscular orthodoxy. She represented a fundamental threat because she faced the community with the extremest logic of its own theology. That is to say, she took literally what her spiritual mentors preached: the supremacy of the Spirit, the autonomous rectitude of the regenerate self, the internalization of authority.[1] Taking the figures of Hutchinson and her eventual chief accuser, John Cotton, as symbolic, the opposed terms of the dialectic they embodied can be regarded as a major element in Puritanism's legacy to the American imagination.

Cotton had been Hutchinson's teacher before he became her judge. He had been the preeminent theorist of the unconditional covenant. But he had developed his radical views while preaching in Lincolnshire in old England as a vehicle for his dissent from prevailing theological and political authority.[2] The journey to New England had brought leadership, and leadership had brought different demands. The potentially subversive ideology Cotton had shaped between the hammer and anvil of Laud and the Stuart kings had to be reforged in the new commonwealth, had to be adjusted to the realities of governance. The revision and the trimming, however, were Cotton's, not Hutchinson's. It may be, as John Winthrop recorded in his journal, that Cotton pronounced sentence on Hutchinson "with great solemnity, and with much zeal and detestation of her errors"; one assumes that he also felt the sting of his own doubtful position.[3]

It is a famous scene. Hawthorne is only the foremost of the novelists and historians who have been drawn to it over the years. Those later Americans have been attracted not merely by the high drama of the episode but by its prophetic implications. In that Massachusetts court-room in March of 1638, the barely emergent culture of the New World acted out a paradigmatic conflict between the competing claims of individual and society, of antinomian self-sufficiency and civic conformity.

Two hundred and eighty years later the drama was reenacted. The outcome and significance were much the same. Emma Goldman was, like Anne Hutchinson, an immigrant in the New World. Like Hutchinson, she terrified the guardians of her society because she believed literally in the creed of the autonomous conscience. And, like Hutchinson, she was put on trial for her belief and then banished from her adopted home.

I do not mean to ignore the passage of three centuries, nor to elide the differences between the Lithuanian Jewish atheist and the English Christian, nor to merge the connivances of J. Edgar Hoover and Julius Mayer with those of Cotton and Winthrop. Nevertheless, the differences between the two episodes do not obscure what is at least a provocative analogous relationship; and I will argue that the resemblance goes much deeper. Hutchinson and Goldman were armed only with their ideas and their rebellion, but the powerful forces arrayed against them apparently judged these lone women to be evenly matched against the cadres of law and order. The atmosphere in both the seventeenth- and twentieth-century courts was charged with the suspicion that everything – the meaning of individual identity, societal cohesion, the future itself – was at stake. Both women were expelled as strategies of what can only be called self-defense.

Goldman was almost surely cheated out of her American citizenship illegally. The chicanery only demonstrates the government's obsessive need to eliminate the challenge offered it by this short, overweight, nearsighted, fifty-year-old immigrant woman. She had hounded the American status quo for three decades and had become perhaps the most widely recognized dissident figure of her time. "Red Emma": In an August 1897 New York *World* cartoon, her oversized, bespectacled eyes are fixed in a wild and menacing glare. Her mouth is a half-open snarl; her hair is cropped licentiously close. "Anarchist Emma Goldman," reads the caption, "who prefers Hell to Heaven" (Plate 32).

The simplification is crude but not altogether misleading. She cer-

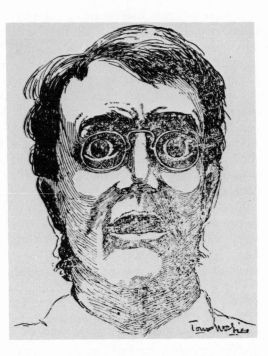

PLATE 32. "Emma Goldman," from the August 1897 issue of the New York *World*.

tainly wanted no part of the *World's* "Heaven," and she did her best to
undo most earthly arrangements as well. Repeatedly, passionately, she
said no: to property, to religion, to the state. In pamphlets, articles, and
books, she searched out and denounced just about every institution of
early twentieth-century American life. She attacked government, the
military, the church, marriage. She was, according to firsthand accounts, an exceptional orator, and she carried her message back and
forth across the country in literally thousands of speeches.

She had less a program than a vision, a dream of a world from which
coercion had disappeared. She held a profoundly romantic conviction of
the perfectibility of unfettered individuality and a corresponding belief
in the corruption of all restraint. She accepted and even insisted on the
furthest logical outcomes of this position. For Goldman, to give one
example, "crime," in anything like the conventional sense, simply did
not exist. In an essay on prisons, she sorts what are called criminals into
four categories. The first consists of political dissidents, such as John
Brown and Industrial Workers of the World strikers. A second group
acts out of mitigating passion. A third is insane. The last and largest
group is what Goldman calls "occasional" criminals, the thieves and

pickpockets and whores and drunks who fill America's jails but who are created by "our cruel social and economic arrangement."[4]

Bourgeois opinion holds prisons to be a sad but necessary discipline, a sordid instrument of order's last resort. Goldman's opinion is that prisons, and the broken laws they revenge, are themselves crimes. The prison does not represent the punishment of deviance from legitimate constraint but the reductive imposition of conformity.[5] Law itself, except that which proceeds from within, is the essential deviation, and this view leads Goldman to the declaration that "everything illegal necessitates integrity, self-reliance, and courage."[6]

If that sounds abstract, Goldman gave the assertion its most notorious specificity in her defense of political assassins. Even more obviously than the rest of her opinions, this one is rooted in her life. On July 23, 1892, Alexander Berkman, Goldman's collaborator, lover, and lifelong friend, attempted to murder Henry Clay Frick. The attempt failed, Frick quickly recovered, and Berkman spent the next fourteen years in prison. Whatever its theoretical sources, Goldman's defense of "propagandists of the deed" was thickly overlaid with her feelings about Berkman's *Attentat*. She considered herself Berkman's unindicted co-conspirator, and she therefore claimed to feel wrongly shielded from sharing his punishment.

It was Berkman more than anyone else (certainly more than Leon Czolgosz, for whom she felt only pity) whom Goldman objectified and justified in her speculations on the psychology of political violence. Such violence, Goldman argued, was the individual's ultimate means of protest against the greater violence of the state. She quoted with approval the writers and scientists who had studied the personality of the *Attentäter* and discovered it to be unusually sensitive, selfless, strongly moved by injustice. Goldman believed that such courageous men as Vaillant, Caserio, Angiolillo, and especially Berkman acted not only for themselves – least of all for themselves – but to precipitate the new society. In short, far from being the beast or lunatic of common perception, the assassin is the supreme humanitarian.[7] Years after Berkman's attempt on Frick, Goldman summarized "the lesson [she] had gained from Sasha's deed." From that time,

> I had ceased to regard political acts, as some other revolutionists did, from a merely utilitarian standpoint or from the view of their propagandistic value. The inner forces that compel an idealist to acts of violence, often involving the destruction of his own life, had come to mean much more to me. I felt certain now that behind every political deed of that nature was an impressionable, highly sensitized personality and a gentle spirit. Such beings can-

not go on living complacently in the sight of great human misery and wrong. Their reactions to the cruelty and injustice of the world must inevitably express themselves in some violent act, in supreme rending of their tortured soul.[8]

Thus did Goldman contribute her portion to the twentieth century's ideology of romantic violence. And thus she anticipated, among others, Georges Sorel's notion of class resurrection through violence, Frantz Fanon's devotion to violence as a means of purification and regeneration, even the pseudoexistential escapades of Norman Mailer. She also anticipated, of course, unintendedly but ironically, the cult of violence at the heart of Fascist and Nazi doctrine.[9]

The unspeakable political and social history of this century would seem to prove that what comes out of the barrel of a gun is bullets. But to say that is not to trivialize the fundamental question Goldman was wrestling with. She wanted to know: What is possible and legitimate for the individual when threatened by the multiple and organized violence of modern reality and the modern state? Far more sober observers than Goldman confirmed her diagnosis of that reality, even when they rejected her prescriptions. Some of them, like Wallace Stevens, studiously constructed worlds elsewhere: The imagination is "a violence within that protects us from a violence without." Goldman longed to build a world here.[10]

If the assassin was Goldman's noble rider, signaling and eventually provoking liberation through his deed, the antithetical figure is the uniformed enforcer, the policeman and particularly the soldier: the man charged with the single mission of repressing freedom by coercion and violence. Consequently, patriotism, defined by Goldman as the noxious mixture of militarism and nationalism, reveals itself as the most dangerous of modern attitudes. She adopted as her own Tolstoy's understanding of patriotism as "the principle that will justify the training of wholesale murderers."[11] She analyzed war, including the recent Spanish–American War, as a function of economic causes: "The lives, blood and money of the American people were used to protect the interests of American capitalists."[12] Not Hearst, but sugar, sent Roosevelt scampering up San Juan Hill.

Chauvinism grew in its virulence and scope after the "easy" war with Spain, but until the outbreak of World War I antimilitarism remained an alternative, and not only on the left. Despite the estimate of Judge H. H. Powers cited in the first chapter, Americans did not unanimously embrace either militarism or imperialism overnight.

The voluminous publications of the Anti-Imperialist League and the personal leadership of such men as William Dean Howells, Carl Schurz, and E. L. Godkin ensured that imperialism would continue to be debated.[13] When William James elaborated on his division of America into the parties of force and education, he did so as a dissent from imperialism:

> Speaking broadly, there are never more than two fundamental parties in a nation: the party of red blood, as it calls itself, and that of pale reflection; the party of animal instinct, jingoism, fun, excitement, bigness; and that of reason, forecast, order gained by growth, and spiritual methods – briefly put, the party of force and that of education.[14]

Though the leaders of these two parties are unnamed, James's intentions are evident. He did his best, in his last years, to lead the party of education himself. And the leader of the party of force and red blood is Theodore Roosevelt.

James had identified Roosevelt as a spokesman for "crude and barbaric patriotism" at least as early as 1895. His attack on Roosevelt's ominously popular speech exhorting Americans to lead "The Strenuous Life" (1899) was ferocious:

> Although in middle life . . . and in a situation of responsibility concrete enough, [Roosevelt] is still mentally in the Sturm und Drang period of early adolescence, treats human affairs, when he makes speeches about them, from the sole point of view of the organic excitement and difficulty they may bring, gushes over war as the ideal condition of human society, for the manly strenuousness which it involves, and treats peace as a condition of blubberlike and swollen ignobility, fit only for huckstering weaklings, dwelling in gray twilight and heedless of the higher life.[15]

Anti-imperialism produced a good deal of verse and fiction and polemic essays; parodies of Kipling's hugely popular poem "The White Man's Burden" became a standard exercise for antimilitarist belletrists. Surely the most famous literary document to come from the debate was Mark Twain's vitriolic attack on America's conduct in the Philippines, "To the Person Sitting in Darkness":

> There have been lies, yes, but they were told in a good cause. We have been treacherous, but that was only in order that real good might come out of apparent evil. True, we have crushed a deceived and confiding people; we have turned against the weak and friendless who trusted us; we have stamped out a just and intelligent and well-ordered republic; we have stabbed an ally in the back and slapped the face of a guest; we have bought a shadow

from an enemy that hadn't it to sell; we have robbed a trusting friend of his land and his liberty; we have invited our clean young men to shoulder a discredited musket and do bandits' work under a flag which bandits have been accustomed to fear, not to follow; we have debauched America's honor and blacked her face before the world; but each detail was for the best.[16]

Emma Goldman shared Mark Twain's opinion of America's foreign conduct, and she shared William James's estimate of Roosevelt, whom she despised as America's "future Napoleon" and the embodiment of "the very worst element of mob psychology."[17] At least in the earliest years of the century, then, Goldman's anarchist reaction to imperialism harmonized with the conclusions of a fair number of quite respectable people.

In the years after Roosevelt's election in 1904, however, anti-imperialism receded from the national agenda. Opposition to nationalism and militarism became increasingly unpopular, and then it remained for Goldman and other elements of the left to carry on the struggle. Some of the most powerful graphics in *The Masses,* for example, are cartoons by John Sloan, Henry Glintenkamp, and Robert Minor that pillory the emergence of the transatlantic military state. The second issue of *The Masses,* in February 1911, includes an essay by George R. Kirkpatrick called "The Boy Scout Movement." This is, I believe, the earliest American interpretation of the scouting movement as essentially militaristic: "an organized . . . subsidized effort for creating the kill-lust in boys, the love of arms, the desire for the military life, and the brainlessly automatic obedience of soldiers."[18]

In the first years of the twentieth century, Goldman's opposition to militarism and war aligned her intellectually and morally with a spectrum of Americans that was, at least initially, quite broad. That alliance gradually shrank and narrowed as the European war drew closer. By the time of America's entry into the war, Goldman continued to stand on the same ground, but she now stood there almost alone. Neither the laborers nor the intellectuals proved immune to the fever of war. Or, to change the metaphor as Randolph Bourne sardonically did: War proved to be the health of the state.[19] In her autobiography, Goldman enumerated some of the men who broke ranks with antiwar solidarity:

The reactionaries were not the only element responsible for the patriotic orgy. Sam Gompers handed over the American Federation of Labor to the war baiters. The liberal intelligentsia, with Walter Lippman, Louis F. Post, and George Creel in the lead, socialists like Charles Edward Russell, Arthur Bullard, English

Walling, Phelps Stokes, John Spargo, Simons, and Ghent, all shared in the glory.[20]

The principles Goldman applied to the police state and the war machine also shaped her understanding of private life. All relationships should consist in the free association of free individuals. Education, for example, will in the anarchist future be "of an entirely spontaneous nature."[21] The conventional schoolhouse is another symbol of repression, and one even more tragic and universal than the prison: more tragic because children are the victims, more universal because while only a relatively few go to jail, virtually everybody goes through the school system.

During the years we are interested in, it was Goldman's views on marriage and sexuality that comprised her most inflammatory cause. And her commitment to anarchist sexuality was not merely theoretical. She took a fairly long series of lovers and always (or almost always) insisted on her sexual equality and freedom as the basis of the partnership. Marriage repelled her as nothing more than systematic exploitation and legalized prostitution.

As we have already seen in earlier chapters, Goldman was by no means the only critic to redefine marriage in terms of prostitution; but she seems to have gone a step further. In Goldman's view, women in a capitalist society have just three choices, and all of them are prostitution. They may enter the labor market, which Goldman calls the system of "industrial prostitution"; they may marry, which entails a lifetime of underpaid prostitution; or they may walk the streets.[22]

Women, in other words, more than men, are the particular victims of what Goldman, in one of her more overwrought phrases, calls "the merciless Moloch of capitalism."[23] (Perhaps overwrought, but recall Ginsberg's use of the same figure half a century later.) And she defended her opposition to woman's suffrage as consistent with both her sensitivity to women's situation and her anarchism. Goldman was opposed to the vote for women principally because she was opposed to the vote. Democracy was merely a governmental snare and a delusion. "The poor, stupid, free American citizen! Free to starve, free to tramp the highways . . . he enjoys universal suffrage." (Goldman was echoing Anatole France's famous gibe, that the rich man and the poor man are equally free to sleep under the bridge.) In Goldman's view, the vote was simply not worth having; it was an opiate and a diversion. What "people of intellect perceived fifty years ago [is] that suffrage is an evil, that it has only helped to enslave people, that it has but closed their eyes."[24]

In addition, Goldman was suspicious about woman's suffrage because of her fears about the purposes to which it would be put. She worried that the deeper ideology of the suffrage movement was actually reactionary. According to Goldman, the typical suffragist insists that the vote "will make her a better Christian and homekeeper, a staunch citizen of the State. This suffrage is only a means of strengthening the omnipotence of the very Gods that woman has served from time immemorial."[25] Goldman had no interest in simply doubling the number of ordinary, law-abiding, middle-class American citizens.

Her demand was that women "cut loose from the weight of prejudices, traditions and customs."[26] Only then would freedom from "external tyrannies," such as that promised by suffrage, be matched by liberation from the more fearsome "internal tyrants . . . the ethical and social conventions" that suffragists as well as conservatives still share. What this will mean, in turn, is that each woman will insist on recognition of her sexuality and will refuse "the right to anyone over her body."[27] As one outcome of this view, Goldman became a tireless propagandist for birth control. She did important pioneering work, for which she was alternately applauded and jailed.

Like the rest of her ideas, Goldman's sexual opinions gained very little purchase on the American consciousness. In part the enemy was Comstock and Comstockery. In larger part, she ran afoul of the prurient puritanism that America seems unable (at least in its masculine half) to outgrow. She provoked winks and leers. She tells the story of the knock, late one night, at her hotel room door, which was followed by a hoarse, whispered invitation to sex. When Goldman shouted through the door that she would awaken the entire establishment, the voice whimpered in retreat: "Please, please! Don't make any scene. I'm a married man, with grown children. I thought you believed in free love."

Thus did Cincinnati understand Goldman's fervent call for sexual equality and fulfillment.

Anarchism in all its implications was Goldman's theme in her life and lectures and writing through the early twentieth century. One measure of her energy, if not of her effectiveness, is the frightened and frightening hostility she evoked. Young J. Edgar Hoover was reduced to incoherence: "Emma Goldman and Alexander Berkman are, beyond doubt, two of the most dangerous anarchists in this country and if permitted to return to the community will result in undue harm."[28] Years earlier, Roosevelt had denounced Goldman as a "pervert" and a "madwoman." To Roosevelt, anarchists like Goldman were mere criminals, though "more dangerous than any other."[29] Roosevelt's capacity for overstatement was, of course, immense. On the subject of Emma Goldman, however, he went no further than scores of his countrymen, from journalists to the clergy to the wage earners and the poor on whose behalf she presumed to dream and to suffer. It was not only official America, nor only entrenched privilege, that rejected what Goldman offered.

To return to the dialectical vocabulary of the first chapter, Goldman was as complete a symbol of the revolutionary future as any other person in these years; and she provoked a counterrevolutionary reply. She seemed to many Americans to represent the disruptive new tendencies against which old beliefs struggled. Since few people either saw or heard her firsthand, and fewer still read her articles and essays, Goldman actually became "Goldman," as perception took the shortcut of newspaper cartoons and of clichés: bombs, flag burning, free love. Be that as it may, in this simplified image of Emma Goldman, Americans came face to face with what they took to be a lifelike portrait of the economic, sexual, and political future. Goldman was a glimpse into a revolutionary new world, and most Americans drew back with a shudder.

We have already seen some of the details of Goldman's thinking. More generally, she claimed anarchism to be "the most revolutionary and uncompromising" of ideas; it is the universal and systematic assertion of "the New" against the multiform claims of "the Old."[30] All forms of government, whether autocratic or participatory, are grounded in violence and are therefore illegitimate as well as unnecessary.

This major premise of Goldman's requires comment. Under the heading of "government," she was either unable or unwilling to distinguish between the Czar's Russia and Roosevelt's America. She seems actually to have believed that only trivial details differentiated the politics of her new home from those of her old. This belief, in turn, was at once nourished and opposed by the ripening Americanism of the early twentieth century that expressed itself in the tripartite phenomenon we surveyed earlier: nativism, jingoism, conformity. To return to the analogic vocabulary of several earlier chapters, Goldman and the American majority assiduously cultivated each other's paranoia. For Roosevelt and Hoover, Goldman was the sinister and exotic Other, conspiring to topple the towers of legitimacy. For Goldman, Roosevelt and Hoover represented systemic repression, equally Other and equally conspiratorial.

If the response of Roosevelt and Hoover seems absurdly disproportionate in its fear and frenzy, so also does Goldman's estimate of Roosevelt and Hoover seem frankly unbalanced. Roosevelt was not Czar Nicholas, after all, and Hoover was not Rasputin (though he would probably have liked to have been). It is possible, and perhaps even plausible, to trace Goldman's ultimate political failure directly back to this fundamental analytic mistake. To put it summarily: The immigrant Emma Goldman brought with her from eastern Europe a philosophy that had been constructed, slowly and over decades, out of the stones of anti-Czarism. The structure was simply not suitable to the climate and landscape of America. James Joll formulates this hypothesis more generally and abstractly: "Anarchism is necessarily a creed of all or nothing, and consequently it has had less success in countries where there is still a hope of winning something out of the existing system."[31]

But all of this, I think, simplifies the situation and diminishes Goldman's significance. She did more than transport and transplant an alien organism that withered in American soil. At least three other events or developments help to explain her ideas and the shape and direction of her career, and they all connect her with specifically American figures and attitudes.

To begin with, if the preceding pages have accomplished nothing else, they have documented the astonishing turbulence and consequent anxieties of early twentieth-century America. The revelations of journalists and novelists and investigators and humanitarians of all ideological stripes proved incontrovertibly the gigantic cleavage that lay between the economic classes of American society; they demonstrated as well the enormous oppression of the poor and of workers. If "conditions" weren't as bad here as elsewhere, they were very bad, at least for "the other half." The brave new technological world we glanced at in the first chapter certainly made middle-class life easier; but before 1917 it did little for the lower classes except to speed up the work of those who labored in factories. If class contrasts didn't actually increase in these years, they became at least more vivid. And if America's poor were better off than the rest of the world's poor, that tenuous consolation paled before the facts: of infant mortality, of child labor and worker injury and industrial disease, of proliferating slums and official brutality. As we have had occasion to note, a good many less incendiary personalities than Emma Goldman expected revolution. So if her analysis was mistaken, it was by no means naïve. She was not alone in seeing "the system" as autocratic in spite of its electoral apparatus.

Second, Goldman was deeply affected by Haymarket. Chronology is important here. Goldman and her sister Helena sailed to America in December 1885. If she brought any ideological baggage with her at all, it was certainly not anarchism (a term she had not even heard). Rather, like millions of others, she carried with her an idealized image of the United States as the land of hope and freedom:

The last day of our journey comes vividly to my mind. Everybody was on deck. Helena and I stood pressed to each other, enraptured by the sight of the harbour and the Statue of Liberty suddenly emerging from the mist. Ah, there she was, the symbol of hope, of freedom, of opportunity! She held her torch high to light the way to the free country, the asylum for the oppressed of all lands. We, too, Helena and I, would find a place in the generous heart of America. Our spirits were high, our eyes filled with tears.[32]

Goldman's personal disillusion commenced promptly. She was manhandled by federal officials, insulted by ordinary citizens, and soon trapped in the bleak poverty of garment work in a Rochester factory. Less than two years later, when the frustration and bitterness of her own eighteen-year-old life were becoming entrenched, the Haymarket bomb exploded, and the shock waves permanently altered her conception of American life. Seven policemen died, and their murderers have never been convincingly identified. But eight anarchists were convicted; and, on November 11, 1887, four of them were hanged. (A fifth was also sentenced to die but committed suicide before the execution.) The prosecution had admitted, indeed had insisted, that anarchism was on trial, that Albert Parsons, August Spies, and the rest were only incidental.

Haymarket had, I think, a double significance. On the one hand, it really did seem to confirm the most sinister interpretation of American political power. Streets and scaffolds covered with bodies and blood. Five men sentenced to death essentially for their ideas. The state violence and the arbitrary extermination of dissenters: These were the hallmarks of life in an autocracy. This is what people who had known pogroms had learned to expect from government.

Haymarket was significant, then, because it occurred. But its other and equally profound significance was that it never occurred again. State oppression, police brutality, organized exploitation of all sorts continued and even arguably worsened. These were not the daydreams of fringe extremists. But neither were they ever distilled again into the same judicial nightmare, never was legal murder to be enacted again in quite the same solemn and almost ceremonial terms.

Thus the centrality of Haymarket to the radical imagination becomes increasingly ironic over time. Goldman is our example, and this paragraph on the twenty-fifth anniversary of "Black Friday" is typical:

November 11, 1887–November 11, 1912! Twenty-five years, an infinitesimal fraction of time in the upward march of the race, but an eternity for him who dies many deaths in the course of his life.

The twenty-fifth anniversary of the Chicago martyrdom intensified my feeling for the men I had never personally known, but
who by their death had become the most decisive influence in my
existence. The spirit of Parsons, Spies, Lingg, and their co-
workers seemed to hover over me and give deeper meaning to the
events that had inspired my spiritual birth and growth.[33]

The irony in such a passage lies in the humanly fortunate but ideologically disappointing fact that, twenty-five years after the execution of the
Haymarket martyrs, they remained the only martyrs to American
anarchism's cause. When does memory become merely memory?
    Yet Goldman was by no means alone in regarding Haymarket as an
enduring, relevant symbol; and if other radicals were most decisively
affected, many members of America's intellectual rank and file were
also moved to varying extents. We have already recalled the episode's
influence on Howells as preface to a discussion of Charlotte Teller's *The
Cage* (Chapter 4).
    Haymarket and the conflicts of the succeeding years mark two ave-
nues of explanation that connect Goldman to American political and
imaginative experience; the third is a path that leads back again to Anne
Hutchinson. One of Goldman's biographers argues that "her ideas were
in part merely logical extensions of the Reformation doctrine of the
priesthood of all believers and of the classical liberal tradition of individual freedom and distrust of the state."[34] A reading of Goldman's
essays and of her autobiography suggests that this judgment is essentially correct; to develop it is to indicate as well the subterranean links
reaching back from Goldman to Hutchinson.
    In her occasional essays and her later memoirs, Goldman consistently
named Peter Kropotkin as her mentor and model. And yet, in the
essays in particular, Kropotkin rarely appears. The writers most often
cited and approved are Thoreau, Emerson, and Whitman. In part the
citations may be a rhetorical device, a strategy of Goldman's to domes-
ticate her subversive ideas for her American audience. In larger part,
though, the personal homage and the philosophical indebtedness are
real. Through Goldman, America in the early twentieth century once
again enacted its perennial dialectic, once again spoke the dissent of self
to the power of collectivity.
    If, for example, Goldman seemed to overvalue and even to mythify
the natural goodness of the individual, she could quote Emerson: "The
one thing of value in the world . . . is the active soul; this every man
contains within him. The soul active sees absolute truth and utters truth
and creates." If she sounded melodramatic in her denunciation of
American government, she could quote Emerson again: "All govern-

ment in essence is tyranny."[35] Or she could appeal to Thoreau: "That government is best which governs not at all"; "a man cannot without disgrace be associated with" the American government; "I quietly declare war with the state."

Through the careers of men like Gandhi and King, Thoreau would exert a powerful influence across the history of twentieth-century resistance. At the beginning of the century, he stirred Emma Goldman with what she understood to be a foreshadowing of her own message: "There will never be a really free and enlightened State until the State comes to recognize the individual as a higher and independent power."[36]

Thoreau was "the greatest American anarchist";[37] and in her autobiography, Goldman tells of a pilgrimage she made in his honor. She went to Concord and found only a quaint old town and a few sleepy inhabitants. It was a present "more ghostlike than the dead," with "no sign that men and women had existed in Concord to whom liberty was a living ideal." She visited with Frank B. Sanborn, Thoreau's biographer, and found him aristocratic in bearing, charming and gracious in manner. Sanborn spoke with pride of his own refusal to pay taxes, of his acquaintance with John Brown, of his friendship with Emerson. Above all, he talked "with reverence of Thoreau . . . the rebel against the encroachments of the State on the rights of the individual."

It is a superb vignette. Emma Goldman, apostle of twentieth-century anarchy, reaching back through the touch of hand upon hand directly to her nineteenth-century forebear. The ideological challenge in the scene was too great for Goldman's patrician host. She told Sanborn that she found his portrait confirming her own conception of Thoreau as "the precursor of anarchism in the United States." The old biographer was scandalized:

> "No, indeed!" he cried; "anarchism means violence and revolution. It means Czolgosz. Thoreau was an extreme non-resistant."
> We spent several hours trying to enlighten this contemporary of the most anarchistic period of American thought about the meaning of anarchism.[38]

It doesn't matter for our purposes, of course, whether Goldman or Sanborn won this argument. The anecdote illustrates what Goldman understood to be the indigenous American sources of her radical position.

She appealed to Thoreau's authority repeatedly in her attacks on government, on all organized efforts to trammel the free individual. And if Thoreau stands behind Goldman, then behind Thoreau, as virtually every student of the subject has observed, stands Anne Hutchinson. I have had occasion to speak of the antinomian impulse in American culture throughout these chapters; Goldman and Hutchinson anchor an ideological span that arches across that culture. Thus Emma Goldman, spokeswoman for "the New" – note that near-allegorical capital letter – was simultaneously the charismatic voice of a long tradition.

But to say that is also to sketch the outlines of a paradox. Though she was despised (or, less often, admired) for what she denied, what Goldman affirmed discloses as well her deep connections with the culture she criticized. In addition and more interestingly, the very terms and forms of her dissent document her inevitable reliance on the old system she was trying to repudiate.

The fullest portrait we have of Goldman, her autobiography, is also the fullest revelation we have of her divided mind. In these thousand closely printed pages, Goldman reconstructed herself and relived her life. The book is a frank and richly detailed chronicle of Goldman's private and public careers. It is also filled with the names and doings of other early twentieth-century radicals, and of their friends and opponents, and it is an indispensable sourcebook for some of the most agitated years of American politics. From the social workers to the "goo-goo's" to the Wobblies to the police, from Theodore Roosevelt to John Reed to Max Eastman to Bill Haywood, all the major actors, and a good many extras along with them, make their entrances and exits. At their center stands Goldman, hectoring, lecturing, writing, resting only in jail. Her centrality, as we have seen, is a defensible tribute to her visibility and to the tenacity and scale of her dissent. Of course, Goldman is the preemptive presence in her memoirs for the simpler, technical reason that the self-centered point of view of autobiography demands it.

It is a simple fact, a question of genre of the most elementary sort, but its implications are far-reaching. What is true of point of view is true of the book as a whole: Goldman necessarily worked inside the imaginative and rhetorical limits set by the bourgeois culture she despised, and she produced an autobiography of the most conventional and conventionally American kind. Goldman's life, as she herself envisioned it, and in the only version of it now available to us across time, fully conforms in its structure, vocabulary, and tone to the received canons of early twentieth-century American aesthetics. Except for the details of its politics, the book is startling only in its close resemblance to so many other American texts in this genre. The aesthetic resemblance suggests as well a more fundamental similarity, Goldman's ultimate dependence on the conception of personality created by the society against which she struggled. What sets out to be a revolutionary testament takes relentlessly conservative shape. *Living My Life* is the story of a conversion; of an education; of goodness endangered, repeatedly betrayed but endlessly resilient. It is an ideological recasting of the rags-to-riches saga. It is the tale of a restless journey: the romance of the self, couched in the most familiar rhythm of the romance form.

The structure is straightforward. For the most part, the story unfolds in a routinely chronological order, from Goldman's early years in eastern Europe and Russia to her three decades in the United States; from her experiences in Soviet Russia after the First World War to her travels in Canada, England, Spain, and elsewhere, to the time of the book's writing, in France, in 1930. The major exception to this uncomplicated linearity occurs in the opening pages; instead of beginning at the beginning, Goldman commences on August 15, 1889, the day of her arrival in New York City from Rochester. From that point, Goldman works backward for two chapters, through the Rochester years, Haymarket, her immigration, her childhood. All of that was preface to her move to New York: "All that had happened in my life until that time was now left behind me, cast off like a worn-out garment. A new world was before me, strange and terrifying" (I:3).

That comes from the book's first paragraph. Goldman, in other words, made a conspicuous effort to rearrange her narrative in order that it call attention to the metaphor of the new world, and the episode serves her conscious design quite well. Twenty-year-old Emma Goldman, with a sewing machine under one arm and all the rest of her worldly goods under the other, preparing "to meet unflinchingly" whatever her new life required, makes a vivid figure. She seems a young and female Franklin, stepping off the ferry in Philadelphia and striding up Market Street possessed only of a couple of loaves of bread and ambition.

The language of "new world," introduced in the first paragraph, recurs throughout *Living My Life*. New York is a new world in 1889, but so also had it appeared when Goldman arrived there four years earlier, as a new immigrant. We have seen that, and we have also seen how the execution of the Haymarket anarchists opened "a new world" (I:10). In short, Goldman creates a prominent motif of conversion; and she continues it. Hearing Johann Most lecture on anarchism brings Goldman to yet another new life, and so does Berkman's attack on Frick, and the assassination of McKinley, and the Ludlow massacre.

Her ceaseless travels across America reenacted the epic tales of the pioneers, the explorers, as she traveled in the doubled New World of her ideology and of American myth. Pioneers (not settlers, for Americans have been impatient with settling) have always preferred the open road to the fence. Goldman, too, whatever may have been the European contribution to her ideas, was searching for the dream that lay hidden somewhere in the New World's secret places. Like her American predecessors, the end she strove toward was less a definite condition than a state beyond definition. The last of the essays reprinted in *Anarchism* concludes with this diapason: "All roads [now] lead to the great social reconstruction. The economic awakening of the working-man, and his realization of the necessity for concerted industrial action; the tendencies of modern education, especially in their application to the free development of the child; the spirit of growing unrest expressed through, and cultivated by, art and literature, all pave the way to the Open Road."[39]

New world; new life; open road. Goldman's extraordinary career revivified the stock figures and phrases of American romance. Yet they remain clichés as well, for all that, and as such they prove an accurate index to her book. For the entire autobiography is cast in such language. The vocabulary is an amalgam of melodramatic excess and stock romantic formulas.

Take, for a randomly chosen example, this evocation of the imprisoned Berkman:

> My Sasha, my wonderful Sasha – he was not only brave, as Ed [Brady] had said; he was a tower of strength. As so often since that day when the steam monster at the Baltimore and Ohio Station had snatched him away from me, he stood out like a shining meteor on the dark horizon. . . . He was like a white light that purged one's soul, inspiring even awe at his detachment from human frailties. (I:177)

The breathless tone and the one-dimensional sentimentality are characteristic of Goldman's voice throughout *Living My Life*. She creates no persons, but rather renders the straw men and women of melodrama. The only distinguishing features admitted are abstract and political. Despite her deep theoretical commitment to individuality, the individuals she met and knew and fought with emerge as mere signifiers in a morality play. What is true of a major figure like Berkman is even more true of minor characters. Kitty Beck, for example, becomes the emblem of self-sacrifice:

> Her life had been very tragic, perhaps because nature had made her all too lavish. Giving was to her a ritual, to serve to the uttermost her only impulse. Whether it was the man she loved, a friend, or a beggar, a stray cat or a dog, Kitty always emptied the fullness of her heart. she could exact nothing for herself. . . .
> Those in her life accepted from her as a matter of course; few, if any, of them understood the craving of her own heart. Kitty was born to give, not to receive. (II:710)

Goldman's allegorical figures, stripped of human personality, inhabit a setting equally devoid of particularity and substance. For all the huge extent of her travels and the variety of her experience, Goldman describes almost nothing in her autobiography (or in any of her other writings). Her life story is meagerly furnished; hardly an image intrudes itself. Those that do typically congeal into treacly slogans: "I woke the next morning with the bright sunshine streaming into my room and wide stretches of blue hanging over the luscious green of trees and lawn. The air was pungent with the aroma of the earth, the lake was vibrant with soft music, and all of nature breathed enchantment. I, too, was under her magic spell" (II:620).

Perception is confined within the limits of formula; nothing is actually described. The symbolic opportunities offered by such derivative settings are correspondingly circumscribed:

> The storm outside had stopped. The air was still, the sun slowly rising and spreading its red and gold over the sky in greeting of the new day. I wept, conscious of the eternal rebirth in nature, in the dreams of man, in his quest for freedom and beauty, in the struggle of humanity to greater heights. I felt the rebirth of my own life, to blend once more with the universal . . . (II:945–946)

The correspondences are as predictable as they are antique, and the entire paragraph could have dropped out of any run-of-the-mill adventure tale. Sentimentality and stock response have replaced sight; the storm, the air, the sun are not really seen, they are given by rote.

The stick people who occupy Goldman's papier-mâché landscapes behave and judge in predictably simplified ways.

– Edward Brady, caught between his love for Goldman and his anger at her independence, "paced the room like a caged lion, turning from time to time to fasten his eyes on me." At the end of a row between them, Goldman shouts: "You're rooted in the old. Very well, remain there! But don't imagine you will hold me to it. You are not going to clip my wings, you shan't stop my flight. I'll free myself even if it means tearing you out of my heart" (I:183, 195).

– A scheme to rescue Berkman from jail "seemed fantastic, the desperate design of one driven to stake everything, even his life, upon the throw of a card. Yet I was carried away by the project . . ." (I:247).

– Goldman visits ailing Justus Schwab (one of the Haymarket anarchists pardoned by John Peter Altgeld): "I found him in bed, a mere shadow of his former self. A lump rose in my throat at the sight of our giant so wasted" (I:282).

– Reverend Dr. H. S. McCowan is vilified by his Detroit congregation for inviting Goldman to speak from his pulpit: The minister is brave and "knew what he was doing; it was only right for him to stick to his guns" (I:205).

– Goldman recalls her admiration for Horace Traubel, and her improved opinion of Debs:

> Another man brought close to me by Horace was Eugene V. Debs. I had met him previously on several occasions and had clashed swords with him in a friendly way over our political differences, but I knew little of his real personality. Horace, an intimate friend of Debs's, made him vibrant to me in the heights and depths of his character. The comradeship I felt for Horace ripened into a beautiful friendship during my visits to Philadelphia. The city's empty boast of brotherly love was redeemed by none so much as by Horace Traubel, whose love embraced mankind. (II:568)

– And finally, this. One Christmas Eve, boxes of presents are delivered to Goldman's apartment: "a wonderful coat with a real astrakhan collar, muff, and turban to match. There were a dress, silk underwear, stockings, and gloves. I felt like Cinderella" (I:333).

Goldman as Cinderella. The image is arresting. It would be pedantic to press the significance of the casual allusion too far. Yet it is not altogether farfetched. It recapitulates in a phrase the problem we have been examining in Goldman's case and have investigated in earlier writers as well: the problem of the misfit between ideological aspirations and imaginative form. If she had paused to think about it, Goldman would have detested the male-dominant, domestic theme that the Cinderella story obviously inculcates. In part my point is that she didn't pause to think about it. She needed a language and a structure, and she took what was at hand, whether it was the well-worn imagery of American romance or the satisfying simplifications of fairy tale.

Goldman's reference to Cinderella also offers oblique entry into the sexual politics of *Living My Life,* the subject that most completely captures the reality of her divided mind. As we have seen, with the philosophically motivated exception of her opposition to woman's suffrage, Goldman associated herself with virtually the whole range of feminist issues. She discusses those issues at length in her autobiography, but she also reveals the coexistence of a quite different ideology. Goldman demanded freedom for herself and for all women, in friendship, in sex, and in motherhood, but she could find no other terms in which to formulate her demands than those handed down by the traditions of romantic love.

Thus, she recalls an afternoon in Baltimore with Robert Reitzel "Unforgettable were the hours I spent with my knight. The sunshine of his spirit drew me into its orbit and made me reluctant to tear myself away" (I:215). There are many such moments in *Living My Life*. Another of them occurs during Goldman's recollection of a night in London with Hippolyte Havel: "We found ourselves, hardly conscious how, in each other's embrace. London receded, the cry of the East End was far away. Only the call of love sounded in our hearts, and we listened and yielded to it. I felt reborn with the new joy in my life" (I:261).

This, too, is typical: the modulation of the motif of the "new life" from the ideological to the sexual. Goldman intends the modulation, because she intends the sexual *as* ideological. She often declared that love was at the core of her anarchism, because love is the most human, the most liberating, and thus the most anarchic of emotions. Yet her efforts to express this conviction always lead into the verbal and conceptual cul-de-sac of romance cliché: "Some day, some day men and women will rise, they will reach the mountain peak, they will meet big and strong and free, ready to receive, to partake, to bask in the golden rays of love."[40] Despite the risk of anachronism, it is hard to call passages like this anything but harlequin love songs.

And such passages abound. No one elicits more of them than Ben Reitman, the bizarre "King of the Hoboes." Where others saw an exhibitionist, a self-promoter, and an unwashed charlatan, Goldman saw his "brown, large, and dreamy" eyes. "His lips, disclosing beautiful teeth when he smiled, were full and passionate." Female Petrarch to Reitman's unlikely Laura, Goldman even transforms her lover's dirty fingernails: "His hands, narrow and white, exerted a perculiar fascination. His finger-nails, like his hair, seemed to be on strike against soap and brush. I could not take my eyes off his hands. A strange charm seemed to emanate from them, caressing and stirring." All in all, confesses the smitten Goldman, "he looked a handsome brute" (I:416). Reitman was utterly unreliable as a colleague and collaborator, but he was apparently an exceptional talent in bed: "That night [with Reitman] I was caught in the torrent of an elemental passion I had never dreamed any man could rouse in me. I responded shamelessly to its primitive call, its naked beauty, its ecstatic joy" (I:420). And if that weren't enough, Reitman followed Goldman into her dreams: "I dreamed that Ben was bending over me, his face close to mine, his hands on my chest. Flames were shooting from his finger-tips and slowly enveloping my body. I made no attempt to escape them. I strained toward them, craving to be consumed by their fire" (I:422).

Goldman herself recognized the distance between Reitman's amatory and ideological performances. Her devotion to him was self-abasing but it persisted nonetheless, and it rebuked her own protestations about the causal link between liberated love and politics.[41]

In Chapter 6, we attended to Kate Chopin's more implicit dramatiza-
tion of something like the same dilemma. "There are no words,"
Chopin wrote, "save the old ones" of romance and chivalry. There are
words for the received, but not for the new. The tension between
prophecy and the limits of language lies at the heart of Goldman's
story, as it did of Edna Pontellier's. The images that Goldman and
Chopin deploy are sometimes strikingly similar. This passage, for example, in which Goldman re-creates her response to Margaret Ander-
son's piano playing, might have been lifted almost verbatim out of *The
Awakening:*

> Margaret's playing was not that of a trained artist. There was a
> certain original and vibrant quality in it, particularly when no
> strangers were present. At such moments she was able to give full
> expression to all her emotion and intensity. Music stirred me
> profoundly, but Margaret's playing exerted a peculiar effect, like
> the sight of the sea, which always made me uneasy and restless. I
> had never learned to swim and I feared deep water, yet on the
> beach I would be filled with a desire to reach out towards the
> waves and become submerged in their embrace. Whenever I heard
> Margaret play, I was overcome by the same sensation and an
> uneasy craving. (II:531–532)

Unlike Edna Pontellier, Goldman did not yield to the desire to extin-
guish herself in the sea, but the familiar coordination between death
and the erotic offers an unnerving glimpse into Goldman's tragic pre-
dicament.

Romantic love was not the only tradition that enclosed Goldman
within its formulas. Religion was another. Once again, in all the more
obvious ways, Goldman repudiated all forms of religion. She was an
atheist by repeated choice. She placed much of the blame for European
and American systems of oppression on institutional religion. She saw
the churches and their clergy as the willing accomplices of exploitation
and bigotry. The liberation of workers, women, minorities – of all humanity – will be a liberation from the superstitions of religion.

Goldman also used religion as a source of adversarial metaphors in her
lifelong debate against socialism. Socialism, she often said, was "essentially another Church with new dogmas" (II:520). Similarly, after a few
months in Soviet Russia, Goldman employed the same religious trope to
emphasize her disillusion. Political prisoners were "social heretics who
were guilty of the cardinal sin against the Communist Church" (II:873).
The Soviet Union had become "the modern socialist Lourdes, to which
the blind and the lame, the deaf and the dumb were flocking for miraculous cures" (II:916). The logic of these metaphors is evident. To Goldman, Marxian socialism and Russia under Lenin both exhibit the repres-

sive hallmarks of earlier religions: conformity, the subordination of humanity to dogma, the cruel treatment of dissenters.

Given these views, the logic that moved Goldman also to associate religion with anarchism in a set of positive correlations is less evident but no less significant. What was distasteful in the case of the Catholic Church or the Socialist Party or the Soviet Union becomes somehow attractive in connection with Berkman and Goldman and their comrades.

Early in the autobiography, Goldman elaborates on that "new world" into which she was born as a result of Haymarket in a language of sustained religiosity:

> I had a distinct sensation that something new and wonderful had been born in my soul. A great ideal, a burning faith, a determination to dedicate myself to the memory of my martyred comrades, to make their cause my own, to make known to the world their beautiful lives and heroic deaths. (I:10)

Later, her experiences on the East Side of New York are a "baptism" (I:121). Berkman's imprisonment was a "fourteen years' Calvary" (I:393).

Perhaps the most astonishing of Goldman's religious figures is this description of a speech she gave in the security of millionaire Alden Freeman's East Orange estate: "The garage where our gathering took place was more comfortable than some workmen's homes. The coloured lights trembled like shadows in the night, throwing fantastic silhouettes. It was a picture suggesting the legendary birthplace of the Christ-child, the hallelujahs changed into a song of freedom and revolt" (I:454).

Goldman notices neither the irony of the setting here (she simply accepted Freeman's radically chic gesture as brave) nor the irony of her symbolism. The allusion to Bethlehem typifies Goldman's recurrent reliance on what might be called a displaced religious discourse. Though she rejected organized religion and any other ideological systems that command their adherents to doctrinal obedience, she also longed for the certitude, the zeal, and the consolation that religion brings to its followers. She wanted to clothe her own ideas in the same mantle of dignity and confidence that religion wears. Above all, she wanted to magnify the scale and significance of her opinions. She thus turned, paradoxically but probably inevitably, to the only vocabulary that was universally understood to hold out such assurances; and thus again her vision of the future was entangled in the debris of the past.[42]

In the first chapter of this book, I proposed that the real revolution taking place in the early twentieth century was the triumph of organization. Max Weber long ago prescribed the lenses through which Woodcock and the other historians I cited observe the movements of hegemony and resistance in these years. The primary fact for our purposes is that the institutions Emma Goldman opposed were growing stronger and larger as she opposed them. Above all was this true of the state. In that sense, her anarchism was not merely entangled in the past, it was essentially *of* the past, retrospective if not retrograde. Barbara Tuchman may miss a few fine distinctions, but the generalization she submits on this matter is sound: Anarchism was "the last cry of individual man, the last movement . . . on behalf of individual liberty, the last hope of living unregulated, the last fist shaken against the encroaching State, before the State, the party, the union, the organization closed in."[43] What appeared to so many of her contemporaries as a call to the revolutionary future was, after all, a retreat from history altogether. Goldman turned her face in dismay from the irresistible tendencies of her time.

Lenin accused Goldman of "bourgeois sentimentality."[44] Theodore Roosevelt would have been dumbfounded, but the charge, to Goldman's credit, is probably about right. Her affirmation of the liberated and self-creating individual is bathed in nostalgia, for all its prophetic apparatus. She did not want simply to replace the current managers of hated institutions with her friends and herself. She wanted to detonate the institutions themselves. She longed to assert and make use of the human spirit; she had no interest in merely "mastering the machine."[45]

Resistance to the machine of organization sometimes took a different but corollary form. Goldman gave one of the main addresses at the International Anarchist Congress in Amsterdam in 1907. In it, she denied that she was opposed to the idea of organization as such. It was only the particular organizations that had evolved in modern society – state, church, army, school – that she rejected. She then went on to redefine the term "organization":

> Organization, as we understand it . . . is a different thing [from state, church, and so on]. It is based primarily on freedom. It is the natural and voluntary grouping of energies for the achievement of results beneficial to humanity. . . . It is the harmony of organic growth which produces variety of color and form, the complete whole we admire in the flower. Analogously will the organized activity of free human beings, endowed with the spirit of solidarity, result in the perfection of social harmony, which we call Anarchism.[46]

In short, Goldman mystifies the idea of organization in order to appropriate it. The antithesis between individual and collectivity dissolves in romantic wishfulness: The machinery of organization is transformed into the flower of organic nature.

In the preceding chapters, we have seen a good many of Goldman's contemporaries either choosing or backing into the same logical cleft stick. Men as otherwise divergent in their views as John D. Rockefeller, David Graham Phillips, and Frank Lloyd Wright all undertook the same sleight of hand. What is ideologically attractive or compulsory is anointed with the oil of organic process.

Goldman clung to this view. In her autobiographical look back at the Anarchist Congress, she changed the vehicle of her metaphor but repeated her organic claims:

> In reality . . . the true function of organization is to aid the development and growth of personality. Just as the animal cells, by mutual co-operation, express their latent powers in the formation of the complete organism, so does . . . individuality, by co-operative effort with other individualities, attain its highest form of development.[47]

Goldman summarized the argument by insisting that anarchism did not have to compel a choice "between Kropotkin and Ibsen; it embraces both" (I:402). Richard Drinnon defends this bristling proposition with about as much sympathy as could be mustered: "She was as keenly aware as Ibsen of the tragedy of the modern individual and mass organization; she was as apprehensive as Kropotkin of the power-obsessed, socially irresponsible individual. Caught between these two positions, she tried to fuse them into a higher synthesis of individualistic communism."[48]

In the event, we are left to contemplate not a "higher synthesis" – the phrase always gives itself away – but a series of contradictions. But in this she is all the more worth our attention. "Conservative Christian anarchist": That was the phrase of Henry Adams with which we began. Its relevance to Goldman has by now, I trust, become clear. Alien as she seemed to her antagonists, the American family resemblance is plain. Like the other men and women in the preceding chapters, Goldman is to be found where Richard Chase located so much of American culture, among the contradictions and extreme ranges of experience.

Epilogue: Hester Street, 1905

Asked if Emma Goldman and Evelyn Nesbit had ever *really* met, E. L. Doctorow is reported to have answered: "They have now."

Calendars and documents inform us that in June 1905, Henry James and Emma Goldman were both present on New York's Lower East Side. They did not in fact meet (either then or now), but they could have. If they had, the scene would serve as emblem for this book, a symbol of the divided mind of turn-of-the-century America.

James and Goldman open and close these essays, first and most obviously, because they confront each other as completely antithetical characters. Everything James was and stood for Goldman was not and denied. On the one ideological boundary of the culture was the aristocratically inclined Anglo-Saxon gentleman and connoisseur of nuance, for whom order made art and art made life. On the opposite boundary was the anarchist immigrant Jewish woman, for whom life was freedom and freedom was the abolition of the encumbering past. Linked together by their systematic difference, James and Goldman express in almost reductive form much of the dialectic that has been the concern of these chapters: the conflict, to return to the language of the first chapter, between tradition and innovation, between control and independence, between order and liberation. James peering anxiously back to some lost condition of well-ordered social harmony, Goldman gazing hopefully ahead toward a future of spontaneous cooperation: Between them, they virtually exhaust the furthest terms of America's early twentieth-century debate.

Upon a closer inspection, however, the facts of the case have proven themselves significant in a rather more complex and more interesting way. James and Goldman exemplify the dialectical shape of American culture not only in their opposition to each other but in themselves as well. This is what we have found. As he turned his face in angry despair away from the American present and toward the betrayed past, James inadvertently helped to invent the future. The style and manner of his retreat from the twentieth century contributed importantly to the making of modernism, which has comprised this century's predominant cultural achievement. And Goldman, as she rejected the American present on behalf of a utopian communitarian future, inevitably cast back to the forms and ideas of the past. Her embrace of what could be was entangled in the vocabulary and images of what had been.

If these formulations seem too neatly symmetrical, they nonetheless serve to isolate accurately the further and final connection between James and Goldman. Both were propelled by a deeply felt dissatisfaction with things as they are, and both yearned throughout most of their lives for what – in completely different definitions – they felt would be more attractive worlds.

At a high but still useful explanatory level of abstraction, the profound differences between James and Goldman are subsumed in a resemblance yet more profound. They both resisted the physical and human environment in which the industrial and organizational revolutions imprisoned them. They therefore imagined what they took to be more humane social and political spaces in which the lives of men and women might flourish, protected from the onslaught of the modern state and its apparatus.

That attitude of dissent, which James and Goldman brought to such climatically opposed extremity, has linked many of the otherwise disparate figures in all these chapters. It is what links them, in turn, to the American antecedents that lie behind them. Finally, it is what links American ideology and American art. Both are poised between memory and desire. Thus, one point of the preceding essays has been to understand America's politics as another expression of its people's imaginative resistance to the given.

To push the speculation too hard or too far would risk confusing the domains of aesthetics and sociology. The rich and multiform experience of twentieth-century America eludes any ultimate reduction; and another point of the preceding essays has been to reproduce the competing attitudes and tones of the turn of the century. Nonetheless, what united a good many Americans in the early 1900s, whether they professed themselves reactionary or radical, was a stance of dissent, coupled with a less certain urge to discover what might be affirmed.

That would have expressed the truer significance of our fanciful meeting between Henry James and Emma Goldman, though neither of them would have paused long enough to puzzle it out. In their rage against the existing order, in their indifference to a clearly defined or programmatic alternative, and in their simultaneous embodiment of past and future, James and Goldman speak to us, choruslike, in American voices. They speak as well for the other writers and artists and public figures whose lives and work have filled these pages.

Notes

<hr style="border:1px double black" />

Chapter 1. The temper of the times

1 Henry Adams, *The Education of Henry Adams* (1907; rept., Boston: Houghton Mifflin, 1973), p. 406.

2 On the word "generation," see especially Karl Mannheim, "The Problem of Generations," in *Essays on the Sociology of Knowledge,* ed. Paul Kecskemeti (London: Routledge and Kegan Paul, 1952), pp. 276–322. The conceptual difficulties attending the notion of generation are addressed by several contributors to the Fall 1978 issue of *Daedalus* (vol. 107, no. 4). See also Ellen Condliffe Lagemann, *A Generation of Women: Education in the Lives of Progressive Reformers* (Cambridge, Mass.: Harvard University Press, 1979), pp. 1–2.

3 Stanley P. Caine, "The Origins of Progressivism," in *The Progressive Era,* ed. Lewis L. Gould (Syracuse, N.Y.: Syracuse University Press, 1974), p. 11.

4 Lawrence Goodwyn, *The Populist Moment: A Short History of the Agrarian Revolt in America* (New York: Oxford University Press, 1978).

5 Richard Hofstadter, *The Age of Reform: From Bryan to F.D.R.* (New York: Knopf, 1955).

6 Gabriel Kolko, *The Triumph of Conservatism* (Chicago: Quadrangle Books, 1967).

7 Allen F. Davis, "Welfare, Reform and World War I," *American Quarterly,* vol. XIX (Fall 1967), pp. 516–533. See also Richard M. Abrams, "The Failure of Progressivism," in *The Shaping of Twentieth-Century America,* ed. Abrams and Lawrence W. Levine, 2d ed. (Boston: Little, Brown, 1971), pp. 207–224.

8 Russel Nye, *The Unembarrassed Muse: The Popular Arts in America* (New York: Dial Press, 1970), p. 257.

9 Donelson F. Hoopes, *The American Impressionists* (New York: Watson-Guptill, 1972), p. 18.

10 Loren Baritz, Introduction to *The Culture of the Twenties* (Indianapolis: Bobbs-Merrill, 1970), p. xvii.

11 Lionel Trilling, *The Liberal Imagination* (New York: Viking Press, 1953), p. 20.

12 Richard Chase, *The American Novel and Its Tradition* (Garden City, N.Y.: Anchor Books, 1957), p. 1.
13 Cited in Chase, *The American Novel,* p.6.
14 Kai Erikson, *Everything in Its Path* (New York: Simon and Schuster, 1976), p. 82.
15 Marcus Klein, *Foreigners: The Making of American Literature, 1900–1940* (Chicago: University of Chicago Press, 1981), p. x.
16 Henry May, *The End of American Innocence: A Study of the First Years of Our Own Time, 1912–1917* (New York: Oxford University Press, 1979), p. ix.
17 John Higham, *Strangers in the Land: Patterns of American Nativism, 1860–1925* (New York: Atheneum, 1978), p. 110.
18 John Thomas, "Nationalizing the Republic, 1890–1920," in *The Great Republic,* Bernard Bailyn et al. (Boston: Little, Brown, 1977), p. 833.
19 See, for example, Robert M. Henderson, *D.W. Griffith: The Years at Biograph* (New York: Farrar, Straus and Giroux, 1970), esp. pp. 158–177.
20 Mark Sullivan, *Our Times: The United States, 1900–1925,* vol. I (New York: Scribners, 1931), p. 64.
21 Wilton B. Fowler, "American Diplomacy in the Progressive Era," in Gould, ed., *The Progressive Era,* p. 153.
22 Ernest May, *American Imperialism* (New York: Atheneum, 1968), p. 3. For a less disjunctive view of the turn of the century – and a more conspiratorial hypothesis about the preceding years – see Walter LaFeber, *The New Empire: An Interpretation of American Expansion, 1860–1898* (Ithaca, N.Y.: Cornell University Press, 1963).
23 H. H. Powers, "The War as a Suggestion of Manifest Destiny," *Annals of the American Academy of Political and Social Science* (September 1898), p. 173. (I am grateful to Professor Robert Regan for directing me to this and the following reference.)
24 E. L. Godkin, "The Imperial Policy," *The Nation,* vol. 66, no. 1717 (May 26, 1898), p. 396.
25 Theodore Roosevelt, "Biological Analogies in History," in *Literary Essays,* vol. XIV of *The Works of Theodore Roosevelt* (New York: Scribners, 1924), p. 69. The passage comes from a lecture Roosevelt delivered at Oxford in 1910.
26 Cited in Claude G. Bowers, *Beveridge and the Progressive Era* (Cambridge, Mass.: Houghton Mifflin, 1932), p. 121.
27 Samuel P. Hays, *The Response to Industrialism, 1885–1914* (Chicago: University of Chicago Press, 1957), p. 48. See also Robert Wiebe, *The Search for Order, 1877–1920* (New York: Hill and Wang, 1967).
28 Cited in Allan Nevins, *Study in Power: John D. Rockefeller, Industrialist and Philanthropist,* vol.II (New York: Scribners, 1953), pp. 243–244.
29 Frank Norris, *The Octopus* (1900; rept., New York: New American Library, 1964), p. 405.
30 See James Weinstein, *The Corporate Ideal in the Liberal State, 1900–1918* (Boston: Beacon Press, 1968).
31 Benjamin Parke DeWitt, *The Progressive Movement* (New York: Macmillan, 1915), p. 320.

32 Alexandra Oleson and John Voss, Introduction to *The Organization of Knowledge in Modern America, 1860–1920,* ed. Oleson and Voss (Baltimore: Johns Hopkins University Press, 1979), p. vii.

33 See, for example, Jack M. Holl, *Juvenile Reform in the Progressive Era* (Ithaca, N.Y.: Cornell University Press, 1971).

34 David F. Noble, *America by Design: Science, Technology, and the Rise of Corporate Capitalism* (New York: Knopf, 1977).

35 *The Masses,* no. 5 (May 1911), p. 3.

36 George Woodcock, *Anarchism: A History of Libertarian Ideas and Movements* (Cleveland, Oh.: Meridian Books, 1962), p. 469. See also Robert F. Wesser, *Charles Evans Hughes: Politics and Reform in New York, 1905–1910* (Ithaca, N.Y.: Cornell University Press, 1967), p. 1.

37 George Santayana, "The Genteel Tradition in American Philosophy," in *Winds of Doctrine* (New York: Scribners, 1913), pp. 187–188.

38 See also Theodore Roosevelt's comments on business and businessmen, cited in Chapter 3, and Frank Norris on the romance of the businessman-hero, discussed in Chapter 6.

39 See Joe Bertram Frantz and Julian Ernest Choate, *The American Cowboy: The Myth and the Reality* (Norman, Okla.: University of Oklahoma Press, 1955).

40 Jay Martin and Gossie H. Hudson, eds., *The Paul Laurence Dunbar Reader* (New York: Dodd, Mead, 1975), p. 341.

41 Daniel Boorstin, Editor's Preface to Hays, *Response to Industrialism,* p. vii.

42 Clifford Geertz, "Art as a Cultural System," *MLN,* vol. 91, no. 6 (December 1976), p. 1478.

43 On Geertz's conception of culture, see also Kenneth A. Rice, *Geertz and Culture* (Ann Arbor: University of Michigan Press, 1980).

44 Robert Macleod, *Style and Society: Architectural Ideology in Britain, 1835–1914* (London: Royal Institute of British Architects, 1971), p. 7.

45 Karl Popper, *The Open Society and Its Enemies,* vol. II (London: Routledge, 1945), p. 256.

Chapter 2: The triumph of reaction

1 Percy Lubbock, ed., *The Letters of Henry James,* vol. II (New York: Macmillan, 1920), p. 384.

2 Graham Greene, *Collected Essays* (New York: Viking Press, 1969), p. 24.

3 Henry James, *The Wings of the Dove,* vol. II (New York: Scribners 1909), p. 283.

4 Leon Edel, *Henry James: The Untried Years* (Philadelphia: Lippincott, 1953), p. 301.

5 Leon Edel, ed., *The Letters of Henry James,* vol. I (Cambridge, Mass.: Harvard University Press, 1974), pp. 139–140. See also James's comments on Ruskin in an article on Venice, in the November 1882 issue of *Century* magazine.

6 Edel, ed., *Letters of Henry James,* vol. I, p. 103.

7 Edith Wharton, *A Backward Glance* (New York: Appleton-Century, 1934), p. 191.

8 Leon Edel, ed., *The Complete Tales of Henry James,* vol. XII (Philadelphia: Lippincott, 1964), p. 14.

9 Leon Edel, ed., *The Complete Tales of Henry James,* vol. XI (Philadelphia: Lippincott, 1964), p. 21.

10 See R. W. B. Lewis, "Henry James: The Theater of Consciousness," pt. II, *The Wings of the Dove,* in *Trials of the Word* (New Haven, Conn.: Yale University Press, 1965), pp. 120–128.

11 See, in particular, Chapter 7, this volume.

12 Edel, ed., *Complete Tales,* vol. XI, p. 405. The "National Poet" is actually never named in the tale. Part of the reason for James's reticence will be suggested in my discussion of the story.

13 Henry Adams, *The Education of Henry Adams* (1907; Boston: Houghton Mifflin, 1973), p. 417.

14 Henry James, *The Golden Bowl,* vol. I (New York: Scribners, 1909), p. 131.

15 Since the extent of Adam's knowledge eventually becomes one of the most baffling of *The Golden Bowl*'s several baffling questions, this casual but reliable narrative comment early in the book possesses a considerable interpretative significance.

16 Henry James, *The Portrait of a Lady,* vol. II (New York: Scribners, 1908), pp. 10–11.

17 Ruth B. Yeazell, *Language and Knowledge in the Late Novels of Henry James* (Chicago: University of Chicago Press, 1977), pp. 128–129.

18 Henry James, *The Ambassadors,* vol. I (New York: Scribners, 1909), p. 89.

19 Henry James, *The American Scene,* ed. Leon Edel (1907; rept., Bloomington: Indiana University Press, 1968), p. 42.

20 Henry James, *Hawthorne* (1879; rept., Ithaca, N.Y.: Cornell University Press, 1966), p. 34.

21 Richard Hofstadter, *The Paranoid Style in American Politics and Other Essays* (Chicago: University of Chicago Press, 1965), pp. 3–40. I use the term while acknowledging the cogency of David Stannard's reservations about it. See *Shrinking History: On Freud and the Failure of Psychohistory* (New York: Oxford University Press, 1982), p. 108.

22 Leon Edel, ed., *Henry James: Selected Fiction* (New York: Dutton, 1964), p. 599.

23 Leon Edel, *Henry James: The Middle Years* (Philadelphia: Lippincott, 1962), p. 21.

24 Leon Edel, *Henry James: The Treacherous Years* (Philadelphia: Lippincott, 1969), p. 350.

25 Leon Edel, ed., *Complete Tales,* vol. XII, p. 203.

26 Hugh Kenner, *The Pound Era* (Berkeley: The University of California Press, 1971), pp. 3–4.

Chapter 3. Restoration as reform

1 Roosevelt probably took the idea for his speech from a February 10, 1906, item in *Collier's,* headed "The Man with the Muckrake Improved."

2 Louis Filler, *The Muckrakers* (University Park, Pa.: Pennsylvania State University Press, 1976), p. 253.

322 NOTES TO PP. 50–64

3 Justin Kaplan, *Lincoln Steffens: A Biography* (New York: Simon and Schuster, 1974), p. 115.
4 David Graham Phillips, *The Treason of the Senate* (1906; rept., New York: Monthly Review Press, 1953), p. 2.
5 Gabriel Kolko made this point rather more harshly: "It is significant that out of the entire muckraking literature, which was in effect a refutation of the existing theories on the character of the capitalist economy . . . no serious social or economic theory was formulated" (*The Triumph of Conservatism* [Chicago: Quadrangle Books, 1967], p. 160).
6 *The Outlook*, vol. 85 (April 6, 1907), p. 805.
7 David Graham Phillips, *The Plum Tree* (New York: Grosset and Dunlap, 1905), p. 19.
8 Lincoln Steffens, *The Shame of the Cities* (1904; rept., New York: Hill and Wang, 1957), p. 2.
9 Theodore Roosevelt, *An Autobiography*, cited in Kaplan, *Lincoln Steffens*, p. 63.
10 In addition to Kolko, *Triumph of Conservatism*, see James Weinstein, "Big Business and the Origins of Workmen's Compensation," *Labor History*, vol. VIII (Spring 1967), pp. 156–174.
11 Antonio Gramsci, *Selections from the Prison Notebooks*, ed. and trans. Quintin Hoare and Geoffrey Nowell-Smith (New York: International Publishers, 1971), esp. pp. 55–60, 242–246, 264–276, 333.
12 The closest person to a biographical "source" for Scarborough was Albert Beveridge, Phillips's roommate at Asbury College (later DePauw University), who in 1905 was serving his first term as senator from Indiana.
13 Cited in David Herreschoff, *American Disciples of Marx* (Detroit: Wayne State University Press, 1967), pp. 117–118.
14 Raymond Williams, *The Country and the City* (New York: Oxford University Press, 1973), esp. pp. 8–45.
15 The protagonist of George Horace Lorimer's *Letters from a Self-made Merchant to His Son* (1902) – that gigantically successful fictional potpourri of advice on getting ahead in business – is also named "John Graham."
16 David Graham Phillips, *The Great God Success* (New York: Grosset and Dunlap, 1901), pp. 24, 28–29.
17 Political dissent in the Protestant tradition, as well as in literature, has of course frequently been associated with demands for simplicity of language.
18 Jacob Riis, *Theodore Roosevelt the Citizen* (New York: Outlook Co., 1904), p. 102.
19 See Chapter 2, p. 27, this volume.
20 Cited in Abe C. Ravitz, *David Graham Phillips* (New York: Twayne Publishers, 1966), p. 91.
21 See Chapter 5, pp. 122, this volume.
22 David Graham Phillips, *The Second Generation* (New York: Grosset and Dunlap, 1906), p. 73.
23 Recall the refounding of Antioch College, in 1919, on the influential "work–study" pattern. The point was not merely to provide financial aid but to knit together academic theory and "real" work in a student's career.

24 Edmund Morris, *The Rise of Theodore Roosevelt* (New York: Coward, McCann and Geoghegan, 1979), pp. 328, 796.

25 Cited in John Morton Blum, *The Republican Roosevelt,* 2d ed. (Cambridge, Mass.: Harvard University Press, 1977), p. 23. On a visit to the United States in 1913, Rupert Brooke made a casual but exceptionally shrewd observation, and one that can also be used to gloss Roosevelt's character. When Brooke attended his first baseball game, Harvard versus Yale, he was more attracted by the goings-on in the stands and along the sidelines than on the field. The frenzied athleticism of Harvard's cheerleader seemed, to Brooke, "wonderfully American, in its combination of entire wildness and entire regulation, with the whole just a trifle fantastic" (*Letters from America* [New York: Scribners, 1916], p. 43). Brooke is surely right about the paradoxically American nature of this simultaneously wild and well-regulated young man. And he might easily have been describing that earlier Harvard athlete and slightly "fantastic" cheerleader to the nation, Theodore Roosevelt.

26 Ann Douglas turns to Roosevelt briefly at the conclusion of her superlative study, *The Feminization of American Culture* (New York: Avon Books, 1978), pp. 397–399. I would offer the additional suggestion that Roosevelt simultaneously conforms to and reverses the formula developed in that book.

27 Cited in Ernest Fischer, ed., *The Essential Marx* (New York: Herder and Herder, 1971), p. 102.

28 Marx repeated this figurative definition in the first chapter of *Capital* (London: Dent, 1972), p. 8.

29 See John Burchard and Albert Bush-Brown, *The Architecture of America: A Social and Cultural History* (Boston: Little, Brown, 1961), pp. 238–239.

30 Albert Fine, "The American City: The Ideal and the Real," in *The Rise of an American Architecture,* ed. Edgar Kaufmann, Jr. (New York: Praeger, 1970), p. 52.

31 Frederick C. Howe, *The City: The Hope of Democracy* (New York: Scribners, 1905), p. 7.

32 See Jill Conway, "Jane Addams: An American Heroine," in *The Woman in America,* ed. Robert Jay Lifton (Boston: Houghton Mifflin, 1965), pp. 247–266.

33 David Graham Phillips, *The Conflict* (New York: Grosset and Dunlap, 1911), p. 31.

34 Burchard and Bush-Brown, *Architecture of America,* p. 201. See also Chapter 7, p. 227, this volume.

35 Claude G. Bowers, *Beveridge and the Progressive Era* (Cambridge, Mass.: Houghton Mifflin, 1932), p. 319. W. J. Ghent pursued the logic of the analogy through to the prophecy of a fascist America, in *Our Benevolent Feudalism* (New York: Macmillan, 1902).

36 Herbert Croly, *Progressive Democracy* (New York: Macmillan, 1914), p. 19.

37 See, among many other sources, Mark Sullivan, *Our Times: The United States, 1900–1925,* vol. I (New York: Scribners, 1931), p. 530; and James D. Hart, *The Popular Book: A History of America's Literary Taste* (Berkeley: University of California Press, 1950), chaps. 11, 12.

38 Maurice Thompson, "The Prospect in Fiction," *The Independent,* vol. 52, no. 2685 (May 17, 1900), p. 1182.

39 Kenneth Lynn, *The Dream of Success: A Study of the Modern American Imagination* (Boston: Little, Brown, 1955), p. 151.

40 Eugene V. Debs, "Industrial Unionism," reprinted in *Eugene V. Debs Speaks,* ed. Jean Y. Tussey (New York: Pathfinder Press, 1972), pp. 132–133; paragraphing simplified.

41 Lawrence Goodwyn, *The Populist Moment: A Short History of the Agrarian Revolt in America* (New York: Oxford University Press, 1978), p. xi.

42 Ibid., p. 157.

43 Ibid., p. 270.

44 We shall discuss this argument again, in Chapter 6 and in Chapter 10.

45 David Graham Phillips, *The Price She Paid* (New York: Appleton, 1912), p. 97.

46 David Graham Phillips, *The Worth of a Woman* and *A Point of Law* (New York: Appleton, 1908), pp. 81–82.

47 Sacvan Bercovitch, *The American Jeremiad* (Madison: University of Wisconsin Press, 1978), p. 6.

Chapter 4. It couldn't happen here

1 David M. Parry, *The Scarlet Empire* (1906; rept., New York: Arno Press, 1971), p. 10.

2 Kenneth M. Roemer, *The Obsolete Necessity: America in Utopian Writing, 1888–1900* (Kent, Oh.: Kent State University Press, 1976), p. 3.

3 Mark Sullivan, *Our Times: The United States, 1900–1925,* vol. II (New York: Scribners, 1932), p. 328. See also Oscar Cargill, "A Robber Baron Revises *The Octopus,*" in *Toward a Pluralistic Criticism* (Carbondale: Southern Illinois University Press, 1965), pp. 118–130.

4 Mark Sullivan, *Our Times: The United States, 1900–1925,* vol. I (New York: Scribners, 1931), p. 373.

5 John L. Thomas, "Nationalizing the Republic, 1890–1920," in *The Great Republic,* Bernard Bailyn et al. (Boston: Little, Brown, 1977),p. 862.

6 The New York *Times* notice appeared on June 16, 1906, and the *Arena* review in the September issue.

7 Richard Hofstadter, *The Paranoid Style in American Politics and Other Essays* (Chicago: University of Chicago Press, 1965), p. 29.

8 Sidney Lens, *The Labor Wars: From the Molly Maguires to the Sitdowns* (Garden City, N.Y.: Anchor Books, 1977), p. 93.

9 Cited in Lens, *Labor Wars,* pp. 89–90.

10 John Graham Brooks, *American Syndicalism* (New York: Macmillan, 1913), p. 84.

11 Morris Hillquit, *History of Socialism in the United States* (New York: Funk and Wagnalls, 1903).

12 The best-informed guide to this history remains Daniel Bell's *Marxian Socialism in the United States* (1952; rept., Princeton, N.J.: Princeton University Press, 1973).

13 Cited in Bell, *Marxian Socialism,* p. 70.

14 William English Walling, *Socialism As It Is* (New York: Macmillan, 1912), pp. 175–203.

15 E. J. Hobsbawm, *The Age of Revolution, 1789–1848* (New York: New American Library, 1962), pp. 84–85.

16 Charlotte Teller, *The Cage* (New York: Appleton, 1907), p. 308.

17 Transcribed in Edwin Cady, *The Realist at War* (Syracuse, N.Y.: Syracuse University Press, 1958), p. 74.

18 Cited in Robert L. Hough, *The Quiet Rebel: William Dean Howells as Social Commentator* (Lincoln: University of Nebraska Press, 1959), p. 37.

19 Ibid., p. 63.

20 Kenneth Lynn, *William Dean Howells: An American Life* (New York: Harcourt Brace Jovanovich, 1970), p. 2

21 In a letter to William Cooper Howells, cited in Lynn, *Howells,* p. 295.

22 Lynn, *Howells,* p. 53.

23 Alfred Kazin, *On Native Grounds: An Interpretation of Modern American Prose Literature* (1942; rept., New York: Harcourt Brace Jovanovich, 1970), p. 110.

24 I shall have occasion again to comment on the persistence of Haymarket in the American imagination in Chapter 10. It suffices to remark here that *The Cage* takes a great historical liberty that nonetheless illustrates the potent significance of the episode and its perception as a climactic encounter in the struggle against industrial capitalism. Teller resolutely and unapologetically diverts Haymarket's anarchists into precursors and even allies of socialism.

25 Vol. 62 (March 7, 1907), p. 559.

26 Bullard, a prominent socialist, published this and several other books under the name Albert Edwards.

27 Arthur Bullard, *Comrade Yetta* (New York: Macmillan, 1913), p. 41.

28 Jack London, *John Barleycorn* (New York: Grosset and Dunlap, 1913). See Andrew Sinclair, *Jack: A Biography of Jack London* (New York: Harper and Row, 1977), p. 174.

29 The most useful comprehensive account of London's social views probably remains Philip S. Foner's *Jack London: American Rebel* (New York: Citadel Press, 1947).

30 Cited in Donald R. Glancy, "Socialist with a Valet: Jack London's 'First, Last, and Only' Lecture Tour," *Quarterly Journal of Speech,* vol. 49 (1963), p. 31.

31 *The Masses,* vol. X, nos. 1, 2 (November–December 1917), p. 17.

32 Citations from the speech are taken from the published version, in Jack London, *Revolution and Other Essays* (New York: Macmillan, 1910), pp. 3–38.

34 Charles Child Walcutt, "Jack London," in *Seven Novelists in the American Naturalist Tradition* ed. Walcutt (Minneapolis: University of Minnesota Press, 1974), p. 147.

35 Jack London, "The Dream of Debs," in *The Bodley Head Jack London,* vol. 1, ed. Arthur Calder-Marshall (London: Bodley Head, 1963), p. 246.

John Ames Mitchell's *The Silent War* (1906) bears interesting resemblances to "The Dream of Debs." Mitchell also combines radical indignation with a sympathetic rendering of capitalism. Mitchell creates a People's League, whose object is to take control – peacefully and politically – of the American government and to enact an equitable income tax. Mitchell's allegiance to the goals of the People's League is pronounced. But the plot he goes on to manufacture makes his ambivalence strikingly clear. The League is taken over by the murderous Committee of Seven, who replace electoral maneuvering with extortion and homicide. As in London, when the people actually organize themselves, they inevitably become dangerous and tyrannical. And, just as London's point of view in "The Dream of Debs" resides with a rich but decent man, so too Mitchell's hero, struggling against the barbaric Committee of Seven, is an honest, admirable millionaire.

36 London, "South of the Slot," in *Bodley Head Jack London*, vol. 1, p. 193.
37 Jack London, *Martin Eden* ed. Sam S. Baskett (1909; rept., New York: Holt, Rinehart, 1966), p. 245.
38 Cited in Baskett's Introduction to *Martin Eden*, p. vii.
39 Cited in Joan London, *Jack London and His Times* (New York: Doubleday, Doran, 1939), pp. 356–357.
40 Jack London, *The Assassination Bureau, Ltd.* [completed by Robert L. Fish] (New York: Penguin Books, 1978), p. 19.
41 Carolyn Willson, " 'Rattling the Bones': Jack London as Socialist Evangelist," *Western American Literature*, vol. 11 (1976), p. 136.
42 Ninetta Eames, "Haunts of Jack London," *Cosmopolitan* (December 1905), p. 230.
43 New York *Times Book Review* (February 7, 1915), p. 43; *The New Republic*, vol. II, no. 20 (March 20, 1915), p. 187; *The Outlook*, vol. 109 (March 3, 1915), p. 542; *Book News Monthly*, vol. 33 (August 1915), p. 565.
44 Joseph Freeman, *An American Testament* (New York: Farrar and Rinehart, 1936), p. 88.
45 Lewis Mumford, *The Golden Day: A Study in American Literature and Culture* (Boston: Beacon Press, 1957), p. ix.
46 John Hart, "Heroism through Social Awareness: Ernest Poole's *The Harbor*," *Critique*, vol. 9 (1967), p. 84.
47 Ernest Poole, *The Harbor* (New York: Macmillian, 1915), p. 5.
48 Maurice Beebe, *Ivory Towers and Sacred Founts: The Artist as Hero in Fiction from Goethe to Joyce* (New York: New York University Press, 1964), p. 114.
49 For a comment on the significance of this discrimination for literature, see Warner Berthoff, *The Ferment of Realism: American Literature, 1884–1919* (New York: Free Press, 1965), p. 28n.
50 Daniel Nelson, "The Making of a Progressive Engineer: Frederick W. Taylor," *The Pennsylvania Magazine of History and Biography*, vol. CIII, no. 4 (October 1979), p. 454.
51 On the subjects discussed here, see Robert H. Wiebe, *The Search for Order, 1877–1920* (New York: Hill and Wang, 1967), and Samuel Haber, *Efficiency and Uplift* (Chicago: University of Chicago Press, 1964).

52 More's review appeared in 1916; it was reprinted under the title "Economic Ideals" in *A New England Group and Others,* the eleventh series of Shelburne Essays (Boston: Houghton Mifflin, 1921). The citation is taken from the reprinted text, p. 242.

53 There is an interesting resemblance between this and the Jamesian dissolutions observed in Chapter 2. America's imperturbable political sluggishness apparently drives both right and left beyond frustration, toward figures (at least) of annihilation.

54 Ernest Poole, *The Bridge* (New York: Macmillan, 1940), p. 259.

55 Irving Howe, *World of Our Fathers: The Journey of the East European Jews to America and the Life They Found and Made* (New York: Simon and Schuster, 1976), p. 323.

56 Kazin, *On Native Grounds,* p. 120.

57 This is not to deny the book's dramatic problems. Walter B. Rideout has adroitly traced *The Jungle's* modulation from "fiction toward another kind of statement." What begins in rich confusion and complexity ends as tract (*The Radical Novel in the United States, 1900–1954* [Cambridge, Mass.: Harvard University Press, 1956], pp. 35–36).

Chapter 5. On being black

1 Dudley Randall, "Booker T. and W.E.B.," in *Poem Counterpoem* (Detroit: Broadside Press, 1966), p. 8. Courtesy of Dudley Randall.

2 Theodore Rosengarten, *All God's Dangers: The Life of Nate Shaw* (New York: Knopf, 1975),p. 543.

3 W. E. B. Du Bois, "The Evolution of Negro Leadership," *Dial,* vol. XXXI (July 1, 1901), pp. 53–55.

4 Arthur Wallace Dunn, *From Harrison to Harding,* vol. 1 (1922; rept., Port Washington, N.Y.: Kennikat Press, 1971), p. 358.

5 Booker T. Washington, *Up from Slavery* (1901; rept., Garden City, N.Y.: Doubleday, Doran, 1944), p. 10.

6 William Bradford, *History of Plimoth Plantation* (Boston: Wright, 1898), pp. 90–91.

7 W. E. B. Du Bois, *The Souls of Black Folk* (1903; rept., Millwood, N.Y.: Kraus-Thomson Organization, 1973), p. 43.

8 Ralph Ellison, "Hidden Name and Complex Fate," in *Shadow and Act* (New York: New American Library, 1966), pp. 148–168.

9 Stephen Jay Gould, *Ever since Darwin* (New York: Norton, 1977), p. 208.

10 Relevant portions of Engels's essay are reprinted in Lee Baxandall and Stefan Morawski, eds., *Marx and Engels on Literature and Art* (St. Louis: Telos Press, 1973), pp. 54–56.

11 Ibid.

12 August Meier, *Negro Thought in America, 1880–1915* (Ann Arbor: University of Michigan Press, 1966), p. 114. See also Donald J. Callista, "Booker T. Washington: Another Look," *Journal of Negro History,* vol. XLIX, no. 4 (1964), pp. 240–255.

13 Sacvan Bercovitch, *The Puritan Origins of the American Self* (New Haven: Yale University Press, 1975).

14 Sterling Brown, "Negro Poetry and Drama," ed. Robert Bone (1937; rept., New York: Atheneum, 1969), p. 113. Gilbert Osofsky's enumeration of turn-of-the-century comedies recalls the abusive norms that obtained in theatrical presentations of black people on the American stage. *The Coon at the Door, The Coon Musketeers, Dat Famous Chicken Debate* ("Resolved, That Stealing Chickens Ain't No Crime"), *Dat Watermillyun, The Coonville 'Ristocrat Club, The Coon and the Chink, Jes' Like White Folks, In Bandanna Land* – these and others like them were successful, profitable comedies. They were populated by characters with names like Doolittle Black, Pompey Ducklegs, Useless Peabody, Moses Abraham Highbrow, and Julius Crow (Gilbert Osofsky, *Harlem: The Making of a Ghetto,* 2d ed. [New York: Harper and Row, 1971], pp. 38–39).

15 Robert Sheldon, *The Nigger* (New York: Macmillan, 1910), p. 81.

16 Joseph Wood Krutch, "Eugene O'Neill," in *Literary History of the United States,* ed. Robert E. Spiller et al. 4th ed. (New York: Macmillan, 1974), p. 1237.

17 Sterling Brown, "Negro Character as Seen by White Authors," *Journal of Negro Education,* vol. II (April 1933), pp. 179–203.

18 Ben B. Lindsey and Harvey O'Higgins, "The Beast and the Jungle" (1909), reprinted in *Years of Conscience: The Muckrakers,* ed. Harvey Swados (New York: World Publishing, 1962), p. 43.

19 William Archer, *Through Afro-America* (1910; rept., Westport, Conn.: Negro Universities Press, 1970), pp. 25–26.

20 Thomas Nelson Page, *The Negro: The Southerner's Problem* (1904; rept., New York: Johnson Reprint Co., 1970), pp. 100, 114.

21 Archer, *Through Afro-America,* p. 24.

22 William Jennings Bryan, "The Race Problem" (1903), reprinted in *William Jennings Bryan: Selections,* ed. Ray Ginger (Indianapolis: Bobbs-Merrill, 1967), p. 70.

23 Cited in C. Vann Woodward, *Tom Watson: Agrarian Rebel* (1938; rept., New York: Oxford University Press, 1969), p. 432.

24 Brown, "Negro Character," pp. 194–195.

25 W. E. B. Du Bois, "The Study of the Negro Problems" (1898), reprinted in *W.E.B. Du Bois Speaks: Speeches and Addresses, 1890–1919,* ed. Philip S. Foner (New York: Pathfinder Press, 1970), p. 111.

26 Du Bois, "Study of the Negro Problems," p. 116.

27 W. E. B. Du Bois, "A Pageant in Seven Decades," in *W. E. B. Du Bois Speaks,* ed. Foner, p. 37.

28 Gertrude Himmelfarb, *Darwin and the Darwinian Revolution* (New York: Norton, 1968), p. 432.

29 Frank L. Baum, Introduction to *The Magic of Oz* (Chicago: Reilly and Lee, 1919), p. 11.

30 See, among other sources, Richard Hofstadter, *Social Darwinism in American Thought,* rev. ed. (Boston: Beacon Press, 1955), esp. Chap. 9, and Thomas

F. Gossett, *Race: The History of an Idea in America* (New York: Schocken Books, 1965), esp. chap. 11.

31 Nathaniel S. Shaler, "European Peasants as Immigrants," *The Atlantic Monthly,* vol. XXXVII (May 1893), pp. 646–655. Though his subject is European immigration, Shaler cannot resist several abusive asides directed toward American Negroes.

32 Franz Boas, "Race Problems in America," *Science,* vol. XXIX (May 28, 1909), pp. 839–849; first delivered as an address to the American Association for the Advancement of Science, Baltimore, 1908.

33 The ninth, tenth, and eleventh editions span the years from 1875 to 1920; for most purposes, the tenth edition was a reissue of the ninth.

34 A. H. Keane, "Negro," *The Encyclopedia Britannica,* 9th ed., vol. XVII (Philadelphia: Stoddart, 1884), pp. 325–326. The eleventh edition was slightly more tentative in its racism than its predecessors had been and slightly more cautious in its deployment of quantitative "proof." The conclusions of W. F. Willcox in the eleventh edition about black inferiority are nonetheless indistinguishable from those propounded in the ninth edition by A. H. Keane: "The negro would appear to stand on a lower evolutionary plane than the white man, and to be more closely related to the highest anthropoids. . . . Mentally the negro is inferior to the white. . . . The arrest or even deterioration in mental development is no doubt very largely due to the fact that after puberty sexual matters take the first place in the negro's life and thoughts" (Walter Francis Willcox, "Negro," *The Encyclopedia Britannica,* 11th ed., vol. XIX [New York: Encyclopedia Britannica, 1911], p. 344).

35 See Raymond Williams, *Keywords: A Vocabulary of Culture and Society* (New York: Oxford University Press, 1976), pp. 226–230.

36 The "scientific" dogma of inequality was widely circulated through a large number of popularizations published during these years. Such books as William P. Calhoun's *The Caucasian and the Negro* (1902), Carlyle McKinley's *Appeal to Pharaoh* (1907), Robert Wilson Schufeldt's *The Negro* (1907), and William Pickett's *The Negro Problem* (1909) all retailed in one form or another the vulgar gospel of white supremacy.

37 Winthrop Jordan, *White over Black: American Attitudes toward the Negro, 1550–1812* (Baltimore: Penguin Books, 1969), esp. pp. 3–43. See also George M. Frederickson, *The Black Image in the White Mind: The Debate on Afro-American Character and Destiny, 1817–1914* (New York: Harper and Row, 1971); chaps. 8–10 are particularly relevant to our purposes.

38 Dunbar's novel *The Sport of the Gods* (1902) is regarded as the first serious and extended treatment of black life in New York; the seriousness is attenuated by the book's plantation overtones. See Eugene Arden, "The Early Harlem Novel," in *Images of the Negro in American Literature,* ed. Seymour L. Gross and John Edward Hardy (Chicago: University of Chicago Press, 1966), pp. 106–114.

39 See Francis E. Kearns, ed., *The Black Experience* (New York: Viking Press, 1970), p. 282.

40 Charles Waddell Chesnutt, *The House behind the Cedars* (1900) (New York: Collier Books, 1969), p. 239.

41 Du Bois, *Souls of Black Folk*, p. 3.

42 Henry James paid grudging, condescending tribute to the book when he asked: "How can everything so have gone that the only 'Southern' book of any distinction published for many a year is *The Souls of Black Folk*, by that most accomplished of members of the negro race, Mr. W. E. B. Du Bois?"(*The American Scene* [1907; rept., Bloomington: Indiana University Press, 1968], p. 418). James may have offered a more significant though unacknowledged homage in the organizing rhetoric of *The American Scene*. We examined at the end of Chapter 2 James's speculations on the connection between fences and civilized decency. Just before he wrote those paragraphs, James may have read these lines (in which Du Bois is trying to sort out for himself the joyless poverty of the rural Black Belt): "There is little beauty in this region, only a sort of crude abandon that suggests power, – a naked grandeur, as it were. . . . I think I never before quite realized the place of the Fence in civilization. This is the Land of the Unfenced. . . . Here lies the Negro problem in its naked dirt and penury. And here are no fences. But now and then the criss-cross rails or straight palings break into view, and then we know a touch of culture is near" (*Souls*, p. 120).

43 Charles Crowe, "Racial Massacre in Atlanta, September 22, 1906," reprinted in *The Segregation Era, 1863–1954*, ed. Allen Weinstein and Frank Otto Gatell (New York: Oxford University Press, 1970), p. 113.

44 See W. E. B. Du Bois, "The Souls of White Folk," in *Darkwater: Voices from within the Veil* (New York: Harcourt, Brace, 1921), pp. 29–52.

45 Meier, *Negro Thought in America*, pp. 110–111. The quotations from Du Bois in this paragraph are from *Souls of Black Folk*, pp. 203, 109.

46 Arnold Rampersad, *The Art and Imagination of W. E. B. Du Bois* (Cambridge, Mass.: Harvard University Press, 1976), pp. 170–174.

47 W. E. B. Du Bois, *The Quest of the Silver Fleece* (Chicago: McClurg and Co., 1911), p. 75.

48 A passage like this suggests the probable influence of Norris and his "epic of the wheat" upon both the symbolism and the rhetoric of *The Quest*.

Chapter 6. Woman's place

1 Eleanor Flexner, *Century of Struggle: The Woman's Rights Movement in the United States*, rev. ed. (Cambridge, Mass.: Harvard University Press, 1975), chap. XIX, pp. 256–270.

2 Cited in Samuel P. Hays, *The Response to Industrialism: 1885–1914* (Chicago: University of Chicago Press, 1971), p. 73.

3 This action provided some of the background for Arthur Bullard's *Comrade Yetta*, discussed in Chapter 4, this volume.

4 Margaret Sanger, *Family Limitation*, 5th ed. (New York: n.p., 1916), p. 3.

5 These were some of the women who worked on the important congressional study "Report on the Condition of Woman and Child Wage-Earners

in the United States," 19 vols. (Washington, D.C.: Government Printing Office, 1910–1911). Elizabeth Lewis Otley prepared vol. VI, *The Beginnings of Child Labor Legislation in Certain States; a Comparative Study* (1910). Helen L. Sumner prepared vol. IX, *History of Women in Industry in the United States* (1910). Mary Conyngton prepared vol. XV, *Relations between Occupation and Criminality of Women* (1911).

6　Alice Rossi, *The Feminist Papers: From Adams to Beauvoir* (New York: Columbia University Press, 1973), p. 568.

7　Charlotte Perkins Gilman, *Women and Economics* (Boston: Small, Maynard, 1898), p. 174.

8　These passages are taken from Charlotte Perkins Gilman, *His Religion and Hers: A Study of the Faith of Our Fathers and the Work of Our Mothers* (1923). They are cited in Mary A. Hill, *Charlotte Perkins Gilman: The Making of a Radical Feminist, 1860–1896* (Philadelphia: Temple University Press, 1980), p. 269.

9　See Carl N. Degler, "Revolution without Ideology: The Changing Place of Women in America," in *The Woman in America*, ed. Robert Jay Lifton (Boston: Houghton Mifflin, 1965), pp. 193–210.

10　Gilman, *Women and Economics,* p. 168.

11　Winifred Kirkland, "The Joys of Being a Woman," *The Unpopular Review*, vol. VI, no. 11 (July–September 1916), pp. 44–57.

12　Mrs. S.P. Ravenel, "The Eternal Feminine," *The Unpopular Review*, vol. VI, no. 12 (October–December 1916), pp. 348–366.

13　See Jill Conway, "Jane Addams: An American Heroine," in Lifton, ed., *Woman in America*, pp. 247–266.

14　Allen F. Davis, *Spearheads for Reform: the Social Settlements and the Progressive Movement, 1890–1914* (New York: Oxford University Press, 1967).

15　Cited in Davis, *Spearheads for Reform*, p. 243.

16　In Margaret Tims, *Jane Addams of Hull House, 1860–1935* (New York: Macmillan, 1961), p. 49.

17　Jill Conway, "Women Reformers and American Culture, 1870–1930," *Journal of Social History*, vol. 5, no. 2 (Winter 1971–1972), p. 167. See also William H. Chafe, *Women and Equality: Changing Patterns in American Culture* (New York: Oxford University Press, 1977), pp. 39–42.

18　Kate Chopin, *The Awakening* (1899; rept., New York: Norton, 1976), p. 8.

19　See, for example, George M. Spangler, "Kate Chopin's *The Awakening:* A Partial Dissent," *Novel*, vol. III (Spring 1970), pp. 249–255.

20　Ellen Glasgow, *Virginia* (1913; rept., Garden City, N.Y.: Doubleday/Old Dominion Edition, 1929), p. 474.

21　Louis Auchincloss, *Ellen Glasgow* (Minneapolis: University of Minnesota Press, 1964), p. 6.

22　In her autobiography, Glasgow cast a complementary but harsher light on her attitudes toward her region. "It may be an unrecognized law or our nature that we should be drawn back, inevitably, to the place where we have suffered most" (*The Woman Within* [New York: Harcourt, Brace, 1954], p. 209).

23 Edith Wharton, *A Backward Glance* (New York: Appleton-Century, 1934), p. 5.

24 Edith Wharton, *French Ways and Their Meaning* (New York: Appleton-Century, 1919), p. 97.

25 Edith Wharton, *A Motor-Flight through France* (New York: Scribners, 1908), pp. 28–29.

26 Edith Wharton, "Souls Belated," in *The Greater Inclination* (New York: Scribners, 1899), pp. 83–84.

27 Wharton, *A Backward Glance,* p. 207.

28 Edith Wharton, *The House of Mirth* (1905; rept., New York: New American Library, 1964), p. 131.

29 See Chapter 2, this volume. See also Cynthia Griffin Wolff's brilliant analysis of this scene in *A Feast of Words: The Truimph of Edith Wharton* (New York: Oxford University Press, 1977), pp. 112–133.

30 James Lomax and Richard Ormond, *John Singer Sargent and the Edwardian Age,* exhibition catalogue (London: Leeds Art Galleries and the National Portrait Gallery, 1979), pp. 65, 68.

31 Edith Wharton, *The Custom of the Country* (1913; rept., New York: Scribners, 1956), p. 578.

32 Henry James, *The American Scene,* ed. Leon Edel (1907; rept., Bloomington: Indiana University Press, 1968), p. 102.

33 On a grander scale, Undine rather recalls Sir A. B. C. Beadel-Muffett, K.C.B., M.P., James's portrait of the twentieth-century celebrity in "The Papers."

34 Frank Norris, *The Responsibilities of the Novelist* (1903; rept., New York: Greenwood Press, 1968), p. 69.

35 Cleanth Brooks, R. W. B. Lewis, and Robert Penn Warren, *American Literature: The Makers and the Making, Book C: 1861–1914* (New York, 1974), p. 1594.

36 Cynthia Griffin Wolff's commentary on this novel includes an illuminating discussion of the Jacobean source of Wharton's title. *The Custom of the Country,* a play by John Fletcher and Philip Massinger, tells of a land where women, upon their betrothal, are offered as property at public auction. Wolff quotes a key passage from the play: "O the wicked Custom of this Country,/ The barbarous, most inhumane, damned Custom./ . . . That when a Maid is contracted/ And ready to the tye o' th' Church, the Governour,/ He that commands in chief, must have her Maiden-head,/ Or Ransom it for money at his pleasure./ . . . all/ Your sad misfortunes had original/ From the barbarous Custom practis'd in my Country." This is a world, as Wolff, puts it, "whose moral center has been lost – a world where everything is for sale. A world like that of Wharton's novel" (*A Feast of Words,* p. 247).

        The novel appeared in 1913. In that same year, George J. Kneeland published *Commercialized Prostitution in New York City,* an attempt, according to the Introduction by John D. Rockefeller, Jr., to set forth "as accurately and fully as possible the conditions of vice," to provide a "dispassionate, objective account of things as they were" ([New York: Century Company, 1913], p. x).

Kneeland's book is a sordid encyclopedia of data that he accumulated in a year-long, street-by-street survey. Along with his dreary revelations about methods and prices, drugs and disease, Kneeland records some of the metaphorical language in which the trade expressed itself: "A madame who conducts a prosperous business in a tenement in West 58th Street sends a letter to her former customers announcing the removal of the 'library.' The use of the word 'library' to indicate the resort and of 'books' to indicate inmates is a popular one. Another madame urges her former patrons to renew their 'membership in the library'; 'new books,' she asserts, are 'on file in our new quarters' " (pp. 27–28).

Chapter 7. Building the past and the future

1 Henry-Russell Hitchcock and Philip Johnson, *The International Style: Architecture since 1922* (New York: Norton, 1932), p. 19.
2 Frank Lloyd Wright, *An Autobiography* (New York: Horizon Press, 1977), p. 175.
3 Brooks Adams, *The New Empire* (1902; rpt., Cleveland, Oh.: Frontier Press, 1967), p. xxix.
4 Henry-Russell Hitchcock, *Painting toward Architecture* (New York: Duell, Sloan and Pierce, 1948), p. 17.
5 Lewis Mumford, *Roots of Contemporary American Architecture* (New York: Reinhold, 1952), p. 14.
6 This paragraph summarizes information provided in Marcus Whiffen's superb survey, *American Architecture since 1780: A Guide to the Styles* (Cambridge, Mass.: MIT Press, 1969), esp. pp. 147–171.
7 George Santayana, "The Genteel Tradition in American Philosophy," in *Winds of Doctrine* (New York: Scribners, 1912), p. 188.
8 David Watkin, *Morality and Architecture: The Development of a Theme in Architectural History and Theory from the Gothic Revival to the Modern Movement* (Oxford: Oxford University Press, 1977), p. 17.
9 Cited in Watkin, *Morality and Architecture*, p. 19.
10 Frank Lloyd Wright, Preface to *Ausgeführte Bauten und Entwürfe;* reprinted as "The Sovereignty of the Individual," in *Frank Lloyd Wright: Writings and Buildings,* ed. Edgar Kaufmann and Ben Braeburn (New York: Meridian Books, 1960), pp. 94–95.
11 Thorstein Veblen, *The Theory of the Leisure Class* (1899; rpt., New York: Huebsch, 1918), pp. 153, 154.
12 Mumford, *Contemporary American Architecture,* p. 7.
13 Walter C. Kidney, *The Architecture of Choice: Eclecticism in America, 1880–1930* (New York: Braziller, 1974), p. 7.
14 Cited in Charles C. Baldwin, *Stanford White* (New York: Dodd, Mead, 1931), p. 363.
15 Kidney, *Architecture of Choice,* p. 3.

16 Ralph Adams Cram, *My Life in Architecture* (Boston: Little, Brown, 1936), p. 105.
17 Whiffen, *American Architecture since 1780*, p. 176.
18 Cram, *My Life*, p. 17.
19 Ralph Adams Cram, *The Gothic Quest* (New York: Baker and Taylor, 1907), p. 23.
20 Ibid., p. 22.
21 Ibid., p. 27.
22 Ibid., p. 155.
23 Cram, *My Life*, pp. 28–29.
24 Ibid., p. 275.
25 See chap. VI of Cram's *The Substance of Gothic* (Boston: Jones, 1917).
26 Cram, *Gothic Quest*, p. 45.
27 Cram, *My Life*, p. 37.
28 Cram, *Gothic Quest*, p. 60. Like so many other artists of his generation, Cram had his Japanese interlude. He traveled in Japan, admired its "ancient and august civilization," published on Japanese art, and designed an unbuilt project for the new Japanese parliament houses.
29 Cram, *My Life*, p. 182.
30 Montgomery Schuyler, "Architecture of American Colleges: No. 3, Princeton," *The Architectural Record*, vol. XXVII, no. 2 (February 1910), pp. 148–149.
31 Cram, *Gothic Quest*, pp. 73, 74, 75.
32 Ibid., p. 40.
33 Cram, *My Life*, p. 20.
34 Ibid., p. 306.
35 Cram, "The Development of Ecclesiastical Architecture in England," in *Gothic Quest*, p. 117. The essay was originally published in 1905.
36 In Chapter 3, p. 81–2, this volume.
37 Cram, *Gothic Quest*, pp. 176, 177.
38 Cram, *My Life*, pp. 249–250.
39 Peter Davey, *Architecture of the Arts and Crafts Movement* (New York: Rizzoli, 1980), p. 52.
40 *A Handbook of Information concerning the Cathedral-Church of Bryn Athyn, Pennsylvania*, 9th ed. (Bryn Athyn, Pa.: General Church Book Center, 1967), pp. 4–5.
41 See John Dos Passos, *Mr. Wilson's War* (Garden City, N.Y.: Doubleday, 1962), pp. 39–40.
42 Cram, *My Life*, p. 121.
43 Cited in Royal Cortissoz, *John La Farge: A Memoir and a Study* (Boston: Houghton Mifflin, 1911), pp. 68–69.
44 See, in Chapter 5, p. 146–7, this volume, the discussion of the tournament.
45 Robert Judson Clark, ed., *The Arts and Crafts Movement in America, 1876–1916* (Princeton, N. J.: Princeton University Press, 1972).
46 In Ralph Barton Perry, *The Thought and Character of William James,* briefer version (New York: Harper Torchbooks, 1964), p. 240.

47 See Calvin Tomkins, *Merchants and Masterpieces: The Story of the Metropolitan Museum of Art* (New York: Dutton, 1970), pp. 245-261.

48 Henry Adams, *Mont-Saint-Michel and Chartres* (1913; rept., Garden City, N.Y.: Anchor Books, 1959), p. 106.

49 Cram, *My Life,* p. 226.

50 See Wayne Andrews, *American Gothic: Its Origins, Its Trials, Its Triumphs* (New York: Random House, 1975).

51 Adams, *The New Empire,* p. xxix.

52 Russell Sturgis, "The Warehouse and the Factory in America," pt. 1, *The Architectural Record,* vol. XV, no. 1 (January 1904), pp. 1, 2.

53 Russell Sturgis, "The Warehouse and the Factory in America," pt. 2, *The Architectural Record,* vol. XV, no. 2 (February 1904), p. 133.

54 Peter Bonnett Wight, "Utilitarian Architecture at Chicago," *The Architectural Record,* vol. XXVII, no. 2 (February 1910), p. 190.

55 Ibid., p. 192.

56 John Burchard and Albert Bush-Brown, *The Architecture of America: A Social and Cultural History* (Boston: Little, Brown, 1961), p. 242. My entire discussion of industrial architecture is indebted to this compendious and useful study.

57 Cited in W. Hawkins Ferry, "Albert Kahn, 1869-1942," in *The Legacy of Albert Kahn,* ed. William A. Bostick (Detroit: Detroit Institute of Arts, 1970), p. 11.

58 Ibid., p. 11.

59 Cited in *Albert Kahn: Architect Abroad* (Ann Arbor: University of Michigan Press, 1973), p. 7.

60 Cited in *The Legacy of Albert Kahn,* p. 19.

61 Hitchcock, *Painting toward Architecture,* p. 20.

62 Nikolaus Pevsner, *Pioneers of the Modern Movement from William Morris to Walter Gropius* (London: Faber and Faber, 1936), p. 34.

63 Hitchcock, *Painting toward Architecture,* p. 20.

64 Vincent Scully, Jr., *Frank Lloyd Wright* (New York: Braziller, 1960), pp. 13-14.

65 Henry-Russell Hitchcock, *In the Nature of Materials* (New York: Duell, Sloan and Pierce, 1942).

66 Peter Collins, *Changing Ideals in Modern Architecture, 1750-1950* (Montreal: McGill University Press, 1965), pp. 286-287. See also Vincent Scully, Jr., *Modern Architecture: The Architecture of Democracy* (New York: Braziller, 1961), pp. 19-22.

67 E. Baldwin Smith, Preface to Frank Lloyd Wright, *Modern Architecture: Being the Kahn Lectures for 1930* (Princeton, N.J.: Princeton University Press, 1931), n.p.

68 Wright, *Modern Architecture,* p. 8.

69 This passage is taken from the first full reprinting of the 1901 version of the lecture, in Kaufmann and Braeburn, eds., *Wright: Writings and Buildings,* p. 55. Wright claimed to his audience in 1930 that he was literally rereading the text of the earlier speech: "Here is the manuscript. We will begin, twenty-

seven years later, again" (p. 7). Despite this statement, the 1930 text differs at nearly every point from that of 1901, and I shall suggest later some of the reasons for the changes. Both texts will be cited in the following discussion; they will be distinguished as "Hull House" and "Princeton," respectively.

70 Frank Lloyd Wright, "In the Cause of Architecture," *The Architectural Record,* vol. XXIII, no. 3 (March 1908). Reprinted in Frederick Gutheim, ed., *In the Cause of Architecture* (New York: Architectural Record Books, 1975), p. 61.

71 H. H. Arnason, *History of Modern Art* (Englewood Cliffs, N.J.: Prentice-Hall, 1968), pp. 145–146.

72 Frank Lloyd Wright, from *The Living City,* reprinted in Kaufmann and Braeburn, eds., *Wright: Writings and Buildings,* p. 261.

73 See Robert C. Twombly, *Frank Lloyd Wright: His Life and His Architecture* (New York: Wiley, 1979), pp. 37–38.

74 Wright, *An Autobiography,* p. 174.

75 Cited in Burchard and Bush-Brown, *Architecture of America,* p. 261.

76 Vincent Scully, Jr., *American Architecture and Urbanism* (New York: Praeger, 1969), p. 123.

77 Wright, *An Autobiography,* p. 194.

78 See Wright's comments on Unity Temple in *An Autobiography,* p. 178. On Ruskin's views, see Kristine Ottesen Garrigan, *Ruskin on Architecture: His Thought and Influence* (Madison: University of Wisconsin Press, 1973), esp. chaps. 2, 3.

79 John D. Rosenberg, *The Darkening Glass: A Portrait of Ruskin's Genius* (New York: Columbia University Press, 1961), p. 71.

80 Wright, "The Sovereignty of the Individual," p. 89.

81 Ibid.

82 Scully, *American Architecture and Urbanism,* p. 185.

83 Wright, *Modern Architecture,* p. 77.

84 Wright, "Sovereignty of the Individual," p. 93.

Chapter 8. Innovation and nostalgia

1 Charles Ives, *Essays before a Sonata and Other Writings,* ed. Howard Boatwright (New York: Norton, 1962), p. 123.

2 Henry Cowell and Sidney Cowell, *Charles Ives and His Music* (New York: Oxford University Press, 1955), p. 72.

3 Charles Ives, *Memos,* ed. John Kirkpatrick (New York: Norton, 1972), p. 114.

4 Ives, *Memos,* p. 115.

5 For these anecdotes and others, see "Some Quarter-Tone Impressions" in Ives, *Essays,* pp. 110–111.

6 Ives, *Memos,* p. 45.

7 Ibid., p. 115.

8 Ibid., p. 116.

9 Ibid., p. 116.

10 Ibid., p. 49.
11 From an interview with Myrick, included in app. 18 of Ives, *Memos*, p. 269.
12 Cowell and Cowell, *Ives and His Music*, pp. 53–54n.
13 Cited in Cowell and Cowell, *Ives and His Music*, p. 48.
14 Ives, *Memos*, pp. 55–56. See Allen Forte's fine analysis, "Ives and Atonality," in *An Ives Celebration*, ed. H. Wiley Hitchcock and Vivian Perlis (Urbana: University of Illinois Press, 1977), pp. 159–186.
15 Cited in Cowell and Cowell, *Ives and His Music*, p. 136.
16 Ives, *Memos*, p. 138.
17 Ibid., p. 28. The reference is to Philip Hale, music critic for the Boston *Herald*, who reviewed a performance of *Three Places in New England* in 1931.
18 Transcribed in David Wooldridge, *From the Steeples and Mountains: A Study of Charles Ives* (New York: Knopf, 1974), p. 174.
19 Cited in Cowell and Cowell, *Ives and His Music*, p. 97.
20 See Chapter 3, p. 64, this volume.
21 Ives, *Essays*, p. 28.
22 Ibid., p. 62.
23 Cited in Cowell and Cowell, *Ives and His Music*, p. 59.
24 Ives, *Essays*, p. 160.
25 Transcribed in Wooldridge, *From the Steeples and Mountains*, p. 176.
26 See Robert M. Crunden, "Charles Ives's Place in American Thought," in *An Ives Celebration*, ed. Hitchcock and Perlis, pp. 4–15.
27 Ives, *Essays*, pp. 184, 186.
28 Ibid., p. 62.
29 Ibid., p. 80.
30 Cited in H. Wiley Hitchcock, *Ives* (New York: Oxford University Press, 1977), p. 75.
31 Hitchcock, *Ives*, p. 75.
32 Ives, *Essays*, p. 128.
33 Ibid., p. 189.
34 Ives, *Memos*, p. 133.
35 Transcribed in Wooldridge, *From the Steeples and Mountains*, p. 158.
36 Ives, *Essays*, p. 13.
37 A different perspective on Ives's work – which would anchor a different essay than this one – would attend to his pioneering use of American musical materials at a time when such materials were almost universally assumed to lie beneath serious artistic notice.
38 Ives, *Essays*, p. 23.
39 Ibid., p. 36.
40 Ibid., p. 39.
41 Ibid., p. 48.
42 Ibid., p. 67. The reference is to the death of Ives's father.
43 Interview in Vivian Perlis, *Charles Ives Remembered: An Oral History* (New Haven, Conn.: Yale University Press, 1974), p. 74.
44 Ives, *Memos*, p. 130.
45 Ibid., p. 95.

46 Cited in Hitchcock, *Ives,* p. 73.
47 Cited in Rosalie Sandra Perry, *Charles Ives and the American Mind* (Kent, Oh.: Kent State University Press, 1974), p. 92.
48 Ives, *Memos,* p. 97.
49 The useful phrase comes from an article by Robert M. Crunden, "Charles Ives' Innovative Nostalgia," *The Choral Journal* (December 1974), pp. 5–12.
50 Ives, *Memos,* pp. 28, 30. "Rollo" was Ives's imaginary nemesis; he appears regularly in Ives's prose, always as the small-minded and dull adversary.
51 The series of quotations is from Ives, *Memos,* pp. 141n, 134, 133, 134.
52 Ibid., pp. 135, 134, 41, 131, 41.
53 Ives, *Memos,* p. 44n.
54 Ives, *Essays,* p. 84.
55 Ives, *Memos,* p. 132.
56 Frank Rossiter, *Charles Ives and His America* (New York: Liveright, 1975), p. 320.
57 Terry Eagleton, *Marxism and Literary Criticism* (Berkeley: University of California Press, 1976), p. 8.
58 The "Founding and Manifesto of Futurism" announced, "We will glorify war – the world's only hygiene – militarism, patriotism" (February 20, 1909). The manifesto also committed the futurists – logically if nonetheless viciously – to "scorn for women." For a discussion of the developing attitudes of the group to women, see Caroline Tisdall and Angelo Bozzolla, *Futurism* (New York: Oxford University Press, 1977), chap. 8.
59 See Tisdall and Bozzolla, *Futurism,* pp. 163, 200–209. H. H. Arnason surely over-rates the political significance of the movement when he accuses it of serving as "a pillar of Italian fascism" (*History of Modern Art* [Englewood Cliffs, N.J.: Prentice-Hall, 1968], p. 212).
60 The series of quotations in this paragraph is from Ives, *Essays,* p. 99; *Memos,* pp. 135, 134–135; and *Essays,* p. 97.

Chapter 9. Realism and modernism

1 Bruce St. John, ed., *John Sloan's New York Scene: From the Diaries, Notes and Correspondence, 1906–1913* (New York: Harper and Row, 1965), p. 258.
2 Cited in Frederick A. Sweet, *Miss Mary Cassatt* (Norman: University of Oklahoma Press, 1966), p. 196. See also James R. Mellow, *Charmed Circle: Gertrude Stein and Company* (New York: Avon Books, 1975), pp. 25–26.
3 Hilton Kramer, "Shedding Fresh Light on the Art of Kandinsky," *New York Times,* sect. 2 (January 17, 1982), p. 1.
4 Paul Schweizer et al., "The Rise of the Avant-Garde in America," in *Avant-Garde Painting and Sculpture in America, 1910–1925* (Wilmington: Delaware Art Museum, 1975), p. 9.
5 Milton W. Browne, *American Painting from the Armory Show to the Depression* (Princeton, N.J.: Princeton University Press, 1955), p. 103.
6 *New York Scene,* p. 288.

7 John McCoubrey, *American Tradition in Painting* (New York: Braziller, 1963), p. 43.

8 Lloyd Goodrich, *John Sloan* (New York: Macmillan, 1952), p. 5.

9 Van Wyck Brooks, *John Sloan: A Painter's Life* (New York: Dutton, 1955), p. 43.

10 Mahonri Sharp Young, *The Realist Revolt in American Painting* (New York: Watson-Guptill, 1973), p. 143.

11 John C. Van Dyke, *American Painting and Its Tradition* (New York: Scribners, 1919), p. v.

12 Chase was actually the eleventh member of the Ten, replacing Twachtman after the latter's death in 1902.

13 Henry James, "The Madonna of the Future" (1874), in *The Complete Tales of Henry James,* vol. III, ed. Leon Edel (Philadelphia: Lippincott, 1962), p. 15.

14 *New York Scene,* p. 270.

15 Ibid., pp. 183, 166.

16 Kenyon Cox, *The Classic Point of View* (1911; rept., New York: Norton, 1980), p. 23.

17 Cox was by no means alone in his admiration of Blashfield's achievement. William Walton praised Blashfield's ability to mingle "realistic or historic personages" with "abstractons and personifications" and to do so "without apparent incongruity." The Washington panel, according to Walton, is "very luminous and beautiful in color. . . . In the center, throned high against a baldachin, like many a gentle Renaissance Madonna, sits Columbia or *Patria,* the saints and supporters below being quite adequately replaced by the various graceful personifications appropriate to the theme, among which appears, quite prominently at the right, Washington, in full Continental costume, and very dignified and appropriate." And so on. (William Walton, "Recent Mural Decorations by Mr. E. H. Blashfield," *Scribner's Magazine,* vol. XXXVII, no. 3 [March 1905], p. 382).

18 Patricia Jobe Pierce, *The Ten* (Concord, N.H.: Rumford Press, 1976), p. 3.

19 Cited in Bennard B. Perlman, *The Immortal Eight: American Painting from Eakins to the Armory Show* (New York: Exposition Press, 1962), p. 143.

20 Theodore Roosevelt, "Dante and the Bowery," in *Literary Essays,* vol. XIV of *The Works of Theodore Roosevelt* (New York: Scribners, 1924), pp. 439–440. The essay was first published in *The Outlook* (August 26, 1911).

   Edgar Saltus published a rhapsodical account of the architecture of New York in *Munsey's Magazine* in 1905. It opens with this dialogue between imaginary tourists:

   " 'What do you know of New York?' said one wanderer to another.
   " 'Only what I have read in Dante,' was the bleak reply."

   Saltus corrects the tone of the respondent with the comment, "Dante told of the inferno. He told, too, of paradise. Manhattan may typify both" (Edgar Saltus, "The Most Extraordinary Panorama in the World," *Munsey's Magazine,* vol. XXXIII, no. 4 [July 1905], p. 381).

   Perhaps Roosevelt had read the Saltus piece. In any case, the two citations suggest that this Dantesque vocabulary – with its intimations of urban sublimity – was current during Sloan's first years in New York.

21 *New York Scene*, p. 283.

22 Cited in Charles H. Morgan, *George Bellows, Painter of America* (New York: Reynal, 1965), p. 70. Recall the similar attacks on fictional realism quoted in Chapter 3, p. 72, this volume.

23 John Sloan, *Gist of Art* (New York: American Artists Group, 1939), p. 3. In discussing the "realist revolt" of the Eight, I am actually referring, of course, only to the four Philadelphians listed here by Sloan, along with their sometime leader Henri. I am not concerned with the impressionism of Lawson, the picturesque postimpressionism of Prendergast, or the Puvis-esque romanticism of Davies. I use the term "the Eight" with this distinction in mind for economy's sake.

24 McCoubrey, *American Tradition*, p. 9.

25 Robert Henri, *The Art Spirit* (1923; rept., Philadelphia: Lippincott, 1960), p. 217.

26 Cited in Helen Appleton Read, Introduction to *Robert Henri and Five of His Pupils* (1946; rept., Freeport, N.Y.: Books for Libraries Press, 1971), n.p.

27 Cited in Matthew Baigall, *A History of American Painting* (New York: Praeger, 1971), p. 177.

28 Harold Rosenberg, *The De-definition of Art: Action Art to Pop to Earthworks* (New York: Horizon Press, 1972), p. 26.

29 James Hoopes discusses this article in his book *Van Wyck Brooks: In Search of American Culture* (Amherst: University of Massachusetts Press, 1977), pp. 74–75.

30 Richard Drinnon, *Rebel in Paradise: A Biography of Emma Goldman* (Chicago: University of Chicago Press, 1961), p. 157. Recall Marx's own inference, from his critique of the division of labor, that "in a communist society there are no painters but at most people who engage in painting among other activities." (From *The German Ideology* [1846], cited in Lee Baxandall and Stefan Morawski, trans. and eds., *Marx and Engels on Literature and Art* [St. Louis: Telos Press, 1973], p. 71.)

31 McCoubrey, *American Tradition*, p. 44.

32 *New York Scene*, p. 42.

33 Cited in David W. Scott, *John Sloan* (New York: Watson-Guptill, 1975), p. 35.

34 Donald Braider, *George Bellows and the Ashcan School of Painting* (Garden City, N.Y.: Doubleday, 1971), p. 26.

35 *New York Scene*, pp. 113, 118.

36 Ibid., pp. 194, 192–193, 197.

37 Ibid., p. 61.

38 Ibid., p. 164.

39 Ibid., p. 259.

40 Ibid., p. 313.

41 Ibid., p. 316.

42 Ibid., p. 475.

43 Ibid., p. 306. See also Joseph J. Kwiat, "John Sloan: An American Artist as

Social Critic, 1900–1917," *The Arizona Quarterly*, vol. 10, no. 1 (Spring 1954), pp. 52–64.

44 Sloan, *Gist of Art*, p. 3.

45 See, for example, Goodrich, *John Sloan*, p. 44.

46 Henry May, *The End of American Innocence: A Study of the First Years of Our Own Time, 1912–1917* (New York: Oxford University Press, 1979), p. 315.

47 *The Masses*, vol. VIII, no. 9 (July 1916), p. 5.

48 Max Eastman, *Enjoyment of Living* (New York: Harper and Row, 1948), p. 404.

49 *The Masses*, vol. V, no. 4 (January 1914), p. 3.

50 Cited in Goodrich, *John Sloan*, p. 47.

51 Irving Howe, "To *The Masses*–With Love and Envy," in *Echoes of Revolt: The Masses, 1911–1917*, ed. William O'Neill (Chicago: Quadrangle Books, 1966), p. 7.

52 Cited in Lee Benson, "Doing History as Moral Philosophy and Public Advocacy," a paper delivered at the meeting of the Organization of American Historians, Detroit, Mich., April 1, 1981, p. 14.

53 Benson, "Doing History," p. 14.

54 Eastman, *Enjoyment of Living*, p. 412.

55 Cited in Brooks, *John Sloan*, p. 96.

56 McCoubrey, *American Tradition*, pp. 45–46.

57 Harold Rosenberg, *The Anxious Object: Art Today and Its Audience* (New York: Horizon Press, 1964), p. 191.

58 Royal Cortissoz, "The Post-Impressionist Illusion," *The Century Magazine*, vol. LXXXC, no. 6 (April 1913), pp. 805–815.

59 "Cubists and Futurists Are Making Insanity Pay," New York *Times*, pt. 6 (March 16, 1913), p. 1.

60 Justin Kaplan, *Lincoln Steffens: A Biography* (New York: Simon and Schuster, 1974), p. 199.

61 *Camera Work*, no. 23 (July 1908), p. 10.

62 Cited in Jonathan Green, ed., *Camera Work: A Critical Anthology* (Millerton, N.Y.: Aperture, 1973), p. 16.

63 William Innes Homer, *Alfred Stieglitz and the American Avant-Garde* (Boston: New York Graphics Society, 1977), p. 3. For a somewhat different account of avant-garde developments in the prewar years, see Gail Levin, *Synchronism and American Color Abstraction, 1910–1925* (New York: Braziller, 1978), pp. 10–16.

64 Abraham Davidson, *Early American Modernist Painting: 1910–1935* (New York: Harper and Row, 1981), pp. 2–3.

65 Homer, *Alfred Stieglitz*, p. 83.

66 Cited in Homer, *Alfred Stieglitz*, p. 67.

67 Denman Ross, *A Theory of Pure Design* (Boston: Houghton Mifflin, 1907), p. 61.

68 Ibid., p. 187.

69 Barbara Rose, *Readings in American Art, 1900–1975* (New York: Holt, Rinehart and Winston, 1975), p. 13.

70 Robert Doty, *Photo-Secession: Stieglitz and the Fine-Art Movement in Photography* (New York: Dover, 1978), pp. 28, 31.

71 Green, *Camera Work,* p. 21. The internal quotation is from a review of Marsden Hartley that appeared in the October 1909 issue of *Camera Work.*

72 *Camera Work,* no. 16 (October 1906), p. 51.

73 Doty, *Photo-Secession,* p. 57.

74 Charles Caffin, *Photography as a Fine Art* (New York: Doubleday, 1901), p. 38. Nonetheless, Sadakichi Hartmann used the February 1904 exhibition of the Photo-Secession as the occasion to complain about the continuing "aesthetic" preoccupations of Stieglitz, Keiley, and Steichen ("A Plea for Straight Photography," *American Amateur Photographer,* no. 16. [March 1905], pp. 101–109).

75 Cited in Homer, *Alfred Stieglitz,* p. 70.

76 See Calvin Tomkins, "Profile," in *Paul Strand: Sixty Years of Photographs* (Millerton, N.Y.: Aperture, 1976).

77 Cited in Doty, *Photo-Secession,* p. 63.

78 Jonathan L. Doherty, *Lewis Wickes Hine's Interpretive Photography* (Chicago: University of Chicago Press, 1978), p. viii. Alan Trachtenberg locates Hine's work in its social and ideological contexts in *America and Lewis Hines: Photographs 1904–1940* (Millerton, N.Y.: Aperture, 1977).

79 Cited in *Paul Strand,* p. 21.

Chapter 10. A glimpse into the twenty-first century

1 See Larzer Ziff, *Puritanism in America: New Culture in a New World* (New York: Viking Press, 1973), pp. 61–64.

2 See, for example, the series of sermons Cotton preached in exposition of 1 John.

3 Cited in Perry Miller and Thomas H. Johnson, eds., *The Puritans,* vol. I (New York: Harper Torchbooks, 1963), p. 135.

4 Emma Goldman, "Prisons: A Social Crime and Failure," in *Anarchism and Other Essays* (1910; rept., Port Washington, N.Y.: Kennikat Press, 1969), p. 121. The fourfold division of crime follows Havelock Ellis.

5 Prison reform, in the general direction of self-governance and rehabilitation, was a principal concern of Progressives; but one finds nothing quite like Goldman's radically antisocial premises and conclusions. See, for example, Thomas Mott Osborne, *Society and Prisons* (New Haven, Conn.: Yale University Press, 1916).

6 Emma Goldman, "Anarchism: What It Really Stands For," in *Anarchism,* p. 71.

7 Emma Goldman, "The Psychology of Political Violence," in *Anarchism,* pp. 85–114.

8 Emma Goldman, *Living My Life,* vol. I (1931; rept., New York: Dover, 1970), p. 190.

9 See Henry Bienen, *Violence and Social Change* (Chicago: University of Chicago Press, 1968), esp. pp. 72–73.

10 The Stevens passage comes from near the end of his essay "The Noble Rider and the Sound of Words," in *The Necessary Angel* (New York: Vintage Books, 1965), p. 36. It should be inserted that Goldman later claimed to have reversed her acceptance of political violence sometime before the First World War (*Living My Life*, vol. II [1931; rept., New York: Dover, 1970], p. 536).

11 Emma Goldman, "Patriotism: A Menace to Liberty," in *Anarchism*, p. 134.

12 Goldman, "Patriotism," p. 140.

13 See E. Berkeley Tompkins, *Anti-Imperialism in the United States: The Great Debate, 1890–1920* (Philadelphia: University of Pennsylvania Press, 1972), esp. pp. 134–139, 290–296.

14 Cited in Ralph Barton Perry, *The Thought and Character of William James*, briefer version (New York: Harper Torchbooks, 1964), p. 240.

15 Cited in Perry, *Thought and Character*, p. 246.

16 Mark Twain, "To the Person Sitting in Darkness" (1901), reprinted in Bernard De Voto, ed., *The Portable Mark Twain* (New York: Viking Press, 1966), pp. 611–612.

17 Emma Goldman, "The Traffic in Women" and "Minorities versus Majorities," in *Anarchism*, pp. 196, 80.

18 *The Masses*, no. 2 (February 1911), p. 17.

19 Randolph Bourne, "The State," in *The Radical Will*, ed. Olaf Hansen (New York: Urizen Books, 1977), p. 359.

20 Goldman, *Living My Life*, vol. II, p. 641.

21 Emma Goldman, "Francisco Ferrer and the Modern School," in *Anarchism*, p. 169.

22 Goldman, "The Traffic in Women," p. 184.

24 Emma Goldman, "Woman Suffrage," in *Anarchism*, p. 204.

25 Ibid., 203.

26 Emma Goldman, "The Tragedy of Woman's Emancipation," in *Anarchism*, p. 230.

27 Goldman, "Woman Suffrage," p. 217.

28 Cited in Richard Drinnon, *Rebel in Paradise: A Biography of Emma Goldman* (Chicago: University of Chicago Press, 1961), p. 215.

29 Cited in Drinnon, *Rebel*, p. 19.

30 Goldman, "Anarchism," pp. 54, 53.

31 James Joll, *The Anarchists* (Boston: Little, Brown, 1964), p. 275.

32 Goldman, *Living My Life*, vol. I, p. 11. See also the section titled "The Lure of America" in Irving Howe, *World of Our Fathers: The Journey of the East European Jews to America and the Life They Found and Made* (New York: Simon and Schuster, 1976), pp. 34–36.

33 Goldman, *Living My Life*, vol. II, 508.

34 Drinnon, *Rebel*, p. 141.

35 Goldman, "Anarchism," pp. 58, 62.

36 Henry David Thoreau, *Civil Disobedience* (1849; rept., New York: Holt, Rinehart and Winston, 1948), pp. 281, 284, 299, 304.

37 Goldman, "Anarchism," p. 62.

38 Goldman, *Living My Life,* vol. II, pp. 584–585.
39 Emma Goldman, "The Modern Drama: A Powerful Disseminator of Radical Thought," in *Anarchism,* p. 277.
40 Emma Goldman, "Marriage and Love," in *Anarchism,* p. 245.
41 On Ben Reitman, see Drinnon, *Rebel,* pp. 122–126.
42 Note the similar concatenation of religious and romantic vestiges in W. E. B. Du Bois's *The Quest of the Silver Fleece;* Chapter 5, p. 154, this volume.

   I referred in an earlier chapter to R. W. B. Lewis's speculations on the interaction between the secular and religious planes of discourse; Chapter 2, p. 22, this volume.
43 Barbara Tuchman, *The Proud Tower: A Portrait of the World before the War, 1890–1914* (New York: Macmillan, 1966), p. 113.
44 Goldman, *Living My Life,* vol. II, p. 766.
45 Margaret S. Marsh, *Anarchist Women, 1870–1920* (Philadelphia: Temple University Press, 1981), p. 15.
46 Cited in Drinnon, *Rebel,* p. 106.
47 Goldman, *Living My Life,* vol. I, p. 402.
48 Drinnon, *Rebel,* p. 107.

Index

345